AUTOBIOGRAPHY

MEMORIES AND EXPERIENCES

OF

MONCURE DANIEL CONWAY

VOLUME II

AUTOBIOGRAPHY

MEMORIES AND EXPERIENCES

OF

MONCURE DANIEL CONWAY

VOLUME II

DA CAPO PRESS • NEW YORK • 1970

A Da Capo Press Reprint Edition

This Da Capo Press edition of *Autobiography, Memories,
and Experiences of Moncure Daniel Conway* is an un-
abridged republication of the first edition published in
Boston and New York in 1904.

Library of Congress Catalog Card Number 76-87495

SBN 306-71402-7

Published by Da Capo Press
A Division of Plenum Publishing Corporation
227 West 17th Street, New York, N. Y. 10011

Manufactured in the United States of America

AUTOBIOGRAPHY

OF

MONCURE DANIEL CONWAY

IN TWO VOLUMES

VOL. II

Moncure D. Conway

AUTOBIOGRAPHY

MEMORIES AND EXPERIENCES

OF

MONCURE DANIEL CONWAY

IN TWO VOLUMES

VOL. II

BOSTON AND NEW YORK
HOUGHTON, MIFFLIN AND COMPANY
The Riverside Press, Cambridge
1904

CONTENTS OF VOLUME II

CHAPTER XXXII

CHAPTER XXXIII

CHAPTER XXXIV

CHAPTER XXXV

CHAPTER XXXVI

CHAPTER XXXVII

CHAPTER XXXVIII

CHAPTER XXXIX

CHAPTER XL

CHAPTER XLI

CHAPTER XLII

CHAPTER XLIII

CHAPTER XLIV

CHAPTER XLV

LIST OF ILLUSTRATIONS

AUTOBIOGRAPHY

OF

MONCURE DANIEL CONWAY

CHAPTER XXVIII

Discussions in London concerning slavery and the negro — My " Testimonies concerning Slavery " — A disclosure about the Confederacy — Commemoration of John Brown — Thackeray — George Cruikshank — Charles Dickens — My journalistic work — The Shakespeare tercentenary at Stratford-on-Avon — Howard Staunton — Mrs. Shakespeare's second marriage — Illness and death of our child Emerson — Excursion on the Continent — A visit to Dr. Strauss — Gervinus — A week at Ostend — Residence at Notting Hill — Professor Cairnes — J. S. Mill — Helen Taylor.

THE paradoxical ideas of Carlyle on slavery, impressive by reason of his absolute veracity and remoteness from the partizan arena, were quoted by men not free from partizanship. One Sunday evening I was taken by Tom Hughes to a room where the elder Macmillan received his friends. Conversation began on the American situation, and some participant spoke to me sharply. Thereupon Hughes broke out on my assailant with a severity from which the company could not recover. Herbert Spencer said to me in a low voice, " A good many intelligent people do not hold the same views of the negro and his position as those of the abolitionists."

I was invited to join the newly formed Anthropological Society, and did so, but found that it was led by a few ingenious gentlemen whose chief interest was to foster contempt of the negro. One of these, Dr. James Hunt, published a pamphlet entitled " The Negro's Place in Nature." Huxley pointed out to me privately the fallacies of Hunt, and I made speeches in the Anthropological Society, but it became plain to me that antislavery sentiment in England was by no means so deep as I had supposed. I felt certain that I could name half a dozen great English writers, read and honoured throughout America, who by a public declaration could have shamed our government out of its pretexts for not dealing genuinely with its only real enemy — slavery. With the hope of effecting something in this direction, I wrote the book printed at the end of 1863, " Testimonies concerning Slavery."

From this work, never published in America, and long out of print, I quote a paragraph of the Introduction : —

I have long believed that the friends of liberty can help America much more by rekindling their old watchfires, which sadly need fuel, than by advocating this or that measure or man that may be for the time associated with the struggle. What America needs now is not a sultry indulgence but a bracing criticism, always supposing that criticism to be made in the interest of liberty and not of slavery. It is related that, at the Federal repulse at Charleston, a negro who bore the flag crawled a long distance amid a storm of shot and shell, dragging his wounded body, but still holding up the flag. When he regained his companions, his only words were, " I did not let it (the flag) touch the ground once." Let the voices of all true men keep it ever before the rulers of America, that her banner is far nobler so long as a negro holds it up with devotion, as too pure to touch the ground, than if it should wave over every fort and city of the South tainted with compromise or soiled with slavery.

I had privately told this story of the negro and the flag to Browning, and he told me he had repeated it in several companies. I afterwards regretted having printed it, for Browning would probably have made it into a lyric.

John Bright was pleased with my " Testimonies " and did much to promote its circulation ; indeed, all of my personal friends were satisfied with it. It was the best I could do at such a distance from America, and under circumstances that rendered it impossible to correspond with my friends in Virginia ; but I do not now read the book with satisfaction. It contains a chapter on the negro which I sometimes think of reprinting, but so far as the war is concerned the book by no means represents the conclusions reached by studying facts afterwards revealed.

While writing my " Testimonies," I received the following : —

SIR,—I have not the honour of your acquaintance and therefore my signature would be of no value. The substance of this note, however, may be important to you.

A short time since the representative of the Southern States in Europe submitted to the governments of France and England propositions for the practical abolition of slavery, on condition of recognition and material assistance, viz. : that the children of slaves born after a given period should *be free*. This, which is the only possible way of abolition, may now be withdrawn, but the information may be useful to you and I therefore enclose it. Yours truly, LIBERTAS.

I paid little attention to this anonymous note, but it was recently recalled to me by a manuscript in possession of the Du Bellet family, Paris. Mr. Du Bellet, whose widow (*née* Moncure) is my relative, was a native of New Orleans and a barrister. He happened to be in France in 1861, and though holding no commission from the Confederacy devoted himself to its interests in Europe, his command of French enabling him to assist the Confederate agents. Mr. Du Bellet left a narrative of negotiations in Paris at that time, shown me by his family. Of Mr. Du Bellet I never heard until thirty years after the war, but he records that he urged upon Slidell in Paris, and on other foreign agents of the Confederacy, the necessity of immediate emancipation. He also wrote to the Confederate government in Richmond declaring that as the war would certainly end slavery, even were the South victorious, they should at once utilize emancipation.[1]

---

[1] I reported the existence of this Du Bellet MS. to our national librarian, and a typewritten copy is now in the library at Washington.

My cousin, the late P. V. Daniel Jr., then president of the Richmond and Petersburg R. R., was in constant communication with Jefferson Davis, and I am informed by his daughter, Mrs. Cautley, that when President Lincoln's proclamation was read by her father he informed his family that President Davis had some time before tried to bring the Con-

On December 2, 1863, a public meeting convened by the Emancipation Society was held in the Whittington Club Hall to commemorate the fourth anniversary of the execution of John Brown. The chair was taken by William Malleson, who in his opening speech related the mythical story that on his way to the scaffold Brown stopped and gave a kiss to a little negro girl. The meeting had been convened to listen to an address from myself, and this was published by the society. In it I said, " Brown's plan was the best his eye could scan ; but it would only have done in Virginia what he had already done in Kansas, — free a few slaves. But God's plan was a different one from that. It included the placing of the angel Justice side by side with the fiend Oppression, that the world should see them ere the foot of the one was planted on the neck of the other."

I am now certain that no god had anything to do with the affair except the phantasmal god of war worshipped by Brown, and that the biblical captain who revived that deified wrath inflicted on America sequels of slavery worse than the disease.

---

federacy to a policy of emancipation. She remembers her father saying that Mr. Davis told his Cabinet that France could not recognize the Confederacy without England, and England would not recognize a slave-holding nation. The proposal was successfully opposed by A. H. Stephens and Robert Toombs, who thenceforth were hostile to Davis. Cousin P. V. Daniel Jr. agreed with Davis, but his relative, John M. Daniel, editor of the *Examiner*, while suppressing the proposal, bitterly attacked Davis. In November, 1864, Davis proposed to his Congress that 40,000 slaves should be employed on fortifications, etc., and rewarded with freedom at the end of the war. The *Examiner* approved of the negroes' employment, but declared the offer of freedom as a " reward " a surrender of the Southern position, which was " that while living with the white in the relation of slave he is in a state superior and better for him than that of freedom." However, the demand of Davis was conceded. In giving freedom to every slave that rendered it service the Confederacy curiously coincided with the policy which for a year prevailed in the United States : any slave escaping into the Union lines was free, provided he could show that he had helped the enemy ; if he had befriended us he was assumed to belong to a loyal man and must be returned to bondage !

Bayard Taylor told me that he once visited the studio of Baron Marochetti with Thackeray, who pointed to a sculpture of St. George and the Dragon and said, " Every man has his dragon ; mine is dining out ; what 's yours ? " " The same," replied Taylor.

Carlyle, who had known Thackeray from his youth, told me that at times he (Thackeray), having some urgent work on hand, escaped from invitations, callers, and letters, and went off from his house without leaving any address. One night a messenger came to him (Carlyle) from a public house near by with a request from Thackeray for the loan of a Bible. I sometimes saw Thackeray ; his hair was so white that I supposed him old until it was announced at his death that he was only fifty-two.

The death of Thackeray, December 24, 1863, caused universal distress. The day of his burial at Kensal Green cemetery (December 30) was beautiful, and a large throng surrounded his grave. Starting out on foot for the cemetery I overtook George Cruikshank, whom I well knew, and we walked together. He was much shocked at the death of his friend. For there had been no premonitions ; Thackeray had cheerfully bid his family good-night ; in the early morning his servant entered his room and placed beside him the usual cup of coffee ; entering later, he noticed the coffee untouched. Thackeray died of an effusion on a brain that weighed $58\frac{1}{4}$ ounces, — the average weight of the masculine brain being less than four pounds.

George Cruikshank received my compliments for his vigour at seventy-two with his usual discourse on the advantages of teetotalism. He was a small, thick-set man, with a pale face so singular that it might have been strikingly homely if it had not been intellectual and benevolent. " I am getting to know this road well — very well," he said. " Many a fine fellow has been buried at Kensal Green, but never a finer or a truer than Makepeace Thackeray. How little did they know the man who thought him a hard, cold, and cutting blade. He was much more like a sensitive, loving little girl." I never was more impressed than at this moment with Cruikshank's genius for seeing; his phrase interpreted certain lines under Thackeray's eyes, lines of wondrous tenderness, as if their light were flowing out to all on whom he looked. "Here is one picture I have in my mind of him," said Cruikshank; "he was coming from Ireland across the Channel, with his wife and children, one an infant. There was a fearful storm all night, and the Channel horribly rough, and Mrs. Thackeray was seized with a brain fever. And through all that terrible night, from shore to shore, sat Thackeray, motionless, bearing the infant in one arm, sustaining the wife with the other, utterly unconscious of the prevailing terror, — for there was danger. His poor wife never recovered from brain fever, and was worse than lost to him forever." Cruikshank had been Thackeray's teacher when the author aspired to be an artist; "but," he said, "he had not the patience to be an artist with pencil or brush. I used to tell him that to be an artist was to burrow along like a mole, heaving up a little mound here and there for a long distance. He said he thought he would presently break out into another element and stay there."

Cruikshank spoke of his venture in 1841, "The Omnibus," of which Laman Blanchard was editor and Thackeray the chief contributor. "It would be more pleasing to think of Thackeray as resting by the side of Douglas Jerrold, but Jerrold was not buried at Kensal Green. I remember well the day when we were standing beside the grave of the poor suicide Laman Blanchard at Clapham Way, and Jerrold said he wished to be buried at a spot hard by, which he pointed out; and there he was buried. Poor Blanchard!"

Cruikshank did not go on with his memory of Laman Blanchard, who, unable to recover from the shock of his wife's death, killed himself two months after it, February 15, 1845. For at this time the hearse passed us, and my companion's lip quivered and his eye grew moist. John Leech came up. The two artists looked into one another's eyes and shook hands, but no word passed.

Nearly every literary man in London was present. I particularly remarked the emotion of Charles Dickens.

After the funeral I walked away with Robert Browning, and we were presently joined by Dickens, to whom the poet introduced me. Dickens warmly admired Browning, and I was told he once said to a friend that he would rather have written " Colombe's Birthday " than any of his novels. As my road lay in another direction, I mounted an omnibus and sat beside the driver, who inquired if Charles Dickens had been at the funeral, adding, " I would just like to see that man." When I told him Dickens had passed on ahead he lashed his horses, but Dickens had disappeared, and Browning was with Tom Taylor. But the driver was partly consoled by seeing the author of his favourite play, " The Ticket-of-leave Man."

Dickens was a wonder. The more I saw of London the more I loved and honoured the London Dante who had invested it with romance, and peopled its streets and alleys with spirits, so that the huge city could never more be seen without his types and shadows. He had his limitations, no doubt; had he been born in France, where genius is free to deal with every side of human life, Dickens might have been greater. To me he remained the chief marvel of his time. I felt some satisfaction in telling him that Oliver Twist, Little Nell, and other children of his had been far back in the forties our beloved friends in a Virginian village of which he had never heard ; that I had myself lost my position as a model schoolboy and been flogged for jumping out of the school window and playing truant in order to see him alight from the stage-coach in Fredericksburg; and that his description of the fearful roads by which he journeyed thither hastened the building of a railway.

Of Dickens's readings no description can convey any adequate impression. He was in himself a whole stock company. He seemed to be physically transformed as he passed from one character to another ; he had as many distinct voices as his books had characters ; he held at command the fountains

of laughter and tears. Dickens's voice in its every disguise
was of such quality that it reached all of those thousands
in St. James's Hall, and he stood before us a magician. When
he sat down it was not mere applause that followed, but a
passionate outburst of love for the man. Dickens was a unique
man. He had graduated from Grub Street to the palace,
and his writings insinuated themselves equally into the hearts
of rich and poor, learned and illiterate.

The year 1864 had opened happily for wife and myself.
The Mason incident had cleared away, and letters came from
America full of the old friendship. My "Testimonies concerning Slavery" was circulating largely, and also my article
on "Benjamin Banneker, the Negro Astronomer," reprinted
from the "Atlantic Monthly" by the "Ladies Emancipation
Society;" my congregation was rapidly growing, our means
increasing. We found our best amusement in strolling along
the quaint shops and through the Zoölogical Gardens with
our two children. My journalistic work was not under orders,
but selected by myself. My duties were thus always congenial,
and at times delightful.

For one week in the April of 1864 I moved in an enchanted land. It was at Stratford-on-Avon, during the celebration of the tercentenary of Shakespeare. That poet, with
all his miracles, hardly imagined more beautiful masques
than those amid which we moved during those fair days. A
grand pavilion for theatrical performances had been raised,
vast tents for concerts, and a gallery containing all the great
Shakespearian subjects ever painted, with the thirty famous
portraits of the poet, — all these were open for the throng
of pilgrims from every part of Europe who day by day, nay
hour by hour, were charmed away from the hard contemporary world as Ferdinand and Miranda by the pageants of
Prospero. Now we were listening to the songs of Shakespeare
set to music of the early English composers, then to Mendelssohn's "Sommernachtstraum;" one night we laughed at
Buckstone's Andrew Aguecheek, on another saw beautiful
Stella Colas shine on Juliet's balcony like a star, and every

night some exquisite play. The grand old Mayor Flower at
" The Hill," his son Charles at " Avonbank " near the church,
and his son Edgar in the village, kept open house ; there were
daily banquets ; pretty barges, laden with pretty ladies, floated
along with the swans on the Avon ; excursions were made to
Ann Hathaway's cottage and to Charlecote Hall, scene of
the legendary deer-stalking incident. There was a grand dinner, with a Shakespeare text for every dish, and wine and
toast ; there were five discourses about Shakespeare in the
old church by Bishops Trench and Wordsworth ; and finally
there was as magnificent a fancy dress ball as was ever
known, — every one being in a Shakespearian character.
The gentry from all Warwickshire and from other counties,
and many from London, France, Germany, were present, and
the dance went on till dawn.

During all this festival I sat in the ancient Red Lion Inn
for a large part of each night, — save when on duty as Mal-
volio at the ball, — surrounded by the relics of Washington
Irving, writing my description of the wondrous affair for
" Harper's Monthly." A daily letter was due to the " Morning Star " in London, one or two to the " Commonwealth "
in Boston, but I found writing a joy, and grudged every
moment that sleep claimed from my real dreamland.

I made during the fête the acquaintance of Howard Staunton, the acute editor of Shakespeare, and almost the only unbiased critical investigator into the personal life of the poet.
Staunton was then about fifty, with a ruddy English colour
and clear-cut features. His step was elastic, his movement
quick, and, being myself a good walker, we enjoyed rambles
together. I told him how much I had valued his standard
work on Chess, but he had long given up the game. " It not
only took up too much time," he said, " but I found that it
demoralized players. Men have hated me and said mean things
about me merely because I beat them at chess." Staunton had
long before reached the conclusion I had just come to that
Shakespeare's widow had married Richard James, but I
warned him that if he touched the romantic sentiment invest-

ing Ann Hathaway he might suffer as much as if he had beaten the accepted writers at chess. We examined the register of burials in the church, and felt certain that the carefully bracketed names were those of one and the same person.

Aug. 8 $\begin{cases} \text{Mrs. Shakespeare} \\ \text{Ann, uxor Ricardi James} \end{cases}$

The register, it is said, is not the original one, but this only makes it more certain that the copy is exact, for at a later time no one would have ventured to bracket the wife of Shakespeare with another Ann ; and certainly no clergyman or clerk would have omitted to add " uxor Gulielmi Shakespeare " to his widow's name, while being so particular about the wife of one Richard James. Staunton had made a search in the old town records after the James family, and found that it was a well-known name but belonged to people of much lower position than the Shakespeares. He had found one item which suggested to him that the Richard James whom Shakespeare's widow married was a Stratford shoemaker and a pious ranter. Staunton invited me to visit him at his house in London, where he would show me the notes he had made on the matter; but I was prevented from doing this, and he died not long after. But knowing well the exactness of Staunton, I have adhered to his theory, — of which, indeed, I find some confirmation in Shakespeare's dislike of Puritanism, and still more in the epitaph of his daughter, Mrs. Hall. No such words would have been inscribed on her grave had she not been among pharisaic people.

> Witty above her sexe, but that's not all,
> Wise to salvation was good Mistris Hall;
> Something of Shakespeare was in that, but this
> Wholly of Him with whom she's now in bliss.

My return from the fairyland beside the Avon was into a cloud. I found my wife sitting with anxiety beside our little Emerson. Knowing how important was the fulfilment of my contract as commissioner of the " Morning Star " at Stratford, she had not telegraphed me of the child's illness, — the sequel of measles, — not immediately dangerous. My wife was a believer in homœopathy, and our invalid was attended by Dr. James John Garth Wilkinson, well known in our Concord circle by his book, "The Human Body and its Connection with the Human Soul." He was a grand sort of man, with a powerful will, and his devotion to the child gained our gratitude. It was a long illness, but some improvement came in May, and our doctor advised us to go into the country.

We went to Wimbledon, where our friends Mr. and Mrs. Henry Whitehead took us as lodgers in their charming homestead, Warren Farm. Here Emerson steadily improved, and we had fair prospect that he would recover. But where is there any escape from man's supplement to nature's destructiveness? Near the middle of July the military review and rifle practice began at Wimbledon, and the cottagers were given notice to leave. We concluded to try Brighton, but the change was fatal.

Oh, how we nursed that child! My wife was nearly worn out. Night after night I paced the room with my sweet child in my arms. As the homœopathic doctor in Brighton had been a personal friend of the Rev. F. W. Robertson I supposed him competent, but what was my horror at his intimation that he had consulted the "spirits" about the remedies! Here were we, Ellen and I, haters of war, who could not be left in our quiet Wimbledon Vale by the infernal bullets; and with all our dislike of "spiritualism" had fallen into the hands of a spiritualist physician!

In the evening before the morning of burial my wife desired some flowers, and I went out to buy them. It was late, and I could find no florist shop open; but there was one grand establishment where I supposed I could find residents who would promise to let me have the flowers very early in the morning. The large glass conservatory was lighted, and I hurried to the door and knocked, — knocked again, and louder. There was no answer, and straining my eyes against the glass of doors and windows I found that the seeming illumination was all from the street lamps outside. Within was silence and emptiness. A dread came upon me. Was I looking into little Emerson's grave and finding that all the bright hopes, all the visions of immortal life, were but projections from earthly lamps on emptiness? Somehow I felt that in the illusion under which I had fairly battered at the door there was a sort of mockery.

In the early morning, between seven and eight o'clock, I went out and managed to get the white flowers. I find a note by my wife: "Saturday, 6th of August, we placed his body in the ground near F. W. Robertson, on a high hill overlooking the sea, and a little stone cross above, twined with ivy." So even then we were trying to cling to the cross.

Ralph Waldo Emerson had once called on us, after we had a house in Concord, and seeing my two sons, he said of his namesake, "Little Emerson is beautiful and winning, but I think you will get more satisfaction out of the elder boy (Eustace)." So it proved.

The words of Shylock are far-reaching: "The curse never fell upon our race till now; I never felt it till now." I had caught a glimpse of sullen spite in nature glaring through her veil of violets and tinted skies. It was not merely the child's premature death that was unpardonable, but the prolonged cruel incidents of it. The sweet little one — he was nearly three years of age — did not indeed suffer much physical pain from the hydrocephalus that caused his death, but during the four months preceding death (August 4) he was so sadly puzzled by his inability to walk, the cessation of our merry strolls. I hear now his little voice saying, " I wish I could get well," or, seeing our distress, "Kiss me, kiss me again, mamma." Day by day, hour by hour, the child was more and more deeply entwined with our heart-strings. And poor little Eustace, in his sixth year, who had so petted Emerson, wandered about helplessly.

My vacation began with August, and we started off with our one child for a tour. We went to Paris and tried to forget our grief amid the manifold beauties of the city. We passed over to Germany and Switzerland. The thin and worn

condition of my wife, which had been giving me anxiety,
began to disappear, but we really found no consolation for our
hearts. We could only weep silently together. I received a
letter from Browning in which he said : " If I, who cannot
restore your child, *would*, He who can, *will*." It made us
both love the poet more, but our visions of immortality must
have unconsciously grown dim.

I had with me a letter from Dr. Brabant of Bath to
Strauss, and to meet him we visited Heilbrönn. I was welcomed by Strauss and his attractive daughter, — he had
for some time been separated from his wife, a brilliant, but
incompatible actress. We went on a long walk beside the
Neckar, and he inquired about Parker, Emerson, and the English liberals. I asked him whether he knew of any work
worth reading concerning immortality. He said after some
reflection, " No. It appears to me a purely anthropological
problem." And on that point no more was said.

Strauss was in his fifty-sixth year. There was as yet no
grey in his dark hair; his features were fine, his mouth especially delicate, as if related to his sweet voice ; his dark eyes
candid and tender. He pointed out to me near an ancient
church traces of the holy fountain which gave Heilbrönn its
name. He said, with his gentle smile : " The theory of the
priests is that the fountain ceased to flow when I came here
to reside."

After my memorable day and evening with Strauss, we
travelled to Heidelberg to visit Gervinus, — whose English
was fluent enough to enable me to enjoy his conversation at
the breakfast to which he invited me. We reached Frankfort
on Goethe's birthday, and found the city decorated. We
explored the Goethe Birth-house (a museum), and tried to
forget our pain amid the festivities. We enjoyed our sail on
the Rhine, under a beautiful sky ; we visited grand cathedrals
and art galleries in Germany and Belgium ; and on the last
day of August (1864) arrived at Ostend.

Finding our London friends, Mr. and Mrs. William Neill
and their little son Harold for our child to play with, we

remained a week at Ostend. I there wrote a sermon for the formidable day when I must again stand before my sympathizing congregation. I also wrote down some notes concerning persons met on my little tour. I find it written concerning the conversation of Strauss : —

He felt oppressed at seeing nearly every nation in Europe chained by an allied despotism of prince and priest. He studied long the nature of this oppression, and came to the conclusion that the chain was rather inward than outward, and without the inward thraldom the outward would soon rust away. The inward chain was superstition, and the form in which it bound the people of Europe was Christian supernaturalism. So long as men accept religious control not based on reason, they will accept political control not based on reason. The man who gives up the whole of his moral nature to an unquestioned authority suffers a paralysis of his mind, and all the changes of outward circumstance in the world cannot make him a free man. For this reason our European revolutions have been, even when successful, mere transfers from one tyranny to another. He believed when writing the " Leben Jesu " that in striking at supernaturalism he was striking at the root of the whole tree of political and social degradation. Renan had done for France what he had thought to do for Germany. Renan had written a book which the common people read ; the influence of the " Leben Jesu " had been confined to scholars more than he liked, and he meant to put it into a more popular shape. Germany must be made to realize that the decay of Christianity means the growth of national life, and also of general humanity.

As Strauss could speak little English, and my German was not equal to profound themes, we now and then resorted to Latin words. What I have just written was gathered from our conversation, and must not be taken literally. But what he said to me about immortality — that it was a purely anthropological problem — is exact, for on that I had meditated every day since I left him, and again as I looked out from Ostend over the shoreless sea.

It was at Ostend, strolling amid the happy promenaders on the Digue, bathing in the translucent waves, observing

the happy peasantry, above all the crowds of merry children
on the beach, that our spirits found some relief and repose.
The old Belgian town took hold of our affection; we made
some acquaintance with the market women and tradespeople;
we found the seaside luxuries wholesome and cheap; and in
after years, being not permitted to bathe together on English
beaches, we found happy vacations in dear old Ostend.

From my wife's diary: "Sept. 11. Monc preached for
the first time since our loss, and broke down completely.
. . . Sept. 21. My darling's birthday (Emerson),— a regular
cloud and sunshine day. Eustace says he guesses God got
the rainbow for Emerson."

Returned to London, we found pleasant lodgings at 28
Notting Hill Square. The house was kept by a childless
couple (Hepple), who were not only kind but amusing. The
husband passed all his time in genealogical investigations,
and we had not been in the house a month before he had
traced us both back to royal families. Our new residence had
been selected in that region in order to be near our friends
of Aubrey House. To our delight our friends Professor
Cairnes and his wife took the only other apartment to let in
the house. This admirable man was thoroughly instructed
in American affairs. He knew our constitutional history, and
the causes of the anomalies and compromises which had led
to the war. He was well acquainted with all the legal, economic, and international questions involved, and being withal
a man of sweetness as well as light, I could consult him about
all my articles written for either country. Professor Cairnes
was a tall, handsome man, younger than his published works
had led me to suppose. Though sadly afflicted with rheumatism, his countenance was always beaming with humour. His
lovely wife was gracious, witty, always cheerful, and my wife
found her friendship a great resource. The intimate friends
of Cairnes were his confrères in economic studies, — John
Stuart Mill and Professor Fawcett. Now and then we all
went to dine with Mill and his stepdaughter, Helen Taylor,
who lived in a pretty house at Cray.

In personal appearance John Stuart Mill resembled Edgar A. Poe. His delicate mouth, almost feminine, — which twitched nervously at times, — and the small chin, were in contrast with the breadth and height of his brow.

Although Mill was more eager to listen than to talk, we managed to throw the burden of conversation upon him, and never failed to go away enriched by his ample knowledge and ideas. Many a new view in philosophy, religion, and sociology grew in me from his casual suggestions made without the slightest doctrinaire spirit. When led to speak of eminent contemporaries from whom he differed, he did so with a look of deference. There was pathos in his expression when he spoke of Carlyle, and said, " Then Carlyle turned against all his friends." [1] Emerson he had met in 1848, and though he had no liking for any transcendentalism, held him in great esteem.

On the evening of our first visit to Mill, Professor Cairnes and the ladies drove to the station and our host walked with me. He turned the conversation on Emerson, and I told him how when I was a youth in Virginia sharing the conventional notions of those around me, a sentence quoted from Emerson in a magazine had awakened in me a new thought and aim which ultimately revolutionized my life. Mill paused on the road and said, " That is something that should be engraved on a man's tomb." Although in his countenance there was a tinge of melancholy, it was serene; and there was some twinkle in his eyes when he uttered an epigrammatic criticism on one or another politician who had acquired popularity or power. He was a man of delicate sentiment, elegant manners, and affectionate nature. By the personal care he had given to the culture of his stepdaughter, a care maternal as

---

[1] Carlyle told me of the burning of the MS. of his first volume of the *French Revolution*, which he had submitted to Mill for criticism. Mill submitted it to Mrs. Taylor, whose maid used the pages to light the fire. "The beautiful young man rushed in on us deathly pale, almost speechless with horror, and we had to give our attention to his condition before we could consider my own."

Saint Véran, Avignon
Oct. 23. 1865

Dear Sir

I cannot thank you enough for Mr
Wendell Phillips' admirable speeches. I was
not aware that he was so thorough an adherent
of not only representation of minorities, but what is
much more, personal representation – the representation
of every elector: that great idea of which the credit,
though Mr Phillips seems to give it to me, is exclusively
due to Mr Hare. It is hardly possible to state the merits
of the principle more forcibly, or with a more thorough
understanding of all its importance, than Mr Phillips
has done. It is indeed at once a direct corollary from
the first principles of democracy, and a most powerful
corrective of all evils liable to arise from the forms
of democratic government hitherto in use. That Mr
Phillips should have taken it up, and in the manner
he has, is most cheering and auspicious. I was not
aware of the publication he mentions, and should
like very much to see it.

I beg that you will express my warmest thanks to Mr Phillips for his correction of my unintentional misrepresentation of the Abolitionists — to whom, I hope I need not say that I meant no disparagement having always regarded them as the élite of their country not to say of their age, I have been much gratified by receiving so strong a confirmation, from such authority of my opinion concerning Tocqueville. which I shall now hold with increased confidence,

I have not, however, been convinced by Mr Phillips' argument against an educational qualification. It is very true that intelligence, and even a high order of it, may be formed by other means than reading, and even (though, I think, rarely) without the aid of reading: but not, I think. intelligence of public affairs, or the power of judging of public men; have perhaps in exceptional cases, too few to affect the practical conclusion. At the present crisis, however, the securing of equal political rights to the negro is paramount to all other considerations respecting the suffrage, I should be glad to think 'that you are strong enough to reject a compromise admitting reposes on an educational qualification common to them with the others. As things look now, it seems as if even that would be a thing to be thankful for.

The author of the article "Enfranchisement of Women" would have been well rewarded by the progress which that question is making, had she lived to see it. Nothing would have gratified her more than to hear on such high authority that the cause to which she was so earnestly devoted had been in any degree forwarded in America by what she wrote.

I am Dear Sir
yours very truly
J. S. Mill

Do you wish the two numbers of Mr Garrison's paper to be returned?

well as paternal, she was able to appreciate his philosophy, learning, and his unique personality.

Some of my most instructive conversations with Mill and Helen Taylor related to their observations of the French people and their religion in the provinces. They felt that the central figure of the Madonna was more elevating in their humble homes than any form that Protestantism could offer. Helen Taylor told me that once when they were in Scotland she called on a poor woman who had lost her little son. The mother was inconsolable, and said, " What troubles me is, they be all men folk up there and won't know how to do for him."

I had heard that when Mill and Helen Taylor visited the Parthenon, where there was some discussion as to the spot on which the statue of Athene had stood, the young lady moved to a certain point and said, " I believe it stood here." Curtius and his party heard of it and reached the same conclusion. I asked her about it and she said her reason was that if it had been a Catholic church the Virgin would have stood at that spot.

CHAPTER XXIX

My reviews of Browning — The wrapper of his poems — Carlyle's account of the marriage of the Brownings — Browning's father — " Mr. Sludge, the Medium " — Margaret Fuller Ossoli — The sisters Eliza and Sarah Flower, Browning and W. J. Fox — A visit to Tennyson at Farringford — Mrs. Cameron — A romance at Freshwater — " The Promise of May " — Tennyson's dread of both agnosticism and orthodoxy.

MEETING with Robert Browning was like a fine morning. His whole handsome countenance smiled, not his mouth merely or even chiefly, and his greeting was to tell something pleasant. For some years I lived in Delamere Terrace near his house in Warwick Crescent, and sometimes joined his walks. He had been friendly with me from the first, having read an article I had written in America about his poetry. The large three-volume edition of his poems had just appeared when I arrived (1863), and I wrote two extended reviews of it, one in the " Westminster Review," the other in the " Englishwoman's Journal." He recognized the papers as indicating loving study of his writings. I was able also to do him some practical service. Finding that he had no adequate arrangement in America for the publication of his works or those of Mrs. Browning, I offered to undertake that matter for him, and succeeded. He showed his gratitude by presenting me with a copy of the original edition of his first poem, " Pauline," which many years later I found was one of the five or six copies discoverable.

Browning was much interested in America. Mrs. Conway, who had been requested to act in London in the interest of the Concord Bazaar for the benefit of the " freedmen," hinted to Browning that an autograph of his would be valuable. Thereupon he took out a large bundle of papers, — manuscripts of his early poems (" Sordello " was in a separate wrapper) ; he removed the parchment wrapper of the poems, and showed us the sentences — Greek, Latin, English — with which it was covered. This parchment wrapper was duly forwarded to Mrs. Horace Mann, but who was the purchaser I know not. It would be a relic of interest to the Browning Society in London. Before sending it to America I made a copy which I conclude to insert here. The figures affixed to each quotation refer to the translations that will follow : —

Ἀλλὰ πᾶν τοματὸν (καὶ) πένητα . . . . (1)

Ἐνικήσαμεν ὡς ἐβουλόμεθα (2)

| To-day Venezia, June 2 1838 | Saturday, May 27, 1837 Tuesday, June 18, 1837, July 30, 1837, Aug. 7. Jan. 5, 1838, March 6, 27. Feb. 23, 1840.   ΘΔΕΑ |

"Εξ ὧραι μόχθοις ἱκανώτατα · αἱ μετ' αὐτὰς
γράμμασι δεικνύμεναι ΖΕΘΙ λέγουσι βροτοῖς (3)

Ἡβῶοις, φίλε θυμέ · τάχ' ἄν τινες ἄλλοι ἔσονται
ἄνδρες, ἐγὼ δὲ θανὼν γαῖα μέλαιν' ἔσομαι. (4)

Τεθνηκὼς, Ζωῶ φθεγγόμενος στόματι. (5)

Ὦ ἄνα . . . . . οὔποτε σεῖο
λῆσομαι ἀρχόμενος οὐδ' ἀποπαυόμενος,
ἀλλ' αἰεί πρῶτον σε καὶ ὕστατον ἔν τε μέσοισιν
ἀείσω · · σύ δέ μοι κλύθι καί ἐσθλά δίδου. (6)

Tu fulminibus frange trisulcis. (7)

Πάντη δ' ἀθανάτων ἀφανῆς νόος ἀνθρώποισιν. (8)

Χ' οὕτως ἄν δοκέοιμι μετ' ἀνθρώπων θέος . . . (9)

Ego quid ater
Hadriæ novi sinus et quid albus
Peccet Iapyx. (10)

Then I said, I will not make mention of Him nor speak any more in his name ; but his word was in mine heart as a burning fire shut up in my bones, and I was weary with forbearing and I could not stay.

[Here in the Greek 1 Corinthians xiv. 8, 9.]

Ὡς παράξενοι χαίροντες ἰδεῖν που ὁδοῦ
καὶ οἱ θαλλαττεύοντες ἰδεῖν λιμένα
οὕτω οἱ γράφοντες βιβλίου τέλος.

Tomorrow, and Tomorrow and Tomorrow.

On Browning's parchment the sentences were irregular, some of them curving about to find room; one passage was all in capitals and run together like a single long word; the accents were hardly decipherable; no translations nor references to sources were given. The difficulties of presenting the document in any useful way were so great that I had nearly concluded not to attempt it, but a friend submitted it to a scholar not to be baffled by difficulties, namely to Professor W. K. Prentice of Princeton. This ingenious and learned gentleman sent light through the whole thing, as my reader will find by bringing together the figures I have above appended to Browning's lines with those that number Professor Prentice's notes here subjoined : —

1. This is translated by Wharton (Sappho, Ode ii, 17) : "But I must dare all, since one so poor . . . ," and this is probably what the line meant to Browning. But it is quite uncertain whether these are the words of Sappho herself or of Longinus, who quotes the ode, or partly of one and partly of the other. Consequently it is uncertain what the words really mean, and they are omitted from most editions of Sappho. Longinus ("On the Sublime," chap. 10) is the only source for this ode.

2. "We conquered as we wished."

3. "Six hours are quite enough for toil: those thereafter, expressed in writing, say LIVE! to mortals." — Anthologia Palatina, x. 43 (anonym.).

4. "Rejoice thou in thy youth, dear heart! Soon there will be others ; but I, dying, shall be black earth."— Theognis, 877 f.

5. "[For now the corse from out the sea hath called me home,]
   Dead, (yet) speaking with a living tongue."
   Theognis, 1230.

But this distich was written originally, as Athenæus (x. 427 b) says, of a conch-shell, which was used as a horn to call the poet home, perhaps to his dinner.

6. "O Lord, [thou son of Leto, child of Zeus], thee never
   Will I forget, beginning nor when I make an end ;

But even thee first, last and midmost
Will I sing : then hear me thou, and grant me good."
Theognis, 1–4.

7. " Shatter thou with three-cleft thunderbolts ! "

8. " But the thought of the immortals is altogether secret unto men." — Solon, frag. 17.

9. " And thus would I appear a god among men . . ."

10. " I know what Hadria's gulf is when it darkens, and what mischief bright Iapyx doth make." — Horace, Caron. 27, 18–20.

11. " As travellers rejoice to see [how far they have come ?], and mariners to see the port, so scribes to see the end of the book."

In 1863, and for a number of years after, Robert Browning was by no means the famous man he afterwards became. Complaints of obscurity in his writings were still heard among literary men. Tennyson, to whom Browning introduced me, told me he thought his poems powerful but too " rough." Anthony Froude had a similar feeling. Browning had then more' admirers in Boston than in London. William Henry Channing and I had an enthusiasm then shared only by Dante Rossetti. Channing told me that the obscurity of " Sordello " lay in the fact that in the original edition there was no punctuation at all : he had taken his pencil and punctuated the book and it was comprehensible enough. A Browning Club was suggested in my article (1864) in the " Englishwoman's Journal."

When " Dramatis Personæ " appeared, the first review of it was written by myself, from the proofs Browning gave me, for the " Morning Star." I found fault with the closing verse of " Gold Hair " for its apparent sanction of a dogma (Human Depravity), and he thought I had missed his meaning. A review which I thought grossly unjust appeared in one of the quarterlies and I wondered who could have written it. " A man who sometimes invites me to dinner," said Browning.

Carlyle objected to all rhymed and measured poetry, but he must have made some reservation in favour of Browning.

The men did not meet often, but were always cordial. I never heard Browning speak of Carlyle but with homage except on the appearance of his " Shooting Niagara."

One evening when I was with the Carlyles the talk fell on the Brownings; and the same night I wrote down my recollections: —

Carlyle. I remember Browning as a fine young man, living in the neighbourhood of Croydon. I liked him better than any young man about here. He had simple speech and manners and ideas of his own. A good talk I recall with him, when I walked with him to the top of a hill, which had a fine prospect. When he published " Paracelsus " I did not make much out of it: it seemed to me to have something " sensational " as they say about it; but that and his other works proved a strong man.

Miss Barrett sent me some of her first verses in manuscript. I wrote back that I thought she could do better than write verses : I saw little usefulness in them. She wrote me then saying, " What else can I do? Here I am held hopelessly on a sofa by spinal disease." I wrote taking back all I had said. Her father was a doctor late from India — harsh and impracticable; his lightest utterances must stand out hard as the laws of the Medes and Persians. He saw her a moment every day as a physician; then she was left alone. Then she read some compliments of Browning's to her poetry.

Mrs. Carlyle (interposing). Oh no, Mr. Browning never wrote a word about her.

Carlyle. Ah well, you shall tell it all revised and corrected when I get through. — Then she wrote something about him, comparing him to a nectarine.

Mrs. Carlyle. Oh!

Mr. Ballantyne. A pomegranate.

M. D. C.

" And from Browning some pomegranate which cut deep down the middle,
Shows a heart within blood-tinctured of a veined humanity.

Carlyle. I stand corrected. Well: Browning becomes interested in that and other poems, and resolves to find her out. He has no clue to her except an acquaintance with her wealthy uncle, John Kenyon. He writes to John Kenyon asking for an introduction. How was it then, madam?

Mrs. Carlyle. Mr. Kenyon was absent. As soon as he

returned he wrote a note to Mr. Browning saying that his niece was a confirmed invalid — never saw any one, nor left her couch — and that an introduction was impossible.

Carlyle. Ah yes, — meanwhile Browning hearing nothing from Kenyon determined not to stop on ceremony and went to Dr. Barrett's house. The servant man had been taking too much beer; thought Browning a doctor, and admitted him. He went into the study where Miss Elizabeth was reclining. They had a conversation; liked each other; and she made arrangements for him to call again. He did so, and the spinal disease passed away; the spell-bound princess was reached by her knight; took up her bed and walked; one day went all the way to Marylebone church, where they were married. Then they could not face the angry father, and went to Italy. Kenyon supplied the money; and when he died left them more. She was never suffered by her father to see him again — not even when he was dying. She caught sight of him through an open door. Now, madam, you may give the history in chronological order.

Upon which Mrs. Carlyle dressed up a few points in his narrative. In our talk Mrs. Carlyle said she had tried to read " Sordello," but could not tell whether Sordello was " a book, a city, or a man."

The house of the Brownings in Warwick Crescent was of rather dark interior, and the mixture of old Italian tapestries and furniture with modern things was not attractive. The family consisted of Robert Browning, his father, his sister Miss Browning, and his son Barrett, whom they called " Pinna." This youth petted a white owl, which indeed had a high place in the affections of the whole family. Old Mr. Browning was extremely interesting. Dante Rossetti contended that there was something Semitic in Robert Browning's countenance, and although there was less suggestion of that origin in his father's look, plausibility was lent to the supposition by the fact that he had been a clerk of the Rothschilds, and also by his Hebrew learning. The original name, Browning told me, had been De Bruni. I was told by an old friend of the elder Browning that he was a good deal of a humourist; he was clever in drawing pleasant sketches and

caricatures of his friends, and writing amusing verses beneath
them. I found his conversation particularly instructive in
folk-lore. The old gentleman's brain was a storehouse of literary and philosophical antiquities. He seemed to have known
Paracelsus, Faustus, and even Talmudic personages personally. He was modest with his learning, a perfect gentleman.

Miss Browning was in every way attractive, and with a wit
and tact that appeared more French than English.

Browning was a cautious believer in "clairvoyance." There
was a famous "medium" in London, Mrs. Marshall, whose
performances puzzled me. Browning attributed them to
"clairvoyance;" he had no faith in the theory of spirits, and
a dislike of spiritualists in general, of Hume in particular.
Hume I had met at the house of Mr. and Mrs. Spencer Hall,
— where he recited a comic piece in verse, — and could appreciate the portraiture of "Mr. Sludge, the Medium."

After Browning had enraged the spiritualists by that poem,
I mentioned to him in a note a story which had been put into
circulation in America, and which I wished to stigmatize in
one of my letters to the "Cincinnati Commercial." It was
that at some séance in Italy where Hume was present, the
spirits had placed a wreath on the head of his wife instead of
on himself, which made him jealous and angry. He wrote me:
" What you call the ' ridiculous story ' of Hume's spirits passing me by to crown my wife and so gaining him my enmity,
was told by Hume in a spiritualistic journal — and I remember that the article containing the story invited me to say
what I pleased in reply. Had I condescended to reply it would
have been simply to the effect that I could desire no better
evidence of Hume's nature and practices than this lie, which
no doubt seemed to him exactly the thing to believe."

Browning said to Mrs. Conway that when people talked
about his wife he had a sort of "jealousy" of her being spoken
of by persons who knew little or nothing of the kind of woman
she was. One day when I was in his library Browning took
down his wife's Bible, — Hebrew, Greek, and English, — and
pointed to her notes (on the wide margins), which were nu-

merous and critical, including a number of more exact ren-
derings. " What is that for learning ? " he said.

When Queen Victoria desired to meet Carlyle, and the
Dean and Lady Augusta Stanley arranged the matter (March
4, 1869), Robert Browning, Sir Charles and Lady Lyell, and
Mr. and Mrs. Grote were also invited. In a letter to his
sister, — too intimate to be copied here in full, — Carlyle remarks with some humour that the Queen said to Browning,
" Are you writing anything ? " Browning had just been publishing the longest poem ever written. The poet told me, by
the way, that after the publication of " The Ring and the
Book " he met Carlyle and told him that if he had now reached
the public it was by telling his story over ten times. " It was
like bawling into the ear of a deaf man."

After that introduction to the Queen, Browning was courted
by the aristocracy. He was above all an artist, and knew well
the philosophy of Emerson's quatrain : —

> Quit the hut, frequent the palace —
> Reck not what the people say;
> For still where'er the trees grow biggest
> Huntsmen find the easiest way.

But I always felt that his serious friendships, since those of
his youth, had mainly been with Americans. He spoke with
much feeling of Margaret Fuller. " From her plague-stricken
ship poor Margaret wrote my wife a letter. After a long time
it reached us, but so blurred that we could make out very
little, the paper so foul that we burnt it." He loved to talk
of the Hawthornes, who had lived near him in Florence, and
of the Motleys and the Storys. Americans with good introduction were received with open arms. He came in one day
and found my wife sitting with his sister, and said to her with
a glow of satisfaction, that he had just black-balled an editor
who had tried to stir ill-feeling between America and England. He enjoyed some of our American writers, admired our
women, and liked our sparkling Catawba, to which I had the
pleasure of introducing him in the days when old Longworth
made wine fit for any poet.

The friendships of his youth were sacred to Browning, and they were chiefly with those who had built up the peculiar character of my South Place chapel. The first review ever written of him was by my predecessor, W. J. Fox, M. P. To Eliza Flower he wrote shortly before her early death in 1846: "I never had another feeling than entire admiration for your music — entire admiration. I put it apart from all other English music I know, and fully believe in it as the music we all waited for. Of your health I shall not trust myself to speak; you must know what is unspoken." I always believe she was Browning's first love.

I believe that the advanced rationalism for which our chapel became distinguished in Mr. Fox's time was primarily due to Robert Browning. In his early youth he was precociously sceptical, and undermined the faith of Eliza Flower's sister, Sarah, now known to the world as Sarah Flower Adams, author of "Nearer, my God, to Thee!" From their home at Harlow Sarah wrote, November 23, 1827, a strange letter to Mr. Fox, whose daughter, Mrs. Bridell-Fox, gave me the subjoined copy: —

You did not ask me to write, and perhaps will be little thankful for what you are like to receive, a regular confession of faith, or rather the want of it, from one whom you little suspect guilty of the heinous sin of unbelief. It reads like half jest: never was I more serious. My mind has been wandering a long time, and now it seems to have lost sight of that only invulnerable hold against the assaults of this warring world, a firm belief in the genuineness of the Scriptures.

No, not the only one. I do believe in the existence of an All-wise and Omnipotent Being — and that, involving as it does the conviction that everything is working together for good, brings with it comfort I would not resign for worlds. Still, I would fain go to my Bible as I used to — but I cannot. The cloud has come over me gradually, and I did not discover the darkness in which my soul was shrouded until, in seeking to give light to others, my own gloomy state became too settled to admit of doubt. It was in answering Robert Browning that my mind refused to bring forward argument, turned recreant, and sided with the enemy. And when I went to Norwich musical festival, oh, how much I lost! In all the choruses of praise to the Almighty my heart joined, and seemed to lift itself above the world to celebrate the praises of him to whom I owed the bliss of these feelings; but the rest of the " Messiah " dwindled to a mere musical enjoyment; and the consciousness of what it might once have been to me brought the bitterest sensations of sadness, almost remorse.

And now, as I sit and look up to the room in which I first had existence, and think of the mother who gave it, and watch the window of the chamber in which she yielded hers, in death as in life a fervent Christian, that thought links itself with another, — how much rather would she I had never been, than to be what I now am.

I have a firm belief in a resurrection, — at least I think I have, — but my mind is in a sad state ; and before that goes, I must endeavour to build up my decaying faith. How is it to be done ? I want to read a good ecclesiastical history. I dare not apply to papa. I dare not let him have a glimpse at the infatuation that possesses me. Had he been less rigid in his ideas of all kinds of unbelief, it would have been better for me. But I have had no one either to remove or confirm my doubts, and heaven alone knows what uneasiness they have given me. I would give worlds to be a sincere believer ; to go to my Bible as to a friend in the hour of trial, feeling that whatever might befall, *that* would never desert me, and defying the world to rob me of its consolations.

My life has been like a set of gems on a string of gold, — a succession of bright and beautiful things, without a dark thread to dim their lustre. But it will not be always thus. It is not thus now, and some resources I must have against the evil time which is beginning to set in. The very study will be a delight, even if it has not the desired result. The consciousness that I have not examined as far as in me lies, weighs heavily upon me, and to you I now look to direct my inquiries. 'T is a bold step, and I wonder how I could bring myself to it. I have often longed to speak to you, but *that* I could not do. And now it seems as if I could not bear to speak to any one, but I want quietly to read in my own room. What ? Why, any books that you would deem suitable.

I shall soon be at home (London), and if you will lend them, and let me read them, my mind will, at all events, be relieved from whatever portion of guilt may mingle in its present uneasiness.

I hope this will not worry you. I would not be one to add
to the annoyances that visit you ; but that you have a sincere
regard for me I now believe, and how it is returned let this
confidence which you possess, unshared by any one beside,
bear testimony.

I long to come home. Harlow is not what it once was, and
it has added to the feeling of loneliness which has been coming on. Though I may often be mirthful, I am not always
happy. But I am in a sad mood this morning, and to-morrow may be brighter in the heavens and in the heart. So I
will not write any more than one thing, and that you know
already, that I am yours affectionately,   SALLY.

Burn, and forget, — not me and those books, — but the
letter and low spirits.

Mr. Fox had been up to that time a liberal Unitarian, but
his opinions had by no means reached the phase indicated in
the above letter. His rationalism, however, took a new departure a year or two later, and after a careful study of his
works and those of Sarah Flower Adams, I am convinced that
her doubts, or perhaps his efforts to remove them, did away
with his faith in a biblical revelation. Thus Robert Browning, as I believe, had something to do with the preparation
of my chapel for the freethought which now characterizes it.

I believe the sisters Flower inspired both " Pauline " and
" Pippa Passes." Long before I knew the relations between
Browning and those ladies, I had felt that Pippa's voice told
the secret of the poet's experiences. At a meeting of the
London Browning Society (May 23, 1884) I said : " My first
meeting with Pippa stands apart in memory, unique, indescribable, — like falling in love." But deep answers only to
deep. Seven years later I learned how the singing of Eliza
had enchanted his heart; and that before he was sixteen his
unconscious influence, like that of Pippa, had wrought far-
reaching effects on and through Sarah, whose genius was just
flowering.

In my memorial discourse on the death of W. J. Fox
(June 12, 1864) I alluded to a favourite anthem of his, from
Browning's " Paracelsus," and it was sung by the choir.

> I stoop
> Into a dark tremendous sea of cloud.
> It is but for a time: I press God's lamp
> Close to my breast: its splendours soon or late
> Will pierce the gloom: I shall emerge some day.

I afterwards heard that Browning was present. It was
Sarah Flower Adams who, with the assistance of Mr. Fox,
compiled and largely composed the "South Place Hymn-
Book" (published in 1841), and set in it those lines from
Browning. I also find some record of experience in the quotation from Jeremiah on the old parchment cover of his
poems (*supra*). In her heart, too, the old fire burned, after
its light had sunk, and along with the lines from "Paracelsus" appeared, for the first time (1841), her famous hymn,
"Nearer, my God, to Thee?" She pressed the lamp close to
her breast, but its splendours could not disperse the gloom
of the agonies of the world. For in the same year that her
famous hymn was written, she wrote also her wonderful poem,
"Vivia Perpetua," in which Vivia says : —

> There are some mysteries; I scarce begin
> To thread them, but from out them up springs love,
> Flies through them like a bird along a grove,
> And sings them to forgetfulness, in joy.
> But one e'en now doth come to hold her mute:
> Oppression yet doth crush with iron foot. . . .
> Our power is so much weaker than our will, —
> But Love omnipotent !

In these lines Sarah Flower Adams laid her finger on the
defect of all theological theism. Robert Browning, no doubt,
tried to limit the scepticism he had awakened, but his familiar
argument, that good comes out of evil, did not reach the
theistic dilemma: infliction of pain for good purposes may be
the necessity of limited power, but how is it pardonable in
unlimited power? Sarah Flower Adams aspired to her God,
not everybody's God ; but everybody is now singing the hymn
so many years heard only in our chapel. And perhaps not
one who sings it realizes that it was written by a disbeliever
in Christianity.

I do not think that Browning continued his old relations with W. J. Fox, M. P., whom he described to me as " a man of genius apt to put out his talent to work for him." He may have shared the feeling of some that Eliza Flower really died, like Ottilia in Goethe's " Elective Affinities," of a struggle between her moral sentiment and her passion for W. J. Fox (long separated from his wife). The affection of the minister for Eliza Flower had given rise to much gossip, and after entering Parliament her friends thought him more distant. He never spoke a word against Fox, but said little about him, and I now believe that this silence was due to the painful memories with which the orator was associated.

In our walks Browning generally broached the religious topic. As the minister of South Place I may have been unconsciously a sort of ghost from his past. I do not remember that he ever referred to the Bible as an authority, but he had read it critically. In one of his later poems I noted that he quotes, " In *a* beginning God made heaven and earth." In the original Hebrew there is no article before " beginning," and " In *the* beginning," is misleading. Browning followed the Talmud, according to which there were several beginnings which were disapproved by the deity, but at length " a beginning " which he pronounced " exceeding good," i. e. exceeding the previous ones. My own belief is that the meaning can only be preserved by reading " In beginning."

Browning was not conventionally orthodox, but it was a necessity of his genius to project a divine drama into the universe. He hated to give up anything scenic, even a day of judgment. In one of our talks he said, " If a man can summon his workmen and tenants at the end of the week or the year, and settle with them, why should not God so summon mankind at the end of life? " So hard did he try to believe. I once asked him how anybody was suffered to doubt about a truth of such stupendous importance as immortality. " Because," he said, " such certainty would not be consistent with the discipline of life. Were there no doubt, faith would not be faith." Yet he never explained why omnipotence could

not effect all the discipline without the ignorance, and without
evil. But I doubt if Browning conceived of any omnipotent
being. He was only clear in criticising my sceptical positions,
and I could never get him to define his own positions. There
was no mysticism about him, no accent of the pietist nor of
the moralist, and it appeared to me curious that this man of
the world should make more of theology than of ethics. To
my expression of that surprise Browning answered, " Moral
character and action depend so much on circumstances that
it is almost impossible for men to judge each other fairly."
He was of course equally tolerant in religious matters, but so
animated in discussing them that I have known him stop on
the pavement to impress his point. This interest in speculative religion may have been to some extent an inheritance,
but not from his father, who appeared to have little interest
in theology. The family had belonged to the Congregation-
alist (or Independent) denomination, and Browning sometimes went to the little chapel of Mr. Foster in Camden
Town. One evening this minister, very liberal, preached on
nature, and Browning meeting him at the door said, " It was
interesting, but I should have preferred that instead of describing nature you had told us the impression made by
nature on you."

But it was only in private that I recall any sign in Browning of interest in religious subjects. In society he was always
the man of the world, and he frequented society. A young
American admirer told us she had found him " dinner-eed to
death." Another tale went that on being verbally invited to
dinner he made a note of the date and then said, " Of course
you mean next year "? There never was a more delightful
table-talker. But with all this he never appeared to me really
English. He had not the ruddy complexion due to his large
and fair face ; he was so cosmopolitan, he had such taste for
beauty in woman (often undraped in his poems), and such
passion for the Greek language, that I suspect there may
have been some Brunidean clan in ancient Hellas. Browning was a fair amateur sculptor : when I first called on him,

with my letter from Curtis, he was modelling a fine head of Keats.

Browning had few intimate literary friendships. He liked to talk with George Eliot and Lewes, but was rarely at the Priory on their Sunday evenings, when others were usually present. He had more friends among the London artists. He cared little, I think, for English politics, and his interest in the affairs of France and Italy appeared to me rather that of a spectator looking down on the arena. I could never discover whether he sympathized with Mrs. Browning's admiration for Napoleon III, but once at my table when Mazzini was mentioned he said with genuine feeling, "Poor Mazzini!" William Malleson, an intimate friend of Mazzini and enthusiast for his cause, was troubled by the exclamation. But I had often reason to recall it with sympathy, and its indication of the remoteness of Browning from the rush and roar of European politics. His interest was in individual minds and characters, and not in people herded together either in political or sectarian masses. Above all he appreciated and loved the "Eternal Feminine," and merited the warm friendship he enjoyed of ladies.

My first experience of an old-fashioned English inn was in Tennyson's country. It was at Freshwater, and from my tidy room in the Albion I had a beautiful outlook over the bay. On my way, travelling on an old stage-coach, I heard a good deal said about a romance in the neighbourhood. A young officer of high family had formed an engagement of marriage with a pretty "servant girl." The match was opposed by his family, but he persisted. No clergyman in the island could be found to perform the marriage service, and one had to be imported for the purpose. There were circumstances in the life of the "servant girl" which led the neighbours to take deep interest in her. She was refined and educated, and the Tennysons acknowledged her as a friend, and were present at the wedding.

On arrival I sent from the inn my letter from Browning, and received an invitation from Mrs. Tennyson to dine at

Farringford at eight. I thus had a good afternoon for strolling on the cliffs, though such is the perversity of my own nature that I soon get tired of external nature, unless I meet her in the excursions of Wordsworth or some other poet. So the best part of my afternoon was passed at the house of Mrs. Cameron, already well known to me by her artistic photographs. She was the first person in England to make the large portraits and copies of pictures, and was a much valued friend of the Rossettis. Mrs. Cameron was the widow of a distinguished officer in India, where she was much admired in society, being not only handsome but of fine intelligence. She had at that time been an amateur in photography, and after her husband's death concluded to increase her means by the improvements she had discovered. When I visited her, and had admired her portraits of Tennyson and Sir Henry Taylor, she spoke of Tennyson as her best friend, and alluded to the great service he had recently rendered to her. I then learned that the romance I had heard about on the coach had occurred in her house. The " servant girl," so called, whom the officer had just married, had been an inmate of her own family ; and she related to me the brief story which, she declared, she had no objection should be made public. She was once walking in the streets of Cork, when a lovely child offered to sell her flowers. Struck by her appearance she made some inquiries, and, finding that the child was an orphan and without relatives to object, she took her into her own family and had her carefully educated. She turned out to be in every respect a lovely girl, worthy of any position. Mrs. Cameron presented me with a picture of the bride, who was certainly refined and beautiful enough to be set in the poetry of Tennyson, where I think I have met her. She was finely educated, and was accomplished in music. All of this went on while the Camerons were in affluence. When Mrs. Cameron, who had no children of her own, became a widow in reduced circumstances, the grateful adopted daughter insisted on doing the work of a housemaid. The Freshwater legend was that the young officer had seen her sweeping the steps in front of Mrs. Cameron's pretty cottage. In fact, however, the young man, who had acquired some distinction by a philosophical essay, had visited the Tennysons, and on his way back called to get Mrs. Cameron's portrait of the poet. The graceful young girl met him at the door, and being a man of some genius as well as taste, he asked Mrs. Cameron about her. Mrs. Cameron told him that she was taking care of the house because she was grateful, but was a real lady; she regarded her with as much honour and affection as if she were her daughter. The Tennysons were greatly pleased by the betrothal, and when, on account of the objections of the officer's aristocratic relatives, the village clergyman refused to perform the ceremony, Tennyson brought one from a distance, and I think the wedding festival was at his house, Farringford. The Tennysons withdrew from the village church, and the clergyman was becoming unpopular.

Although I have placed this visit to Mrs. Cameron in June, 1863, I am not certain that it may not have been on one of my later visits, — for the Isle of Wight and Lymington, while Allingham was there, were my favourite haunts, and my adventures were duly chronicled in my " South-Coast Saunterings in England " (" Harper's Magazine "), where, however, the times and seasons of my adventures are not noted. When I was there the officer had shortly before taken his bride to India, where his career was philosophical rather than military; he founded at Calcutta a Positivist church.

I was the only guest at Farringford. Mrs. Tennyson was attractive, and lighted up the table by her cordiality and pleasant voice. After dinner the poet took me up to his study, where he sat smoking his pipe — having given me a cigar — and talking in the frankest manner. Among other things he told me of the people who waylaid him, the incidents being sometimes amusing. Two men, for example, having got into his garden separately, one climbed a tree at the approach of the other. The other, seeing him, called out softly, " I twig ! " and immediately climbed another tree. And yet he declared that no man was more accessible to any one who had any reason for wishing to see him. So I, for one, certainly found, the hospitalities of Farringford having been offered to me beyond my willingness to accept them.

It had been a stormy evening and the night was of pitchy darkness when I started out, against invitations to remain, to go to the "Albion." Tennyson insisted on showing me a nearer way, but in the darkness got off his bearings. Bidding me walk close behind him, we went forward through the mud, when suddenly I found myself precipitated six or seven feet downward. Sitting in the mud, I called on the poet to pause, but it was too late; he was speedily seated beside me. This was seeing the Laureate of England in a new light, or rather, hearing him under a novel darkness. Covered with mud, groping about, he improved the odd occasion with such an innocent run of witticisms and anecdotes that I had to conclude that he had reached a condition which had discovered in him unexpected resources. His deep bass voice came through the congenial darkness like mirthful thunder, while he groped until he found a path. "That this should have happened after dinner!" he exclaimed; "do not mention this to the temperance folk."

Next morning I was punctual to an appointment Tennyson had made to take me around his manor and favourite cliffs. Mrs. Tennyson met me with the explanation of our fall: she had directed the gardener to make an addition to a walk in the garden which required a deep cut of which Mr. Tennyson had not been informed. She expressed more regret than was necessary, but smiled at the drollery of her husband's account, and declared the place should be named Conway Walk.

Tennyson was in every way different from the man I expected to see. The portrait published with his poems in America conveyed some of the expression around his eyes, but not the long head and the long face. Moreover, of all the eminent men I have met, he was the one who could least be seen before he had spoken. His deep and blunt voice, and his fondness for strong Saxon words, such as would make a Tennysonian faint if met in one of his lines, his almost Quaker-like plainness of manner albeit softened by the gentle eye and the healthy humanity of his thought, did not support my precon- ception that he was the drawing-room idealist. When in speaking of Robert Browning with high estimation he yet wondered at "a certain roughness" in his poems, it rather amused me ; for Browning put the utmost daintiness — while Tennyson put all of his roughness — into his talk. He did not seem to me a typical Englishman, despite his passionate patriotism. He said but little about the war in America. I think Browning in his letter may have intimated to him that I was much concerned about the slaves and friendly to Eng- land, for he evidently restrained himself in his resentment of the abuse of England in America. Such resentment I consid- ered natural and just, so there was no controversy in that direction. It was the day after I had written my letter of June 10, 1863, to the Confederate Mason, but I cannot re- member our conversation about that, nor indeed about any- thing. In his library Tennyson put me in an easy chair, then went on telling good anecdotes, — these not about his contemporaries, but concerning personages of a past genera- tion. But I admired him most out on the cliff. When he had accompanied me along the sea on my way to the station, then turned and walked slowly back, I gave a look at him from a hundred yards distance, and he appeared to me the ideal Prospero summoning around him the beautiful forms that will never fade from his isle.

Tennyson wrote me a letter in response to my book, " The Sacred Anthology," a copy of which I sent him. He wished me to print an edition of smaller size, which one could carry on his walks. He was astonished to find that the non-Chris- tian peoples were so exalted in their religion and ethics, and no doubt startled to find how many ideas in his own poems had been anticipated by Oriental poets.

In later years I had reason to deplore the extent to which Tennyson was ignorant of the non-Christian people in Eng- land. In November, 1882, his drama " The Promise of May " was performed at the Globe Theatre in London, and although

I should have been distressed as a freethinker had the audience applauded Tennyson's notion of our tribe, I was troubled at the utter failure of his religious play, knowing how he would be hurt by it. I was not there the first evening when Lord Queensberry made a scene by protesting from his box against the calumnies against Secularists. It was suspected by some that Queensberry had been enticed by the manager to make a " scandal," for it was the means of crowding the house the second night. Lord Queensberry had taken a box for this occasion also, and invited Mrs. Conway and myself into it, but promised he would not make any demonstration. A Sunday had intervened between these first two representations, and several utterances had been cut out; among them what the girl said of her lover, " Yet I fear he is a freethinker." This had been greeted on the first night with loud laughter.

But no chord in the public breast was touched. The pathos had the effect of bathos ; the audience grew serious only when humour was attempted, and roared with laughter at the solemn parts. The Laureate had evolved his typical freethinker in his library. Had he, instead of wandering about incognito among farmers, as he once did, made some excursion among the Secularists in London, he would have discovered that though the sceptic may be unhappy, he is the last man to make others unhappy. It would be impossible to find more affectionate and tender-hearted and benevolent men than Darwin, Huxley, Tyndall, and other eminent unbelievers. Freethinkers have as much devotion as the orthodox, though it is lavished on human beings.

The play revealed Tennyson's weak point as a poet. He could not invent a plot. He was the inspired story-teller, but the story had to be given. His Ulysses, Princess, Arthurian Idylls, all his great works, are the exquisite telling of old tales. Of his four dramas neither had the least chance of popular success; but the " Falcon," the " Cup," and " Queen Mary " had plots of classic origin, and being finely mounted and acted did no injury to the poet's fame. In the " Promise of May "

the Laureate attempted a plot of his own, and it turned out
to be a mixture of a police court seduction case and a curate's
sermon.

It is doubtful whether any play with a theological purpose
had been put on the stage since Marlowe's " Barabbas." That
play represented a Jew evolved out of Marlowe's inner consciousness who went about committing every kind of crime
from the pure love of it. In the following century that play
was travestied by Cyril Tourneur in " The Atheist." Shakespeare had answered Marlowe's Barabbas with Shylock, showing that the Jew was a man impelled by human motives. If
Tennyson's play had appeared two centuries before, it might
have been a sort of reply to Cyril Tourneur's " Atheist,"
showing that the unbeliever had at least humanly conceivable
motives for his deeds. A further comparative study was suggested by the fact that Marlowe was personally an atheist and
that many were made sceptics by Tennyson's " In Memoriam."
Tennyson, as his poem " Despair " shows, waged war against
the orthodox dogmas that seem cruel as much as against atheism. A friend of his told me that he was once at a dinner
company at Farringford when in the evening they all went to
a window to witness the burning of dry brush-wood in the
garden. There were in the company a Roman Catholic baronet and his wife, and Tennyson said loudly, " Lady ——,
how would it do to throw a man into that fire to burn through
eternity? That's what you believe is going to happen to me
because I don't believe the creeds ! " The lady was embarrassed, but Tennyson was excited and persisted in the attack,
until her husband took him by the arm and said, " Ah, she
does n't pretend to know anything about such things ! "

CHAPTER XXX

WHEN at the close of 1863 the Committee of South Place chapel had urged a permanent settlement, we agreed to remain for six months. The ladies of Concord and Boston had appointed Mrs. Conway to collect contributions in England in aid of the coloured freedmen. While she was successfully occupied with that work, and I was writing articles for English and American papers, we felt that we were serving our country as well as if residing in it.

I had been preaching at South Place pretty regularly for five months before my regular ministry began, February, 1864. The society had originated under the American apostle of universalism, Elhanan Winchester, during the French Revolution, which he interpreted by the Book of Revelation, and the society now passed to another American who had come over to interpret the new revolution in America. During its threescore years and ten the society had passed from Winchester's rudimentary universalism through phases of faith leading to the humanized theism of W. J. Fox. In rewriting my old discourses I discovered how conservative my theology had been in Cincinnati, even when the seceders went off to found their " Church of the Redeemer." At South Place the old sacramental vessels were preserved only as relics, the communion-table was used only for the flowers set there every Sunday : one relic, the fine gown worn even by W. J. Fox, I was the first to discard. There was a pleasant vestry in which was always placed a decanter of port or sherry for the preacher's refreshment. The high " pepper-box " pulpit and the straight-backed pews remained until 1876, when the whole interior was renovated. It is a building of excellent acoustical qualities with deep galleries, and can seat nearly a thousand. The congregation contained no workingmen so-called, and the few artisans in it were persons of fair education. The members were mostly middle-class people of literary tastes, and trained in families whose vital religion was the new Reformation. This Reformation of varied phases — some illusive while those affecting freedom of thought steadily prevailed — had been fruitful in individual characters. I was the pastor of the veteran radicals even when they were too infirm to attend the chapel. James Watson, whose memory extended to the prosecutions of Thomas Paine and his friends, and who had himself been in prison for selling Paine's works, was a serene man of such clear mind that I could hardly realize his age. William Lovett, the old chartist, who wrote several useful books on sociological and educational subjects, was a charming old radical to talk with. I conducted the funerals of Watson and Lovett and cherish the souvenirs sent me by their families, a large engraving of Romney's Paine, and a portrait of Madame Darusmont (Fanny Wright).

London was a different city in those days from what it had become only twenty years later. In 1864 the Soho region was still phenomenal for villainy. It was something to be seen, and I remember passing through the besotted streets under guard of a policeman. But fifteen years later Wentworth Higginson, who was visiting us, related with sorrow the destructiveness of time on old institutions : he had gone alone through the whole Soho district, but, alas, without having his pocket picked even of its half-visible handkerchief. Field Lane, where Dickens located Fagin's school for pocket-picking, was, in 1864, a place still suggestive of such dens: an uninhabited old shanty was pointed out as the very house of Fagin, and I tried to make out the itinerary of Oliver Twist and the Artful Dodger. The Seven Dials, where sots drank their gin in rooms still

UNITARIAN CHAPEL, FINSBURY

retaining traces of a fashionable past, was a place to avoid, but the district of St. George's-in-the-East was a show-place of orgies. It is near that region that Swedenborg was buried in a pretty churchyard. I have sometimes sat beside his tomb and watched the children seeking in that green garden asylum from the miserable scenes outside, and wondered that the great mystic should have seen his first visions in the thick of London city. A little farther amid the docks I saw a ritualist clergyman, celebrating on Good Friday the "Stations of the Cross." A small procession of his congregation (St. Peter's) followed the draped cross, and at its several stations paused to sing hymns; but an English rector in monkish dress and the intoned ceremonies enraged the crowds, which jeered at the ritualists. Across the Thames I found and entered the old Tabard inn from whose yard the pilgrims used to start for Canterbury. On it there was a bit of some carven figure out of which the imagination might restore the head of either a horse or a pilgrim.

The gallows still had its place outside the grim Old Bailey prison. On what was I believe the last public execution — that of the men of Manila concerned in the "Flowery Land" murders — I went out in the early morning to observe the crowd, but intending to avoid the spectacle of the law's imitation of the murderers. But even then, hours before the event, every street and alley leading to the prison was crammed. The crowd was brutal, many of both sexes being already tipsy. With some difficulty I reached a point near Smithfield where the executions by fire and stake, deemed civilized in their day, supplied the right moral point of view for the scene of legal murder. As I was surveying the mass of people, the church bell began to toll, the boisterous throng was smitten silent, and far away I beheld the white-robed victims swinging in the air. The men hung there from nine till noon.

During the first years of my ministry at South Place the means of reaching it from Camden Town were inconvenient. After I had reached the underground railway at Portland Road it only took me to Farringdon Street. From that point

I made my way on foot through Smithfield, then an open
" common." Smithfield, long consecrated in my sentiment by
the ashes of its martyrs, became more sacred as the arena
where the unchurched heretics and their opponents carried
on their debates. Every Sunday there were separate groups
each surrounding its leader, but generally they all amalga-
mated around the central combat between the " atheists " and
the " orthodox." The whole thing was picturesque. No ordinary pulpit eloquence could fascinate me so much as the
vigorous unadorned argument of men whose freedom showed
what fruit is borne by wooden stakes quickened by fire and
blood.

I was drawn into the Smithfield conflict. It appeared
grievous that the " atheists " should be offered no alternative
but the dogmas of their evangelical antagonists, and one
morning I advanced from the outskirts of the crowd and
challenged the statement of the chief unbelieving orator,
Bradlaugh. My statement, made in a friendly spirit from an
unorthodox point of view, and presenting a new kind of
theism, commanded respect from the heretics, but vexed the
orthodox. Afterwards I left home early on Sundays to participate in the debate before going on to my chapel. I derived help for my ministry from these open-air meetings. I
was feeling the pulses of London, realizing what problems had
been evolved by the conditions of that great world, and gaining knowledge of the task before me.

I felt it as an affliction when the police began to make the
outdoor disputants " move on." It was at once pathetic and
comical when the more pertinacious of the speakers were
occasionally seen walking backwards and gesticulating at
their moving audience, as if followed by a mob. Finally the
huge meat market was built and the glorious liberties of
Smithfield became a memory.

Not far from us in Camden Town lived the vigorous freethinker and reformer, George Jacob Holyoake, the last man
imprisoned in England for atheism. In my Cincinnati
"Dial" (November and December, 1860) I printed an article

concerning him entitled "Sketch of a Leading English Atheist." Holyoake at fifty had apparently not suffered much by his six months' imprisonment and his many editorial and lecturing labours; he was rather boyish in appearance, and his almost feminine voice in public speaking conveyed an impression of immortal youth.

The lady who wrote the sketch of Holyoake published in my "Dial," Miss Sophia Dobson Collet, resided just opposite us in Lansdowne Terrace. She was deformed but happy; her refined countenance was full of intelligence and vivacity. Her culture — both literary and musical — was wonderful. She had attended the concerts of Mendelssohn in London, knew the Novellos, and could identify every character in Miss Shepard's famous "Charles Auchester." It was from her that I heard of Miss Shepard's "Rumour," never published in America, in which figure Beethoven (Rodomont), Disraeli (Diamid Albany), and Louis Napoleon (Porphyrio). Miss Collet had known Emerson and heard all of his lectures in London in 1848. (Emerson remembered her and asked me about her.) Although she wrote the sympathetic sketch of Holyoake she did not share his opinions. She had sat under the ministry of W. J. Fox at South Place; had been intimate with Eliza Flower, the composer of South Place music, and Sarah Flower Adams, its hymn-writer, and had herself written several hymns and tunes sung in the chapel. She occasionally came to South Place, but had not passed with the congregation into its rationalistic phases of belief, and her spirit had found its support in Frederic Denison Maurice. My wife formed a fast friendship with the sweet neighbour and was able to enliven her existence. She had a strong desire to meet Robert Browning and Thomas Hughes, and we secured them for a Sunday evening dinner, where she and Browning had a talk concerning their old friends.

Miss Collet's brother, C. D. Collet,[1] editor of the "Diplo-

---

[1] C. D. Collet had been a well-known radical and editor in his day. He had, however, been carried away by the strange theory of Mr. Urquhart and Edmund Beales that Lord Palmerston was the paid agent of Russia.

matic Review," had been the musical director of South Place
in the days of the sisters Flower, when its choir was regarded
as the finest in London. He retained this position for a time
after my arrival. Increasing deafness caused him to resign,
but he kept a seat in the gallery near the choir, and was there
every Sunday. He always stopped to speak to me, and one
morning told me that he had not for a year been able to hear
a word from the pulpit. Gradually the music too became inaudible to him, but still he sat there, his daughter beside him.
One morning when the blond and picturesque old gentleman
did not appear, I knew that his end must be near, and so it
proved.

I received a letter from Horace Greeley, dated April 17,
1864, reproaching me sharply for not returning to join in the
presidential campaign. In it he said : —

There was no year of our great trial which was not one of
intense agony to me, as to thousands beside who would gladly
have been buried in the darkest corner of Siberia, only that
we knew that would not do. And we are still in the whirlpool, with no assurance of a safe deliverance. It is by no
means certain that the Copperheads will not choose the next
President — being enabled to choose him because many are in
Europe who should be here in the thickest of the fight.

This letter from one I held in high esteem troubled me. I
replied that I did not see how in America I could do more
than I was doing ; I was writing to the " Tribune " occasionally, regularly to the " Commonwealth " and the Cincinnati
" Gazette," — writing three or four letters every week —
bringing the views of eminent European friends of America
and emancipation to bear on our situation ; that I was receiving assurances from Phillips and others that my letters were
doing good service ; that should I return the discussion of my

I found that my old friend not only saw the hand of Russia and Palmerston in all the base political intrigues of Europe, but also in those of
America, — even of our civil war. He used to load me with his paper,
the *Diplomatic Review*, which despite its wild notions concerning Palmerston contained valuable information.

Mason correspondence might be revived to the detriment of our cause ; but that, nevertheless, if he thought otherwise and would guarantee me a place where I could write and speak freely, I would return. Horace Greeley returned no answer, but I was engaged as the regular London correspondent of the " Tribune."

The cause in which I was interested was liberty; I would not have advocated bloodshed even for emancipation, though anxious since war had come that it should be the means of destroying slavery. I would have considered the Union apart from emancipation not worth one man's blood. I was thus too different from other Americans — even from my antislavery colleagues — to be directly useful in the republican campaign. I had no faith that war could achieve any permanent benefit to white, or black, or to any nation, while the President and the people recognized only the military method of pacification and emancipation. There was thus no place for me in militant America.

London had cordially offered me what my native country had not — a field for the exercise of the ministry for which my strange pilgrimage from slaveholding Virginia and Methodism to freedom and rationalism had trained me. So, despite Horace Greeley's reproach, reason bade me stay where I was wanted for tasks to which I felt that I could bring some competency. So it was that, having gone to England for a few months, I remained more than thirty years.

Unitarianism in England possessed characteristics which promised better for a free lance than the more organized denomination in America. This was largely due to the influence of two men, — John James Taylor and James Martineau.

Mr. Taylor, though not aged and his faculties still in full vigour, had retired from the pulpit ; he was, however, much occupied by duties relating to the liberal movement which he had largely moulded, and I could not venture to see him personally as often as his kindness warranted. But his warm interest in the call for aid to the American freedmen in America, which my wife had in hand, brought me into sufficient contact with him to realize the sweetness of his heart and the elevation of his mind. His serene spirit had risen above all egotism and pride.

James Martineau was very different from Taylor. The leader of Unitarians *malgre lui*, he was alarming most of their preachers by his far-reaching researches, involving negations whose corresponding affirmations were not yet clear.

I find among my notes one dated October 26, 1864 : —

Went to the Unitarian Ministerial Conference at Mr. Ireson's church, Islington. Mr. Martineau opened the topic after tea: it was, how far the phrases applied to Christ in the New Testament — e. g., Lord, Saviour, Prince, etc. — were really characteristic of Christ, and had any meaning for us now. It was the most powerful piece of theological statement I ever heard. He proved conclusively that these names all referred to the idea of a kingdom of Christ, begun after the alleged ascension. The great characteristic of modern theology was, he said, a shifting of the scene of Christ's power and influence from heaven to earth, from a future to history, — consequently those phrases and titles have no religious meaning for us now. It was very sweeping. Mr. Aspland, J. J. Taylor, Solly, Coupland, Means, etc., spoke. I was the only one out of the fifteen present, I believe, — certainly the only speaker, — who heartily and entirely agreed with Martineau.

In addition to this memorandum I remember that in closing the discussion Martineau said he must decline to answer any of the arguments that had been adduced from consequences. The fact that the fallacious titles and phrases were used in their own Unitarian hymns and literature, and that all these might have to be expurgated, could not be legitimately weighed against the claim of truth and fact.

Though a leader of Unitarians, Martineau was not a leader of Unitarianism. He had in his mind an ideal English church, though for the moment it consisted of himself and his chapel. It was to gather under its wings all the religious minds, and make the nation a fountain of living waters for all races, without any doctrinal Christianization of them. He was jealous of everything that tended to detach the Unitarian spirit and critique from the general religious life of the country, or organize it into a distinct church. It was here that his contempt for "consequences" had serious effects. On one occasion, when there was reported at the annual meeting of the Unitarian Association a large bequest left it, Martineau declared that the money would tend to entrench in a sort of fortress a spiritual movement that should be perfectly free. The sectarian wing of the association was strong, but the personality and moral genius of Martineau prevailed. I doubt whether in Christian history there can be found another instance of a religious association rejecting a large bequest of money.

None of Martineau's large works convey the right idea of his peculiar power. While unequalled as a preacher, his attempts at systematizing what cannot be systematized are chiefly useful as proving the impossibility of any science of religion. As a sympathetic minister he could console the sorrowful by pointing out the means of distilling some good from things evil; but when he has to carry this out into all its corollaries, the generalization breaks down. Martineau vainly attempted to carry into theism the optimism essential to it, and admits that suffering is refining only to the already refined. His great works on ethics and religion, with all their beautiful pages and their learned surveys of human evolution, must remain as monuments of the failure of theistic philosophy to meet the evil and agony in nature.

The last sermon I had heard in America was from Ralph Waldo Emerson.

After Theodore Parker went silent his society in Boston listened to Emerson whenever he could be secured. When he was to give the Sunday discourse the hall was crowded with the most cultured people in Boston and its suburbs, and some came from Salem, Lynn, Concord. Familiar as I was with his lyceum lectures, they could not with all their charm prepare me for this inspiration, this fountain of spiritual power, this pathos. And this was the man who was lost to the pulpit because the Unitarian Church preferred the sacramental symbols of a broken body and shed blood in ancient Judea to the living spirit rising above all symbols! Great as Emerson was in literature, his hereditary and natural place was in the pulpit, which his essays did indeed leaven, under whatever sectarian forms, but only along with more admixture of chaff than of honest meal.

With Emerson's wonderful sermon still ringing in my ears I went to hear James Martineau. His chapel was a relic of the time when among dissenters there was a cult of ugliness, — fine architecture and stained glass being decorations of the "Scarlet Woman." In the gloomy little chapel I waited until the man should appear whose "Endeavours after the Christian Life" had brought me help in my early solitude. When Martineau presently ascended the pulpit I was impressed by his noble figure, but when his face shone upon us through the gloom, when his gracious and clear voice was heard, I said, this is a potential Emerson! It is an Emerson not banished from his pulpit, but held fast thirty years as a Unitarian leader!

This first sermon was disappointing in that it lacked warm blood. But I heard Martineau again and again, and discovered that he was a new type of preacher, that he was deeper than his books, and I must take heed how I heard. He was presently to me the great preacher. He did not work the miracle we witnessed when Emerson reascended the pulpit. That cannot be done in a gown, beneath which wings must be folded. But this minister was meeting the spiritual need and hunger of best men and women. In his audience of three or four hundred none had come except by inward attraction. They did not come for God's sake, for conformity or non-conformity, but were individual minds taking to heart things generally conventionalized. There sat Sir Charles Lyell, who had established a new book of Genesis, and who with his distinguished lady kept abreast of religious studies;

there was Miss Frances Power Cobbe, author of " Intuitive
Morals ; " there was the preacher's son, Russell Martineau,
the Hebraist whose veracity prevented his acceptance of a
place among the revisers of the Authorized Version (1881),
being forewarned of the retention of certain consecrated
mistranslations ; there were students of the Unitarian Divinity College (now Manchester College, Oxford) trained to
become its teachers, — such as Estlin Carpenter and Drum-
mond. But it would be a long catalogue that should name
the distinguished men and women who found their nurture or
their nourishment in that small chapel, and who in the beauty
and exaltation of Martineau's discourse did not envy the
cathedrals their fine arches and flaming windows.

A seat was always ready for me in the pew of Sir Charles
and Lady Lyell. It added to my happiness to witness that of
these eminent friends in listening to the discourses of Martineau, each of which invariably surpassed the previous one.
On one occasion as we walked away together Sir Charles
said, " what strikes me with wonder is that so many people
crowd to listen to the immense quantity of stupid sermons
preached every Sunday while it is possible to hear such a discourse as that."

When, as time went on, I gradually knew more about those
gathered around Martineau, and the widely different opinions
developed under his teaching, this seemed an especial sign of
his art. He was preëminently the pulpit artist.

Emerson's remark, that there was more progressiveness and
more enthusiasm in Unitarian ministers of orthodox ante-
cedents than in those of Unitarian birth, is true. They whose
freedom has involved struggle carry heat into their ministry.
But this is at some cost. The career of Martineau, born
among liberal thinkers, suggests that the better service may
be done by those who have had no personal quarrel with the
dogmas they clear from the paths of others. Less smoke
mingles with the flame of their lamp.

It was a relief after so many weary years of strife and
polemics in America to have no further need to preach about

slavery and dogma. I was not in an aggressive spirit, and got on fairly well with the right-wing Unitarians in England, occasionally preaching in their chapels. Two or three, familiar with my heretical course in America, kept a suspicious eye on me. I was invited to the annual festivals of the association, and at their first soirée after my settlement was called on for a speech. I meant my remarks to be particularly friendly all round, but something in them, or possibly in himself, excited old Dr. Aspland, who spoke with severity of the presumption of rationalists in supposing their opponents less candid than themselves. Dr. Aspland was a venerable white-haired gentleman with a ruddy, broad, benevolent countenance ; he was a historic figure in English Unitarianism, and without knowing the cause of his rebuke I received it in silence.

I had for several years been passing into religious states derived purely from my own experience. At one point or another things caught from some master slipped from me, and new thoughts — or thoughts of Thoughts — had surprised me. Even after I had parted from the traditional Christ, I had preached at Cincinnati a series of sermons on " Characteristics of Christ," in one of which I was uncritical enough to speak of the healing miracles as attributable to the power of a perfect man combined with the potency of faith in those healed. I had for years been too much absorbed in slave emancipation to study books on my shelf demonstrating the late origin of such narratives.

When in London I was able to pull myself together, I found that my flesh and blood Jesus was as yet really a vision. I had been too busy for a thorough critical inquiry into the evidence even of his historical existence. The man I now had in mind was not a mere dead Jew, nor was he on the other hand an ideal human character. I was prepared to find in Jesus, could he be proved historical at all, a man with some faults, but the preliminary question was, what had we to do with Jesus at all ? The answer then appeared to be — nothing, except that he and his supposed teachings had become in the religious developement of Christendom a sort of language

through which alone the people could be reached. But to
acknowledge this was to recognize that he was in some sort a
"providential man," — not exactly supernatural, but raised
up by God for a certain "mission." Nothing could have been
a more comfortable Christology in religious London in the
years following Darwin's great discovery. The " Origin of
Species " had been published only a few years, but already
the demands of orthodoxy on faith were lowered. Insistence on detailed dogmas was relegated to the conventicle : the
educated forces of both church and chapel, Unitarian or
Trinitarian, were concentrated on the task of defending their
common foundation — belief in the divine existence and government. When John Morley was spelling God with a small
" g " a hallelujah could be raised for Herbert Spencer's
spelling unknowable with a big " U." It was a great day for
theists, especially for those who ascribed to Jesus any exceptional place in the order of the world.

It is now strange to me that in those early years in London
I did not recognize in the collectivist deism a mere " ism."
Some years before I had declared at Cincinnati that Jehovah
was a war-god to be classed with Mars, but it was long before I realized the meaning of Confucius in saying, " To worship a god not your own is mere flattery." I called myself
a theist without reflecting that a worshipper of Mumbo-Jumbo
was equally a theist. But I can now see repeated in my experience, in quasi-embryonic changes, the spiritual history of
the early believers who lost their friend and brother, Jesus,
by his absorption into a giant Omnipotence, — impartial
source of good and bad.

Really my theism had brought me unrest. The experience
that gave birth to my fable of the monk and his Christ vision
(chapter xviii) had made way for another that reversed the
story. I had clung to a vision of the god instead of the man,
and my living Jesus was leaving me, — as if saying, " Since
thou hast stayed I must flee." I could not worship the
creator of this predatory universe, an unmoral cosmos evolv-
ing all evils and agonies, and at the same time genuinely

love a man because of his abhorrence of the cosmic horrors and all inhumanity. For a time I tried to satisfy my heart by projecting my lost Jesus into the Cosmos-deity. He was a Father, he was Love, he was the Supreme Light. I still made melody in my heart with the dear old hymns —

> Thou hidden love of God whose height,
> Whose depth unfathomed no man knows ! —

and

> Come, O thou traveller unknown,
> Whom still I hold but cannot see !

But how can one's heart sing, "Thou hidden cosmic Love" without laughing (till he cries !). No, — I could not feel what my dear Professor Clifford called "cosmic emotion;" and in this unrest moved with conscious purpose, where I had before unconsciously moved, on my "earthward pilgrimage."

There was one notable difference between England and America with regard to the ethics of heretical thought. In America it had become axiomatic among unorthodox scholars that their convictions must be boldly avowed. But in England the intellectual men, even in the middle of the nineteenth century, generally regarded it as the truer morality to keep to themselves novel and disturbing ideas or discoveries. After the revolutionary publication of Darwin in 1859, the press and pulpit were so filled with controversies that it was hardly possible to observe the admonition against casting pearls before swine. Tennyson, who substantially agreed with Martineau's views, regretted their publication; and even Matthew Arnold in his first heretical steps censured Colenso for not writing in Latin. With regard to Tennyson it should be said that his favour for exclusively esoteric expression of sceptical ideas was due to his tenderness for human minds and hearts, and his dread that they should lose the consolations of childlike faith as he had lost them. This Martineau recognized, but wrote to Tennyson's son, " I cannot see that we are entrusted with any right of suppression when once profoundly convinced of a truth not yet within others' reach." Indeed I believe that Martineau was the first scholar of high social position who entered on a ministry quite uncommitted to any sect, and absolutely consecrated to the search for truth.

But Martineau had entered into this outspoken rôle through the scientific threshold. His ancestors were men of science and he himself began his studies with the intention of becoming a civil engineer. It was the imprisonment of Richard Carlisle and his wife for publishing the religious works of Thomas Paine, and the general peril of free inquiry and printing, that induced the young aristocrat to leave his scientific plan and devote himself to religion.

Carlyle was talking one evening of Socinianism — he never called it Unitarianism — and said he had once or twice met Martineau, but not enough to form any judgment about him. Most men of his acquaintance who went as far as Martineau went farther; they were apt to keep silent in such matters. " I remember well," he said, " going to your chapel to hear the famous Mr. Fox. He was eloquent; it was like opening a window through London fog into the blue sky. But I went away feeling that Fox had been summoning those people to sit in judgment on matters of which they were no judges at all." In this Carlyle was mistaken, the audience at South Place being in chief part educated gentlemen and ladies who were centres of influence.[1] " I remember well," continued Carlyle, " when Strauss's Life of Jesus appeared in England that a number of men I knew, who had long held the same views but never dreamed of publishing them, were shocked; some who agreed with him could not forgive him for publishing his views, and called it a punishment when he married an actress and was divorced." In speaking of Martineau again, Carlyle said he had once travelled with two or three friends from Scotland to London. The conversation was mainly on religious and philosophical subjects, and of a critical and

[1] In November, 1865, some gentlemen, among them P. A. Taylor, M. P., and Karl Blind, leased Cleveland Hall, Fitzroy Square, for Sunday evenings, in order that I might " address the working classes." This continued for a year, but the place was filled by well-dressed people of the lower middle class.

destructive kind. "Martineau sat in a corner of the compartment leaning back with his eyes closed during the talk, but I am well persuaded that he heard every word that was said."

William Johnstone Fox, M. P., is the most notable instance with which I am acquainted of a man of genius so entirely concentrated on the issues of his own time that his fame had passed away with them. He was for nearly twenty years the most famous orator in England ; neither Bright nor Cobden could be compared with him ; but in 1864, ten years after his public career had closed, the people generally who had idolized him hardly knew that he was living, and the new generation had no knowledge of him.

Fox was residing with his wife at 3 Sussex Place, Regent's Park, where we sometimes passed an evening with him. He was a picturesque figure there in his elegant drawing-room ; his white hair parted in the middle fell in wavelets beside his serene and broad forehead, and his countenance held a rosy tinge still (his seventy-eighth year). He talked much of Browning, whom he knew when he (Browning) was hardly out of boyhood, and whose poems — as well as Tennyson's — he was the first to review with praise. Browning, he said, used to "spout" poetry when he was a boy. In talking of our South Place hymn-book, I ascribed a tune to the wrong composer. "It was not by him," said Mr. Fox, but did not give the true name, which I afterwards found was Eliza Flower. Jealousy of Eliza Flower had caused a separation between Mr. and Mrs. Fox, and I concluded that her name was not now mentioned by them.

The orator under whose voice vast crowds in all the halls of England had bent, as Froude said, "as forests beneath the storm," was not without some of the old fire, and the charm was still in his voice. His love of art and beauty which had educated Unitarians out of their lingering notion that godliness was akin to ugliness was visible in the decoration of the room, and even in his velvet coat, which harmonized with his armchair. He listened with pleasure to the stories I told him

W. J. FOX

of emigrants from his congregation whom I had known in America, and also to what Longfellow had told me of his visit to South Place: when he entered, a stranger to all present, they were singing his " Psalm of Life " — the first time he had ever heard any poem of his sung as a hymn. Longfellow was charmed by the sermon, which was on Shakespeare. After the service he spoke to the preacher and went home with him to dinner, — all of which Mr. Fox remembered. He spoke with admiration of Margaret Fuller, whom he had entertained, also of Emerson and Theodore Parker.

Mr. Fox was still able to pass an occasional evening with Mr. and Mrs. William Malleson; his old friends Mr. and Mrs. Peter Taylor and my wife and myself were always present. We sometimes played " Spanish Merchant," or perhaps whist; then read a play of Shakespeare, each one of us taking a character. The play was selected in order that we might listen to the sonorous voice of Fox in some favourite character. I well remember the impressiveness of his interpretation of the king in Part I of Henry IV.

It was indeed a precious experience to know the man who was the chief orator of the Corn Law agitation; who helped to found the " Westminster Review; " at whose feet in South Place chapel had sat Hazlitt, Thomas Campbell, John Stuart Mill, Douglas Jerrold, Leigh Hunt, Serjeant Talfourd, John Forster, Crabb Robinson, Browning, Macready, the Novellos, Hennells, Brabants, Brays, Howitts, Cowden Clarkes, Harriet Martineau, Helen Faucit, Sarah Flower Adams, and her sister Eliza Flower.

My old friend Mr. Lyon told me that during the Corn Law agitation so many pious dissenters were enlisted that the meetings were apt to be solemn. Some of the young people wished to have dancing in the halls after the speaking was over, but were afraid of offending the pious. This was mentioned to Fox who, after an eloquent speech, rose again and cried, " I am in favour of free trade in hops! " Thenceforth the gatherings often ended with " hops."

Mr. Fox died on June 3, 1864. I assisted his old friend,

the Rev. Mr. Malleson, at his burial in Brompton Cemetery. On June 12 a memorial service was held in our chapel, and my discourse, listened to by his old friends and printed by the society, seemed to link me to the intimate history of the progressive movement he so long led.

But by the historic chapel itself I was linked to a far larger movement, — the great and solemn procession of the generations of martyrs, aspirants, leaders who, suffering and labouring for beliefs not ours, yet by their fidelity and freedom rendered possible in London a congregation holding truth supersacred. Their monuments were close around us; our chapel was built on hallowed ground. Dean Stanley told us of an English bishop who visited the graveyard of City Road Temple and asked the sexton if it had ever been consecrated. "Yes," was the reply, "by holding the remains of the servant of God, John Wesley." Near by are Bunhill Fields, consecrated by the dust of the saints of dissent, the homes of More and of Milton, Smithfield with its ashes of martyrs; and nearer still the cemetery of the Quakers, where amid many graves but one is marked, — this by a small headstone bearing the name of England's greatest religious genius, George Fox. From these graves arose a cloud of witnesses to surround me when in the course of my ministry occurred our memorial services in honour of some of their successors: W. J. Fox, Lincoln, Cobden, Dickens, Maurice, Mazzini, Mill, Strauss, Livingstone, Lyell, Clifford, "George Eliot," Dean Stanley, Darwin, Longfellow, Carlyle, Emerson, Louis Blanc, Harriet Martineau, Mary Carpenter, Colenso, Renan, Tennyson, Huxley.

CHAPTER XXXI

PETER ALFRED TAYLOR, M. P. for Leicester, though not an impassioned orator was an eloquent speaker, and the only thorough republican of high position and wealth I ever knew in England. He was a leader in the agitation against the game laws, and the Sabbath laws, and against tithes. He and his wife Mentia, a lady of finest culture and literary taste, made their beautiful mansion, Aubrey House, a centre of liberal thinkers, writers, artists, — a veritable *salon*. At their receptions I met young writers and artists who afterwards became famous, and Mrs. Taylor formed there a "Pen and Pencil Club" at which our sketches were read or exhibited. A privately printed volume of the essays is treasured by the survivors of that delightful club.

Peter Taylor freely gave money to the leagues defending the antislavery cause in America, and to those of the "liberators" of Poland and Italy. He was the treasurer of the Italian agitators especially, and Mazzini passed nearly every evening of his sojourn in London at Aubrey House. Radical leaders of other countries also visited Aubrey House, but I thought Mazzini slightly jealous of any competition with Italy in English interest. He evidently thought that the "initiative" of world-renovation belonged by transcendent necessity to Italy. I met Mazzini continually. His circle was my own. His fellow exile, Venturi, had married Miss Ashurst, a sister of the wife of the Hon. James Stansfeld, M. P. Mr. Stansfeld got into trouble by receiving letters for Mazzini. This was necessary even though the letters were addressed to "Mr. Flower" (Fior di Mazza?). Mazzini had yet another name for London. In my address-book (1863) I find: "Seignior Ernesti (Joseph Mazzini), 2 Onslow Terrace, Brompton, S. W. (between 11 and 6)." We must not write to or ask for him under his real name. In the poor little lodging house he had two small rooms. At one time he was so poor that a few friends quietly made up a "testimonial."

There was a Mazzini cult, and to some extent my wife and I shared the enthusiasm, though we did not include in it any passionate interest in Italian unity. It was impossible to resist the personality of Mazzini, and I thought even his accent added to the charm of his conversation. He appeared to me an illustration of Heine's belief that the beauty of Italians is due to the sublime works of art surrounding their mothers. His life had been, as Peter Taylor said, "one long sacrifice," and there was in every feature, and especially in his great dark eye, a melancholy rarely relieved even by a smile.

We were all surprised when, early in 1864, our radical friend, James Stansfeld, was appointed by Palmerston Junior Lord of the Admiralty. Soon after that the Greco regicide plot was announced. Mazzini called on me and declared that Greco was a mere decoy of Napoleon III to arrest the republican propaganda of Garibaldi and himself. Stansfeld said that he did not suppose there was anything seditious in the correspondence, — Mazzini, being sometimes absent from London, needed a friend to receive his letters, — but offered his resignation, which was not accepted. During the discussion in the House of Commons, Sir H. Tracey read an old letter of Mazzini concerning Gallenga's declaration to him of his purpose to kill Charles Albert. Mazzini discouraged him, but, said his letter, "he ended by convincing me that he was one of those beings whose purposes are a matter between their own consciences and God, and whom Providence from time to time lets loose upon earth (like Harmodius of yore) to teach despots that the limit of their power rests in the hand of one single man." Gallenga — a brilliant man — I had met in America, where, however, he had again gone (1864) as a Confederate sympathizer to write for the London " Times." So much was I hypnotized by Mazzini that I was ready to gloze over all this. Nor did I doubt that the Greco plot was a trick of Napoleon III. But if so it was a mismove. English people were not so much concerned about the security of the Emperor as about their mails; Italian enthusiasm revived, and Garibaldi was invited to England.

There was a great sensation about this visit of Garibaldi. The Palmerstonian or right-wing liberals were allies of Napoleon III since the commercial treaty obtained by Cobden, but they could not offend the radicals by preventing the visit. It was decided that the aristocracy should monopolize Garibaldi and keep him from mingling with the radicals, and especially from consultation with Mazzini. He had accepted an invitation to pass several days at Aubrey House, and there I met him. He saw with delight for the first time a portrait of Cromwell. It represented the Protector refusing the crown, and Garibaldi knew English enough to exclaim, " Noble fellow, noble fellow — not to accept it ! "

Garibaldi — Karl Blind assured me that he was of German extraction, and that his name combined *Gar* (war) and *Bald* (bold) — was nobler in looks than Cromwell, but his boldness was confined to the battlefield. The eye of Napoleon III was on him there at Aubrey House, where he was surrounded by Mazzini, Venturi, Saffi, Karl Blind, Freiligrath, Ledru Rollin, Louis Blanc, and other great refugees. But he was drawn away by the aristocracy to be fêted. The grandeur of the popular reception given him in London had attracted the attention of all Europe, but not less the demonstration in Covent Garden Opera House, where the aristocrats imprudently carried him. He was treated like an emperor in that city where Louis Napoleon had lived so long in obscurity. Enormous flowers decorated his private box, where lords and ladies in official robes surrounded him. Worse than all, the opera was " Masaniello," and a furore was excited by the line "O santo ardor di patrio amor."

The prospect of seeing Garibaldi pass on a triumphal march through the United Kingdom was intolerable to Napoleon III. All he had to do was to suggest a possible withdrawal from the free-trade treaty; John Bull's heart was thus touched; and Gladstone, who was managing the matter, determined that Garibaldi was too ill to continue his visit. The opera of " Masaniello " made way for a diplomatic performance of a famous scene in " The Barber of Seville," — with the modification that, whereas in the play Don Basilio is genuinely persuaded by the lovers that he is ill, Garibaldi never felt in better health than when the commercial lovers, Napoleon III and Britannia, suddenly hustled him out of England.

When tricks are done on our side, how easy it is to pardon them! I could not forgive Gladstone or Napoleon III, but could recognize legitimate stratagems — if not quite noble — in devices of " liberators."

Mazzini told me that when he and Garibaldi occupied Naples the priests wished to excite hostility to them among the people by a disappointment on the fête of St. Januarius. The annual liquefaction of the blood of St. Januarius attracts great crowds, but it had been announced that the blood would not liquefy that year. But Garibaldi and Mazzini (both unbelievers in Christianity) informed the priests that if the blood did not liquefy as usual St. Januarius church would be perpetually closed. So the blood liquefied on time, and the miracle was thus turned into a divine sanction of the Republic.

In Rome also, during the brief existence of the Republic there, came a fête at which the people were accustomed to see the dome of St. Peter's illuminated. Mazzini, hearing that it had been prophesied by the priests that the Republic would end that and other celebrations, commanded the officials of St. Peter's to do exactly as usual, and on their refusal appointed special officers, who took care that nothing should be omitted. Mazzini said he believed he could do more towards removing popular superstitions by securing the foundations of free government than by offending the common sentiment of the people.

About Garibaldi there remained something child-like to the end. When, after the Crimean war, Savoy and Nice were about to be annexed to the French Empire, Garibaldi hastened to Turin and presented himself to my cousin, John Moncure Daniel, United States Minister. He said that he had come to ask him to annex Nice to the American Republic and throw over it the "powerful protection of the American banner!" He declared himself proud of being a citizen of the United States, and said that his "fellow citizens of Nice loathed the French." My cousin, Frederick Daniel, Secretary of Legation under his brother, tells me that a good many Italian Mazzinists visited the legation, and that the minister told them that while he sympathized with their cause he could do nothing for them.

In 1865, after the Union cause had triumphed in America, Mazzini spoke to me and wrote to me urging the duty of the new emancipated America to enter on her mission of universal liberation. In one letter (May 25) he wrote: —

DEAR MR. CONWAY, — The heroic struggle in your native land is at an end. Ought it not to be the beginning of a new era in American life?

The life of a great nation is twofold: inward and outward. A nation is a mission — a function in the development of mankind — or nothing. A nation has a task to fulfil in the world for the good of all, a principle it represents in a mighty struggle which constitutes history, a flag to hoist in the giant battle to which all local battles are episodes — going on in the earth between justice and injustice, liberty and tyranny, equality and arbitrary privilege, God and the devil. The non-interference doctrine is an atheistic one. To abstain is to deny the oneness of God and of mankind.

There is a time, a period, during which the implement must be fitted up, the *power* for action organized. That period requires *abstention*. You have gone through that period. It was right that the founders of the United States should say to them: "Abstain from all European concerns." It would be mere selfism if they took that rule as a permanent one.

You are now powerful with a *tested* power. You have asserted your *self*. You have by the abolition of slavery linked yourselves with the condition of Europe. The four years' list of noble deeds achieved by you all *must* be a christening to the mission of which I speak. You have shown yourselves great: you have, therefore, great duties to perform.

You must represent the republican principle, which is your life, not only within your boundaries but everywhere, whenever it is possible to do so.

Europe — the republican Europe — expects you to do so. You *can* be a leading power amongst us ; therefore, you *ought* to be such a power.

All this is far higher than any consideration of safety. Still even *that* consideration is something. What you have done, and the applause of all struggling countries, have alarmed all the European monarchs. Depend upon it, they will not leave you at rest. The imperialist scheme, the Spanish scheme, the Austrian scheme, will go on. The Mexican affair is a programme.

You must interfere if you want to avoid being interfered with. You ought to grasp the opportunity. Your prestige is immense. You are in one of those decisive moments given by victory which was — on a smaller scale — before Garibaldi, after he had conquered Sicily and Naples. He might have achieved anything, had he not yielded to monarchies' bidding; you may *now* achieve anything.

League yourselves with all our republican national parties. Let your representatives abroad be instructed to put themselves in contact with us and to give a word of encouragement to our efforts, a pledge of alliance with our future.

Go to Mexico : go quickly : ensure a victory. Defeat the usurpers before they have reinforcements.

Let your proclamations say that you go, not for conquest's sake, but in the name of a principle, because you feel called to check the interfering progress of despotic monarchical schemes.

And help us to act *simultaneously* both in France and Italy, against Austria and against the Empire. A sum of fifty thousand, of thirty thousand dollars — a steam-frigate sent — of course not officially — at our orders — will enable us to ensure triumph not only for ourselves, but for yourselves too.

Why am I saying this? Why do we not collect money in our own countries ?

Of course, we can. But it would take six months, one year. And everybody will know it. And every (monarch) will be on the alert. Now, if you go to Mexico, action on our side ought to be sudden and simultaneous.

I write these things to you, because you have friends in the United States to whom you may, perhaps, communicate these ideas and who may find it advisable to embody them into facts. If so, the transaction ought to take place secretly and quickly.   Ever faithfully yours,

JOSEPH MAZZINI.

I quote from another letter dated October 30, 1865: —

DEAR CONWAY, — You ask my opinion about the coloured-men-suffrage question. Can you doubt it?

You have abolished slavery ; you have as a crowning to your glorious struggle, as a religious consecration to battles which otherwise would have only been deplorable events, decreed that the sun of the Republic shines on all, that he who breathes the air of the Republic is free, that, as God is one, so on the blessed soil where liberty is not a mere hap-and-hazard *fate*, but a *faith* and a gospel, the stamp of mankind is one. Can you mutilate this great principle? Can you cut it down to the monarchical half-freedom standard? proclaim the existence of the half-man? enthrone a dogma of half-responsibility? constitute on the Republican American land a middle-ages class of political serfs? Is there liberty without the vote? Is not political liberty the sanction, the guarantee of civil liberty? Is not the vote the stamp of self-asserting human nature through the moral world, as the right of labour and property is its self-asserting stamp through the physical world? Will you turn, by denying this, your democracy to an incipient aristocracy? Will you decree that colour is *moral subalternation?* Ignorance is, indeed, but you did *not* choose educated intellect as a test for the electoral right. Had you done so, objections might arise on a different ground, but you could not be accused of betraying the very principle you have been proclaiming of applying a different rule to two sections of God's children ; of saying: " These coloured men will be called on to be the armed apostles of national union and to give their life for it, but their life will not be represented in the councils of the nation."

The Mazzinists supposed that Robert Browning sympathized with the strange delusion which inspired his wife's poem, "Napoleon III in Italy." This I doubted, and I felt that Mazzini held corresponding delusions. With my abhorrence of war I could not espouse his scheme for European conflagration, with the United States for participant, and his letter of May 25, 1865, was not communicated to any one, and here appears for the first time. I was rather embarrassed in this matter. As minister of South Place chapel I was intimate in the circle of Mazzini's particular friends. Mazzini was to them not only representative of the European republic — yet in dreamland — but a sort of high priest of the religion on which it was based. His faith in it was absolute, resting not on scientific premises, but on a vision of the eternal reasonableness of things. One day when we were alone I ventured to press a little on his theism, for I was beginning to realize that it was of a type that included the sword as a means of establishing the divine Republic. I suggested that his theism seemed to verge on optimism : if God created all things and governed the world his worshippers might claim the existence of the Papacy as its sufficient authority. He said that in that direction one might indeed be driven into Pyrrhonism, but went on to appeal to the spiritual intuitions and the facts of moral consciousness as the supreme truth. This, of course, did not meet the dilemma, because it left no tribunal to decide between the moral consciousness of Mazzini and that of the Pope ; nor between the method of warfare, common to both, and my own principles against war.

My friend Miss Ashurst Biggs once reproached me for inconsistency in not entering into the cause of Italian liberty with the same zeal as for negro liberty. I surprised her by saying that although, after war had unhappily broken out between North and South, I had sustained the side that seemed likely to liberate the slave and remove our country's source of discord, I never advocated negro insurrection, and had opposed coercion of the seceded States.

Mazzini's theism was not shaken by the consideration that

under God his republic had been given by Garibaldi to the monarchy, but mine was shaken by the assassin's transfer of the negro race in America into the hands of an ignorant slaveholder. Andrew Johnson, made President by the bullet of Wilkes Booth, going about with his unctuous phrase, " when it pleased Almighty God to remove Abraham Lincoln," was enough to make every earnest soul an atheist so far as that deity was concerned. Nevertheless, when such a soul started out to discover a deity totally free from complicity with the assassin, he would find it difficult to discover one, and probably take refuge with a deity whose predetermined violences were on the believer's own side.

My experience is that long labour against injustice done to a race not our own has a tendency to diminish reverence for things consecrated by nationalism. Having lost my early devotion to the " sacred soil " of Virginia, having learned to look upon disunion as flinging open the portals of freedom and justice for a race not my own, I could not share Mazzini's creed about the sacredness of Rome and the importance of Italy's reintegration to the everlasting purposes. I began to inquire in each case not about boundaries without souls, but whether the individuals inside them enjoyed freedom.

When Mazzini died (1872) the feeling among us all in London was profound. My friend Peter Taylor M. P. wrote me a heart-broken note, in which he said : —

His friends — I among others — pleaded with him to leave the fight, and live his last few years among us in peace and literary activity only. We said, " You have put your country on the road to progress; you have gained independence ; the rest is a work of time, of more time than is yours. Disappointment and apparent failure will attend the first steps." We failed because he was no egotist. While there was anything not achieved, and while he had power to move, he could not rest. Had he consented to end his political life before he yielded his mortal life he would have received this side the grave the laurels that now will adorn the cemetery.

On the day of Mazzini's death I visited Carlyle, and told him I should hold at South Place a memorial service in honour of that man. Carlyle talked freely about him, and I wrote down as nearly as I could what he said.

I remember well when he sat for the first time on the seat there. A more beautiful person I never beheld, with his soft flashing eyes and face full of intelligence. He had great talent, — certainly the only acquaintance of mine of anything like equal intellect who ever became entangled in what seemed to me hopeless visions. He was rather silent, spoke chiefly in French, though he spoke good English even then. It was plain he might have taken a high rank in literature. He wrote well, as it was, — sometimes for the love of it, at others when he wanted a little money, but never what he might have written had he devoted himself to that kind of work. He had fine tastes, particularly in music. But he gave himself up as a martyr to his aims for Italy. He lived almost in squalor. His health was poor from the first ; he took no care of it. He used to smoke a great deal, and drink coffee with bread crumbled in it ; but hardly gave any attention to his food. His mother used to send him money ; but he gave it away. When she died she left him as much as two hundred pounds a year, — all she had, — but it went to Italian beggars. His mother was the only member of his family who clung to him. His father soon turned his back on him ; his only sister married a strict Catholic, and herself became too strict to have anything to do with Mazzini. He did see her once or twice, but the interviews were too painful to be repeated. He desired, I am told, to see her again when he was dying, but she declined. Poor Mazzini ! I could not have sympathy with his views and hopes. He used to come here and talk about the " solidarity of peoples ; " and when he found that I was less and less interested in such things, he had yet another attraction than myself which brought him to us. But he found that she also by no means entered into his opinions, and his visits became fewer. But we always esteemed him. He was a very religious soul. When I first knew him he reverenced Dante chiefly, if not exclusively. When his letters were opened at the post-office here, Mazzini became, for the first time, known to the English people. There was great indignation at an English government taking the side of the Austrian against Italian patriots ; and Mazzini was much sought for, invited to dinners, and all that. But he did not want the dinners. He went to but few places.

JOSEPH MAZZINI

He formed an intimacy with the Ashursts, which did him
great good, — gave him a kind of home circle for the rest of
his life in England. At last it has come to an end. I went
to see him just before he left London for the last time, passed
an hour, and came away feeling that I should never see him
again. And so it is. The papers and people have gone away
blubbering over him, — the very papers and people that denounced him during life, seeing nothing of the excellence
that was in him. They now praise him without any perception
of his defects. Poor Mazzini! After all, he succeeded. He
died receiving the homage of the people, and seeing Italy
united, with Rome for its capital. Well, one may be glad he
has succeeded. We wait to see whether Italy will make anything great out of what she has got. We wait!

On March 17, 1872, the audience assembled in South Place
chapel to do homage to Mazzini included his most eminent
friends, but I could say nothing about Italy. I could only
speak of the fidelity and personal greatness of the man, for I
was already beginning to realize that the method of violence
for any high aim was a gigantic mistake. I saw that all
Mazzini's self-sacrifice had gone to strengthen the throne of
Napoleon III, and to bring on that war in which his ideal
of Italy had been crucified between Napoleon III and Bismarck.

On hearing of the outbreak of the Franco-German war,
Mazzini, who read Shakespeare, exclaimed, " A plague o'
both your houses ! "

Among the refugees in London from the revolutions of
1848 the most resourceful was Karl Blind. He possessed
some means, had a good mastery of English, and was an excellent writer in German. He was the London correspondent
of every radical journal in Germany, also of one in Vienna,
his letters keeping them abreast of general literature and
science in England. Meanwhile his erudition in German philosophy — he was of course a freethinker — and his knowledge
of Teutonic mythology and folk-lore, enabled him to write
useful articles in English magazines.

He brought with him to London his wife and her two

children, Ferdinand and Mathilde, who adopted the name of Blind.

In 1866 the family was overwhelmed and all the world startled by the attempt of Ferdinand to shoot Bismarck, and his suicide. The young man had been finely educated both in England and in Germany. His sister Mathilde gave me some account of him. After his graduation he made a tour through Germany, to study the different kinds of scientific agriculture. Mathilde showed me a letter from her brother to a friend in Germany, in which he declares that Bismarck is steadily leading Germany into war, and as he is too high for the law to reach, he can only be dealt with by an individual. One passage in Ferdinand's letter is very remarkable, being written in 1866, and I quote it literally : " As I wandered through the blooming fields of Germany, that were so soon to be crushed under the iron heel of war, and saw the numbers of youths pass by that were to lose their lives for the selfish aims of a few, the thought came quite spontaneously to punish the cause of so much evil, even if it were at the cost of my life."

The wild deed which struck so close to my friends, not simply the Blind family, but the families of their eminent fellow exiles, did them only evil. It called out many classical anecdotes and quotations in honour of regicide. The theory of the radicals, that Bismarck was saved by wearing a coat of mail, did not affect the masses in Europe; young Blind had sacrificed himself to give Bismarck the halo of a Man of Destiny. The republican leaders were thrown against the sharp horns of a dilemma : they must either justify Ferdinand or disarm the Revolution.

I may mention here a strange incident that occurred thirteen years later, when I was residing at Hamlet House. An agreeable young gentleman came from Ohio with an introduction from an eminent friend there. He talked pleasantly, and my wife invited him to stay to dinner. He told us a good deal about our Cincinnati friends, and I asked what I could do for him. He said that he desired to make the acquaintance of Karl Blind, and I gave him my card for introduction. After a few games at billiards, he left for his hotel, and I never saw him again.

Two days later Karl Blind came to my house pale with agitation, and told me that a man sent to him by me had proposed a scheme for killing the Prince of Wales!

Horrified, we drove swiftly to a hotel which he had mentioned to me, but he was not there, and apparently had not been there. Blind regretted, as I did, that he had not at once arrested the man instead of ordering him out of his house; he had a notion, I believe, that he was a guest in my house. At any rate, he was lost in the multitude, and though we took advice, nothing could be done.

In answer to my report to my friend in Ohio, a letter said that the young man had previously been in an insane asylum, but his friends supposed him cured, and the physicians thought that a foreign tour might entirely restore his physical health. He had been a peaceful patient, and his suggestion of assassination was unaccountable to them.

The Blinds entertained a good deal. Mathilde possessed beauty, and from the first was distinguished for her literary culture. Her acquaintance with the languages and literatures of Germany, France, and Italy was marvellous. The delight of Mazzini in her society seemed to some of their political friends to be of importance to the affairs of Germany and France; for Mathilde was well acquainted with such matters and keenly interested in them. Her poems are full of thought, and had she been writing in her native language, I feel certain that she would have reached wide fame. Her brother Rudolf, an artist, their beautiful half-sister Ottilia (now Mrs. Hancock), the entertaining conversation of their mother, combined with Karl Blind's ability and knowledge, made their house a sort of *salon*. There we used to meet the admirable Freiligrath and Ledru Rollin, and if any interesting man came, especially from Germany, we were sure to meet him at one of those Sunday evenings in Winchester Road.

CHAPTER XXXII

Parliament — Brougham, Russell, Derby, Dufferin — Aristocracy — Robert
Lowe — Shaftesbury — Disraeli — Palmerston — Bulwer — Gladstone —
Cobden — His acquaintance with Jefferson Davis — Scene in the House of
Commons following Cobden's death — The funeral of Palmerston — The
death of President Lincoln — The canonization of Lincoln — The course of
Sumner — Letters from Sumner — His attack on England — Consecration of
the sword, and its always broken promises.

It is my conviction that between 1860 and 1880 the English
Parliament reached its high water mark of ability, whether
considered individually or collectively. This may be considered a senile delusion, though I should consider it a childish
delusion to consider the Parliament opening with the twentieth century equal to that of thirty years before. The figures
surviving from the past struggles mingling with those of the
later generation in the House of Lords gave me a new sentiment about the hereditary House. Especially impressive was
Lord Brougham's thin, bent form moving amid the scene of
his historic labours, and it was pleasant to observe that every
peer of whatever party greeted him as he passed.

The Liberal leader in the House of Lords, Lord Granville,
had a handsome and beaming countenance, strikingly like
that of the poet Longfellow; his speaking was pleasant and
to the point. Lord John Russell was so famous that I was
surprised at his small stature. There was a story that he once
wrote a poem, in which the highest flight of imagination was
in the line, " The red rose and the yellow orange." But Lord
John was by no means so prosaic as the humourists made out;
his speeches, always uttered from long experience and wide
information, were never dull. No debater in that House, however, could be compared with the Conservative leader, Lord
Derby. Darwin might have written on him a study of politi-

cal evolution ; every clear-cut feature, every hair on the shapely head, every tone of his penetrating satire feathered with well-bred grace, indicated a leader organically made for his place. I heard his famous speech attacking the government in February, 1864. Sydney Smith was never more brilliant than Derby in his description of Lord John Russell's foreign policy. He pictured him as Bottom wishing to play every part, quoting the phrases of Shakespeare with consummate art, and ended with, " The noble Lord's motto seems to have been ' Meddle and Muddle.' *Nil quod non tetigit, et nil tetigit quod non conturbavit.*" It was all said in the impetuous style that made Bulwer describe him as " the Rupert of debate." Lord John Russell's face bore a sardonic smile during the vivisection, but there was something anæsthetic in Derby's gracious manner and tone. To the banter Russell only said it was of course very fine, as it all came from Shakespeare.

The debates in the House of Lords interested me as presenting the reactionary and the liberal interpretations of the British Constitution and of English history. The interpretations were not contrarious, but recognizable as the two wings which had steadily borne the nation through the storms of centuries. The speeches generally indicated the close study of a leisure class, and absence of that influence from the *aura popularis* which affects men depending on popular suffrage. These lords, assured of their position, without any interest to elbow any one in order to rise higher, reminded me of the old race of Virginian statesmen. Living on their estates, supported by the labour of their slaves, they had leisure to give their attention to large subjects. The speeches of Pendleton, Crump, John S. Barbour, Robert E. Scott, Travers Daniel, to which I used to listen, were marked by wide information, not merely political, but literary and historical. There was comparatively little of the spread-eagle bombast of the demagogues. The English radical threats of sweeping away the House of Lords did not excite my sympathy. Opposed as I am to the American bicameral system, I knew that in England its only alternative would be an elective — always a rotten-borough — senate. The only conceivable value of a second chamber is an independence of the popular breath which might enable it to check popular passion.

What nonsense we are brought up in about the horrors of hereditary legislation! All legislation is hereditary. How do the American masses get their votes? By birth.

On February 10, 1866, I had a place in the House of Lords to witness the opening of Parliament by the Queen. Since the death of the Prince Consort she had been in deep retreat, and this first step towards a resumption of her functions caused universal satisfaction. The peers and peeresses prepared to welcome her with an enthusiasm and display now historic. Lord Granville had secured for me a fine seat among the peeresses, and I believe that every gem, necklace, coronet, robe, and decoration belonging to the nobility of England was worn that day. The fullest of court dress was worn by the several hundred ladies, and the scene billowy with necks and shoulders. For once I saw the ideal legislative assembly, — the ancient Witenagemote, with best men and women in consultation.

There were whispers of disappointment when the Queen appeared. The fine robes and insignia she ought to have worn were displayed on a table near her; save for some slight badge, and the Koh-i-noor on her forehead, she was still in sombre raiment. She was the only homely woman in the House, and her homeliness, emphasized by her sombre dress, was the more pronounced by contrast with the beautiful and superbly costumed Princess of Wales. Instead of reading her address to Parliament as usual, it was read by the Chamberlain. Through it she sat as if carved on the throne; when it was finished she arose, bowed slightly, kissed the Princess of Wales, and disappeared through the back door.

As my political philosophy assigned to a monarch the sole *métier* of being charming and ornamental, and thereby holding the chief place secure from usurpation by presidency (*könig im fröck*), this withdrawal of the Queen from her functions impressed me as a danger. There was a vigorous republican agitation going on in England, and it was frequently said that the practical extinction of the Court had demonstrated the uselessness of the throne. I remember being at a dinner of the Urban Club, St. John's Gate, of which I was a member, when young Mr. Babington, a kinsman of Lord Macaulay, refused to rise to the toast to the Queen, avowing, when his conduct was challenged, his republican opposition to monarchy. There was a noisy discussion, but a goodly number defended Babington's right to so express his opinion. It became plain to me that the Queen was not then popular. The republican organizations were enfeebled by Andrew Johnson, and died under Grant's administration. It was really an American movement, and I knew well that " republicanism " in England would mean an imitation of our quadrennial revolutionary presidential campaign, and our bicameral Congress. The French say, " the better is enemy of the good." In so-called political reform the better often destroys the good without succeeding to it.

Congress was an inferior body to Parliament, and I felt that it was because neither senator nor representative possessed the personal independence of the peer and the commoner. The superiority of the peer especially consisted in his not having to keep his eye on the hustings, while his subordination to the Commons in any trial of voting strength made it all the more necessary that his argument should be sound and lucid.

But there was already a danger that the House of Lords might lose this independence through intimidation by the menaces of the increasingly enfranchised masses. I used to meet the accomplished Lord Dufferin, a constant friend of the Union cause in America, and asked him whether it would not be wise for the Lords to demand a law definitely securing their right to throw out a measure twice, the said measure to become law without any action of the Upper House if the Commons should pass it a third time. Lord Dufferin declared he would strongly favour such a change, and he had no doubt a majority of the peers would rejoice in it. But subsequent observation convinced me that the Commons would never agree to it, as a good many of them, in order to please their constituents, sometimes vote for a measure they secretly hate because they know the Lords will throw it out. The House of Lords has thus often served as a scapegoat.

Several of the peers mingled in the debates with a tone that seemed to recognize the approaching democracy; the Duke of Argyll, Lord Kimberly, and several bishops were somewhat restless, as if they would prefer to be in the fray of the other House. But as a rule the Lords presented the aspect of having reached the Happy Isle. There was never any sarcasm or bitterness in their encounters; a "palpable hit" that drew no blood was the aim of each antagonist.

At the table of the Duke and Duchess of Argyll, at Argyll Lodge, Kensington, I first met a number of lords who, like themselves, were deeply interested in the antislavery cause. Afterwards I met other aristocratic families, several members of which came to South Place chapel. I discovered that Bunyan's line, "He that is down need fear no fall," has a corollary: he that is so solidly up that he neither fears a fall nor aspires to climb may illustrate humility as much as he who is down. It is not snobbery but common sense which recognizes the superiority of the English aristocracy to the English middle class. Arthur Clough hinted this with his Chartist and Irishman: "Is not one man, fellow men, as good as another?" "Faith," replied Pat, "and a deal better too!" The English race has spread through the world doctrines of equality, while at home their aristocratic institutions have inevitably bred an inequality not simply of position, which might be outgrown, but of character and manners. All the social tiers beneath the aristocracy strive upward, and by their pushing ambition, their snobbery, their contempt for the class beneath them, their elbowing each other to get ahead, they are apt to become vulgarized. It is the fatal necessity of the aristocracy, in reaching social supremacy by birth and without any trick or snobbery, to create inferior classes beneath them. But one must be blind not to recognize the superiority of the average nobility in elegance, repose, simplicity, freedom from pretence, and tact in establishing without airs of patronage pleasant relations with persons of any and every rank.

However democratic the upper middle classes may become, they rarely rid themselves of snobbery. Gladstone was once summoned as a witness in a case that concerned the Duke of Newcastle. Asked whether he was intimate with the duke, he replied, " As intimate as our difference in rank permits." Gladstone was Prime Minister, and the duke inferior to him in everything but birth.

It was with extreme interest that I witnessed and watched the competition of Disraeli and Gladstone as to which should outbid the other in lowering the franchise. Disraeli had set out to " educate the Tories," — as a phrase ascribed to him went, — and had plainly taken the " unjust steward " of the parable as his model. Seeing that Gladstone, by the aid of John Bright, would surely enlarge the popular franchise, and that if the Liberal party got all the credit of such enlargement the Conservative party must be permanently excluded from power, he changed all the accounts between the old Tories and the masses and was duly received into their habitations. Lord Derby refused to commend the ingenious steward ; he described Disraeli's large step towards democracy as " a leap in the dark," and soon after resigned his leadership. The retreat from official life of the most brilliant man in the House of Lords marked the close of an epoch. On the other hand, the most brilliant commoner on the Liberal side, the Right Hon. Robert Lowe, refused to take Gladstone's " leap in the dark." I never heard in the House of Commons a more powerful speech than that of Lowe in parting from the chief to whose government he belonged. He knew that his place in the Cabinet was to be filled by the leader of the independent benches, — John Bright. But John Bright felt that some line must be drawn in lowering the franchise, and spoke vaguely of a " residuum." Robert Lowe, amid the breathless stillness of the House, turned

towards John Bright, and, alluding to the opera of " Don Gio-
vanni," said that the heavy footsteps of the Commandant's
statue had been heard, and the stony figure now entered, saying, " John, you have invited me to supper and I have come ! "
Alluding to the proposal for an educational test, he said, " I
suppose we must teach our masters to read." All through
the speech there were felicitous touches, but the main force
was in the prophetic though quietly uttered statement of the
revolution that was being wrought merely for the sake of
transient party interests.

Lord Shaftesbury revealed to me the large residuum of intolerance lurking within me. My dislike was not caught from
Carlyle, who in a Latter Day Pamphlet spoke of him as the
"universal syllabub of philanthropic twaddle," but from the
way in which his mere rank was utilized by the whole world
of English cant. Pious and evangelical meetings advertised
his expected presence as theatres might draw with a star
actor; but those who went to worship a live lord in the
beauty of holiness found no star unless on his breast. There
were occasional instances in which the popular snobbery was
enlisted in behalf of charities, but these were apt to be mixed
with some pietism, and weighed but little against his obstruc-
tion of the right and the need of the unchurched people to
enjoy their museums and galleries on Sunday. In this long
struggle against the offering of human sacrifices to the Sabbath I was for many years engaged, and had a belief that
Shaftesbury was not honest in persuading workingmen that
their weekly day of rest was endangered by an enlargement
of their freedom on that day. But during the conflict of the
ablest women against Shaftesbury's Factory Acts, I concluded
that he was merely weak-minded. The workmen were using
his soft heart and softer head to rid themselves of the competition of female labour by telling doleful tales about the
way in which women were overworked and their children suffering. In vain we pleaded that there were a million more
women than men in the country, that they had to support
themselves, and that they could not do so if they were pre-

vented from selling their time and their toil on equal terms. Workingman selfishness succeeded through Shaftesbury's sentimentality, and multitudes of women were excluded from factories because forbidden to work full time.

If either of the Fates had anything to do with giving Lord Derby such a lieutenant in the Commons as Disraeli, she must have been in a jocular mood when it was done. If Derby was the Conservative leader by structural evolution, Disraeli was the chief Tory commoner by a sport of nature; no one could look at him without seeing that his natural place was to be acting Mephistopheles in Her Majesty's Theatre rather than that of the political cynic in Her Majesty's House of Commons. Derby believed in something; but beneath every affirmation of Disraeli there was an undertone of scepticism. He once said to W. J. Fox, M. P., my predecessor at South Place: " I am much misunderstood; my forte is revolution." His literary career began with " The Revolutionary Epick." He carried his cynical Christianity to the extent of propounding the unanswerable theory that Judas deserved canonization, since he had performed a disagreeable function without which the Scriptures could not have been fulfilled, and there could have been no salvation for mankind. Such was the leader that the bishops had to follow, while he must have laughed in his sleeve at them. He denounced the " mass in masquerade" of Ritualism, but dated a note " Maunday Thursday." A professor told me that, having on some occasion to see Disraeli, he was received in the library, and Disraeli, pointing to his books, said, " Most of them are the classics and theology, — my favourite studies." But, said my informant, " It is certain he could not read the one nor understand the other."

With all this, I found myself enjoying Disraeli's eminence and influence. There was something so picturesque in a Jewish lad bringing the royal family and the aristocracy to his feet. He had done it, too, in the wise and gentle way of Solomon, who reigned forty years and won foreign kingdoms by unbroken civility and friendliness. Professor Fawcett, who entered Parliament with a reputation for radicalism, and for especial antagonism to Disraeli, told me that Disraeli was the first to extend his hand and welcome him into the House. He was gracious to opponents, and his success as a leader was largely due to his greater eagerness to bring forward the young and modest members of his party than to display himself; in this being notably distinguished from Gladstone, who overshadowed even his own Cabinet. He also had the sense of humour in which Gladstone was so sadly deficient. Disraeli's speeches were more plausible than profound, but, despite an occasional *soupçon* of affectation, they sparkled with genius and were delivered with ease and grace. Whenever a speech of ornamental character was needed, Disraeli was the only member of either House who could utter it perfectly. It was said that the high old Tories were jealous of the enthusiasm of the Queen for him, gained by the pretty things he said at times concerning her and her family. When the Princess Alice of Hesse died of diphtheria caught by a kiss to her dying child, Disraeli, in his touching speech, alluded to the incident as one that deserved to be engraved on an intaglio; and it was said Lord Salisbury whispered, "Blood will tell." But it would have been better for Lord Salisbury if he had possessed some taste for such gems.

Disraeli was also Solomonic in his appreciation of the influence of women. His wife was very homely, but in her pallid, almost weird face and deep-set eyes was visible the power that made her his good genius. His attentiveness to her in company was beautiful. He sympathized with every effort to advance women, and at a drawing-room meeting held to advocate a measure pending in Parliament to enfranchise women, where I was present, it was authoritatively announced that Disraeli would vote for the measure. Miss Frances Power Cobbe arose and said, "Mr. Gladstone, however, has declared that he will oppose it; and this government opposition will be fatal to us. Let him be known as ' William the Woman-hater.'"

Soon afterwards the Tory ladies formed the "Primrose

League," — from Disraeli's favourite flower, — and though an opposition " Liberal League " was formed, it was feeble ; and the Liberal party has suffered ever since through the alienation of eminent women by Gladstone. The women had with infinite toil secured a majority of Parliament, partly through Disraeli's adhesion, for their enfranchisement, which was to be added as a rider to a bill for the extension of the franchise introduced by Gladstone. But Gladstone declared he would withdraw the bill if the rider were added. The members of his Cabinet who favoured the rider, even Fawcett, left the House when the vote came on, and with them many private members. The woman suffrage was thus lost after it was achieved, the defeat being apparently final.

But I have gone ahead of my chronicle. Gladstone was not prime minister of Parliament at the time when I first began to recognize its greatness, but Palmerston, the cynical old politician whom every radical was bound to dislike but could not help regarding with interest. In fact, he was such a historic figure that it seemed unfair to measure him by any standard that had grown up with Young England. Old as he really was, he was so full of life, and was so mentally active, that his small figure and rosy cheeks, quick movement and fashionable dress, conveyed an impression of youthful- ness until he spoke : then one perceived, not by his voice but by his thoughts and phrases, that he belonged to a past gen- eration. He had an air of being unable to understand that a Parliament had grown up able to rebel against his control. It was a considerable part of Richard Cobden's task to watch Palmerston. I remember on one occasion the old Premier trying three times in different forms to bring forward some evasion of the Speaker's ruling. Each time Cobden inter- rupted him with a point of order. Palmerston sat smiling, and occasionally turning toward his vigilant critic with a droll sort of " you-be-damned " look. For he evidently knew that on a point of procedure Cobden was always right.

The bizarre career of Disraeli was even surpassed by that of Palmerston. He had incurred charges of treason, of forging public documents, of sanctioning the murderous outrages of Sir John Bowring on the Chinese, of selling his influence to Russia for its payment of a gambling debt of £20,000, and appointing a disreputable fellow (Hart), who secured the money, to be consul at Leipzig ; he had been dismissed from the premiership on a complaint of the Queen that he withheld information from her and altered measures after she had signed them. These charges were poured into my ear by anti-Palmerstonists, but only one interested me, that of the Queen. It rather pleased my republican ideas that Palmerston, having offended the Queen, should three years later become her prime minister.

My boyish memories of the parental *index expurgatorius*, which included Bulwer's novels, invested that famous author with some romance. He was curious enough in appearance to have stepped out of his own fantastic "Strange Story." His head was a sort of caricature, the jutting forehead and deep-set eyes being as a sort of make-up.

The amusing day in the House of Commons was that set apart for the annual motion to enfranchise women. It was under the care of Jacob Bright, though his famous brother, John, steadily voted against it, and silently. Beresford Hope always led the opposition to its foregone result, and evidently took pleasure in tormenting the ladies behind their grating by making fun of them. I remember his description of the bill to "enfranchise the failures of the sex."

Another annual was the motion to legalize marriage with a deceased wife's sister. For a time the Commons passed it every year and the Lords regularly refused approval. I remarked that after such disapproval the House of Commons never sent it up again during the same session ; and may add that I reached the conclusion that the Commons never insisted on this bill because they did not wish it passed by the Lords, as it might have been had they returned it twice. The Lords, and especially the bishops, were well pleased to have the bill sent up every year, as it enabled them to boast of their power to veto the House of Commons. But it was all a sham affair.

The friends of the measure in the Commons did not demand a second vote in the same session, because they knew they would not get a majority. This is the only measure quoted in support of the Lords' right of veto, and many foreigners are deceived by it. No measure sent up by the House of Commons three times in the same session can fail to pass. Gladstone's measure of Home Rule for Ireland, whose defeat by the Lords excited so much wrath, would have become law had his government not known that the Commons did not mean it to become law, and that they would not have given it a majority the first time but for their certainty that it would fail in the Upper House.

Gladstone was the most famous orator of England to the outside world, but this reputation was largely due to his limitations. He uttered innumerable commonplaces with an air of profundity; he never worried the average man by any original thought or idea; and he pleased the great mass by speeches that were in large part preaching. The preaching was always orthodox, and it was just that mixture of Anglicanism, Evangelism, Puritanism, and Philistine moralism which supplied three fourths of the pulpits (both Church and Nonconformist) with quotations. Of all the great laymen he was the only one left who seriously defended the orthodox dogmas. Other statesmen might utter compliments to Christianity without going into particulars; they might value the Christian system as a national institution; but the defence of the orthodox dogmas in detail had long been only professional and salaried but for Gladstone; and now that he is dead it would be hard to find any Englishman of recognized scholarship and competency, not in orders, who would defend orthodox dogmas. Although Gladstone's parliamentary sermons did not of course go into articles of faith, he printed numerous theological tracts of the kind, and his speeches were sufficiently suffused with the moral accent related to dogma for responsive chords to be touched in church, chapel, and conventicle.

Gladstone's lack of humour raised more laughs than most

people's humour. I heard him speak on the reduction of the tax on pepper; and he so ensouled pepper that it seemed to be flying about the hall, and one must cry, "Pepper for the masses!" An Oxford professor told me that just before a formal meeting of the Faculty of Lincoln College it was learned that Gladstone was on a visit to the Master of Christ's College. They wished to have him at the meeting and get a speech out of him, but the difficulty was that they had no subject to discuss. But one professor remembered that there had been some question whether about twenty old books that had always been on a shelf in a corridor should not be removed to the library, and they resolved to make that motion, though quite unimportant, an excuse for getting up a discussion. Gladstone came with his host and took the discussion seriously. "Gentlemen," he said, "it was remarked by the distinguished professor who raised this important discussion that he did not wish to take the responsibility of changing the location of these volumes without receiving an order from the entire Faculty, and it seems that the Faculty hesitate to take the responsibility. Gentlemen, there have been times when the Faculty of Lincoln College has assumed great responsibility, and I trust that it is still prepared to assume great responsibilities when changes become necessary. We live, Gentlemen, in times when emergencies arrive," — and so on proceeded Gladstone with solemn periods for fifteen minutes about a matter which the professors supposed would bring out some witty anecdotes, but had not expected would afford them just the kind of amusement received.

Gladstone was not beloved. He was a strong statesman without being a great man. He was so entirely occupied by official duty that no room seemed to be left for those apparently small but really vital personal sympathies and relations which belong to real greatness. I was several times in evening companies where he was present. When he entered it was as if in state; all talk and mirth were suspended, and we stood around and bowed to him and his wife and his escort, he returning our bows all around as if we were some delegation.

He would move near the hostess, introductions would follow, but there was no free and easy chat with individuals. Happily he did not remain long on such occasions, and the young people were enabled without much interruption of gaiety to cherish a remembrance of the " Grand Old Man." He was an institution ; how can one love an institution? A member told me that he asked another Liberal why he disliked Gladstone ; the reply was, " Oh, he is always so damnably in the right! "

No doubt I shared at that time the strong feeling of the Italian, French, and German refugees, and their circle in London, against Gladstone, on account of the treatment of Garibaldi ; but both the statesman as well as my humble self was to have a good many instructive experiences, and in the course of time, when I saw Gladstone save England from four wars, and even mobbed and literally hustled with his wife from their house into the street because of his resistance to a warlike project against Russia, I recognized in him the true representative of English humanity.

Richard Cobden fairly fulfilled my ideal of a parliamentary leader. There was in his look, his clear eye, in the mingled dignity and graciousness of his manner, the flash as of some unsheathable Excalibur guarding the nobler from the baser England. I used to watch him from my seat in the Speaker's gallery while discussions were going on, such as those involving the United States, and recognized a man without egotism whose every word was that of one knowing the special strength entrusted to him. He fitted exactly a story Emerson told me : when Cobden was in the thick of the struggle against the Corn Laws, one of his little children asked, " Mamma, who is that gentleman that comes here sometimes? " Never was there a more affectionate domestic character.

Soon after my arrival in England I had the pleasure of breakfasting with Cobden in his rooms near Westminster Hall, and wondered at the extent of his knowledge of our affairs in America. Mill, Cairnes, F. W. Newman, and Fawcett were among the few I met in England who had closely studied the constitutional history of the United States, but Cobden knew also the details of our situation. He had travelled in the United States, north and south, and personally knew the leading men in both sections. He had seen a good deal of Jefferson Davis who was even then, he said, thinking of war as a probability. One thing Cobden said astounded me. He had once travelled with Jefferson Davis and McClellan together, and .Davis whispered to him that in case of a war "that man is one of the first we should put into service."

The proceedings in the House of Commons on the day of Cobden's death, April 3, 1865, were affecting. I had a place in the Speaker's gallery, and that which impressed me especially was the way in which the grief of the whole House did away with formalities. As the deep-toned Westminster clock slowly struck four, the members moved in silently as if summoned by a knell, the ministers following. Not one spoke to another. As they sat in silence with their hats on I felt as if once more in a meeting of Friends. At this moment all eyes were turned to the door as the greatest of Friends entered — John Bright. With head bowed under his sorrow, John Bright walked to his place, by the side of which there was a vacancy never to be filled. When Palmerston arose there rang through the hall something like a cry, followed by a deep hush. As the white-haired old man, who had seen the leading men of more than two generations fall at his side, began to speak, his voice quivered, and recovered itself only when it sank to a low tone that was deeply pathetic. Having recounted the instances in which Cobden had been signally useful to his country, each instance followed by the refusal of proffered honours and emoluments, he said, "Mr. Cobden's name will be forever engraved on the most interesting pages of the history of this country." When Disraeli arose to speak concerning the man whom he had met only in combat, his touching tribute made me feel how irresistible is the force of a right and true man. No mere politician could ever have brought a lifelong antagonist to stand by his grave and say, "I believe that, when the verdict of posterity is recorded on his life and conduct, it will be said of him that, looking to all he said and did, he was without doubt the greatest political character the pure middle class of this country has yet produced, — an ornament to the House of Commons and an honour to England." Then, as if trying to lift a great burden, arose John Bright. Twice he tried to speak, and his voice failed; at length with broken utterance, he said a few words, the last being, " After twenty years of most intimate and brotherly friendship with him, I little knew how much I loved him until I had lost him." As the large, manly orator spoke these simple words, plaintively as a child, his tears came thick and fast, and a wave of emotion passed through the House and galleries.

Six months after the death of Cobden died Palmerston. When Palmerston begged Cobden to enter his Cabinet the answer was, " I am necessarily your lordship's antagonist." After forty years the England of Cobden seems tending to absorption in the England of Palmerston, but in 1865 the two were distinct as positive and negative poles. In his eighty-one years Palmerston had followed England. When England wore shoebuckles and queues he wore them; when England shed those old leaves he shed them. A Tory when England was tory; a Whig when England was whig; a Liberal now proposing reforms, now paralyzing them, he was faithful to his motto, "*Flecti non frangi.*" Braver men who would not bend were broken, but Palmerston was in miniature his nation, which in its history had not been broken because it could bend. His funeral brought out all the surviving splendours of the old régime. I followed the cortège from Cambridge House, and saw him buried in Westminster Abbey between Pitt and Fox, with Canning at his feet, and the statue of Chatham rising above him.

When the hearse with its forest of plumes started from the enclosure of his mansion, it was followed by the solemn royal coaches, but the procession was made gay by the procession of gaudy mayoral coaches, — brought from Edinburgh, Liverpool, and other cities, — and by the forty costumed corporations. Like some huge primeval saurian with glittering scales

passing to its fossil bed, the Palmerston cortège slowly crawled
to the Abbey. The Prince of Wales (Edward VII) and the
Duke of Cambridge entered with the Dean, and half the
"nobility" of England were present. The procession had
come through sunshine, but just as Lord Thynne was reading
about the trumpet that was to sound, a storm broke over the
Abbey, which became so dark that the clergy were nearly invisible. The rain fell heavily, the wind howled about the old
walls, and in that darkness the body was lowered, — gold rings
instead of dust falling on the coffin. It was grand to hear the
voice of the invisible organ coming out of the darkness to accompany the choristers singing "His body is buried in peace."
When the grave was covered over the sun came out again,
lighting up the monuments, but the vast swarm of people
outside had been dispersed by the storm.

No saint in history ever had so magnificent a funeral as
this worldly old lord.[1] That evening I passed with Carlyle,
who told me many interesting incidents and anecdotes about
Palmerston, ending with the words, "Farewell, old friend;
many a man of less worth will be seen in your place!"

But how slight was the excitement caused by the death of
either Cobden or Palmerston compared with that which filled
Great Britain when President Lincoln fell. The fête of victory in America had extended to England, and at Aubrey
House there was a grand dinner company. John Bright was
present, — probably his first appearance in company after
the death of Cobden. Before the dinner had ended the butler
came in and whispered to Peter Taylor, who sprang to his
feet and said the newsboys were crying the murder of Lincoln. We all arose, the gentlemen rushing to the street to
get the papers. It was between nine and ten in the evening
when we received confirmation of the appalling news.

After the death of Lincoln my tribute to him appeared in
the June "Fortnightly Review," — "Personal Recollections

---

[1] But the most wonderful and affecting funeral I ever witnessed was that of
Charles Dickens. The Abbey was surrounded by thousands of the poor, many
of whom were weeping.

of President Lincoln." I said all that it was possible for me to say in appreciation of him as a striking personality. In "Fraser" for June my article went into the political situation entailed. I had high hopes that Andrew Johnson, who had shown some strength of character, might prove a better President to carry out emancipation than Lincoln, for Lincoln had fallen on the very day when he had celebrated the fall of the Confederacy by repeating promises, to the white South alone, that filled antislavery people with anxiety. There was fear that we should find him thereafter ready to amnesty slavery itself.

Abraham Lincoln, ten years before his election to the presidency, was for a short time in Congress. His brief career there was marked by one proposal and one utterance. The proposal was that there should be added to a measure for abolishing slavery in the District of Columbia a provision for the rendition to their owners of slaves escaping into the District, which otherwise might be crowded with negroes seeking asylum there. He was the same man when (see chapter xxiii) he said to our deputation: " Suppose I should put in the South these antislavery generals and governors ; what could they do with the slaves that would come to them ? "

His notable utterance in Congress was his description of military glory as " That rainbow that rises in showers of blood — that serpent eye that charms but to destroy."

When he became President, Lincoln wrote privately to a Quaker: " Your people have had and are having very great trials on principles and faith. Opposed to both war and oppression, they can only practically oppose oppression by war."

But the very State that fired on Fort Sumter had candidly indicated to the new President, before that event, how both secession and oppression could be vanquished without war. Representative Ashmore of South Carolina said in Congress : " The South can sustain more men in the field than the North. Her four millions of slaves alone will enable her to support an army of half a million."

President Lincoln had only to use the war power thrust into his hand by slavery to proclaim those four millions free; the boasted commissariat of the Southern army would have existed no longer when every Northern camp was the slave's asylum; slavery, the *teterrima causa*, would have needed every Southern white to guard it. Repeatedly was this urged on the President, along with the fact that every loyalist's slave might be paid for with a month's cost of war.

In his message to Congress, December, 1863, the President said: " Of those who were slaves at the beginning of the rebellion full 100,000 are now in the United States military service, about half of which number actually bear arms in the ranks, — thus giving the double advantage of *taking so much labor from the insurgent cause*," etc. The President had precisely the same right to take 4,000,000 of black labourers from the insurgent cause as 100,000, with the million-fold " advantage " of preventing the war altogether. After 300,000 soldiers had been slaughtered, thousands of families draped in mourning, commerce by land and sea paralyzed, hostility towards England and France engendered, thousands of fugitive slaves thrust back into slavery, and billions of money wasted, the President came no nearer meeting oppression with liberty than to put his livery on 100,000 negroes, set them to cut the throats of their former masters, and sow new seeds of race hatred.

The evils of slavery as a domestic institution were mere pimples compared with the evils of war. The greater evils of slavery were that it kept the country generally in a state of chronic war, now and then breaking out into acute eruptions, such as the murderous robbery of Mexico and the outrages on Kansas. When secession seemed to be slavery withdrawing from its aggressiveness, antislavery men welcomed it; when the firing on Fort Sumter seemed to be another war on liberty, we felt that liberty had to be defended. Even when it was plain that the war was being waged by the President, not for liberty, but solely for the Union, the probabilities that it would somehow eradicate the root of discord from the nation, rendered it necessary to support the Northern side, there being no prospect of stopping the war. But slavery originated in war, and in 1864 it became clear that the war which we were trying to turn against slavery was protecting it. Habeas corpus was suspended; free speech suppressed; men were drafted and torn from their families by violence to fight the South; slaves were armed and put on much less than the pay given white soldiers; and in 1864 the first attempt to reconstruct a rebel State — Louisiana — was by forcing the loyal negroes to work for their old masters (all rebels), albeit for paltry wages. The disloyal whites were to have suffrage, but not the blacks. The prospect was that in all the reconstructed States slavery was to return as serfdom.

Most of the letters received from my American friends were full of despair, and one from Senator Sumner was pathetic.

WASHINGTON, July 30 (1865).

DEAR MR. CONWAY, — If I have not written to you before it was because my engagements left me no time, and now that Congress has closed I can do little more than make my apologies.

I thank you for your vigilant testimony to the good cause, which has suffered infinitely, first, through the terrible tergiversation of the President, and secondly, through the imbecility of Congress, which shrank from a contest on principle. If Congress had willed it, we could have carried a bill for *political* rights as well as for *civil* rights and on precisely the same argument, — that it was needful in the enforcement of the prohibition of slavery. I tried hard, but could not bring Congress to this duty, but I do not give it up.

The President is singularly reticent, but his prejudices are strong. With Seward as counsellor, nobody can tell what he will forbear. His policy has been arrested by Congress, but this has been by a deadlock rather than by establishing a contrary system. Meanwhile all true Unionists from the South testify alike. Unless something is done they will be constrained to leave their homes. On this the testimony is concurring, whether from Texas or N. Carolina. Gov. Hamilton has left Texas, but cannot return. •Other Unionists are following his example.

I have succeeded during this term in creating a commission for the revision and consolidation of the statutes of the United States. I have also carried through the Senate bills, that have already passed the House, for the introduction of the metric system of weights and measures. Add to these, I stopped in the Senate their bad Banks Bill repealing our neutrality statute, after it had passed the House *unanimously.* These are incidents of the service which I mention with personal satisfaction. And now for the future! God is with us. I shall fight the battle to the end. You will also.

Every sincerely yours,
CHARLES SUMNER.

After all, the metric system was never adopted. But what mattered such things at a moment when the United States was being driven daily towards the fearful precipice? The pathos of Sumner's letter was the evidence in it that he had been excluded from the arena. All he could now say was, " God is with us."

It had troubled me much that in September, 1863, Senator Sumner had delivered in New York an arraignment of England which seemed to me unjust, and still more, in 1864, that he had not arraigned President Lincoln for his policy in Louisiana. This policy Senator Sumner defeated after Lincoln's reëlection, but during his strange nine months' silence I expressed my lamentation that the President should have for the time overborne the voice of our Abdiel in the Capitol, of the fidelity of whose heart there could be no misgiving. Four months after the President's assassination came the following letter from Senator Sumner: —

BOSTON, 15th Aug., 1865.

MY DEAR SIR, — I honor you so much for the dedication of your genius so completely to the cause of Human Freedom, that I cannot be angry even when I think you do injustice to a fellow laborer like myself.

It was a mistake to imagine that I have ever intended to support the Banks reconstruction policy. My hostility to it was declared often to Gen. Banks and to the President himself. Down to the last moment I was not without hope that I might induce the President to change his mind. On one occasion he said to me, "I cannot answer your argument, but I think it can be answered." "No, not if you take till Doomsday," I replied.

And when I found the President persevering, I determined to oppose his Louisiana scheme. You know the result. People from New Orleans say that Gen. Banks now declares "that all the rebel States, not omitting Louisiana, must be kept out of the Union for some time to come."

There was another moment more interesting if possible than that of Louisiana, where I thought you did me injustice. It was in the autumn of 1863, when, as I knew, we were on the brink of war with England. Throughout the month of August Lord Russell had point-blank refused to stop the rams. On the 4th Sept. Mr. Adams wrote, "This is war." On the 10th Sept. I spoke in New York according to the information in my possession, feeling that possibly at the last moment I might obtain a hearing, and determined at least that, if war came, my speech should portray the character of the relations England would have assumed. It was an anxious, painful moment, and I spoke according to my conscience as well as knowledge, knowing well that I should expose myself to misconception and to reproach, but resolved to make my appeal. *The rams were stopped two days before my speech was made.*

If you will kindly look at that speech you will see that it was no perfunctory effort of haste or passion, but that it was done carefully and solemnly; that at the time our peril from England was greater than from France, and that, therefore, England occupied more attention; that curiously, and here is a curiosity of diplomacy, Louis Napoleon, who has always been against us, has carefully avoided stinging and offensive letters, so that positively we have nothing to object to France, except (1) the concession of belligerency, (2) the proffer of mediation, and (3) the Mexican invasion, while hardly a packet came without an offensive despatch from Lord Russell; and you will see that in my speech I did not fail to expose the conduct of Louis Napoleon fully and strongly, so that the French translator did not dare to reproduce that part of the speech.

This being so, I was astonished and pained when I found myself charged with having *said nothing of France* and done injustice to England. I cannot do injustice to England. I know her and love her too well.

But I have always opposed at home all complicity with

slavery, and when I saw England, by that most unhappy and utterly indefensible concession of belligerency — prelude to the tragedy of our war without which it would have been very brief — I felt unhappy as when Daniel Webster supported the Fugitive Slave Bill. You will understand this illustration. But enough of these things.

The contest now assumes a new form. The President [Johnson] has failed us. I saw him often down to the day of leaving Washington, and I had every reason to suppose that there was the utmost harmony between us. Indeed, he said to me, "There is no difference between us. You and I are alike on this question."

But God is stronger than the President. Our cause cannot be lost. There is present uncertainty and solicitude, but we shall prevail. Of this be sure, and what a country we shall then have! Good-bye!   Ever sincerely yours,

CHARLES SUMNER.

That Sumner had privately pleaded against the proposed serfdom in Louisiana no assurance was needed. His leniency to Lincoln in public, no doubt, appeared to him necessary to defeat the Democratic (proslavery) candidate, and the President was reëlected with Andrew Johnson as Vice-President, — the man who, in Tennessee, had pleaded that the only way to save their slaves was to come back into the Union.

Sumner's inopportune diatribe against England appears to me the greatest error of his life. It came at a time when all England was coming to our side, and when the moral unanimity was of practical importance. I knew well the design of Seward to supersede Sumner as chairman of the Senate Committee of Foreign Affairs, — a removal that he would have patriotic as well as personal reasons to dread, — and could only explain the attack at that moment as made under a kind of duress. The speech would have been fair enough when settlements were to be made, but the ingenuities of professional advocacy were not yet in order. The recognition of the Confederacy by England as a " belligerent " was not in hostility ; President Lincoln was, by exchanges of prisoners and otherwise, himself recognizing it as such ; and had not England recognized the " belligerency," it must have made itself an

CHARLES SUMNER

auxiliary in the war on the South, dealing with them as pirates and outlaws. Senator Sumner's own complaints at home of the repudiation by the administration of any antislavery purpose in the war, and the assurance through Minister Adams that slavery would not be affected by the war, were the official instructions of Earl Russell. The case against England was good in law, but it was unfair to bring in the count about slavery. In 1862 the Alabama escaped because of the sudden illness (lunacy) of the Queen's Advocate, Sir R. P. Harding, at the critical moment. After that no privateer escaped ; two days before Sumner's attack on England, the rams were stopped. Lord John Russell's " offensive " despatches were fair rejoinders to the efforts of Seward to foment trouble, of which Sumner himself informed me (see chapter xxii). For Lord John I had no admiration, but he stopped four Confederate rams at a cost to England of nearly three million pounds, and under his " neutrality " the Union got a thousandfold more from England than the Confederacy.

Before the war Sumner, in an oration on " The True Grandeur of Nations," said : " War is known as the *Last Reason of Kings.* Let it be no reason of our Republic ! " Early in the war, October, 1861, in his speech " Emancipation our best Weapon," he proved that the sword could not conquer slavery. The President's refusal to recognize the " belligerency " of slavery was what prolonged the war. Sumner agreed with the rest of us in that, and his discovery, late in 1863, that it was all England's fault, sounded like Seward.

In the above letter, speaking of Johnson, Sumner says : " But God is stronger than the President." " We shall prevail." " And what a country we shall have ! "

What a country ! Poor Sumner presently found himself in a country that degraded him in the Senate, degraded him in his own State, and death alone saved him from witnessing the fulfilment of his worst fear, — uttered beside the fresh grave of Lincoln, — "Alas ! for the dead who have given themselves so bravely to their country ; alas ! for the living who have been left to mourn the dead, — if any relic of slavery is allowed to continue ; especially if this bloody impostor, defeated in the pretension of property in man, is allowed to perpetuate an *Oligarchy of the skin.*"

While recognizing Abraham Lincoln's strong personality and high good qualities, I cannot participate in his canonization. The mass of mankind see in all great historic events the hand of God. Having no such faith, I see in the Union war a great catastrophe. President Lincoln, in disregard of the anti-coercion sentiment of press and pulpit, and without consulting Congress, assumed the individual responsibility of sending a half million men to their graves for the sake of a flag. Wilkes Booth assumed the individual responsibility of sending Lincoln to his grave for the sake of another flag. " In accepting the challenge at Fort Sumter," as Sumner rightly phrased it, Abraham Lincoln decided that the fate of his country should be determined by powder and shot. In the canonization of Lincoln there lurks a consecration of the sword. The method of slaughter is credited with having abolished slavery. But by the same method Booth placed in the presidential chair a tipsy tailor from Tennessee, who founded in the South a reign of terror over the negro race, — which has suffered more physically since the war began than under the previous century of slavery. And the white race has suffered in character to such an extent that our presidential Father Abraham — who persisted in sacrificing his Isaacs instead of the brute caught in the thicket by its horns — could he revisit his country and find us giving up coloured citizens to be freely slain and burned, their blood and ashes still cementing the Union, would feel himself a pilgrim sojourning in a strange land on his way to seek the land of his promise.

Alas ! — the promises of the Sword are always broken ! Always !

CHAPTER XXXIII

EASTER SUNDAY, April 1, 1866, I travelled all night to witness Carlyle's installation as Lord Rector of Edinburgh University next day. The sleeping-car was then unknown, the night was bitter and snowy, and the journey dismal. The first man I met in Edinburgh was Professor Tyndall, who said he believed we two and Huxley were the only men who had undertaken the hard journey to hear Carlyle. Taking my hand he said, "This is the real kind of tie between America and England. Carlyle belongs equally to both."

No reader in the twentieth century can realize the impression made by Carlyle that day. There is no longer the clear historic background behind that figure, — the weary trials, the poverty and want, the long, lonely studies, through which the little boy of fourteen climbed on to a youthful condition still more rugged, and finally, despite his alienation of pulpit and populace, gained this height. As Carlyle entered the university theatre there walked beside him the venerable Sir David Brewster, fourteen years his senior, who first recognized his ability and gave him literary employment. The one now Principal, the other Lord Rector, they moved forward in their gold-laced robes, while professors, students, ladies stood up cheering, waving hats, handkerchiefs, programmes in ecstasy. Near me sat Huxley, and not far away Tyndall, — in whose eyes I saw tears unless my own dim eyes deceived me. Carlyle sat there during the preliminaries, scanning the faces before him, among which were a score that would bring to him memories of this or that quiet retreat in Scotland known in youth or boyhood.

Before he began his address, Carlyle shook himself free of the gold lace gown and laid it on the back of a chair. This movement excited audible mirth in the audience, and the face of the old Principal beamed. For myself I saw in the act the biographer of Cromwell saying, " Take away that bauble! " No stage actor could with more art have indicated that the conventionalities were about to be laid aside. I had, as I thought, seen and heard Carlyle in every mood and expression, but now discovered what immeasurable resources lay in this man : the grand sincerity, the drolleries, the auroral flashes of mystical intimation, the lightnings of scorn for things low and base — all of these severally taking on physiognomical expression in word, tone, movement of the head, colour of the face, brought before us a being whose physical form was a transparency of his thought and feeling.

When Carlyle sat down there was an audible motion, as of breath long held, by all present ; then a cry from the students, an exultation ; they rose up, all arose, waving their arms excitedly ; some pressed forward, as if wishing to embrace him, or to clasp his knees ; others were weeping : what had been heard that day was more than could be reported ; it was the ineffable spirit that went forth from the deeps of a great heart and from the ages stored up in it, and deep answered unto deep.

When Carlyle came out, a carriage was waiting to take him to the house of Mr. Erskine of Llinlathen, but he begged to be allowed to walk. Carlyle had known I was going to Edinburgh, and on arrival I found a note from him asking me to wait for him at the door of the theatre ; I was there, and he desired me to see after the newspaper report. But as we started off to walk he was identified by a delighted crowd who extemporized a demonstration. He found it best to take a cab, but before entering it gave a friendly look on those who were cheering him, — saying, however, softly, as if to himself, " Poor fellows ! poor fellows ! "

The scene I had witnessed was more phenomenal than I could at once take in. It was the revelation of a kind of eloquence and spiritual affluence which set me dreaming. What had the pulpit lost by putting up dogmas that barred Carlyle away from the career in which he might have illumined all Christendom ! The three men who chiefly moulded the thought of their generation in England and America were all trained for the pulpit — Darwin, Carlyle, Emerson : they were all shut out of it by their intellectual honesty and the inability of the churches to recognize the superiority of a great living oracle to the creeds of defunct crania.

I find the following in my note-book : —

April 4. Evening at Erskine's dinner. Present : Thomas Carlyle and Dr. John Carlyle ; Mr. Dundas, lawyer and antiquarian ; Dr. John Brown, author of " Rab," etc. ; Professor Lushington of Glasgow University, whose wife (Tennyson's sister) came in after dinner ; and one or two other gentlemen and ladies. When we followed the ladies to the drawing-room they all wished to be introduced to Carlyle. Presently he came to the far end of the room where I was, and said, "Oh, dear, — I have n't any rest at all — I wish I was through with it." " But," I said, "you are looking better than usual." " Yes — well — it may make me better in the end, but it's tedious work. I am always in company and see nobody preferable to vacuity : ' Please sir, please madam ; might I exchange you for nothing at all ! ' " (A laugh that seemed to do him good.) " I am going up to a smoking-room they've provided me with — will you come with me ? " At the top of the house, the long pipe lighted, Carlyle stretched himself in his favourite home-position on the floor, and began a slow running talk. " Go over the path to Stirling — Dundee, if possible — St. Andrews, you will come down the coast by Kirkcaldy — Ah — a long time since I taught school in that place."

Presently, after some interval of silence, every trace of care and weariness in his face passed away ; with a sweet, child-like expression he looked at me, and knowing well the affection as well as the literary enthusiasm that had brought to his side a young friend of Emerson, he took me into his confidence. In the following report of his talk I enclose in brackets paragraphs that were recorded at somewhat later dates :

It seems very strange as I look back over it all now — so far away — and the faces that grew aged, and then vanished. A greater debt I owe to my father than he lived long enough to have fully paid to him. He was a very thoughtful and earnest kind of man, even to sternness. He was fond of reading, too, particularly the reading of theology. Old John Owen, of the seventeenth century, was his favourite author. He could not tolerate anything fictitious in books, and sternly forbade us to spend our time over the "Arabian Nights"—"those downright lies," he called them. He was grimly religious. I remember him going into the kitchen, where some servants were dancing, and reminding them very emphatically that they were dancing on the verge of a place which no politeness ever prevented his mentioning on fit occasion. He himself walked as a man in the full presence of heaven and hell and the day of judgment. They were always imminent. One evening some people were playing cards in the kitchen when the bakehouse caught fire ; the events were to him as cause and effect, and henceforth there was a flaming handwriting on our walls against all cards. All of which was the hard outside of a genuine veracity and earnestness of nature such as I have not found so common among men as to think of them in him without respect.

My mother stands in my memory as beautiful in all that makes excellence of woman. Pious and gentle she was, with an unweariable devotedness to her family ; a loftiness of moral aim and religious conviction which gave her presence in her humble home a certain graciousness, and, even as I see it now, dignity ; and with it, too, a good deal of wit and originality of mind. No man ever had better opportunities than I for comprehending, were they comprehensible, the great deeps of a mother's love for her children. Nearly my first profound impressions in this world are connected with the death of an infant sister, — an event whose sorrowfulness was made known to me in the inconsolable grief of my mother. For a long time she seemed to dissolve in tears — only tears. For several months not one night passed but she dreamed of holding her babe in her arms, and clasping it to her breast. At length one morning she related a change in her dream : while she held the child in her arms it had seemed to break up into small fragments, and so crumbled away and vanished. From that night her vision of the babe and dream of clasping it never returned.

[The only fault I can remember in my mother was her being too mild and peaceable for the planet she lived in. When I was sent to school, she piously enjoined on me that I should, under no conceivable circumstances, fight with any boy, nor resist evil done to me; and her instructions were so solemn that for a long time I was accustomed to submit to every kind of injustice, simply for her sake. It was a sad mistake. When it was practically discovered that I would not defend myself, every kind of indignity was put upon me, and my life was made utterly miserable. Fortunately the strain was too great. One day a big boy was annoying me, when it occurred to my mind that existence under such conditions was not supportable; so I slipped off my wooden clog, and therewith suddenly gave that boy a blow on the seat of honour which sent him sprawling on face and stomach in a convenient mass of mud and water. I shall never forget the burden that rolled off me at that moment. I never had a more heartfelt satisfaction than in witnessing the consternation of that contemporary. It proved to be a measure of peace, also; from that time I was troubled by the boys no more.]

Ah, well, it would be a long story. As with every " studious boy " of that time and region, the destiny prepared for me was the inevitable kirk. And so I came here to Edinburgh, about fourteen, and went to hard work. And still harder work it was when the University had been passed by, the hardest being to find work. Nearly the only companion I had was poor Edward Irving, then one of the most attractive of youths; we had been to the same Annan school, but he was three years my senior. Here, and for a long time after, destiny threw us a good deal together.

Very little help did I get from anybody in those years, and, as I may say, no sympathy at all in all this old town. And if there was any difference, it was found least where I might most have hoped for it. There was Professor Playfair. For years I attended his lectures, in all weathers and all hours. Many and many a time, when the class was called together, it was found to consist of one individual — to wit, of him now speaking; and still oftener, when others were present, the only person who had at all looked into the lesson assigned was the same humble individual. I remember no instance in which these facts elicited any note or comment from that instructor. He once requested me to translate a mathematical paper, and I worked through it the whole of one Sunday, and it was laid before him, and it was received without remark or thanks. After such long years I came to part with him, and to get my certificate. Without a word he wrote on a bit of paper : " I certify that Mr. Thomas Carlyle has been in my class during his college course, and has made good progress in his studies." Then he rang a bell, and ordered a servant to open the front door for me. Not the slightest sign that I was a person whom he could have distinguished in any crowd. And so I parted from old Professor Playfair.

It had become increasingly clear to me that I could not enter the ministry with any honesty of mind; and nothing else then offering, to say nothing of the utter mental confusion as to what thing was desired, I went away to that lonely straggling town on the Frith of Forth, Kirkcaldy, possessing then, as still, few objects interesting to any one not engaged in the fishing profession. Two years there of hermitage, loneliness, at the end of which something must be done. Back to Edinburgh, and for a time a small subsistence is obtained by teaching a few pupils, while the law is now the object aimed at. Then came the dreariest years, — eating of the heart, misgivings as to whether there shall be presently anything else to eat, disappointment of the nearest and dearest as to the hoped-for entrance on the ministry, and steadily growing disappointment of self with the undertaken law profession, — above all, perhaps, wanderings through mazes of doubt, perpetual questionings unanswered.

I had gradually become a devout reader in German literature, and even now began to feel a capacity for work, but heard no voice calling for just the kind of work I felt capable of doing. The first break of gray light in this kind was brought by my old friend David Brewster. He set me to work on the " Edinburgh Encyclopædia ; " there was not much money in it, but a certain drill, and, still better, a sense of accomplishing something, though far yet from what I was aiming at, — as, indeed, it has always been far enough from *that*.

[And now things brightened a little. Edward Irving, then amid his worshippers in London, had made the acquaintance of a wealthy family, the Bullers, who had a son with whom all teachers had effected nothing. There were two boys, and he named me as likely to succeed with them. It was in this way that I came to take charge of Charles Buller, — afterwards my dear friend, Thackeray's friend also, — and I gradually managed to get him ready for Cambridge. Charles and I came to love each other dearly, and we all saw him with pride steadily rising in parliamentary distinction, when he died. Poor Charles! he was one of the finest youths I ever knew. The engagement ended without regret, but while it lasted was the means of placing me in circumstances of pecuniary comfort beyond what I had previously known, and of thus giving me the means of doing more congenial work, such as the " Life of Schiller," and " Wilhelm Meister's Wanderjahre." But one gaunt form had been brought to my side by the strain through which I had passed, who was not in a hurry to quit — ill health. The reviewers were not able to make much of Wilhelm. De Quincey and Jeffrey looked hard at us. I presently met De Quincey, and he looked pale and uneasy, — possibly thinking that he was about to encounter some resentment from the individual whom he had been cutting up. But it had made the very smallest impression upon me, and I was quite prepared to listen respectfully to anything he had to say. And, as I remember, he made himself quite agreeable when his nervousness was gone. He had a melodious voice and an affable manner, and his powers of conversation were unusual. He had a soft courteous way of taking up what you had said, and furthering it apparently; and you presently discovered that he did n't agree with you at all, and was quietly upsetting your positions one after another.]

And now an event, which had for a long time been visible as a possibility, drew on to consummation. In the loneliest period of my later life here in Edinburgh there was within reach one home and one family to which Irving, always glad to do me a good turn, had introduced me. At Haddington lived the Welshes, and there I had formed a friendship with Jane — now Mrs. Carlyle. She was characterized at that time by an earnest desire for knowledge, and I was for a long time aiding and directing her studies. The family were very grateful, and made it a kind of home for me. But when, further on, our marriage was spoken of, the family — not unnaturally, perhaps, mindful of their hereditary dignity (they were descended from John Knox) — opposed us rather firmly.

But Jane Welsh, having taken her resolution, showed further
her ability to defend it against all comers ; and she maintained it to the extent of our presently dwelling man and wife
at Comley Bank, Edinburgh, and then at the old solitary
farmhouse Craigenputtoch, that is, Hill of the Hawk. The
sketch of it in Goethe's translation of my "Schiller" was
made by George Moir, a lawyer here in Edinburgh, of whom
I used to see something. The last time I saw old Craigenputtoch it filled me with sadness, — a kind of valley of Je-
hoshaphat. Probably it was through both the struggles of
that time, the end of them being not yet, and the happy events
with which it was associated, now buried and gone. It was
there, and on our way there, that the greetings and gifts of
Goethe overtook us ; and it was there that Emerson found
us. He came from Dumfries in an old rusty gig ; came one
day and vanished the next. I had never heard of him ; he
gave us his brief biography, and told us of his bereavement
in loss of his wife. We took a walk while dinner was prepared. We gave him a welcome ; we were glad to see him ;
our house was homely, but she who presided there made it of
neatness such as were at any moment suitable for a visit from
any majesty. I did not then adequately recognize Emerson's
genius, but my wife and I both thought him a beautiful transparent soul, and he was always a very pleasant object to us in
the distance. Now and then a letter came from him, and
amid all the smoke and mist of this world it is always as a
window flung open to the azure. During all this last weary
work of mine, his words have been nearly the only ones about
the thing done — " Friedrich " — to which I have inwardly
responded, "*Yes, yes, yes,* and much obliged to you for saying that same!" The other day I was staying with some
people who talked about the "Idylls of the King," which
seemed idle enough ; so I took up Emerson's "English
Traits," and soon found myself lost to everything else, —
wandering amid all manner of sparkling crystals and wonderful luminous vistas ; and it really appeared marvellous how
many people can read what they sometimes do with such books
on their shelves. Emerson has gone a different direction from
any in which I can see my way to go ; but words cannot tell
how I prize the old friendship formed there on Craigenputtoch Hill, or how deeply I have felt in all he has written the
same aspiring intelligence which shone about us when he came
as a young man, and left with us a memory always cherished.

After Emerson left us gradually all determining interests drew us to London, and there the main work, such as it is, has been done, and now they have brought me down here, and got the talk out of me.

I now quote again from my diary : —

April 5. A pleasant smoke and chat with Dr. Carlyle. He told me much that was interesting about the Carlyle family. There are now living four brothers and two sisters. One brother and a sister (married) live in Canada. One lives at Annandale, the middle dale of Dumfrieshire. He, Dr. Carlyle, is six years younger than Thomas. He was induced by a German, with whom he formed a friendship in Edinburgh in early years, to go to Munich to study in his profession. There were also no good medical schools here then. He went a great deal to see Schelling. He belonged to a choice club of German beer-drinkers, who drank, smoked, and gave one another their views on the universe ; and it was from his accounts and stories of these men told to Thomas that the idea of Teufelsdröck came into his head. Dr. Carlyle was in Italy a great deal. He had a hard fever when twenty years of age and his hair fell out. When it grew again it was perfectly white as it is now, making him look older than his brother. The father, who died about 1832, was a worker who united the callings of mason and architect. He was remarkable for his religious feeling and shrewd proverbial wisdom, — his sayings being quite well known and often repeated in Annandale now. He afterwards became a farmer. The mother, who died 1853, was also a woman of character and beauty; in particular had fine, large, dark eyes. She read and understood all of Thomas's works, though the subjects were new to her ; and even persisted in reading and re-reading the " History of the French Revolution " until she comprehended it entirely. She was at first disturbed by Carlyle's new religious views, but when she found he was steadfast and in earnest, she cared for no more.[1] Dr. Carlyle is very remarkable ; knows all languages, and has a fund of information of every kind.

I learned either from Dr. Carlyle or from Carlyle himself that the investments of the latter were many years before

[1] I was told that Carlyle's mother learned to read anew in order that she might read her son's writings, and that the only book that disturbed her was *Wilhelm Meister*, of which she said, " The women are so wanton."

made in America ; and that when the war broke out there he did not withdraw them. He had his reward, and had just received six thousand pounds from Charles Butler, who attended to his affairs in New York.

April 6. Went to dinner at Erskine's. Present: Lord Neave, Sir David Dundas (once in Palmerston's ministry), Admiral Ramsay, Dr. Carlyle, Mr. and Mrs. Patterson, and Lady ——, beside whom I sat, and who was clever. Carlyle appeared happier than I had ever seen him, and was hardly equalled by Lord Neave, most famous of table-talkers. Dundas was a little pompous, — reminding me of Edward Everett, whom he knew and admired, — but had a goodly number of good anecdotes. After the ladies had left the table the dignified Dundas became more free-and-easy and told us of the epitaph of Pitcairn, the lying-in doctor: " Prospicite virgines, retrospicite matrones, et lugete." Lord Neave laid on this an epitaph he professed to have found on a bibulous old Scotchman named Gladstone : " Baccho et Tobacco nimium indulgebat." Dundas told the story of old Dr. Parr's being unable to sleep part the night because awakened by a doubt whether the word *but* in a Latin epitaph should have been *at* or *sed*. Lord Neave and Carlyle thought Parr an ass ; but Dundas told the story of his having said that somebody (I think Dr. Johnson) " may have gone to Abraham's bosom, but if so he would certainly kick that patriarch's guts out." Smollett was talked of, and Carlyle thinks " Humphrey Clinker " one of the greatest books ever written. Nothing by Dante or anybody else ever surpassed the scene where Humphrey goes into the smithy made for him in an old house, and whilst beating the iron, the woman, who has lost her husband and become deranged, comes forward and talks to him as her husband and says, " John, they told me you were dead, —how glad I am you have come," — and his tears fall down and bubble on the hot iron. Carlyle said he remembers no happier day than when as a boy he went off into the fields and read "Roderick Random ; " and how inconsolable he was that he could not get the second volume. Lord Neave said it was difficult to know what to do or say about great books that contain impurities, or how to advise young women. Carlyle said he thought they should be encouraged to read but not talk about them.

Mr. Erskine himself said but little, evidently preoccupied

with his desire to get the full music out of each guest. A descendant of the Earl of Mar, and kinsman of the famous
Erskine, I have no doubt he was a finer man than either.
Carlyle told me Erskine began life as a lawyer but left that
for religion. He wrote much on this subject but lost his Calvinism by going to study in Germany. He was now not in
public favour because of his scepticism, but Carlyle held him
in high esteem.

When we went into the drawing-room, we found there Lady
Sirras and Miss Dobson and others. Carlyle and Lord Neave
kept up a grand conversation, surrounded by a half-dozen
people. Carlyle, appealed to about the French Emperor, said
he thought him a swindler — an intensified pig. Lord Neave
thought there was a swinish and asinine element in the human
bosom which naturally had its external response. Some one
thought the Emperor had done a great deal to rule over
France so long. Carlyle said it only proved the length of ear
of those who recognized a swindler as an Emperor. All the
men in place in France were such as a man would kick if they
wished to black his boots. If the French of old times were
alive, Louis Napoleon would long before have been beheaded.
" Matthew Arnold says that in France England had lost her
prestige. It shows that Matthew is a good deal of a goose
with considerable sense at bottom. The less *prestige* England
has the better: *prestige* is only another word for humbug.
The Frenchmen say so and so of us. Very well — the fact
' us ' remains the same, whatever you say of that fact. "

Sir David Dundas spoke of a commission once appointed
to select four statues to be placed in front of the British
Museum, of which he was a member. Macaulay was on it.
They were not confined to England or to any nation or age.
They agreed upon Shakespeare at once ; then on Newton ;
about Bacon there was a moment's hesitation, when Macaulay started forward and vehemently urged him as one of the
greatest of mankind. Milton was the last chosen. Carlyle
said it was a mistake to put Bacon before Milton. Sir David
demurred a little. Carlyle thought (and Lord Neave rather

agreed with him) that Bacon was much overrated. " Whilst he was in full glory the greatest discovery of his age was made at his very door, — that of Kepler, — and he had no eye to see it." Referring to the line " Brightest, wisest, meanest of mankind," he thought it worthless — the qualities and defects named were impossible in the same individual.[1]

Carlyle found Dundas sensitive to Homeric criticism, and rather maliciously insisted that " Homer was the name ultimately given to a joint stock company of ballad singers."

Carlyle said, " Clough was as fine a soul as England had produced of late, and would have come to something considerable had he not died."

I was entertained at the house of Lady Anna Campbell, to whom I had been made known by the Duke and Duchess of Argyll. She was surrounded by guests, — among them Lady Wynne and Sir Henry and Lady Moncrieff. There was no enthusiasm about Carlyle in the company. It was impossible not to remark the snobbery to which nature is easily turned by human selection, which evolves much more beauty in the high rank than beneath it. Nor is there any such compensation for this as proverbial Tupper thought when he connected superiority in a woman with plainness of face. These noble ladies, with their masses of auburn hair, rosy cheeks, and superb necks, were intellectual, well informed in political history, and sympathetically interested in the antislavery struggle in America.

It was for me curious that a company so brilliant should break up as it did: a bell was rung, six liveried servants came in, and Sir Henry read a long chapter from the Bible and made a long prayer, — which carried me back to my early days in old Virginia. Sir Henry Moncrieff himself was indeed a fair type of the gentlemen of Scottish descent who had originally settled our neighbourhood on the Rappahannock. I had three days before been taken by Dr. John Carlyle to the Signet's Library, where David Laing, the librarian and Carlyle's

---

[1] Of the " Baconian theory " Carlyle once said, " Bacon could no more have written *Hamlet* than he could have created the planet."

university "assessor," made some search about those families in Virginia. We finally reached the conclusion that they were transported after the Kenmore and Mar Rebellion, 1715–16.

Sunday morning I preached at St. Mark's Unitarian church. If Sir Henry's prayer had carried me to old Virginia, the hymns and atmosphere at St. Mark's carried me back to Boston. Dr. William Smith (translator of Fichte) took me out to his country house to dine, and his daughter Lizzie (now the wife of Professor Kennedy of London) in singing for me the old Scotch songs looked like the lass to whom those of Burns were written; but she also carried me back to our Boston circle by her perfect interpretations of Mozart, Beethoven, Bach, and Mendelssohn.

Carrying numerous letters of introduction, I visited Stirling Castle, then went on to the University of St. Andrews, where I was shown about by Lord Archibald Campbell, the Duke of Argyll's son. I dined with Robert Chambers, a hale old man dividing his interest between golf and spiritualism. He was hospitable and entertaining, but I made up my mind that he never wrote " The Vestiges of Creation."

The death of Mrs. Carlyle, April 21, while her husband was still in Scotland, was an event which I felt would be so terrible to him that I feared he might not survive it. I gave him a note she had written to me at Edinburgh in response to some particulars I had sent her on the evening of Carlyle's address. It was, after Carlyle's death, returned to me by Froude, and is as follows : —

5 CHEYNE Row, Chelsea, 5 April, 1866.

MY DEAR MR. CONWAY, — The " disposition to write me a little note " was a good inspiration, and I thank you for it; or rather, accepting it as an inspiration, I thank Providence for it — Providence, " Immortal Gods," " Superior Powers," " Destinies," whichever be the name you like best.

Indeed, by far the most agreeable part of this flare-up of success, to my feeling, has been the enthusiasm of personal affection and sympathy on the part of his friends. I have n't been so fond of everybody, and so pleased with the world, since I was a girl, as just in these days when reading the letters of his friends, your own included. I am not very well, having done what I do at every opportunity — gone off my sleep; so I am preparing to spend a day and night at Windsor for change of atmosphere, moral as well as material. I am in a hurry, but could n't refrain from saying "Thank you, and all good be with you!"

Sincerely yours,
JANE W. CARLYLE.

When I gave Carlyle the letter he said it was the last she ever wrote except one to himself. He was distressed that she had not received his last letter. It was written at Scotbrig, — the letter which of all he had ever written he would have wished her to read, — but had been delayed beyond the one post necessary, and he found it on her table, there placed while she lay dead in the hospital. He told me again of Edward Irving's introducing him to her and of their marriage. " We had a small patrimony; but I had taken up a standard of literature which was by no means of the paying kind pecuniarily, and our means grew smaller daily whilst I worked. Well — well — we had heavy trials ; trials of a kind different from those which commonly befall people ; but in and through them all she never lost her bright smile and her faith. When she was herself ill and suffering severe pain she was never gloomy. And so she went on through life — shielding me from all the sharp corners of everyday life — and now — it is all over ! One instant, and all one's life is shown to be the merest gossamer which a breath may sweep away forever."

He then took me out into the gardens, where we smoked together. He said he must "either get at some work — or die. Only work could make life sufferable for him now." We then took a long walk in Hyde Park, where he asked me about American affairs, and talked in his usual way about universal suffrage. He said he did not see why votes should be given in America to all the white sots in creation and not to the negro, — but it was a *reductio ad absurdum.* He spoke of the Catholic priest in Ireland who had been the only man beside Emerson who made response to " Sartor Resartus " when it was appearing in " Fraser." Carlyle, when in Ireland, had visited the priest, and found him engaged in some religious exercise or penance in his garden, which required that he should not speak. So Carlyle had to wait for some time, and the conversation amounted to nothing, — though the priest was pleasant enough and had a good head.

Froude told me that when Carlyle returned from Scotland he went around Hyde Park with the driver who had driven his wife there on the fatal day, making him show every point in the drive, — the place where the dog had been run over; where he had been hailed and told that the lady was fainting; ending at the hospital, where he gazed on the couch where she was laid.

Carlyle expressed his desire that I should come as often as I could to see him, and I did so. Occasionally Ruskin came, and it was pleasant to see how serene and beaming was his face, so worn and troubled in appearance, when he entered that room at Chelsea. " Mr. Carlyle," he said one evening, " how few people I know who really can sit down at their own little table and pour out their cup of tea from their own little tea-pot, and there think and say what is to them true without regard to the world's clamour ! " Carlyle said: " That used to be the characteristic of the English people : whenever you had an Englishman you had a man with an opinion of his own ; but one does n't find it so now."

The conversation fell upon the cruelty of sports, and Ruskin referred with enthusiasm to Emerson's lines entitled " Forbearance " : —

> Hast thou named all the birds without a gun ?
> Loved the wood-rose, and left it on its stalk ?
> At rich men's tables eaten bread and pulse ?
> Unarmed, faced danger with a heart of trust ?
> And loved so well a high behaviour,
> In man or maid, that thou from speech refrained,
> Nobility more nobly to repay ?
> O be my friend and teach me to be thine !

Ruskin's talk was eloquent, but I found it at times hazy. " As I was this morning labelling some minerals it occurred

to me: Why have n't you something better to do than labelling minerals? Were you the Duke of So-and-So, would you
not be doing nobler work?" Then he sped off to something
different, indicating, however, that he felt somehow that a
man ought to have some relation to the affairs of his country. Carlyle did not respond to this. One evening the conversation related to the clergy. I mentioned, when Charles
Kingsley was spoken of, the large reputation he had in America through his books, "Alton Locke" and "Yeast." Carlyle told us of Kingsley's father, a good old squire, and of
his mother, — a lady who once visited him, bringing her
young son Charles. She was intelligent and of some beauty,
serious and moist-eyed, looking as if she had emotions she
did not care to utter. Probably Charles and Henry inherited
their ability from her. When she came with young Charles,
he sat in absolute silence during the conversation, and presently turned aside and wrote something. When Charles
first preached his liberalism, some one eminent in the Church
denounced him for heresy. At that the elder Kingsley was
much grieved, and Charles said to any doubter of his orthodoxy, " *Mentiris impudentissime!* " Thenceforth a decline.
Ruskin thought there were some good things in " Alton
Locke," but the poor do not always communicate the small-
pox, nor is it the greatest trouble of life not to be able to wed
a dean's daughter. I objected to the falsity of making research end in a church rectorship. Ruskin and Carlyle then
both spoke at length of the troubles that outspoken clergymen like Colenso had suffered. Dean Stanley, said Ruskin,
got on more easily by consummate tact, and uttering his
heresies in the least startling manner, or even in a way that
rendered them least visible at the time they were uttered.
He honoured Stanley for the high position he took in standing by Colenso.

I think Carlyle outgrew some of his heroes. When Germany conferred the Order of Civil Merit on him he was
rather irritated by it. When I mentioned it, he said he should
have been as well satisfied if they had sent him a few pounds

of good tobacco. He had said to Varnhagen von Ense, who called on him with thanks of all Germany for the Life of Friedrich: " I have had no satisfaction in it at all, only labour and sorrow. What the devil had I to do with your Friedrich, anyhow!" My first misgivings about Cromwell came from Carlyle. I had got high ideas of him from the last lecture on " Heroes and Hero Worship," but when I said something in that vein it was plain that he had moderated if not lost his old enthusiasm for Cromwell. He spoke of Cromwell's power, of the strong nose " buttressing the forehead of him," but the only other comment was that it was a grievous thing to break all of the ties binding men to an existing order, whatsoever its evils. In his lectures on heroes there is at every turn a ring of lingering Calvinism. The Cromwellian war was " the struggle of men intent on the real essence of things against men intent on the semblances and forms of things." But when the discovery was made that Puritanism did not represent the real essence of things, but dogmatized on things of which it was most ignorant, Carlyle had more consideration for the " semblances." We were once talking about John Calvin. About the burning of Servetus by Calvin Carlyle said, " Probably there is no greater proof of a man's real belief in a thing than that he is willing to burn his fellow man for the sake of it." I expressed satisfaction that there no longer existed any such real belief. He then went on to speak of the English Church as the " apotheosis of Decency." Speaking of Swedenborg, he described the old inn in the city where Swedenborg had his first vision. " I stopped there when I first came by coach to London. Swedenborg was just crazy enough to be unable to distinguish between inward and outward impressions. The nervous system is so mysterious that I would not assert that his alleged knowledge of the fire at Stockholm when he was at a long distance is impossible, but I have not seen sufficient evidence of it."

Carlyle was very compassionate. I well remember the wrath with which he spoke one evening to Mr. Ruskin and myself of seeing at the Zoölogical Gardens living mice put into the cages of the snakes. He watched a rattlesnake not yet hungry, but with its cruel glittering eye fixed on the mouse, whose every limb was trembling with terror. Such "laws of this universe" as the instinct of snakes to prey on mice did not silence Carlyle's protests against cruelty. It was largely through his influence that vivisection was restricted.

When John Burroughs, laureate of the American birds, went with me one evening to Chelsea, Carlyle astonished us by his knowledge of birds and love of them. The mavis he thought next to the nightingale in song, and then came the blackbird ("not of that species noted for his accomplishment in picking holes in things"). The lark, though monotonous, is always pleasing. He found it a kind of welcomer wherever he went. The linnet was a pleasant bird. The London house-sparrow was impudent as could be, and would hardly get out of one's path. (He imitated its pert look and popping up of its head admirably.) He remembered the dignified unconcern of a cat passing close by about five hundred of them chattering away about their affairs, and bethought him of the Arabian legend that Solomon's temple was erected under the chirping of 30,000 sparrows, — "all met to give a joint disapproval of the project." Leigh Hunt used to send him here and there to listen to the singing of the nightingale. But he could not hear one until on a certain day there came a song which he recognized by Goethe's description: he compared the poet to it — "a voice sounding amid the din like the nightingale — touching and strong." These words told the whole thing. It was not sad, but pathetic and somewhat piercing. It is incomparable. He listened to it fifteen minutes, but never heard the nightingale again. It is passing away from about London. He heard of one lately singing in Green Park. It does n't go farther north than the bottom of Yorkshire. It is said it cannot find farther up what it requires to eat.

Alexander Ireland told me that, after visiting Carlyle in 1833, at Craigenputtoch, Emerson met him (Ireland) with the exclamation, "What a wonderful child!" Never was Carlyle better labelled unless by Emerson's words after his friend's death: "He was a trip-hammer with an æolian attachment." The child in Carlyle was wounded when (1848) Emerson was in his house unable to share his reaction and even carrying off the whole Carlylean congregation! The child in him wept in secret, but his biographer brought the ebullition to light to the distress of Emerson's friends in England. I knew them well, and was among them when Froude's work was published. Although I regretted that the private entry should appear without explanation, it was of too much historical interest to be suppressed. I reproduce it because long acquaintance with the English friends of Carlyle and Emerson made clear to me the circumstances which, for the memory of both and their fifty years of friendship, should now be related. The entry, dated February 9, 1848, is as follows : —

Emerson is now in England, in the north, lecturing to Mechanics' Institutes, etc., — in fact, though he knows it not, to a band of intellectual *canaille*. Came here and stayed with us some days on his first arrival. Very *exotic ;* of smaller dimensions, too, and differed much from me as a gymnosophist sitting idle on a flowery bank may do from a wearied worker and wrestler passing that way with many of his bones broken. Good of him I could get none, except from his friendly looks and elevated, exotic, polite ways ; and he would not let me sit silent for a minute. Solitary on that side too, then ? Be it so, if so it must be. But we will try a little further. Lonelier man is not in this world that I know of.

It was a terrible trial for a man who, after slow years of toil and poverty, had gained the applause of the best heads in his country, to find himself in the position of a "Lost Leader." But it was just that which Emerson's presence in England revealed to Carlyle. The overthrow of kings on the Continent he welcomed with his adherents, because they were sham kings, and in his vision he beheld them succeeded by real kings, by Cromwells or Friedrichs ; but his flock dreamed only of democracy filling their place, and to Carlyle that meant anarchy. Though John Stuart Mill said, "Carlyle turned against all his friends," I think the friends had shaped in themselves out of his "French Revolution" and his "Cromwell" a Carlyle that never existed; in those works he merely cleared sham potentates from thrones they were usurping that the real kings might sit on them. And in their eagerness to find a new leader they also shaped an Emerson that did not exist. For Emerson freely declared his "distrust of masses," and his desire to see individuals developed out of them. Democracy in America meant a majority wielded by slavery. But while presenting no system of his own Emerson refused to accept that of Carlyle; he did not believe that the ideal kingdom was at hand nor lose his hopes of mankind. This was enough for the Carlyleans amid the thunder of toppling thrones and breaking chains. Although Carlyle believed that Emerson's audiences in the provincial institutes were *canaille*, he knew that in and around London it was the best people who were carried away by the enthusiasm for Emerson, — the Martineaus, Hennells, Marian Evans (George Eliot), Matthew Arnold, the Howitts, Sir Arthur Helps, Sir A. Alison, W. E. Forster M. P., Richard Cobden M. P., W. J. Fox M. P., J. S. Mill, Arthur Clough, Monckton Milnes (Lord Houghton), the Carpenters, Dr. Chapman, and others. J. A. Froude met him at Oxford and his life, he declared, was influenced by him. It was impossible for the childlike heart of Carlyle not to feel the pain of this break between himself and his circle. Mrs. Carlyle was in such distress that she complained to Espinasse that he talked too much about Emerson.

"But," says Carlyle in his loneliness, "we will try a little further." A resolution speedily justified. Emerson, surrounded by those whom Carlyle had awakened, was everywhere affirming his love and confidence in him, extolling his honesty and grandeur in uttering his thought even when unwelcome to his friends. Carlyle could hardly fail to know this. He never knew all that Emerson had done for him when he was in poverty. I heard him say that there was "something maternal in the way America treated me," but he never knew that the money sent him for his first books was got by Emerson and his friend Dr. Le Baron Russell going from house to house, man to man, fairly compelling them to subscribe for the volumes. His love of Emerson was never really disturbed; he spoke of him as the "cleanest intellect in this planet." In 1880 I called on him before a journey to America, and as I was leaving he said, "Give my love to Emerson. I still think of his visit to us in Craigenputtoch as the most beautiful thing in my experiences there."

When I returned from America in 1881 Carlyle had sunk very low. His mind was yet in fair strength, and he was reading over the German books which had influenced him in youth. His eightieth birthday had brought him many letters and telegrams of congratulation. "It was one of the unpleasantest days I ever passed. Few people know how miserable a thing is life when the strength has gone out of it. Some of my friends lately sent a doctor here, but it would have been just as useful to pour my ailments into the shaggy ear of a jackass. I said to him, 'The only benefit you could do me would be to mingle some arsenic with this cup of tea, but as the law forbids that, there is no reason for your remaining professionally.' He was a sensible sort of man."

CHAPTER XXXIV

Ruskin — Carlyle and Ruskin — Ruskin's lectures — Contemporary art — " A
Caution to Snakes " — The Rossettis — Dante Rossetti's " Nonsense Verses "
— Rossetti's "Mary Virgin " — " Mary Magdalene " — Rev. Dr. Storrs —
" The Gate of Memory " — Dante and Beatrice — " The fall of the leaf " —
Burne-Jones — Religion and Preraphaelists — Holman Hunt — Ford Madox
Brown — Oliver Madox Brown —Works of F. Madox Brown.

ON one of those blissful mornings which pass the year insen-
sibly from spring to summer, beneath whose glow England
expands like a water-lily on her silver seas, I sat in the
study of the most eminent art critic in the world. The house
at Denmark Hill was embowered with trees — old patriarchs
that had watched over the home for a hundred years. Everything betokened wealth, taste, and elegance. The halls ended
in airy apartments, and these into conservatories lustrous with
floral offerings from every zone. The luminous walls and
tinted ceilings combined to give the best light to choicest
works of art. As I waited in the library, gazing now at the
pictures, and now at the fresh lawns stretching from the low
windows, I seemed to be in the ideal home of a man elected
by destiny to study the beautiful.

He, Ruskin, was affable and kindly in manner, but with
something retractile about him, as of one over-sensitive and
on guard over too quick sympathies. He had the look and
voice of an idealist, but not the calmness of the optimist. He
was emotional and nervous, and his voice, though rich and
sweet, had a tendency to sink into a hopeless tone. His
large, light eye was soft and genial, his mouth thin and
severe. The brow was prominent, and suggested power ; the
chin was receding and weak. I felt at once a discrepancy
between the man and his home ; the home meant content-
ment and peace — the man meant restless striving, ideals

unfulfilled. He showed me exquisite works of art by masters ; but turned away from them, one after another, as if a Tantalus seeking fruits and finding only blossoms.

He spoke eagerly of his American friends, especially of Charles E. Norton and his family. I do not remember his talk except that he bewailed the mere mercantile conditions of domestic service, and thought the negro in a kindly Southern home must be happier by the life-contract that made him a member of the family. Ah, if the Southerners had all been Ruskins ! My call was brief, and I went off with a sorrowful feeling that this charming man, so affectionate and appreciative of feminine beauty, should be alone in that mansion and its pretty gardens. One who had acted as Ruskin's secretary told me that though Ruskin was under fifty, any allusion to his divorced wife made him suddenly eighty.

The affection between Ruskin and Carlyle was beautiful. Carlyle cared little for the arts, but loved any man who had mastered the " art and mystery " of any vocation. I felt it distressing when Ruskin, by a chivalrous blunder, put Carlyle into a false position requiring a public disclaimer. The facts were, as I had reason to believe, that as Carlyle was returning home from his afternoon walk, one or two rough lads observing his striking appearance called out to him. Whether Ruskin was with Carlyle or met him at his door I do not recall, but he either witnessed the incident or Carlyle mentioned it, and went on with some lamentation on the degeneracy of the time; however that may be, Ruskin in hot resentment proclaimed with bitterness that Carlyle could not walk about Chelsea without being jeered at. In fact, Chelsea was proud of Carlyle, who wrote to the " Times " gently that Ruskin's statement was the reverse of the fact. Carlyle was troubled at having to do this, which brought on Ruskin reproofs from the press, but said to me, " The gods could not save Ruskin."

It so happened that this flurry (June, 1867) immediately preceded a lecture by Ruskin on contemporary art at the Royal Institution. Ruskin had not written any reply to Car-

lyle or to the attacks, but before beginning his lecture he said
words nearly like these : " It may be expected that I would
say something concerning the matter which has been publicly
discussed relating to a statement of mine ; but I will only say
here that there are reasons, quite apart from the question of
my accuracy, which prevent me from saying anything on the
subject."

This was said so simply, so quietly, and Ruskin was so unconscious of their pathos, that there was a burst of applause.
He then proceeded with his lecture. Sir Henry Holland was
in the chair, with Earl Stanhope and Sir Roderick Murchison supporting him. In the audience were Sir John Millais
the artist, and his wife — formerly Mrs. Ruskin. Ruskin continued, I believe, to visit Mr. and Mrs. Millais.

In enumerating the characteristics of contemporary art,
Ruskin named first its compassionateness. Eugène Sue had
said, " If the rich only knew ! " and art *did* know the depth
of truth and beauty among the poor. Ancient art honoured
the palace ; that of to-day loves the cottage, — prefers peasants to kings. It was significant that the compassionate art
has its great representative in Edouard Frère — Edward the
Brother. Ruskin exhibited a painting by Frère of a cottage
interior scantily furnished, its only occupant a little girl
scraping carrots. You will observe, he said, the sympathetic
touches of light and shade in this picture. Wherever there
exists sensitiveness to human conditions there is also a sensitiveness to light and shadow. The second characteristic of the
art of the present day is its domesticity. Ancient art waited
in the forum, ours lingers in the nursery. And this, he regretted to say, with all its advantages, was closely connected
with its third characteristic, — shallowness. For people to be
entirely comfortable in their little nests implies some narrow-
ness.

Here occurred an incident unprecedented in the Institution, whose audiences are the *crème de la crème.* An old gentleman who had taken something stronger than cream, now
and then gave vent to his feelings by ejaculating, " Quite

right, that's so," and presently was so continuous that Ruskin
stopped. Tyndall went to him and said mildly, "Come, friend,
leave." " I beg your pardon," replied the old gentleman with
a good humour that made the audience roar, " I 've come to
hear Ruskin. I 'll sit here." Then Tyndall took hold of an
arm, Burne-Jones of a leg, and the man was removed. Tyndall and Jones presently appeared near the lecturer, very
warm, and were greeted with cheers. Ruskin, in proceeding,
read from his notes sentences so oddly appropriate to the occurrence that we were excited to laughter, in which he joined:
" Sequent on the domesticity of art is its eccentricity."
" The sense of everything true is lost in a hubbub of voices."

He went on to say that the art of the present day was
injured by a straining after originality, and the perpetual
introduction of dramatic effects. As ancient art began to emphasize the dramatic element instead of form and colour, it
declined, and at last became vapid. All that was valuable in
modern art was a movement against this vapidity. At the
head of these reformers he placed Rossetti. He exhibited a
painting which he had snatched from Rossetti's studio. It
was painted at the time Rossetti was bursting out into his
passionate religious art. The painting represented the Pass-
over in the house of Joseph while Jesus was a child. Mary
kneeling sprinkles blood on the lintels of the door. Jesus in
a pink gown looks on, while young John fastens a sandal on
his foot — allusion to the words, " the latchets of whose shoes
I am not worthy to loose." The picture was wonderful for
colour, and the figure of Jesus beautiful. The incident, he
said, might have happened in any Jewish home. Another of
this school was Burne-Jones, several of whose designs for
tapestry were hung behind the lecturer. One of these was
Love leading Alcestis, and another the two wives of Jason
hand in hand — Medea and Hypsipyle. The beauty and refinement of these faces were felt by all. He also spoke of
Burne-Jones's fine picture of St. Dorothea. The leading figure of the picture is the angel bringing flowers from heaven ;
the saint's funeral is removed into a corner of the back-

ground. Domenichino, said Ruskin, would have put the angel into the corner, and the corpse in front. But the English and Italian public had exchanged tastes, and London is now frescoed with the bill-poster's "Talking Head," to offset the street frescoes of Verona and Padua. This allusion to the poster of some exhibition at the Polytechnic excited much merriment. Wherever there was frivolity among the people, there was a disposition to gloat over horrible forms. When " Robert le Diable " was performed at the Opera, it was not considered enough that the corpses should rise up in the abbey and become ballet-dancers, but a great stroke was made by having a row of corpses holding candles while the others danced! He showed some grotesque figures by Doré, and said it was a sad symptom that Burne-Jones should have been almost derided while the British public called for Doré to illustrate its Bible. This wretchedness of the public taste rendered it impossible that high English art should exist at present, and as a national art must be produced from a nation's inner life, the real school of art must for a long time be our streets — our chief designs to make the people clean within and without. Baptism is the great sacrament to save the poor just now ; when the rich were inwardly baptized, the poor would be outwardly cleansed.

In 1880 the London Institution announced for St. Patrick's Day a lecture by Ruskin with the sensational title, " A Caution to Snakes." It drew a crowd, but so little was this famous man known personally that he stood for some time near the desk chatting with friends without being recognized. When the applause came he did not appear conscious of it, and went on chatting, and when he began his lecture it was as if he were simply continuing his conversation. He stood with a pictorial background of snakes, indeed framed in an arch of snakes. Alluding to a lecture on snakes, given there by Huxley, he expressed his affection for Darwin and his sincere respect for Huxley. " Professor Huxley knows all about the inside of snakes and I know something about the outside of them, and that is what I mean to talk about." No paper reported this strange lecture, but I made notes, and quote some of them in a detached way.

A snake is a lizard that has drawn in its legs, a duck that has lost its wings, a fish that has dropped its fins, a honeysuckle that has taken on a head.

You will see at the top a representation of Giotto's design for a sculpture on the Campanile at Florence, the " Creation of Eve." That artist in his series of designs for the panels would not adopt the story of any Fall or Serpent. Eve rises up to meet her Creator beneath a tree, and above her head ivy twines around the tree's trunk, a mere suggestion of danger.

Beside this portrait of the spots of an English viper I have placed a decorative design much used by the ancient Greeks. You will observe that the basis of the decoration is a spotted serpent, but it has a flower at the end instead of a head.

The attitudes assumed by serpents are prefigured by the forms of vegetation. Here is a cranberry vine, which creeps along until it shoots up a stem which curves over to its flower, and you will see how like it is to the cobras there erect with curved necks.

This " Eel-pie Island " of ours does not yet know how an eel swims up a waterfall. Imagine yourself with your feet tied together, and the whole of you tied up in a bag, trying to swim up a waterfall many times your own height. How does the eel manage it? God knows! The motion of a serpent, when the whole of his force is put forth, is a kind of skating on this side and that, himself being the ice.

The snake whose bite is most fatal is that which the Portuguese call the " Cobra of Death." It is only three or four inches long, it goes by leaps; but this little pipe-stem creature has only to touch a man with his tooth and death surely follows.

The colours of the fatal serpents are not bright or beautiful ; they are dull, muddy, repulsive.

Though twenty thousand of the Queen's subjects annually die of snake-bites, there is no full treatise in the English language on the poison of serpents.

The upturned face of this rattlesnake has something human about it. This may be partly accidental, and due to the artist ; but really, the interest which has in every country invested these reptiles has been due to the fact that it has seemed a type of degraded humanity. It has an expression of human cunning and malice.

Although much has been said of the serpent's wisdom, it is not nearly so clever as a crab.

At one point Ruskin caused amusement by persuading two reluctant officials to stand up on high chairs, about twenty feet apart, in order to display the skin of a boa constrictor. Ruskin himself then leaped nimbly up on the table before him and stood at one side in order that the skin might be seen. In that prominent position he began describing the action of the boa; how, elastic as any small snake, it seized its prey by the action of a whip-lash; but when the coil was once around the victim, the lash was as a watch-spring with the rigidity of iron. The action of the boa was described with appropriate gesture, the whole being so dramatic as to elicit applause. This appeared to surprise Ruskin, who, looking down, perceived that he was standing on the top of his desk, and then leaped down with a boyish movement and smile.

Of course it could not have been a lecture by Ruskin if it had not closed with a moral discourse. He said that if, to illustrate the subject, he had then and there put serpent poison into the most worthless lout in England, they would have been filled with horror at the crime; yet multitudes of poor louts in the country are poisoned in many ways daily. His own college of " the Body of Christ," Corpus Christi, at Oxford, derived much of its revenue from a public house which poisons a whole village with its adulterated drinks. Another moral was, that wise as the serpent was reputed to be, he was so silly as to swallow his blanket as real food. He was thus a type of educational " cram." Thousands of youths supposed to be undergoing education were simply swallowing books, as the boa does his blanket; they swallow what is laid before them without tasting or knowing what they are eating. In this our youth ought to be wiser than serpents.

Professor Huxley told me that some scientific men present declared the lecture wild. Perhaps that was its chief charm;

there was a wild beauty about all the transfigurations before us of forms towards which our human horror has been bred into an instinct.

There were many opinions of Ruskin with which I could not agree, but I never read or heard a word of his that did not stimulate thought and suggest truth. He was an inspired egoist without egotism, a spirit at once lowly and aspiring, to whom any mistake is forgiven. Wonderful London! Amid the turmoil and fogs of the city, of a mercantile family was born and reared this hyperæsthetic St. George who encountered the Dragon and was devoured.

It was at an early period in my London life that I met the Rossettis. Dante Gabriel Rossetti charmed me by his fine freedom of thought and feeling before I could thoroughly appreciate his works. He was a unique personality, free from prejudice, and absolutely dedicated to Beauty whether blest or unblest. His poems and paintings are so exquisitely exotic that one has to live up to them individually. They have conveyed to the world the impression of a sombre spirit like the great Italian poet whose name he bore; but he was sociable and generous, and had a rich vein of humour. He gave pleasant dinners, at which William his brother, Swinburne, W. B. Scott, Madox Brown, Stillman (when in town) were generally present, and to which I was sometimes invited. He eagerly joined in the talk; he was a fine wrangler; and indeed I think some of his friends took pains to raise discussions that would bring out his wit and the colours of his sensibility. He loved to poke fun at familiar friends, and wrote "Nonsense Verses" about them, some of which I remember. One was on the artist and poet, W. B. Scott, whose "Year of the World" Emerson so admired. Scott wore a wig.

> There is an old party called Scott,
> Who seems to have hair but has not:
> He seems to have sense —
> A still grosser pretense
> On the part of that party called Scott.

Another victim was the Academician Val Prinsep : —

> There is a creator called God,
> Whose creations are sometimes quite odd :
> I maintain — and I shall —
> The creation of Val
> Reflects little credit on God.

At a dinner given to Stillman, at which Whistler (a Confederate) related with satisfaction his fisticuff with a " Yankee " on shipboard, William Rossetti remarked, " I must say, Whistler, that your conduct was scandalous." (Stillman and myself were silent.) Dante Gabriel promptly wrote : —

> There is a young artist called Whistler,
> Who in every respect is a bristler :
> A tube of white lead
> Or a punch on the head,
> Come equally handy to Whistler.

Another rhyme I remember : —

> There's the Irishman Arthur O'Shaughnessy —
> On the chessboard of poets a pawn is he :
> Though bishop or king
> Would be rather the thing
> To the fancy of Arthur O'Shaughnessy.

His quickness in rhyme-making once led his friends to challenge him with certain names, one that of a model named Olive : he instantly produced a verse of which I remember only two lines : —

> There is a young female named Olive
> When God made her he made a doll live.

The paintings of Rossetti were a revelation to me. In my " earthward pilgrimage " they gave me a movable oasis that went with me through every desert of negation, and preserved the beauty in every lost belief. I fancied in his paintings a pilgrimage of the same kind. His earlier ones had dealt with subjects traditionally holy ; but the Madonna drew nearer, and dwelt on earth in the poetic nature of his sister Christina. I can never forget the emotion with which I saw his picture of " Mary Virgin." The Virgin is a lovely maiden, a perfect portrait of Christina, seated beside St. Anna her mother

(Mrs. Rossetti), while their father as St. Joachim is trimming a vine that climbs above the window. Mary Virgin has before her embroidery; she is copying a lily on which two flowers have expanded, while above these is a bud not yet unfolded. The lily has grown high from a vase whose ornaments are symbolical. An angel is watering the stem, this angel being a portrait of his other sister, Maria. The details of the picture are very fine, but it was the general purport that I found so impressive.[1]

In 1856 Rossetti made a drawing of "Mary Magdalene at the door of Simon the Pharisee." He never put this picture on canvas, but painted the head of Jesus, now in my possession. In 1867 he gave me a full-sized photograph of the original drawing; and this picture, which he retouched and inscribed, remains a source of happiness. What has become of the original I know not. After his death large photographs of his pictures were made by Frederick Hollyer and issued to subscribers by his brother William, by whom each is signed, but the "Mary Magdalene" is not among them.

A large company of merrymakers is passing along the narrow street with music, all in rich costumes and garlands, led by the fairest of them — Mary Magdalene. But as they pass Mary sees at an open window a face that makes her pause: the eyes of Jesus have met hers. She is seen ascending the few steps that lead to the door, not heeding the youths trying to restrain her, tearing off her garlands; her long wavy hair floats back, and the pathetically beautiful face is stretched forward, forever turned away from her gay companions, who stand stricken with wonder, to the one face.

[1] The Madonna had already been humanized for me. One of my early discourses at South Place was on "Madonnas of everyday life." It was given on the vigil of Mary, the theme being placarded as usual outside the door. There was a Catholic church back to back with mine, and a lady in seeking for it was misled by the subject into my chapel. This was discovered after service by her inquiring at the door for the holy water. An incident hardly worth mentioning; but it pleased me to think that on the vigil of the Madonna I had so preached as not to awaken in the devout lady any feeling that she was out of place.

From her girdle hangs the antique round flagon of spikenard.

The picture started me on a quest concerning the Magdalene, with the result of my discovery that the story of her immorality and her penitence was not only unauthorized by the New Testament, but inconsistent with it.[1]

---

[1] The late Bishop of London preached an eloquent sermon in St. Paul's cathedral in which he pictured Jesus as having around him all the types of human character. Among these types was "Mary Magdalene, the Penitent." Through the *Westminster Gazette* I asked his lordship his reason for supposing that Mary Magdalene had any more reason for penitence than any other lady in Jerusalem. My note was printed under the heading "A Much-Calumniated Lady." His lordship printed a respectful admission that there was no authority in the New Testament for the received story, but it was an ancient Church tradition.

In 1887 I was visited by the Rev. Dr. R. S. Storrs, who was much interested in this picture, and I afterwards read in the New York *Independent* the report of an address given by him, October 5, 1887, at Springfield, Mass., in which he said : —

" I saw, not a great while ago, in the house of a gentleman then living in Brooklyn, an etching by Gabriel Rossetti, of which I have never seen any other copy, and of which I doubt if any other copy exists. It pictured the Magdalene, riding through the streets of Jerusalem, with a crowd around her. Her tumbled gold of hair fell upon her shoulders, everything in her dress was wanton and lascivious, everything in her face portrayed marvellous beauty, but with animal passion flaming through it. The traces of the passion, however, were of the past. Even as she rode, with the attendants around her, with the crowd of her admirers, with the spangles on her dress, and with the crown of flowers upon her head, she caught the eye of the Christ and saw his face looking from the window upon the street, and her face had blanched to a pallid hue, and she was tearing with trembling and swift hands the crown from her head and the ornaments from her dress, and flinging them into the street before the face and eye of the Son of God. I thought to myself, There is a type of the change in every heart, however sinful, when it sees the face of Christ. Self-rebuke, piercing pangs of remorse rising in it, but at the same time the wondering love, the adoration of the spirit toward him by whom this marvellous and instantaneous change hath been wrought."

The memory of Dr. Storrs was at fault in two details ; she is not riding, and her face is refined ; but no minister can easily see any Magdalene not voluptuous. This is the way the myth grew, — and will grow, — because her supposed sinfulness makes the charm of the romance.

Rossetti's Mary Magdalene was drawn from Miss Siddal two years before she became his wife, and is, I believe, the only portrait of her at that early time. It is beautiful. It is probable that after her tragical death, February, 1862, this portrait possessed too much sacredness for him to give the picture to the world.

There was enough in the romance of Rossetti and his wife to recall that of Jules the Sculptor in Browning's " Pippa Passes." When Rossetti found her she was a model. Holman Hunt painted from her his Sylvia, Millais his Ophelia; but Rossetti saw in her the possibility of a creation higher than pictorial art could produce. He taught her in art and she became an able artist. After her death he collected all her pictures. Among them was a very striking one which she had called " Shipwreck." A group of women on a cliff are endeavouring to rescue those wrecked. In showing us these pictures Rossetti said, " Had she lived she would have done better work than I."

In " Mary Magdalene at the house of Simon the Pharisee," there are thirteen interesting faces. The youth with garlanded head who seeks to restrain Mary resembles the poet Swinburne. There has been this long time a discussion concerning the man who sat as model for this wonderful " Head of Jesus." It is said by one party to have been Sir Edward Burne-Jones, by the other party George Meredith. The picture being celebrated, the claims have been rather warmly asserted. William Rossetti told me that his brother got Burne-Jones to sit for him, but once on receiving a call from George Meredith, who was not unlike Burne-Jones, he took some traits from him. The painting — it is before me as I write — easily reminds me of both of those fine faces, but the hair and beard are drawn from the purely fictitious letter ascribed to Publius Lentulus : " His beard full, of an auburn colour like his hair, not long, but parted." The most wonderful feature is the eye, — luminous, clear, freighted with the serene strength drawing Mary to his feet.

Rossetti had not the least interest in Christian dogmas, and never alluded to them, nor did he ever attend any church or chapel; but he had created out of the Christian legends and symbols a new set, and thus fashioned a poetic religion for himself. Everything had to be transmuted. He paints Mary holding the infant Jesus in leading strings; his little hand grasps at a passion-flower. If he paints a subject from some poem it must first fall into his mind as a seed and flower into a new poem. Such was the "Gate of Memory," which I purchased at Christie's. This beautiful picture was suggested by a poem of W. B. Scott, entitled "Mary Anne." My friend Scott, as I note in his reminiscences, erroneously supposed that his idea was represented in the painting. The poem is of a betrayed woman wandering in London, where she sees a group of innocent children at play; embittered by the recollection of her own former innocence and happiness, she curses the children.

Rossetti told me what he had in mind when painting this picture. The betrayed woman looks through an arched gateway which is the mystical Gate of Memory. She sees there a vision of her childhood when as a harvest-queen children and maidens joined hands and danced around her. She looks in not with anger but with patient sorrow; her head is uncovered save by its abundant hair; she gathers her shawl close around her, for she is in the cold street; and at her feet between her and the vision runs a rat — a symbol of the betrayer's lust that separated her from that flower-crowned self.

When I purchased these pictures Rossetti asked me to lend them to him and I did so; but my wife became anxious lest he might alter them seriously; so we went down to his studio and he smilingly gave them back, admitting that he had thought of retouching them, but concluded like ourselves that they had best remain.

Rossetti was an appreciative friend of my wife, and we generally went to his studio together. We witnessed the progress of some of his pictures, among these "Love leading Dante to Beatrice on the day of her death." On the day when he told us of its completion we hastened to see it, and were there with him alone. He sat beside his work and read to us the poem he had translated from the "Vita Nuova," now and then pausing at some line to look on us as if asking if we realized its depth. The lines especially related to the picture are these : —

> Then lifting up mine eyes, as the tears came,
> I saw the Angels, like a rain of manna,
> In a long flight flying back Heavenward;
> Having a little cloud in front of them,
> After the which they went and said, " Hosanna ; "
> And if they had said more, you should have heard.
> Then Love said, " Now shall all these things be made clear:
> Come and behold our lady where she lies."
> These 'wildering phantasies
> Then carried me to see my lady dead.
> Even as I there was led,
> Her ladies with a veil were covering her;
> And with her was such very humbleness
> That she appeared to say, " I am at peace."

When Rossetti read that the angels said " Hosanna ; and if they had said more, you should have heard," he paused and said, " That is quaint ; " and from that point his voice became lower and subtly sweet, even moving, in the words " I am at peace." The portrait of his wife was on the wall just above his head.

The genius of Dante Rossetti expressed itself in every least line of his countenance. It was as smooth in every part as if carved, but lights and shades passed over it and sometimes shifting colours ; the eyes now drooped, now expanded. That day when the painting he most loved was completed, he was himself a picture never to be forgotten. We comprehended the mystical meaning of that kiss of Eros. For the face of Love was that of the young wife he had lost, and the Beatrice on whom Love's lips were pressed was Mrs. William Morris.

His wife, whom one night on entering their bedroom he had found seated at her toilet-table dead, might well have leaned out of heaven to kiss Mrs. Morris, for it was she who had lifted the soul of Rossetti out of the grave. I have not in my long life known anything more quasi-miraculous than this reappearance in modern London of Dante and Beatrice. There was no slightest consciousness in it, no poetic posing. The superb lady, great-hearted and sincere, recognized the fine spirit to which she was related, and responded to his visions and ideals. He painted from her many of his most high and spiritual pictorial poems. Happily she had a husband who could not only write poems but appreciate the poem lived in his household. Mrs. William Morris had no levity about her; she was long our neighbour, and I had the pleasure of assisting the efforts of herself and her daughters to clear away some of the evils of Hammersmith. Earnest and serious as she was beautiful, her presence lent a charm to every company in which she appeared; and she was honoured by all who knew her and Dante Rossetti as one who thought for herself, and was great enough to live in accordance with her own heart.

Intellectually Dante Rossetti was a freethinker, though in a vague and untrained way. It was, I believe, because the Protestant dogmas had never touched him at all, and the Catholic creeds with which he was more familiar had faded away in the London atmosphere, that he was able to see so clearly whatever was poetic and picturesque in ancient legends and visions. Madonna, Magdalene, damozel, angel, — they all became lovable and familiar phantoms to him, forms of feeling. But as life wore on he more and more felt their unreality; and after the death of a youth he loved (Oliver Madox Brown) in 1874, there was an increasing plaintiveness in his tone which made his friends feel anxious. In 1875 he wrote a sonnet, which his friend Dannreuther set to music, and gave me leave to print it in a piece I was writing ("The Angel of Death").

> Know'st thou not at the fall of the leaf
> How the heart feels a languid grief,
> Laid on it for covering;
> And how sleep seems a goodly thing,
> In Autumn at the fall of the leaf?

And how the swift beat of the brain
Falters because it is in vain,
In Autumn at the fall of the leaf,
Knowest thou not ? and how the chief
Of joys seems not to suffer pain ?

Know'st thou not at the fall of the leaf
How the soul feels like a dried sheaf,
Bound up at last for harvesting ;
And how death seems a comely thing
In Autumn at the fall of the leaf ?

Rossetti had an affection for his pictures ; they were his children, and every one surrounded with personal associations and cherished memories ; his pigments were mixed with his heart's blood. After I had purchased two of his pictures, he wrote to me to come and dine with Madox Brown and Dr. Gordon Hake, — whose poetry we both admired, — and begged me to bring the pictures. When I came he received me as if I had become his kinsman, and handled the dear " little things " as if they were his long lost children. He had not seen them for a good many years. One day I told him I was going north and would stop to see the collection of Mr. Rae, near Liverpool, which contained some of Rossetti's works. Incidentally I remarked that some of my friends in America were interested in him and I hoped that some of his pictures would find their way over there. He perhaps supposed that the Rae collection might be sold, and some of its Rossettis secured by me for American friends. At any rate, in a letter about other matters came this paragraph : —

If we had been longer together the other day, I might have mentioned a point connected with the question as to Rae's collection. This is the fact (important only to myself) that I should really regret the transportation for life of some half dozen pictures which I should like to be visible and attainable at need. Of course I only mention this as a personal feeling, but you will perceive it could not well be otherwise.

This struck me at the time as more peculiar than it seems now (1904). Among all of my pictures those by Rossetti have given me the most constant delight. The " Head of Jesus " has become to me mystically sacred. Memories of my beloved friend who painted it, of the great artist and the brilliant author whose features are visible in it, of that dearest heart that found in it her ideal, enable me in my old age to interpret the innumerable personal associations which have gone to create that ideal being to whom human hearts tenderly sing, — " Lover of my Soul ! "

It is droll to think that in 1867 Ruskin could speak of Burne-Jones as " almost derided," — the artist presently made D. C. L. by Oxford, and ultimately a baronet !

One day I found Burne-Jones at work on a saint — for some church window. " And I almost a nihilist ! " he said smilingly. It was precisely that which made him so happy in such work. When a mind gets entirely outside of all creeds and superstitions he can see them all with an impartial eye as varied expressions of human nature. They become folk-lore, mythology, variegated fauna and flora of the human heart and imagination. The harmony of the world was set in his heart, and I associate his genius with a wonderful decoration he gave to a piano made for a wealthy friend of his. On the lid is a Muse leaning from an oriel of the blue sky ; beneath stands a poet musing ; between them is a scroll inscribed with a bit of old French, " N'oublié pas " — motto of the owner's family. At another end of the lid is painted amid bay-leaves the page of a book, with illuminated letters, the lines being those of one of Dante's minor poems, beginning, " Fresca rosa novella." But these beauties are surpassed when the lid is lifted. Amid the strings, which are exposed, there is a drift of roses, as if blown into little heaps at the corners by the breath of music. On the interior surface is " Terra Omniparens." Between the thorns and the roses sits this most beautiful Mother, naked and serene, with many babes around her. Above, beneath, around, amid the foliations they are seen — impish, cherubic, some engaged in ingenuities of mischief, others in deeds of kindliness and love. Greed, avarice, cruelty, affection, prayer, in all their varieties are represented by these little faces and forms. Some nestle around the Mother; one has fallen asleep in her lap. The fair Mother never smiles nor frowns: she is impartial as the all-nourishing, patient Earth she typifies ; all the discords turn to harmonies in her eternal generation. Her impartial love waits on the good and the evil ; she is one with the art that " shares with great creating Nature."

The paintings of Burne-Jones fascinated me in an especial way. It seemed as if each subject he touched had taken possession of him and selected the pigments of itself. One of his pictures which I saw on the easel — the Wheel of Fortune, with terrible contrast between those at the top and those beneath — impressed me so much that I ventured to ask him if he had any particular description of the goddess in mind. He said he would think about that, and soon after I received a note in which he said : —

You asked me on what my version of Fortune is made. It was a question not easy to answer, I remember — for the first impulse and vision of a picture is not easy to analyze. I think I saw the wheel chiefly, and that something terrible was connected with the thought of it — the sphere and the spokes and tire, and that dread connected with its form was paramount in the first conception. " It was said unto it in my hearing, O Wheel." Do you remember? So the wheel got its Spirit, and its victims — the lucky, and unlucky, and the onlooker.

Preraphaelism, in naming its short-lived periodical " The Germ," was conscious that it was initiative. But in their varied developments the Brothers generally showed a tendency to freethought. Holman Hunt, who painted Christ-legends so devoutly that it was said some pious ladies took prayer-books when they went to his exhibitions, had peculiar conceptions of the gospel narratives which he studied minutely. It was so rare to find a gentleman of culture in London who, unless in holy orders, believed those narratives without allegorical or rationalistic interpretations that Holman Hunt's talk was original. I think he may have been influenced by the Moslem faith in whose atmosphere he resided so much. Moslems accept the gospel miracles literally, and scepticism is unknown among them. He got near to the hearts of the Bedouins, and his conversation about them was profoundly interesting. He discovered that there existed in Palestine a secret sect of Bedouin " spiritualists," and was invited to one of their secret séances ; he attended, but on finding that it was to open with a prayer to Satan (Sheitan) he at once left! As a demonologist I had to deplore the loss of that prayer, and class the scholarly artist with a lady in Hampshire who said to my friend Mrs. Rose Mary Crawshay, " Do you make your children cross themselves when they say the word ' Satan ' ? I do ; I think it safer."

Notwithstanding all that Christian painting, Holman Hunt was not the artist chosen to decorate churches ; most of such work was done by Burne-Jones and William Morris — sceptics. The history of the introduction of Christianity into England was painted on panels in Manchester Town Hall by Madox Brown, who believed in no form of Christianity. The seal of the London County Council was designed by Walter Crane — freethinker and socialist.

With Ford Madox Brown I was on terms of particular intimacy because of his sympathy with my religious heresies. I assisted at the marriages of his daughters (one to Franz Hueffer, the musical critic, another to William Rossetti), and I conducted the funerals of his son and of himself. His quaint house in Fitzroy Square was long the weekly salon of unconventional artists and writers. On a single evening I have met there Turgenief, the Rossettis, Blinds, Stillmans, Holman Hunts, Alma Tademas, William Morris and his wife, Arthur Hughes, Woolner, Garnett, Burne-Jones and wife, Whistler, Ralston ; the poets Allingham, Swinburne, Gosse, Marston. If French artists or authors were in London they generally found their way to Madox Brown, who, though of English parentage, was born in France (1821) and trained in French art-schools.

In the happy household the only son was Oliver, whose death in his twentieth year filled us all with dismay. His precocious genius had already made its mark in art and literature, and the sweetness of his spirit made him the beloved of all. Dante Rossetti loved him as if he were a son, and I shall never forget the agony in his face when he talked to me of Oliver just before my address at the funeral.

Ford Madox Brown, in his letter requesting my services at the funeral, expressed to me his disbelief of all theologies. But although without any of those hopes of future life in which believers find consolation, I never knew in all my ministry, whether among Methodists or Unitarians, more courage than was displayed by this devoted father under unexpected and terrible affliction. Stricken as by a thunderbolt, he was yet not shattered. He set himself to soothe the bereaved ones around him; he sustained them on his great heart; and he never faltered in devotion to his art. The noble and beautiful life went on until, nineteen years later, we laid him at Finchley beside his son and wife. All the artists in London were mourners at that grave. Ford Madox Brown never had an enemy in his life.

I used to watch Madox Brown's pictures as they grew, — his distinctively poetic pictures, such as the Corsair, the Parting of Romeo and Juliet, and King Lear; all full of refined feeling and sincerity; and at length the fruitage of his poetic in his historical work, — represented in those wonderful paintings that glorify the Manchester Town Hall. The knowledge implied in those paintings, dealing with early epochs of British history, the perception at once of the moral, the national, and the picturesque aspect of history, and the mastery of detail in form and colour, make those Manchester panels a national treasure. They are also a monument of the literary combined with the artistic scholarship which alone could have produced them. They are unique, and they show the artist was not to be labelled as of this or that school, but one who developed a school of his own.

CHAPTER XXXV

" ARTEMUS the delicious," as Charles Reade called him, came
to London in June, 1866, and gave his " piece " in Egyptian
Hall. The refined, delicate, intellectual countenance, the
sweet, grave mouth, from which one might have expected philosophical lectures, retained their seriousness while listeners
were convulsed with laughter. There was something magical
about it. Every sentence was a surprise. He played on his
audience as Liszt did on a piano — most easily when most
effectively. Who can ever forget his attempt to stop his Italian pianist — " a count in his own country but not much account in this " — who went on playing loudly while he was
trying to tell us an " affecting incident " that occurred near a
small clump of trees shown on his panorama of the far West.
The music stormed on ; we could see only lips and arms pathetically moving till the piano suddenly ceased, and we heard
— it was all we heard — " and she fainted in Reginald's arms."
His tricks have been attempted in many theatres, but Artemus
Ward was inimitable. And all the time the man was dying.

Never was American in London so beloved. The Savage
Club, founded in 1857, consisted of some half-dozen writers of
plays who dined together every week in an old Covent Garden

inn (Tom Robertson their chief poked fun at them in one of his plays), until one evening some one brought Artemus there; then everybody wanted to belong, and the club entered on its larger career. He was the life and soul of it. Yet all those brilliant articles in " Punch," all those unforgettable dinners, lasted but six months, and the entertainments in Egyptian Hall only seven weeks. When it was learned that the most delightful of men was wasting away under rapid consumption even while he was charming us, the grief was inexpressible.

I was requested by a committee of Americans to conduct the funeral of Charles F. Browne ("Artemus Ward"), and never had a more difficult and sorrowful task. For his unexpected death was a tragedy that almost unnerved me. The chapel in Kensal Green Cemetery was filled to its utmost capacity. All the chief actors and actresses, writers of plays, literary men and women, were present, and sorrow was in every face.

From that time I enjoyed the friendship of many connected with the stage, and became a member of the Savage Club. Possibly I am the only survivor of those who belonged to the Club at that time, when it was a simple affair. We used to dine at Ashley's, which gave us a fair dinner for half-a-crown. We dined early in order to attend some theatre, — all open to Savages. Among them were able men who were writing, adapting, translating the plays that amused the masses of London. George Grossmith Sr., Andrew Halliday, Charles Millward, and Henry S. Leigh were always present; Henry Irving occasionally; but the soul of the Club was Tom Robertson. How we all loved that handsome, witty comrade, and what a joy was the first night of any play of his! I happened to be at the head of the table when the following note was handed to me : —

To the Chairman of the Savage Club:
Dearest of Friends (whoever you may be) : — Please inform the Savage Club that they shall be welcome at the production of my new play, " School," at the Prince of Wales

Theatre this evening. Full dress not required ; a simple mus-
lin and a rose in the hair will be sufficient.

Ever yours,   T. W. R.

Of course we all went, and I think it was on that evening
that his sister, Madge Robertson (Mrs. Kendall), — hardly
out of girlhood, — first appeared on the stage. The theatre
was crowded, the success immense ; we all gathered around
Robertson with felicitations — because of the play and because his sister had given fine promise. This was in 1869.

Yet it was with that same play that the sorrows of Robertson began. For he was accused of having plagiarized from the
" Aschenbrödel " of Benedix. We who knew Robertson personally, and his scrupulous honour, were also familiar with his
previous plays, — " Society," " Ours," " Caste," " Play," etc.,
— and recognized him in every line of " School." But Robertson wrote to us of the Club to meet him there, and we came in
a troubled mood. He told us that while on an excursion with
his wife in Germany they went to a theatre in Berlin and saw
a play in which the fairy-tale of Cinderella was travestied in
a modern plot. He never saw the libretto, and did not take
anything at all from Benedix except the suggestion of utiliz-
ing the plot of Cinderella in a play of modern life. He said
he had now obtained from Germany a copy of " Aschenbrödel," and had placed it with the libretto of " School " in the
hands of John Hollingshead, from whom he would obtain a
judicial decision. We all approved his course and had confidence in Hollingshead, but Tom's particular friend, Andrew
Halliday, a playwright of much experience, said, " Tom, we
all know that those pretty and thoroughly English situations
are yours, and every bit of those witty dialogues; the only
question that can possibly arise would be whether the previous use of Cinderella as a modern heroine should have been
mentioned in your programme."

Cinderella was such a familiar figure of the Christmas pan-
tomimes that Robertson supposed that, there being no question of originality in the case so far as plot was concerned, he
could hardly have credited Benedix without unfairness to his

own play. Nevertheless it was an error of judgment not to mention Benedix, and Hollingshead so decided, while vindicating the originality of Robertson's treatment of the tale.

While everybody else regarded the incident as closed, and never thought of any serious blame attaching to Robertson, it was not the same with himself. When he dined with us at the Club there was less of his old mirth. It was pitiful that while "School" was having a magnificent run, and Madge Robertson having her first success, the admirable author who had evoked the beautiful scenes should be himself inwardly a sort of Cinderella in ashes. However, the Benedix affair was forgotten by the public. Sothern made a great thing of Robertson's "David Garrick," and he went on writing fine plays, — "M. P.," "Home," "Dreams," "Shadow Tree Shift," "The Nightingale." But "War," on which he had put much patient and excellent work, proved a sort of failure. It was his first failure, and told upon him. Also his wife, an accomplished lady of German birth, died. For some time we had observed that he was in poor health, but his death (February, 1871) in his forty-second year was a shock. It was a heavy bereavement in theatrical circles. He was a noble-hearted man, and few English dramatists achieved so much excellent work in such a short time.

One of my earliest friendships in London was formed with William Allingham, a poet of too fine a strain for popularity. My first knowledge of him was through Emerson, who read his wonderful poem "The Touchstone" in the town hall at Concord to the citizens who had assembled at the hour when John Brown was executed in Virginia. The poem was supposed to be by Emerson and went the rounds of the press with his name.[1] Allingham was on the staff of "Fraser's Magazine," to which I too was a contributor.

Allingham was in every way a charming man, and we became attached to him. He was as thoroughly versed in Emerson and Hawthorne and Thoreau and Dr. Holmes as if he had

---

[1] I have several times read *The Touchstone* in public, the last time at a dinner in Brooklyn, on Thomas Paine's birthday, January 29, 1902.

grown up in Boston; he was a rationalist without aggressiveness, able to recognize every poetic legend in Catholicism. He was on terms of intimate friendship with the Carlyles, Tennysons, Brownings, Rossettis, and the Preraphaelists, all drawn to him by his exquisite poems. He was a bachelor for some years after our arrival, and we often had him at our house, and when he was appointed to the customs office at Lymington we greatly missed his friendly face. I visited him there and once had with him a two days' ramble on the coast. His new residence was not far from Tennyson (Farringford), with whom he used to take long walks. When Froude gave up "Fraser" (1874), Allingham became the editor, and we enjoyed his society as of old. He married in that year Helen Paterson, a well known and admirable artist. It was an ideal marriage.

In Carlyle's last years Mrs. Allingham desired to paint his portrait, and Mrs. Alexander Carlyle, who resided with her uncle, undertook to secure her the opportunity. The artist went at the appointed time. Carlyle presently entered and greeted her kindly ; but when a sketch of him was suggested he turned to leave. Mrs. Allingham would have fled, but Carlyle stood between her and the door; so she stood trembling until the niece gave her an encouraging look. The niece then persuaded him to come back and sit down and read his book, which he did with a quiet growl or two. He then appeared to forget the presence of the two ladies. At the end of the hour he took a look at her water-colour sketch, and when he saw his face so deftly drawn he became interested, and invited her to come again. She did so again and again, perhaps a dozen times, and he enjoyed these visits. While she took the sketches he read or talked or dozed, and this lady with her fine tact met all of his moods, added a pleasing episode in his declining life, and painted many excellent portraits of him. One of these I secured, and it was the picture that brought me nearest to the last vision of my great friend.

On November 2, 1867, a dinner was given in Freemason Hall to Charles Dickens, about to visit America. Most of the

Chelsea, 19 Jan? 1866 —

Dear Sir,

I am sorry to report that my
poor Wife is still in the same whirlwhirl
of sufferings, — Neuralgia all the Doctors
call it, but can nowhere to help it; — and
that I fear it will be a long time before
she can see any of her friends.

Yours (in great haste, as always!,
T. Carlyle

men who were carrying on the literary, dramatic, and artistic work of London were present. The ladies, alas — including Miss Dickens, who strikingly resembled her father, and her aunt Miss Hogarth — were put off into a gallery, after the fashion then lingering.

When Dickens entered arm in arm with Bulwer there was wild enthusiasm : behind them walked Lord Chief-Justice Cockburn, small and pale ; the Lord Mayor, with royal air ; Lord Houghton and Sir Charles Russell ; next the Royal Academicians.

When Lord Lytton, the chairman, arose, it was really the novelist Bulwer we beheld, — figure-head of a past generation. There was power in every line of his face, but still something phantasmal. He was curiously awkward in speech at the beginning — a long drawl terminated by a jerk, at which his head was bent forward till the back of it was seen. His gesture in emphasizing anything was to stretch his hand straight out, clasp the fingers tightly to the palm, then draw it in under his arm.

Lord Lytton had not been selected by any snobbish sentiment. It would have been difficult, Thackeray being dead, to find any man more historically fit for the chairmanship than Bulwer. It stands pleasantly in my memory that I saw the old author at his best. For as his speech proceeded his shining thought was unsheathed from the ungainly form, and the queer gestures appeared expressive of individuality.

A score of times Bulwer's speech was interrupted by cheers, but when Dickens arose he had to stand long while the shouts stormed upon him. Men leaped on chairs, tossed up napkins, waved glasses and decanters over their heads, — and there was a pressing up from the lower tables until Dickens was girt about by a solid wall of friends. As he stood there silent I watched his face ; it was flushed with excitement, and those wonderful eyes flamed around like a searchlight. Had Tennyson been there a poem might have been written more pathetic than the address of Ulysses to his brave companions who had " toiled and wrought " with him, when his purpose held "to sail beyond the sunset." Dickens saw before him authors, actors, artists, with whom in early days he had partaken humblest fare: Horace Mayhew, Mark Lemon, Walter Thornbury, Westland Marston, Tom Taylor, Buckstone, Edmund Yates, G. H. Lewes, the sons of Jerrold and Tom Hood, his own sons stood near, as if witnesses to the career whose victories they had followed from the lowly beginning to this culmination.

When the storm of enthusiasm had quieted, Dickens tried to speak but could not ; the tears streamed down his face. As he stood there looking on us in silence, colour and pallor alternating on his face, sympathetic emotion passed through the hall. When he presently began to say something, though still faltering, we gave our cheers but felt that the real eloquence of the evening had reached its climax in the silent tears of Dickens.

There was much talk in the anteroom, and it was late before the company left; but outside a very large crowd of humble people were waiting to catch a glimpse of the great author, and I remarked one aged woman who pressed forward and bowed her face upon his hand.

In 1872 the announcement that Mark Twain was to lecture in St. George's Hall caused a flutter of curiosity. His reputation was wide in England, but it appeared singular that instead of appearing, like Artemus Ward and other American entertainers, at Egyptian Hall or some popular place, he should select the most fashionable hall in London, and charge high prices for admission. The hall was crowded with fashionable people in evening dress, of whom few if any had ever seen Mark. He came on the platform in full dress with the air of a manager announcing a disappointment, and stammered out apologies. "Mr. Clemens had landed at Liverpool, and had fully hoped to reach London in time, but," etc. The murmurs were deep and threatened to be loud, when Mark added that he was happy to say that Mark Twain was present and would now give his lecture. Loud applause and laughter greeted him, and he proceeded to mention several subjects he had thought of for his lecture. "But since my arrival I have found the English people so frantic in their interest in the — Sandwich Islands," — the sentence was cut short by an explosion of laughter. "But before describing the Sandwich Islands," he resumed, — and that was the last we heard of the islands. The lecture was brimful of amusing inventions of far-western life, given with admirable gravity and action. After telling about a wild game of poker he suddenly became unctuous and added, — "All that was long ago. I never gamble *now*" (*sotto voce*, "unless I can make something by it"). So, after a narrative about a duel, he said in an exalted tone: "But I never fight duels now.. If a man insults me, do I challenge that man? Oh, no! (uplifting his eyes piously) I take that man by the hand, and with soft persuasive words lead him to a dimly lighted apartment and — kill him!" The audience was in an ecstasy of delight and laughter from first to last.

Our Savage Club gave Mark a grand dinner. It was not usual for us to come in evening dress, and Mark, who was in full dress, began with, "Pardon these clothes!" After speaking of Hyde Park he got off a satire so bold that it quite escaped the Englishmen. "I admired that magnificent monument [i. e. to the Prince Consort] which will stand in all its beauty when the name it bears has crumbled into dust." The impression was that this was a tribute to Albert the Good, and I had my laugh arrested by the solemnity of those around me. Indeed, one or two Americans present with whom I spoke considered it a mere slip, and that Mark meant to say that the Prince's fame would last after the monument had crumbled.

The death of Mrs. Clemens at the Villa di Quarto, Florence, announced as I write (June, 1904), brings to me cherished memories of my long friendship with her and "Mark Twain." I first really knew them in their beautiful home in Hartford, Connecticut, where I passed some happy days in 1876. The grounds, with their gardens, trees, flowers, were such as one might look for in Surrey, England, as the result of centuries of culture, but the house they surrounded represented the consummate American taste and art. In showing me to my dainty room Mark pointed out the various tubes for calling up servants, coachman, firemen, etc. " There 's one somewhere for the police, I believe," he said, peering around. One morning, when I was writing in my room, Mark walked softly in, holding a letter. " Here 's a fellow who has for some time been trying to get my autograph under the pretence of business. I have to answer his notes, but am playing a game. Mrs. Clemens has been writing my replies, but just for a change we want you to write one." The brief note being dictated and signed " S. L. Clemens per M. D. C.," then directed, Mark went out with a triumphant smile. In the afternoon when we were at billiards a boy of ten years came in with his autograph book, and Mark laid down his cue and carefully wrote his contribution.

Every day we saw Charles Dudley Warner and his wife, near neighbours, and in the evening Rev. Dr. Twitchell came in. In no country have I met a more delightful man in conversation than Twitchell, and his ministerial adventures if printed would add a rich volume to the library of American humour. Mrs. Clemens was not only beautiful but a gracious hostess; her clear candid eyes saw everything, her tact was perfect, and if she entered, the great strong Mark in his stormiest mood would alight as if a gentle bird in her hand.

In 1870 " Mark Twain's " reputation was mainly western, and when he proposed to marry the daughter of Mr. Jarvis Langdon of Elmira, N. Y., this gentleman, as I have heard, desired to know something about his personal character. According to my informant, Mark sent Mr. Langdon a long list of names and addresses, adding, " Any of these persons will certify that I have committed all the known crimes." Of course I do not vouch for the exactness of this anecdote.

Mrs. Harriet Beecher Stowe was residing in Hartford, and one evening — perhaps her birthday — some young people made up a group of " Jarley Wax Works " for her amusement. Mark agreed to be the showman, and we called on her under the pretext of my desire to have a talk with her. The old lady was in fine spirits, and glad to hear from me about the Argylls and other English friends, when she was startled by the invasion of costumed figures. Mark, well advised concerning each character he was to introduce, began with a knight in full armour, saying as if aside, "Bring on that tin-shop," then proceeded with a romance of this knight's gallant achievements. It was all charming, and I never forget the evident affection for Mark felt by his neighbours.

When I sailed for England I carried with me for his London publishers the manuscript of "Tom Sawyer." I read it on the ship, and then recognized that Mark Twain had entered on a larger literary field.

Two or three years later Clemens and his wife came to London, and Charles Flower of Avonbank, mayor of Stratford-on-Avon, begged me to bring them there for a visit. Mrs. Clemens was an ardent Shakespearian, and Mark Twain determined to give her a surprise. He told her that we were going on a journey to Epworth, and persuaded me to connive with the joke by writing to Charles Flower not to meet us himself but send his carriage. On arrival at the station we directed the driver to take us straight to the church. When we entered and Mrs. Clemens read on Shakespeare's grave "Good frend for Jesus sake forbeare," she started back exclaiming, "Heavens, where am I!" Mark received her reproaches with an affluence of guilt, but never did lady enjoy a visit more than that to Avonbank. Mrs. Charles Flower (née Martineau) took Mrs. Clemens to her heart and contrived that every social or other attraction of that region should surround her.

At a dinner company given to these dear friends at Inglewood, our house in London, Mrs. Crawshay brought out a toy "leaping frog" which she had found in Paris. Mark was more amused than I had ever seen him. He got down on his hands and knees and followed the leaping automaton all about the room.

Early in 1879, I think, I was in Paris, and when strolling

along the Champs d'Elysée overtook Mark Twain. We were
both going to call on the American minister. I asked Mark
what he was writing. " Well," he began, " it 's about this : a
man sets out from home on a long journey to do some particular thing. But he does everything except what he set out
to do." He and his family were at the Hôtel Normandie, to
which I at once transferred my lodgings. Mark was working
steadily — indeed hard — on " A Tramp Abroad," and I had
the happiness of making myself useful to his wife in seeing
Paris. In the evening he read us passages he had written, and
the tact and insight displayed by his wife in her comments
were admirable. He worked in the evening and could not go
with us to theatres ; but on Mardigras about midnight he and
I started out in a voiture and looked in on a dozen fancy balls.

Bret Harte I met now and then, and we gave a large dinner party at Hamlet House in his honour. Froude regarded
him as the finest product of the far West, and William Black
was always seeking to have him in his house or on his yacht.
Bret Harte's consulship at Glasgow was a sort of joke. William Black told me that once when he was returning from
a tour with Harte, as they slowly entered a city Bret said,
" What huge ugly place is this ? " " It is," said Black, " the
city in which you have been consul four years." Bret Harte
told my wife that he was coming to her next Monday afternoon, and she probably mentioned it to some friends. But he
did not come, and when chancing to meet him I alluded to
the disappointment he asked forgiveness and said, " I will
come next Monday — even though I promise."

When I first made acquaintance with the London theatres
(1863) Buckstone was still holding the foremost place in that
kind of transitional drama between farce and comedy of which
Warren, in Boston, was the chief representative. Of course
I could not tolerate the notion that anybody could equal
Warren, my first love, but I could not help admitting that
Buckstone was fairly the peer of Burton. Indeed, I think that
he brought out more fully than Burton the whole sense as
well as fun of " The Serious Family."

There were in London some half dozen clergymen — that is, of the English Church — who were theatre-goers, and were troubled at the alienation of the stage from their profession. They made a gallant effort to bridge the chasm by founding the "Church and Stage Guild." I gladly responded to an invitation to unite in this movement, and attended several of the reunions held in a hall in Westminster. A special effort was made to secure the attendance of those who might suppose themselves especially ostracized, such as the ballet girls. These all came dressed with a certain prudishness which amusingly contrasted with the décolletage of the clergymen's ladies, but this did not prevent Edmund Yates from printing in the "World" a satire entitled "Virtue in Tights." I do not remember meeting any of the leading actors there, and this may have had no more significance than the fact that they had no evenings for their dinner companies except Sundays. I think, however, there was among dramatists and leading actors fear of any such alliance. At any rate, I myself soon gave up my connection with the movement for fear of stage puritanization. Already the English theatre had none too much freedom; the finest French plays had much of their pith removed to suit London; and in fact the separation between Church and Stage, superficial under Catholicism, is a birthmark of Protestantism. The theatre, by all dogmatic logic, is the devil's pulpit; but it is ethically valuable as the very organ, by long evolution, of that human nature which Protestantism pronounces accursed.

The English theatre, instead of suffering under the evil eye of religion, had steadily developed human sympathies and principles. It was worth going to the cheap theatres — Sadler's Wells, Adelphi, Victoria, Shoreditch, Grand — if only to see the villain joyous under his hurricane of hisses and the virtuous hero encouraged by exclamations recalling the Methodist conventicle. But in the higher ranks of dramatic art there had been developed a sort of composite character, a mixture of drollery and pathos, whose supreme expression is in our beloved Joseph Jefferson. The master, however, had his forerunners, and among these might be placed Charles Mathews. He was a wonderful artist. Even in the old-fashioned comedies replete with cynicism he could here and there, by an accent, a look, a slight gesture, give a far-reaching touch of feeling. At times one might almost suspect him of putting in gags to the old plays ; this, however, he never did. There had grown up a public sentiment about Charles Mathews something like that felt about Joseph Jefferson. In the fall of 1872 his engagement at the Gaiety Theatre in London was memorable. Although some of us went at first mainly from homage to the most venerable comedian of the time, we continued to attend every play in his repertoire by fascination. Instead of being in decline, he had matured like old wine. His movement on the stage was like that of a youth. The engagement was a continuous ovation. It was supposed that it must have made him a millionaire, and he had to issue a card which began : " Mr. Charles Mathews presents his compliments to the whole human race, and begs to state that, much as he loves his fellow-creatures, he finds it impossible to provide for the necessities of even the small population of London alone."

J. L. Toole I knew personally and in his own home. He was an amiable gentleman of general culture, and in him one might recognize the many qualities of head and heart that went to the making of the unique comedian. Toole drew our tears of sympathy and of laughter simultaneously. Whatever the deficiencies of a piece, he brought out all that was potential in his part with such finish that the figure remained with us as a new creation. His success showed that in the line of art that touches every shade of fun-making from high comedy to fantastic farce perfect delicacy of both word and suggestion is necessary for the truest effect. No actor in London was more beloved than Toole.

I think the elegant drollery of Toole did much to train Londoners for recognition (1877) of the exquisite touches of Joseph Jefferson in such pieces as " Lend me Five Shillings " and the " Cricket on the Hearth." One afternoon I met

Robert Browning on the street, and he said, "I do not remember having had greater delight in a theatre than last night. Lady Carnarvon sent me a request to share her box, and see an American actor, and I went without any expectation. The play was "Rip Van Winkle," and I found myself completely captivated by his acting. The charm was of a kind entirely new to me." [1]

William Winter had accompanied Jefferson to London. His reputation as a dramatic critic led to his being given a dinner, a number of Americans being present. Towards the close of the dinner, while the wines were still freely circulating, a loud discussion sprang up at one end of the long table, and being at the other end I could not hear what was said, but observed Winter gesticulating and some English journalists around him similarly excited. I went up to find what was the matter, and an Englishman said, "Mr. Winter spoke of the third act in Rip Van Winkle in which Jefferson alone appears, confronting the spectres in the mountains; he said that the acting of Jefferson in that act is the finest ever known on the stage, and that none of us denied. But then Mr. Winter went on to declare that it was finer than any acting that ever would be seen on the stage through all time, and because some of us hesitate to accept that forecast he thinks us all donkeys!" Any further results from this curious issue were escaped by our getting a telling speech from Winter, and adjourning to see Jefferson's corroboration of his friend's uncompromising dictum.

I had for some time written occasionally for the London "Daily News," and in 1868 was invited by the editor, Mr. (afterwards Sir) Thomas Walker, to join his editorial staff. I began this regular work in August, 1868, and usually wrote twice every week. I was not restricted to any class of subjects, but it was expected that I would keep the paper abreast of American thought and politics. Soon after I began work on

[1] Joseph Jefferson told me that he met Browning at dinner at Lady Carnarvon's, and several times at his own house, — and was delighted with him.

the "Daily News" a serious incident occurred. The United States minister, Reverdy Johnson, having accepted an invitation to the Sheffield Cutlers' Feast, sat at the same table with Roebuck, who after dinner made a venomous speech against the United States. The general opinion among Americans was that their minister should have left the room. Roebuck said that politics in America had been relegated to buccaneers, and that the best citizens had withdrawn from all connection with politics. This he repeated in a letter to the "Times." When I had controverted this, a worse incident occurred. The city of Liverpool offered the American minister a grand banquet, which he accepted. Among the preparations for this function it was announced that among the guests was to appear Mr. Laird, the man who built the Confederate cruiser Alabama. My article (October 13, 1868), though severe on Roebuck, was tender towards Johnson, and was genuinely meant to save him and the treaty he had made with the English government in settlement of the Alabama matter. The article raised a storm. The London "Standard" said shrewdly that their contemporary had exactly caught the accent of the worst examples of western journalism. The Liverpool papers declared that the dinner was to be politically "neutral." The misstep was made. The result did not fall heavily upon Reverdy Johnson, for his ministerial career was doomed in any case along with the presidency of Andrew Johnson who appointed him; nor did it fall upon Laird and Roebuck: it fell upon England. The treaty concluded with Reverdy Johnson was angrily rejected by the Senate. In April, 1869, I had the pleasure of writing in the "Daily News" a hearty welcome for the new minister, John Lothrop Motley.

No appointment could have been happier. Americans walked proudly. No other American was more honoured among serious readers and thinkers than Motley. In presence, manners, social accomplishments, he was the ideal minister. The misgivings about Grant — and they were many — were cleared away by this one appointment. We were now to have the new and nobler America.

During my life in London there were ten different American ministers to England, and I knew them all. Concerning Mr. Hay's career there I cannot speak, for I returned to America soon after his arrival. But surely none of the rest were received with such welcome as Motley or parted with so sorrowfully. The reputation of the United States never received a more damaging blow than that which humiliated and ultimately proved fatal to Motley. His wife and daughters were the finest types of American womanhood; no receptions in Europe were more elegant than those of the noble minister and his family; and Motley was assiduous as he was polite in all the functions of his office.

On the morning when his removal was announced by cable I went to see him. I found him alone in his office and his pallor frightened me. His voice, however, was calm, and when I desired to know whether he could name a time for some conversation with me on the removal, he asked me to remain then. But he could not understand the event. He was left to amazement and conjecture. He was not conscious of the slightest deviation from his instructions, and could not readily bring himself to believe that the President was capable of sacrificing him because he was the friend of Sumner, who had defeated his (Grant's) Cuban scheme.

In my biographical introduction to Motley's history of the Dutch Republic (G. Bell & Sons), I gave, with the assistance of his daughters, a careful sketch of Motley, and must resist the temptation to repeat it here.

Among the pleasantest of my pilgrimages was one to the regions of Shelley, to his monument in Christ church, and the relics of him in Boscombe House. The great charm, however, of this excursion was due not to the dead poet but to one living, — Sir Henry Taylor, whose " Philip Van Artevelde " had excited enthusiasm among us at Harvard. He still held his position in the Colonial Office, but passed half the year in his pretty cottage, " The Roost, " at Bournemouth. One could hardly imagine a fitter environment for a poet. Lady Taylor (daughter of Lord Monteagle) had wit as well as beauty, and was rich in memories of the eminent people of her time. There were also several daughters. They were all gratified by responses from America to Sir Henry's works, and had just been delighted by a visit from Charles Eliot Norton. Lady Taylor in her girlhood was a pet of Wordsworth, and the intimacy continued to the end of his life. Wordsworth, she said, rarely made a pleasant impression on visitors. If a gentleman had come all the way from America to see him, and he chanced at the time to be interested in the mending of an old glove, he would go on for an hour about that glove. He was very plain in appearance. Once when talking to his wife he said casually, "That was when, as you know, my dear, I was better looking." "But, my dear," replied Mrs. Wordsworth, "you were always very ugly." A lady who took his portrait said she thought lichens were beginning to grow in his wrinkles. Lady Taylor said that Wordsworth had so long lived among the rocks and woods that his naturally rough visage gradually acquired the colour of wood and stone, and he might be almost mistaken for a part of the scenery.

There was a warm friendship between the Taylors and the Tennysons. Lady Taylor told me several anecdotes about the Laureate. At a grand naval review she and a few other ladies had persuaded Tennyson to go, despite his dread of being observed in public. When they were off on a boat, Tennyson turned to her and said with apparent distress, "I knew how it would be, — see that company on the yacht looking at us!" "And we are looking at them," returned Lady Taylor. Tennyson smiled, and for the rest of the day enjoyed the scene.

Sir Henry walked with me to Boscombe House, several miles away. It was a beautiful and soft autumnal afternoon, and the way was through a pleasant landscape. I never saw a man who had so much the look of the poet. He was then about seventy, but save for the white locks that fell around his handsome face the years had touched him gently. He had entered the Colonial Office in 1824, and told me he had served under twenty-two Foreign Secretaries, — the one he liked best being Lord Aberdeen. The first thing he remembered to have done in office was to prepare the materials for a speech by Canning. He had never gained money by his literary work, and never thought of receiving any : his six volumes were labours of love.

Among the many typographical errors in the first edition of Carlyle's autobiographical essays, one amazed the old friends of Sir Henry Taylor, who was described as a man of "masked vivacity." No phrase could be more ludicrously inappropriate, and none more appropriate than what Carlyle really wrote, — "marked veracity." His grave and noble face, snowy beard, and fine figure had attracted the artists, and I once saw a beautiful painting representing him as King Lear beside Cordelia.

Sir Henry had a warm friendship for Carlyle and said he was the only living man of his acquaintance whose conversation equalled that of Coleridge, whom he had also known well. Sir Henry's own conversation was, I am sure, quite equal to that of Coleridge. He spoke in a gentle tone, and had no views to urge with reference to the agitations of the time. Occasionally he spoke as if all these contemporary affairs impressed him as distant dissolving views. "How few of those who at one time seemed to spread themselves over the country have now any sway at all over it! I remember when the one power seemed to be Scott; no two met but to speak of the 'Wizard of the North.' I knew several people who thought him greater than Shakespeare — seriously. But now the young people read Thackeray and Dickens, and think Scott dull. Even Byron has become tedious to the people, with their Tennyson and Browning; and Coleridge, Lamb, Southey — well, they last better, but their day of doom is coming. Wordsworth is one of the few who has gained with posterity. His 'Ode on Immortality,' however, is not so great as Coleridge's on 'Dejection.' But I am not a good reader. I find my office occupation keeps off ill health better than anything else."

F. W. Newman, the guardian of John Sterling's children, informed me in 1863 that he had been told on good authority

that the influence which carried Sterling into the clerical
order was Love. The kinsfolk of his bride elect demanded
that he should be in some profession; he hated all professions and was not in health for any. Newman was convinced
that Archdeacon Hare reconciled Sterling temporarily to the
idea of a Liberal Christianity, but when he (Sterling) first
came to Clifton, " he was secretly already gone far beyond."
These were Newman's words.

A good many young sceptics have been led into "holy
orders" by filial affection, and among these was a poet who
seemed almost a reappearance of Sterling, namely, Wathen
Mark Wilks Call. With him I enjoyed a certain intimacy,
and he told me that, although he was a devotee of Shelley at
the time of his graduation at Cambridge University, Coleridge opened for him a mystical vestibule into the Church
(1843), by which the hopes of his parents were fulfilled.

Call's particular difficulty had been the dogma of eternal
punishment. But once inside, he found that he had been
misled by Mr. Smooth-it-away Coleridge in supposing that
the odious doctrine was no longer insisted upon in the
Church. The story of Aquinas wrestling all night in prayer
for the salvation of Satan gave birth to Call's " Aquinas," —
one of the miraculous poems. The picture of the monk sitting all day as if stone till the sun went out, then flinging
himself on the bare floor, is all touched with pigments of his
own heart's,blood.

The grapple with that one dogma was followed by a revision
of all, with the result that Call quietly retired from the English Church. But he was to learn that the church of that
period, though unable to make a man believe in a future hell,
could do something towards inflicting anguish upon him in
this life. He had a sister with whom he had enjoyed perfect
intimacy, and who was sympathetic with his thoughts. She
bequeathed to him guardianship of her two children who
loved and were beloved by him. When the testamentary
nomination was made in the court of chancery, there was
introduced a postscript from a private letter he had written

indicating his dissent from the creeds of the churches. The children of his sister, herself unorthodox, were thus given over to strange hands. This incident, profoundly mortifying in itself, was the means of spreading abroad his heresies, alienating friends and relatives, and causing sorrow to many. The retreat which he had hoped might be quiet was turned into a violent rupture with a past sweet in associations.

But there followed the compensation. His spiritual and intellectual kindred sought him out; he enjoyed the friendship of the finest spirits of his time. Above all, he made the acquaintance of the one lady perhaps then living whom a very heretical providence might have trained to be his wife.

It was indeed an ideal marriage. Mrs. Call was the daughter of the eminent Dr. Brabant of Bath, financial founder of the "Westminster Review." That admirable and learned gentleman, whom I had the happiness of knowing, had taken the utmost care for the education of this beautiful daughter, — beautiful she was even in advanced age. She was learned in Hebrew, Greek, German, and French. She and her father — as she told me — read together Strauss's "Leben Jesu" when it appeared, and Dr. Brabant resolved that it should be translated into English. She had made the acquaintance of Marian Evans (afterwards "George Eliot"). Miss Evans did not know ancient languages, but had studied German, and Miss Brabant invited her to work with her on the "Life of Jesus." While these two were thus in collaboration, Miss Brabant became the wife of C. C. Hennell, author of the "Inquiry into the Origin of Christianity" which so influenced Theodore Parker. The translation of the "Leben Jesu" was then more than half finished, and the remainder was given over to Miss Evans, except that Mrs. Hennell continued to assist in notes requiring knowledge of Greek and Hebrew. Mrs. Hennell was happy and well-to-do, and by her private direction the "Life of Jesus" appeared with the name of Marian Evans alone, — to the surprise of the latter.

Mrs. Call thus had the intellectual training of being the

wife of the two most scholarly freethinkers of England of that time, and while her opinion or criticism on grave themes carried weight with serious thinkers, her womanly sentiment and delicate humour charmed them.

Mrs. Call's first husband had two sisters; one was Sarah Hennell, who wrote many mystical religious works, the other married Charles Bray of Coventry. They resided at Rose Hill, Coventry. Mr. Bray was the author of a work on the "Philosophy of Necessity," which had much interested Emerson. Mrs. Bray wrote a little book for children on conduct, manners, and duties, — a book that ought to be in every home and school. I know of no other book of the kind.

I remember well the happiness of my first visit to Rose Hill. I went up on Saturday morning and stayed over Sunday. On Sunday after breakfast I was present at the usual religious service of the family, whose members were Mr. and Mrs. Bray and Sarah Hennell. This service consisted of the rendering on the piano of Handel's "Messiah" (the whole) without words or singing. It was a beautiful day, the low windows opened on the flower garden and the landscape dressed in living green and blossoming trees. There we sat, souls who had passed through an era of storm and stress and left all prophetic and Messianic beliefs, but found in the oratorio hymns of an earth in travail.

After the triumphal close of Handel's music had died away, we all walked out, and, passing through the streets of old Coventry, visited the house where Marian Evans lived in loneliness till she was discovered by the Brays. The house was still named Birdgrove, and the sweetest songster in that little grove had been Emerson. The Brays told me much about her early life, whose pathos and sorrow make the melancholy undertone of George Eliot's works. When we returned, Mrs. Bray showed me a sentence written by Emerson in her notebook: "If the law of love and justice have once entered our heart, why need we seek any other?" To this she had added: "*Emerson* (as he sat in the drawing-room window, July 12, 1848)."

Sarah Hennell brought out for me to copy a letter written
to her by her sister immediately after Emerson's visit: —

Yes, we have had the great spirit amongst us, and I feel
as you do how much greater his thoughts, which we had before, have become from the corroboration they have received
from his presence. I have quite a grateful feeling that he
has been under this roof, though only for a few hours; but
alas! we shall see his face no more! He is rolling on the
waves now towards home. He said his wife insisted on being
on the shore to meet him, though they live twenty miles inland. He was taking a rocking-horse for his two little girls,
and a cross-bow for his son; and his eyes quite sparkled
when he spoke of how much they would be grown in nine
months. My head was full of the preparations for our great
juvenile fête on Thursday, when Emerson's letter came to
say he should be here at midnight, to stay only till Wednesday afternoon. So I ran upstairs to put the best room in
order, and directly after in came Mr. and Mrs. Flower and
Kate Martineau. Of course they wanted to see Emerson
above all things, and had invited him to Stratford. Charles
went to meet him at the station. He looked around the drawing-room and said, " Coventry is a very nice place; " and the
next morning was so very easy and pleasant that I wondered
where all my awe had gone to. He talked about Indian mythology and Stonehenge. After breakfast in walked the
Flowers again. They had set off at five, and came to propose
taking him back with them to Stratford, as they had found a
note from him, on reaching home, expressing a wish to " see
Shakespeare." We were rather disconcerted, as Mary Ann
(Miss Evans) had just come, and we meant to have a nice
quiet day all to ourselves. But it was plain Emerson wished
to see Stratford, and we thought it right he should; so we
all set off by train to Leamington, then in cars to Stratford;
and had a most delightful ride, we four in an open carriage
from Stratford again. This was the pleasantest part of the
day to us, and he talked as if we had been old friends. He
was much struck with Mary Ann (Miss Evans); expressed
his admiration many times to Charles, — " That young lady
has a calm, serious soul." He regretted very much he had no
more time to stay among us. He came home to tea with us.
And so he departed, with much warmth pressing Charles to
go and see him in America. It is well for us a great benign

soul does not often come to disgust us with common life. No, that's a very false sentiment: common life would not be common then. It was a comfort the next day to find that Hannah had been providing the needful for common life while we had been soaring aloft, and that the cakes were made ready for the children at night. The fête was most successful. We had a fiddle and flute to make music, and they danced on the grass.

I found that both Emerson and George Eliot cherished the remembrance of that bright day. When Emerson had talked a few moments with her while they were driving, he suddenly said, "What one book do you value most?" She instantly answered, "Rousseau's Confessions." He started, then said, "So do I. There is a point of sympathy between us."

At Rose Hill our even-song was that of the nightingale. Once more I wondered how any of the poets came to report its strain as melancholy. Shakespeare of course saw into this: Juliet finds the song of the lark melancholy, for with the dawn Romeo must leave: glad is the note of the nightingale, for it holds him by her side. Happy and merry were the larks when we walked to Birdgrove Sunday, but sad were they on Monday when I parted from those friends.

If ever there was a cockcrow over yesterday's sunrise, it was Mrs. Humphry Ward's "Robert Elsmere." The plot is interesting enough, but even that sadly provincial: and as for the religious statements, with their air of paradox, they are the commonplaces of two generations before her romance was born. I was glad to see on the New York stage a play made of the story better than the book: the preaching was omitted; Mrs. Robert Elsmere turns her back on her ritualistic adviser, as any sensible English lady who loved her husband would do; Robert Elsmere is seen out on the lawn recovering health from the sunshine, especially that of his wife's affection and sympathy; and everybody was happy except the author, indignant that her gospel should be made a play.

In "Robert Elsmere" there is one piece of originality, — the country squire. Until Mrs. Ward's time, eye had not seen nor had it entered into the heart of man to conceive of an infidel spending many years writing a treatise on St. John's Gospel, persuading a sceptical clergyman to continue preaching the dogmas they both hate, and also treating his tenants with brutality! What is a double-headed girl in a side-show to that?

It is evident that Mrs. Humphry Ward had never really known a freethinker, and it is marvellous that she could have evolved such a chimera from her inner consciousness, when around her were refined and scholarly freethinkers like Call, Mill, Frederic Harrison, Leslie Stephen, John Morley.

The sensation produced by the book was largely caused by the fact that the writer was a granddaughter of the great Dr. Arnold; that she was the daughter of the Rev. Thomas Arnold, who had journeyed to Romanism; and that she was the niece of Matthew Arnold. She was, therefore, the completion of a picturesque family career, and we could all read between the lines revelations in accordance with our Arnold theories.

Mrs. Humphry Ward's other novels I valued highly, but on listening to her lecture to the Unitarians some years ago I concluded that in religious matters she had become the victim, first of her heredity, and secondly of her " Robert Elsmere."

Among the Americans whom I used to meet occasionally was William James Stillman. As consul at Rome and at Crete, and as the hero of the romantic expedition to Hungary to secure for Kossuth the crown-jewels hid by the king, Stillman had a peculiar reputation in London, especially in the circle of the Rossettis, who combined radical ideas about European affairs with artistic ideas of which this American was a cultured and critical interpreter. When in London he attended the weekly receptions of Madox Brown. I used to feel proud that Harvard literary men should be represented in the capitals of Europe by a high-minded gentleman who at the same time was an enthusiast in art studies and a master of English. Stillman was a thorough American. His tall, slender form, his pale and delicate face, his eager movement, were those of the well-bred American ; and though he was intellectually a unique product of our country, he was one of our few foreign agents who had carried republican ideas into his official relations.

I had a little controvery with Stillman in the "Pall Mall Gazette," in which appeared a serious editorial article appreciating highly my little book entitled "Republican Superstitions." I had opposed the bicameral legislative system, and maintained that it had not worked well in the United States. Stillman vindicated the Senate, and for once in his life took the conventional view. It was, however, all amicable. Although we were always friendly, I did not find him much given to conversation; he had many interesting incidents and adventures to tell, drawn from his own experience, — rarely from books, — and was not so entertaining when drawn into argument.

My wife and I knew the beautiful Greek lady who became the second Mrs. Stillman. All that survived of artistic and classic Greece had found its way to London, and there was something picturesque in the fact that the flower of that fine circle should become the prize of the scholar who so thoroughly appreciated the art and literature of that race.

Among my pleasant recollections were entertainments at the house of Dr. Harley, in Harley Street. My friend Mrs. Alec Tweedie, well known by her brilliant writings, has written a sketch of her father's life: "George Harley, F. R. S., or the Life of a London Physician." Mrs. Tweedie developed her wit when she was hardly out of girlhood. When we were invited to the Harleys we felt sure of witnessing some pretty play got up by this youthful dame who possessed varieties of talent, assisted by the large ideas of her father. The admirable physician understood human nature, spiritual and physical, in a way that amounted to genius. At the Harley entertainments the guests passed from the play and mirth of the drawing-rooms to gather at the top of the house where the doctor and his microscopes were revealing wonders.

Dr. Harley's information about the scientific men, and his appreciation of precisely what each had contributed to knowledge, was marvellous. He smiled at the way in which my friend Alexander Ireland had accepted the rumour that Robert Chambers wrote "The Vestiges of Creation." "Let him go to the Chambers publishing house in Edinburgh and ask to see the manuscripts of that book; he will find it all there, and in the handwriting of Mr. Page."

W. S. Gilbert seemed to me the only English writer who could surprise and delight both cultured and uncultured people with absurdities full of sense, and coquetries without vulgarity. I remember William Froude saying, after witnessing "The Pirates of Penzance," that the charm was the way in which our moral notions were mixed up.

Gilbert's fresh blond face and frank expression were pleasant to meet. I first met him at West House, the residence of our American-born Academician George Boughton, where he was lionized more than he liked. He was quick in his movements and talk, and I remember hearing from him a double d—d when some friend told him that "Pinafore" was running at a half dozen theatres in New York. From that Pactolus streaming to the managerial pirates in America not even a silver sand-grain had reached Gilbert.

We used to have a good deal of talk about Gilbert at the Savage Club. The real founder of the club, our beloved Tom Robertson, had also founded the dramatic career of Gilbert. He had recognized Gilbert's genius before the briefless barrister had any ambition beyond writing for magazines, and persuaded him to undertake a Christmas piece for St. James's Theatre, wanted in two weeks.

A privately circulated pamphlet concerning Gilbert, written by Henrietta Hodson, excited much amusement in theatrical circles. The witty and pretty actress was a universal favourite. She had shown herself a real artist in various characters, among others as Ariel, when, along with her brilliant interpretation, she invented the scene of swimming through artistically contrived blue waves. That was at the New Royalty Theatre. I think that after her marriage with Henry Labouchere she became lessee of that theatre, and her quarrel with

Gilbert led to the pamphlet. The wit and humour of it were so exquisite, the delicate caricature of Gilbert so amusing, without bitterness, that her husband was credited with it by a good many. But those best acquainted with her did not believe Labouchere equal to the charming exaggeration. She had learned, she said, that Gilbert had quarrelled with every actor and actress he had anything to do with, and when she was about to work with him, resolved to be the exception to that rule. When he complained that a statue had just been set up for Shakespeare while none yet existed for himself, she had declared that the stupid world would presently awaken to his merits; when he told her that he had recently sent Madge Robertson weeping to her room, she said that it was a proof of the weakness of the human mind that anybody should oppose him in anything. I have not the pamphlet, and but vaguely remember its artistic raillery. Nobody took it *au pied de la lettre*, and Gilbert was not harmed by it.

I had the great delight of being present at the first night of "The Sorcerer," at the Opera Comique. The main importance of that event in the anticipations of the Savage Club was that our youthful George Grossmith was to make his professional début in the title rôle. Nothing ever produced even by that combination — Gilbert, Sullivan, George Grossmith Jr. — surpassed the effect of that evening. I have found good critics who think with me that "The Sorcerer" is the best of the Gilbert-Sullivan operettas, and yet it had not the long runs of "Pinafore" and "Patience." Perhaps it was because Grossmith acquired such fame that D'Oyly Carte could not keep him, and no other sorcerer was possible.

Ah, what exquisite theatrical evenings we had in those days, — with Buckstone, Toole, Lionel Brough, the Mellons, Vezins, Bancrofts, Kendals, Terrys, the Misses Hodson, Oliver, Everard, Farren, to name only a few! The number of brilliant actresses in those days, not only on the stage but performing in private, convinced me that there is a potential actress in nearly every well-bred English woman.

I was among the early members of the Urban Club, which

used to meet in St. John's Gate ; also of the Savage, Savile,
Century (London), Pen and Pencil, New Vagabonds, Bedford Park, and Browning clubs; and my wife and I were
among the founders of the club for ladies and gentlemen
which developed into the Albemarle Club. But the club that
most interested me was the Omar Khayyám, to which I still
belong. It would require many pages to tell my delightful
memories of my brother Omarites, to whom is dedicated my
book on "Solomon and Solomonic Literature." Edward
Clodd, the admirable banker, who began his literary career
with a book on "The Childhood of the World," grew rapidly
into the leadership in such studies, which he now occupies.
Although I must omit much, a pilgrimage we made to the
grave of Edward Fitzgerald cannot be forgotten. Our beloved
artist, Simpson, being in Persia, travelled a long journey to
visit the tomb of Omar Khayyám at Naishapúr. The poet's
hope was that he might be buried where the north wind might
scatter rose-leaves on his grave ; and there Simpson found the
rose-tree, often replanted in the centuries, and brought slips
of it to London. Thistleton Dyer grafted them on an English
stock in Kew Gardens, and we planted two little shoots on
the grave of Fitzgerald at Boulge, Suffolk. Clodd, Simpson,
Clement Shorter, and Edmund Gosse were of the party. The
rector of Debach and of Boulge, Rev. Charles Hume, wrote
to Clodd: " I should *much prefer* the proposed plate of inscription having no reference to a heathen philosopher which
I cannot but think *out of place* in a *Christian churchyard.*"
Despite these italics the plate was carried, and the Rev. Mr.
Doughty, a neighbouring rector, — executor of Fitzgerald, —
met us and made an excellent speech. He spoke for Miss
Holme White of Boulge Hall, who was present with several
other lovely young ladies, who undertook to take care of
our rose-trees. Standing out there near the old church
(October 7, 1893), beside the grave of the poet on whose
mind was grafted the quatrains of Omar, we planted the
grafts. Simpson told us the story of his pilgrimage to Naishapúr, Gosse read a poem, and all of us made speeches.

Then we went over to Clodd's country homestead at Alde-
burgh, "Strafford House," and remained from that Saturday
till Monday. Fill in from your imagination, O my reader, the
charm and beauty of this function, and of our symposia at
Strafford, and yet something will remain for any laureate who
can see the mystical beauty of the Persian *Rosa centifolia*
now annually flowering in Boulge churchyard.

Few dissenting ministers in England avowed unorthodox
beliefs, and in 1876 the ablest of them, J. Allanson Picton,
even suffered persecution. He was of gentle birth, — in the
English sense, — possessed some means, and being more interested in national than in theological questions, left the pulpit
for Parliament. Picton's particular friend, Edward Clodd,
began about that time inviting some of us to Sunday evening
symposia at his house in London, "Rosemont." We usually
had Estlin Carpenter, now professor in Oxford (Manchester
College), Rev. Mark Wilks, and always Picton. I remember
those evenings at Rosemont as a time when we grew. In after
years Picton gave us some admirable discourses at South
Place chapel, which indeed became for several able men the
only place in London in which they could find perfect freedom and an intelligent audience. In 1893, when we opened
the Thomas Paine Exhibition in our chapel, Picton made a
striking address. He told us that his attention was first called
to Paine by Disraeli. He (Picton) had made a speech in the
House of Commons, and Disraeli arose and said the speech
was all taken from "Tom Paine's Rights of Man." Whereupon he concluded that Paine must have been a man of sense,
and began reading him, and with satisfaction. He alluded to
a bit of Paine's brain exhibited (now in my possession), and
spoke of the thought that once flashed through that substance
darkened by time, and influenced the political history and
conditions of Europe and America. Picton is a writer of
power, but singularly unambitious, and has published little.

Sunday evening was also the time when George Eliot and
G. H. Lewes received their friends. Their residence, "The

Priory," was a quaint old house inside a pleasant little garden, through which one passed to the door. The library of Mr. Lewes, on the ground floor, was suggestive of work. The sitting-room, where their friends were received, though elegant, was not richly furnished. I was not intimate in the house, and went but rarely. I had told Robert Browning that I would like to see George Eliot, and a general invitation for Sunday evening came. She received me pleasantly, and we had some conversation about Emerson, whom she held in warm remembrance, but I think it was the man rather than the author she esteemed.

Although George Henry Lewes did much to further my literary aims, printing my articles in his " Fortnightly Review," and engaging me on the " Pall Mall Gazette," with which he was at first connected, I did not find him personally attractive. I can never consider a countenance homely if there is in it both " sweetness and light," but with all his talent Lewes did not have a pleasing voice, nor any look of sensibility. There was, however, always a quick attention on his part and deference whenever George Eliot said anything.

On my first evening at the Priory those present were all leading Positivists, with the exception of John Morley, who was a cautious sympathizer with them. Once or twice Herbert Spencer was present, but I was disappointed in not finding there Robert Browning. Probably they arranged for private talks with Browning. The only woman I ever met at the Priory was Madame Bodichon, whose acquaintance I had made in Cincinnati. She was English (though her deceased husband was a foreigner), a friend of Mrs. Browning, and very attractive. I was told that after the social disfavour with which George Eliot's irregular marriage was received was put to confusion by her literary renown, a number of ladies of high position had sought her acquaintance without success. She maintained her old friendship with Mrs. Bray of Coventry and Mrs. Call. Whether George Eliot suffered much by separation from general society I do not know, but I always feel that her writings suffered by it. Strong and interesting as her female characters are, few seem drawn from living models.

Although much was said after Charles Reade's death of his unqualified faith in conventional dogmas, I can hardly suppress a suspicion that it was a sort of hoax. I met him occasionally at the Sunday evening companies of actors and actresses, where he was a lion, and seemingly a thorough man of the world. He was ruddy, but had the look of a preoccupied man, and rarely smiled. I called on him once at his house, "Naboth's Vineyard," at the desire of my friend Mrs. Lander (née Davenport) in connection with a theatrical project of hers. He sat at a table in the corner of a large dingy room, before him the big brown sheets of a play he was writing. Our matter was discussed in a businesslike way, but I could not harmonize the man with his novels, which indicate so much humour and delicate sentiment. Several times he was with us at our special Savage Club dinners. When we entertained Mark Twain, I sat near Reade, and when Mark began his speech in his humorous drawling way the novelist said to those around him, "Oh, that accent! that accent!" He presently listened with interest, but did not laugh with the rest. I never met him in the house of any literary men, and have an impression that the enthusiasm with which Americans read "Christie Johnston," "Peg Woffington," and some of Reade's larger novels, was unknown in London.

Winwood Reade, cousin of Charles, was much more talked of among men of letters. The little I saw of him enabled me to understand why he was so greatly beloved by all who enjoyed his friendship. His last work, "The Outcast," was felt by those who saw the admirable man wasting away with rapid consumption to be a fearful tragedy depicted by a fine genius from his own agonies.

Winwood Reade was only thirty-seven when he died (1875), but few at twice that age have known so much of life and of the world. His wide travels were an accompaniment of his pilgrimage through the creeds to his religion of theologic Nihilism. All efforts of friends, relatives, publishers, to induce him not to publish his religious views were in vain, because the views were religious. He believed that the real civilization and the development of man were impossible until the beliefs in Christianity, in a personal God, and in personal immortality, had ceased. Such beliefs, he declared, bound the human mind and energies to a system that consecrated the evils of nature (which could not possibly be the work of a benevolent deity); and mankind could not put forth their genius in perfect freedom while the present life was regarded as subordinate to another.

In all this I am impressed by two things. First, the closeness with which Winwood follows the Greek myth, that when Prometheus brought heavenly fire to man, that he might be a god and creator of his own world, he first of all took away man's belief in immortality : it is said Prometheus left man the *hope*, but perhaps that was a later addition. The second thing I find striking is that the whole enthusiasm of Winwood's siege against the fundamental beliefs is based on his perfect faith in Progress.

But faith in Progress is fundamentally belief in God.

Winwood Reade's two books impressed me with the belief that but for the ghoul Consumption he might have proved heir to the sceptre of Carlyle, and humanized it with more art. His fine personality was revealed to me by my dear friends Dr. and Mrs. Humphrey Sandwith, members of my congregation, in whose house Winwood died. Dr. Sandwith (who had known him at college) and his wife persuaded him, when his illness began, to reside in their villa at Wimbledon. There he had all the alleviations that medical science could bring ; there, embowered with trees, the invalid, seated on the veranda, looked forth on the golden gorse of the common, listened to the merry laughter of children, and was soothed by songs of the nightingale and the skylark.

But one unpleasant incident marred the " passing " of Winwood Reade. His two loving friends could not leave him when he got very low, but nursed him themselves. The pain had ceased, his mind was serene and clear. One afternoon

when he was sweetly sleeping they strolled into the garden
for a few moments, and what was their horror on their return
to find a fanatical woman at Winwood's bedside exhorting the
helpless man to flee from the wrath to come! Dr. Sandwith
and his wife told me that they managed to eject the ' wretched
creature' without trouble, but the incident gave them their
first glimpse into the Salvationist insanity. Probably the experience did not harm Winwood, who had especially studied
the varieties of pious fanaticism in Africa and the East.

I do not blame those poor creatures who disregard all decency in trying to save souls from hell. These doctrinal night-
mares are to them frightful realities. Sir James Stephen told
me that the last time he visited Carlyle, not long before his
death, the aged man looked into the large coal fire and said,
" How would it feel for a man to be put into a vast fire like
that for all eternity? My father, who had as strong a brain
as any man I ever knew, believed with absolute certitude that
the greater number of human beings will suffer in literal fire
without any end at all!" Sir James said that he wondered
whether at last the old man's intellect was giving way, and
merely said that he regarded such notions of the future as
having sprung up in ages of frightful tortures and punish-
ments by savage governments. My own belief was that the
remark was but a continuation by Carlyle of the general revision of his past that went on in his last years. When he had
ceased to write, he used to read over the German and other
works which had influenced his mind; and when he could no
longer read, and was not being read to, his tenacious memory
travelled over his early days.

When "Peter Ibbetson" and "Trilby" appeared, the
world was astonished by the appearance of a new genius, but
those who knew Du Maurier personally were not surprised.
He was a beautiful kind of man, dainty in even common talk;
so evidently a poetic being that his sketches in " Punch "
always appeared to me to suggest further resources. Everybody loved him; he passed years in those delineations of
English society whose satire was so sweet that it never made

an enemy. While the French blood was sufficiently evident in his personal appearance and in the extraordinary quickness of his perceptions, one could not converse with him without being struck by the purity of his English. His complexion was fresh and fair, but without the English ruddiness; with his frankness there was a charming *finesse*, and one felt in him a refinement rare even in the great English writers. It may be doubted whether any of Du Maurier's English or American contemporaries could have written a defence of nudity in art so plain spoken as that in "Trilby" without calling Mrs. Grundy to her guns. As this exquisite artist put it, the statement hardly appeared paradoxical.

Du Maurier was fortunate in his marriage, but his income was not large. They had a pretty home at Hampstead, the interior being harmoniously beautiful. There was nothing that I can recall in the decorations indicating that he or his wife had caught the fancy of his friends for Queen Anne furniture and Morris wall-papers.

My personal knowledge of Du Maurier was really derived from occasional entertainments of small companies in his house; and especially from a memorable one in which he spontaneously gave us an artistic diversion. He brought out a large easel covered with layers of paper and, with a stick of charcoal in his hand, began in his humorously grave way to tell us some incident. Now and then he made a mark on the paper as if by unconscious gesture, hardly looking at it; but, little by little, we saw coming out of these accumulated strokes a face that evoked a burst of laughter. I regret my inability to remember Du Maurier's delicious little fable, of which I find no written note. My impression is that we first saw a despairing and dishevelled artist without work, an untouched canvas before him; next, a matron, with flourishing gown and bonnet, attended by a young edition of herself, whose portrait she desired; presently, unless I am mistaken, the shrinking maiden and the artist making eyes at each other while the work is going on, — I rather think to the distress of the wealthy matron, who means her daughter to marry a lord.

Though my impressions are vague about the tale, I remember
well the delight and laughter of all present, and the charm of
the man as well as the fascination of the story-teller with the
subtle surprises touched in here and there as if unintention-
ally. The only wonder is that from such an imagination the
incomparable novels did not flower long before.

CHAPTER XXXVI

Paris — Exposition, 1867 — Mi-Carême — Emperor and Empress — Maximilian — July 4 — Tallandier — Ledru Rollin — Louis Blanc — Anti-Russian feeling — Stockholm — St. Petersburg — Moscow — Professor Busleaf — Eugene Schuyler — Baronial hospitality — Among the peasants — Travelling with the Czar — Nijni-Novgorod Fair.

THE chief delight in Paris is to be there. With what gentle ecstasy did I wander through the fascinating streets and boulevards, the parks, where there were singing fountains, where earth, sky, and human life were a romance into which I felt myself easily woven!

In 1867 it was announced that the Exposition would be opened by the Emperor on April 1, and it was my pleasant journalistic duty to be present. During the preceding week Paris swarmed with foreigners, and the theatres entertained them with spectacles requiring no knowledge of French. Neilson and Carvalho were singing in the "Magic Flute" at the Lyrique, Patti at the Grand Opéra; Adah Isaacs Menken was dashing up the rocks at the Gaiété as Mazeppa, lashed to a real horse; and there were splendid ballets of the Deluge and of Paradise, — in which last Abingdon was drawing crowds by her interpretation of Eve. The wise serpent turned into a handsome youth and tempted Eve by holding before her a hand-mirror.

The Mid-Lent fête preceded by a few days the opening of the Exposition. Along the boulevards ballet-dancers, female pages, Apollos, Venuses, crowded by day; and in the evening there were, it was said, a hundred bals masqués. I visited those at the Châtelet Theatre and the Grand Opéra. Gay were the revels and startling the costumes; but in none any drunkenness or rudeness. At the Opéra Ball a small troop of soldiers entered at half-past five, took their place in front of the band on the stage, and thence, with slow tread, inevitable but without severity, moved across the room. It was strange to see the contrast of the absolute vacancy behind these soldiers with the leaping and laughing crowd retreating before them: a few more wild arms flung about, nymphs and goddesses borne aloft on young men's shoulders, and the scene dissolved into a multitude of fantastic dances under the bright moon, until the imperial sun sent its troop of beams to clear the outside theatre also.

It was understood that there would be no ceremony at the inauguration, but that the Emperor and his suite would visit the Exposition on April 1, after which it would be open to the public. He arrived as the clock struck two, attended by his ministers and the Corps Législatif. The most prominent figure near the Emperor was Drouyn de l'Huys, a handsome, broad-faced man of fifty years, who wore his insignia proudly. Thiers, with the historic halo about him, was in countenance the most intellectual man present.

Many who then first saw the Empress must have been disenchanted. Instead of the refined and stately lady of the portraits, here was a small woman with heavy underface and unhealthy complexion. The Emperor's face was a study. A few feet behind him, as he stood receiving the guests, I remarked the sculptured figure of a young woman with a laughing face, the chin resting on her hand; at the next step one discovered that this happy face was a mask which the hand had just removed, disclosing behind it a care-worn countenance, in pathetic contrast with the mask. It may have been this sculpture that suggested to me the mask of the crowned man who smiled so blandly on those about him. For I wrote this note on the evening of the day on which, as my invitation required, I had been presented to the Emperor and Empress in the Exposition (Art Gallery), and when I did not know the humiliation he had suffered that very morning. The Dutch forehead, the hooked nose propping it, the feeble under lip and retreating chin, might all have been carved wood for any indication of feeling on them. But at that moment Napoleon III knew that Maximilian was on his way to execution in Mexico, and that he was the executioner. The Emperor and his wife departed, I rushed to the American section. I found there a good large room with just two objects visible — Church's great painting of Niagara and Lawrence's portrait of Emerson. Other Americans who had also come with enthusiastic expectations recalled that it was All Fool's day; but somehow this exhibition made on me a mystical impression. America's greatest physical wonder and the man to match it were sufficiently representative of the real and unimported America. There were a number of unopened boxes strewn about, from which our clever imitations of what was better done elsewhere would emerge.

At the close of June I revisited the Exposition. Paris was all efflorescent for the newly arrived Sultan. I had a good place, as the representative of " Harper's Magazine," to witness the reception of the Orientals by the Emperor in the Palais d'Industrie. There was no Père Pudeur in those days, and Baron Haussmann, Prefect of the Seine, had filled the room with beautiful women, whose charms were liberally displayed in both Eastern and European costumes. Beside the Emperor stood Princes Jerome and Murat. The approach of the Sultan was reported by the blare of trumpets, which, from being faint, gradually became louder, until his Majesty entered. Next Abdul Aziz walked his three sons, and behind them the Viceroy of Egypt and eight Turkish ministers. Of all these the one most plainly arrayed was the Sultan, who was also simple in his manners.

This reception was on Sunday. Next day, July 1, was the g..nd fête of the Exposition. Of the 16,000 persons in the Palais d'Industrie, and the many high personages, just two really interested me, — Rossini and Félicien David. The two composers sat together, — handsome and portly Rossini, David dreamy as his " Desert," — while a thousand instruments and voices rendered the hymn composed by Rossini for the occasion. It consisted of a grand overture, followed by vocal parts. When the voices ceased, the instruments entered upon a grand march. Among the orchestral instruments were enormous bells and cannon, outside the building, the performers upon which sat with telegraph batteries for keys. When the bells rang outside and the cannon thundered their notes, the audience was lifted as by a whirlwind of enthusiasm.

M. Rouher read the report of the Commission of Prizes, and the Emperor gave a well-delivered address. The artist Cabanel was the first to receive a prize ; he was a short, thickset man with a young face but grey hair, his face pale and thin as if from overwork. Next, Meissonier, small, active, precise in movement, Italian in complexion. I was much impressed by the lowly manner and intellectual look of the Roman friar, Father Secchi, — whose meteorological and astronomical clock was the wonder of the scientific world, — when he advanced to receive a gold medal, and was decorated with the Cross of the Legion of Honor. The chief sensation was when the young Prince Imperial, with considerable grace, started forward and took his father's place in order to present the Emperor with the gold medal awarded for the best model of a labourer's cottage.

Next day the execution of Maximilian in Mexico was announced. A telegram had been handed to the Emperor during the prize-giving, and if it contained the gruesome tidings he certainly commanded his face well. All noticed that " Yankee Doodle " and the " Star-spangled Banner " were not included among the national airs. I was at the house of Frolich, the artist, whose albums of " Mademoiselle Lili " were delighting Americans, on the afternoon of July 2. Madame and her little Lili were merry and entertaining in the beautiful interior, when Frolich entered and announced with agitation that Maximilian had been shot.

The tragedy in Mexico, pronounced by Rouher " the one blot on a beautiful tableau," proved a blot so vast that little else could be seen. Every one saw at the door of the Tuileries the mangled corpse of a prince, and beside it a deranged princess. The grand military review prepared for the Sultan was postponed. We Americans found ourselves under the Mexican shadow. Two Fourth of July celebrations had been arranged, one at the Pré-Catalan (Bois de Boulogne), the other, a dinner at the Grand Hôtel. A request came that both should be cancelled. The Committee of the Open Air Fête consented, but the Committee of the Dinner insisted, alleging that it was a private one for Americans. After a warm discussion and a promise by the committee that there should be little speaking and that cautious, the officials retired. General Dix opposed the banquet, from which he was conspicuously absent, as also was George Bancroft, then in Paris, who sent no letter in response to his invitation.

About three hundred ladies and gentlemen were present at the Grand Hôtel. James Milliken of Philadelphia presided. Only a third of the company raised their glasses to the health of President Johnson, and the refusal of many to rise to a toast to the Emperor threatened trouble. Governor Curtin, J. W. Forney, Judge Allison, and others were called for but kept silent. The only extended speech was by Elliot Cowdin, who spoke of the services of France to America.

Most of us were feeling the dinner dull, when suddenly Dr. Mary Walker extemporized a sensation. Over her famous "American dress" (masculine) she wore a large sash of stars and stripes; in this costume she walked up to the head of the table before the company, and before the amazed Milliken could interfere uttered a tribute to "Our soldiers and sailors," dramatically kissed the flag she wore, and glided to her seat. Dr. Mary Walker did not wait for the dancing that followed, and when she left received an ovation from the French crowd in the courtyard on account of the glorious independence of her trousers, nowise concealed but decorated by her patriotic sash. The applause must have been for Dr. Mary Walker's independence; uglier dress was never worn.

The three later expositions in Paris, all of which I witnessed, were by no means so entertaining as that of 1867. They were larger and the edifices grander, but the democratic spirit of uniformity and of curbing eccentricity was apparent.

In 1867 there was no Tartufe to insist on dressing tribal visitors to suit English matrons, no restriction on the amusements. The entertaining barbarians brought with them their actual manners and costumes: the remotest provinces of Europe were represented by their genuine peasants. The ethnography of the Exposition was perfect. Artists who have since become rich and unambitious were then aspirants and did their very best for the Exposition. Every nation also aspired to make a fine show at Paris, and achievements in the means of mutual destruction invaded but slightly the beautiful cosmos which made the Champ de Mars the arena of peace. I occasionally entered the hall where the great chess-players competed: Steinitz, De Vere, Kalisch, De Rivière, Czarnowski, Golmayo, Rousseau, Lloyd, Dr. Richardson of Boston, and others waged their wars on chequered fields. Alexander the Great is said to have been ashamed of his interest in that game, but the world might be happier if Alexander had confined his struggles to the chess-board.

When the Exposition was first planned, the French government had sent out to all countries requests for seeds of their characteristic flowers: there was a universal compliance; the seeds were sown in carefully designed beds of the park around the Palais d'Industrie, and sprang up finely; every zone had set in Paris its floral autograph.

One soft morning it occurred to me to walk away from the building, and pause here and there to listen to the general sound. The sharpest noises were the first to lose distinctness: the loudest machine did not reach so far as the orchestral violin; the vast roar of the machinery was subdued to a solemn bass; the human tongues and the pianos became as the dreamy croon of summer bees; the Russian organ, like a great musical loom, overbore all sounds and wove them — and finally itself — into one grand, ineffable voice.

The Exposition set me dreaming of the Federation of the World.

If, as an Eastern proverb says, for one whose leg is broken the whole world limps, it is equally true that the world moves

gaily for one on whom Fortune smiles. Although my wife and
I were getting on comfortably in London in 1867, we had
to economize more than I liked; but during the early part of
the Exposition Mr. Fletcher Harper of New York, whom I
did not know, sent me an invitation to dine with him at the
Grand Hôtel, and there made with me a generous contract
to write for "Harper's Magazine," my engagement to begin
with an article on the Exposition. Next morning in my Hôtel
de Louvois, my window opening over the green square and
its fountain and children, I began the descriptive article, and
all the horizon of humanity was aglow as if with a dawn.

When I had returned to London, I was one day telling
Louis Blanc of the beautiful things I had seen and the brilliant fêtes and theatres. He said, " That is the way of the
Empire; it says to the people, 'amuse yourselves; so long as
you let politics alone you can enjoy yourselves just as you
please. Amuse yourselves; leave government to us!' But it
cannot last."

The French exiles in London were admirable men. There
was about them none of the melancholy of Mazzini, nor any
disposition to conspire against Napoleon III. They all knew
English, and utilized their exile to study English literature
and search the history of their own country recorded in English archives. One was scholarly Tallandier, who had become
professor of the French language and literature at Stonyhurst,
but sometimes came to London. From him I first gained a
knowledge of the importance of Rabelais, from whose works
he compiled a volume for French schools. Tallandier told me
that a great architect of his acquaintance in Paris had set
himself to make an exact design of the imaginary Abbey of
Theleme so minutely described by Rabelais, and told him that
if such an edifice were to be erected, it would be the most
perfect building ever known.[1]

[1] When a Rabelais Club was formed in London by Sir Walter Besant,
Mr. Knight, and the Pollocks, I attended some of their dinners, and was
much impressed by the enthusiasm of these English writers for the old
French author. Sir Walter Besant's romance, *The Abbey of Thelema*, is,

Ledru Rollin was a large and amiable man, with a strong, solid brow and head.

Victor Schoelcher I had rarely met in London, but had an interview with him after his return to Paris. He was just then in the struggle to exorcise religion from the new constitution, and told me that although the great majority of the legislators were as heretical as himself, he was the first who had ever from the tribune declared himself an atheist.

With Louis Blanc and his wife we formed a close friendship in London. Froude believed that Blanc had some Napoleon blood in him, on what grounds I know not. Small in form, he was great in intellect and heart, and a genuine orator even in English, despite the insuperable accent. His thought was quick as light; whatever point might be raised having any connection with political or social subjects, his brightening eyes would swiftly announce that he had explored it, and the result was stated with lucidity and with the logic that in him was organic as his eye. He was without any consciousness of his extraordinary powers of conversation. In his memory were stored by his experiences many quaint and pertinent incidents. He was once visited by a socialist pauper who urged him to demand equal distribution of property. Louis Blanc requested him to go at once to Rothschild, and ask for half his treasures; and if the baron objected, he must say, "You are welcome to come and take mine. Is n't that fair?" If Rothschild was convinced, the socialist might return to him (Blanc), and he would arrange the decree. He told me of two veteran radicals in Paris, who had worked together fraternally for many years: one of them remarked that Louis Napoleon was a fool; no, said the other, he is a knave. On that issue they quarrelled, and never spoke to each other again. Some fundamental problem in religion being raised, Louis Blanc, reserved on such things, said that he once heard two Frenchmen discussing immortality, one denying, the other affirming. Eugène Sue, who sat near, inter-

I think, one of his happiest works. This club always opened with a toast, not to the Queen, but to "The Master."

rupted their talk, and said, "I consider you both equally audacious men." Louis Blanc and his brother Charles (afterwards Minister of Fine Arts) were twins. When dining with them in Paris, I mentioned the rumour that they were the originals of the melodrama "The Corsican Brothers," and that the incident of one feeling at a great distance the danger menacing his brother, and hastening to him, was founded in fact. They both smiled and said that they were familiar with the legend, which was an extreme exaggeration. Madame Blanc was, I believe, an Alsacian, and a lady of much good sense; but she could hardly manage a conversation in English. They had no children.

Among the English and the German "radicals" the Napoleonic prophecy was proverbial, "all Europe must become either Cossack or Republican," and there grew in me enough of this superstition to make me feel that there must be something preternatural in Slavic Satan. Simply as a demonologist I must go to Russia. Thomas Paine, writing from England (1788) to Jefferson, said: "The enmity of this country against Russia is as bitter as it ever was against America, and is carried to every pitch of abuse and vulgarity." During my sojourn in England this hatred against Russia was as strong as in Paine's time. For every humane action by Russia, even for the emancipation of serfs, some diabolical motive was imagined. The friendship displayed by Russia for the United States did not conciliate even the radical sympathizers with the North. In 1865 I made the acquaintance of Prince Galitzin at Ostend, and my conversations with him — he spoke English — awakened me to the fact that the anti-Russian feeling in England was based on pure ignorance. In the year following I wrote for the "Fortnightly Review" an article entitled "Russia and America," which was not inspired by friendship for Russia, but by fear that the dispute between England and America might issue in war.

In 1867 I was invited by Messrs. Cassell to become editor of a daily paper they were about starting, "The Echo." It was in many ways tempting, but I declined, and it passed into the care of Miss Frances Power Cobbe, whose articles in it displayed varieties of ability that astonished even her admirers.

In 1869 I devoted my summer vacation to Russia. At Berlin I found my American friend, Rev. Joseph Jenckes (Episcopalian). We travelled to Copenhagen, where there was an admirable exposition, and thence to Stockholm. There I visited the old house of Swedenborg, and at the Thiergarten, which exhibited several Swedenborgian relics, discovered on the top of his little organ pieces of music black with dust, which had belonged to Swedenborg, but had escaped notice.

From the day of reaching St. Petersburg I felt that I was in a country concerning which all my prejudices had been misleading. We could not speak Russian, but we could appreciate the grandeur of Isaac cathedral, the tenderness of the sacred pictures, the greatness of the art galleries, and the gentle, happy faces of the people. At a summer garden in the city's outskirts we witnessed the dances of the folk, and the play of a high fountain with changing colours, in which finally arose three Graces. It was all artistic, merry, innocent, in every respect superior to the gardens for amusement which I had seen in England and Germany.

I travelled alone to Moscow, where my friend Eugene Schuyler, Chargé d'Affaires, had secured for me a room in the house he was occupying. With Schuyler for interpreter, I made sufficient acquaintance with Russia and its people to feel ashamed for the English that prejudice should blind them so generally to this great country whose character and social conditions are of phenomenal interest. In the superb club at Moscow, whose hospitality was accorded me, I found as many magazines in Russian as are published in England or in America in English. There were monthly or quarterly periodicals devoted to agriculture and to the several sciences and to art and literature. Instead of finding an oppressed people, I found a people enjoying a personal liberty unknown either in England or America, — no sabbatarian laws, no restrictions on freedom of speech, no limitations on any conduct not criminal, and no fictitious crimes made by arbitrary statutes.

An English scholar, W. S. Ralston, having perfected himself in Russian learning, found in England that his special knowledge appealed to no interest; he struggled against poverty and starvation in London until his heart broke, his mind gave way, and he ended with suicide.

Ralston, who was highly appreciated in Russia, gave me introduction to Professor Buslaef of Moscow. It was a main object with me to study the demonology of every country I visited, and Buslaef had studied and reproduced all the mediæval frescoes and mural paintings in his country. He did not speak English, but brought into our interviews his daughter of seventeen years, who had been well taught by her English governess, and interpreted intelligently between us. The professor gave me his volume of plates, and so lucidly explained them that wherever I went thereafter the ancient church walls were luminous with the light of ages.

The satire of Shakespeare in "Twelfth Night" on the anguish of Christians when their kindred ascend to paradise is not applicable to the Russian believers. I attended a grand banquet in celebration of a nobleman's entrance on eternal bliss, and his son's succession to the title and estates. The table, at which a hundred aristocratic guests were seated, was loaded with luxuries; the finest wines were quaffed; and the happiness of all, including the late ascended gentleman, was recognized in festal speeches.

I was invited with Schuyler to pass a few days at the residence of a wealthy baron twenty miles out of Moscow. We arrived on Saturday morning and drove through a large park to the palatial mansion. The weather was hot, and we were introduced into a very large boudoir, its walls flowers, where, around a central fountain, the baroness and her four daughters, half reclining, were enjoying sherbets and cigarettes, a little stand with these luxuries being beside each. They were all dressed in snowy gowns, and the daughters, between seventeen and twenty-three years of age in appearance, remarkably fair. They all spoke English, French, and German, but the baron and his two sons knew only Russian and German. The ladies arose and received us graciously, and the baroness ordered for us cigars, caviare, and vodka.

After we had conversed a few minutes, Schuyler told the young ladies that I was a personal friend of John Stuart Mill, whereupon they all came and bowed low to me, declaring (in perfect English) that Mill's book demanding freedom for woman was their Bible. " Yes," said the eldest, " I sleep with that book under my pillow."

About noon we all went to an ornamental water in the park for a bath. There were marble benches, and stairs to the water, — the ladies going to one side of the pond and the gentlemen to the other, bathing dresses being entirely dispensed with. After this, further siesta, cigarettes, and conversation. This conversation was mostly on books. The ladies were well acquainted with the best English and French literature, and were delighted at what I could tell them of the authors personally.

The dinner was at four, and lasted two or three hours. Schuyler and I were somewhat embarrassed by the variety and quantity of the wines. The baron every now and then ordered a new vintage to be brought, and I have a note recording nine different wines, which we could not refuse without offence to our effusive host. But we managed to make some disappear otherwise than down our throats.

On Sunday we were taken on an excursion to Troitska (Trinity) Convent, probably the oldest in Russia, founded by St. Sergius, the saint who in Russia stands next to St. George. Sergius began his conversion of the " heathen " by converting a bear. The convent contains a vast accumulation of religious antiquities, the most interesting being a large agate, whose marking, apparently natural, is a figure in priestly robes kneeling before a cross. Schuyler told me that the genuineness of the picture had been much discussed, and the opinion of scientific men was that it is a sport of nature, as it would be more miraculous to imagine an ancient monk knowing any lost art by which such veining could be made in the grain of the agate without detection by experts.

Finding that I was especially interested in folk-lore and demonology, one of the young ladies, also interested in such subjects, proposed that I should remain a day longer and accompany her to an estate of her father's, where there was a village of peasants formerly their serfs. If I should go without any one who knew them, she said, they would be shy of telling anything about their superstitions.

Eugene Schuyler, who had to return to Moscow, cast an envious eye on me as in the bright summer morning I started off in a dog-cart driven by the loveliest of charioteers. She had loaded the vehicle with delicacies, to give to the sick and aged among the peasants. They were just as much attached to them, she said, as when they were their serfs. They all remained at their work, and in the same houses, and the Czar's act of emancipation had produced no convulsion or trouble at all.

When we reached the village the young lady was everywhere saluted. She drove around to call on each invalid, and after the benefactions took me to visit an old widow versed in folk-lore. When we entered she told the woman what I desired, and the humble hostess led me by the hand to a corner of the room to a special decorated chair just beneath a holy picture. Much of the information she gave me is strewn about in my " Demonology and Devil Lore," but I may say here that after making further studies of Russian folk-lore, I have been interested to remember how free the peasant woman's versions were from the sombre and weird superstitions of earlier times. The " domovoi " (house-spirits), which once terrorized Slavic families, are now occasionally mischievous but really good-natured sprites. The vampire is no longer dreaded.

After making my notes in the widow's cabin, I went through the village and noted the communal signs. Over one door is painted a plough, over another a mule, and so on with other costly things that all have need of. Each villager secures an appointed time when he may use that which belongs to all. There was unconscious poverty in this and other villages which I visited, but no squalor, no violence, and no painful scenes. The Russian peasantry impressed me as the happiest I had seen in any country. And there is nothing better than happiness. They have each their parcel of land, untaxed, and perfect freedom. They have their Sunday festivals and dances, no anxieties about their souls, and no politics to divide and excite them. They have their pretty sweethearts and wives. They have no strikes, no ambitions. Ignorant they may be, in a bookish sense, but how many bookish people are ignorant of things known to these humble folk, who live amid their fruits and harvests, bees and birds?

After a happy week in Moscow, I travelled to the great Fair at Nijni-Novgorod. The journey was more than twenty-four hours because the Czar was on our train, and at every town and village through which we passed he was received with ceremony. In each case the train stopped about fifty yards short of the town, and the Czar was out there received by the authorities, who proffered on a silver waiter a roll of bread and a little salt. The Czar touched the bread in the salt-cellar, then took a bite of it. A chorus of maidens or of little girls in white raiment sang his welcome, a brief address was made and responded to; and, having eaten their bread and salt, and become their inviolable guest, the Czar passed on into and out of the town.

It was impossible to look without a certain homage on this Czar who has passed into history as the assassinated emancipator. He was a tall, slender man, perfectly simple and lowly in his manner, his countenance intellectual and refined, his voice gracious, and even tender. Although his escort was in uniform, he himself wore the ordinary dress of a citizen with a hardly observable decoration. And this man, who liberated more people than Lincoln, without shedding a drop of blood, and secured to each emancipated family a piece of land, and was slain like Lincoln, finds no place in the Anglo-Saxon halls of fame!

Arriving at Nijni-Novgorod in the evening, I found it beyond the region of hotels, and was glad enough to find a liquor shop that could give me a pallet in the corner of a small eating-room. They knew no English, but some German, and I could manage with that. I was too tired to be suspicious.

The fair was already busy at sunrise. The scenes and wonders of that fair were incomparable, unique. Ah, the revelation of races, complexions, costumes, voices, languages! How delightful! My heart responded to the Vedic prayer, " Unwearied may I dwell on the many-coloured world!" I heard and heeded the Mollah's call to prayer, and in the cool marble mosque had it in my heart to thank Allah that no Moslem was ever converted by any missionary. And with the same sympathy I listened to the choirs in the Russian and the Greek churches. Through the interminable little path-streets, amid booths, tents, shows, I wandered during most of the day ; then rambled through the old town to the river with the intention of taking a bath. But I found it more interesting to lie on the sands and observe the " many-coloured " enjoying themselves in the water. Men and women were swimming and splashing gaily in proximity, all *in puris naturalibus.* An official who spoke fair English said to me : " All the women who go in naked are respectable ; no prostitute ever does that. It is a sort of religious duty to go under water on Saturday in this region." The paradisaic innocency of the scene was broken in only one instance. A beautiful girl of about eighteen years administered a resounding slap to the cheek of a youth who in some way had offended her. He cried repeatedly, " Vena vott " (my fault), but she straightway left the river with a burning face, dressed herself, and departed. All the time he stood near, clasping his hands, and crying piteously, — " Vena vott ! "

Poor unconscious reptile, who had revealed to an Eve that she was naked, and left thorns where just now were lilies !

Of my six weeks' stay, in this first visit to Russia, I must content myself with gathering here only a few notes. But every day was crowded with precious experiences and charming surprises. At the fair I observed closely the Cossacks, and felt ashamed that I had ever thought of those simple, manly people as vile. The Russians, the most slandered people on the face of the earth, discovered to me how much I had yet to learn of the rich varieties of fruits that grow in the garden of the earth. I envied my friend Schuyler his residence among them, the happiness of which he fully appreciated. We used to sit together at our déjeuner, enjoying our buckwheat and caviare, and realizing that it was more the loss of Anglo-Saxondom than of Russia that this land was "caviare to the general."

CHAPTER XXXVII

INTO the scientific life of London I entered with religious earnestness. I had brought letters from America to Sir Charles and Lady Lyell, who were hearty sympathizers with the anti-slavery cause. They were liberals in religion, generally attending Martineau's chapel, and sometimes South Place, — which had inherited the good-will of scientific and literary men from the time of W. J. Fox, who gathered such men around him. At the house of the Lyells I met men of science — among others Huxley, Sir Roderick Murchison, Tyndall, Dr. Carpenter, Sir Francis Galton, Sir Joseph Hooker, Sir William Grove, and Mrs. Somerville. Huxley gave me admission to the regular lectures at the Royal College of Surgeons, and Tyndall sent us invitations to the Royal Institution. Faraday was getting old, but I heard him twice. I made the acquaintance of the Wedgwoods, whose house in Regent's Park was a centre of hospitality. Mr. Wedgwood was a philologist and his wife a sister of Charles Darwin. At their house I met Dr. Erasmus Darwin, brother of Charles, a grand looking and learned man. Thus I resumed with enthusiasm the scientific studies begun under Agassiz and Baird.

I found in 1863 a great stir in London scientific and theological circles on account of a discovery in France. Sir Charles Lyell, in his "Antiquity of Man" (1863), had said "human remains will be detected in the older alluvium of European valleys," and within three months his prophecy was fulfilled. The prehistoric jaw found at Abbeville being dead yet spoke, and in such a non-Mosaic way that a sharp controversy arose. Early in May a conference of scientific men met in Paris, then adjourned to Abbeville. For one week the attention of scientific Europe was concentrated on that international Congress gathered around a brown bone, and awaited its verdict with more interest than for tidings from the battlefields in America.

Years before, a professor of geology at Cambridge (England) had discovered in Kent's Cavern (Torquay) human bones along with flint implements and the bones of fossil animals, but fear for the Mosaic record induced this pious geologist to keep his discovery secret. The fossils had to be rediscovered. This was done by Mr. Pengelly.

By Sir Charles Lyell's introduction I was able to explore Kent's Cavern, under the guidance of Pengelly. The discoveries continually made were so momentous that the government had put the place under guard. Far in the depths of the "Hole" — as the folk called it — we watched the workmen, and I saw a bit of some extinct animal picked out. Pengelly told me that shortly before an aged woman of the bone-picking profession, seeing him at the door of the cave examining a pile of bones, offered him three ha'pence for them. When he declined, the bone-picker, thinking she had not offered enough, said, "Well, I *can't* give any more, they're an uncommon bad lot." The clergyman frowned on these researches, and a pious lady of his flock asked Pengelly whether the strata above the bones were six thousand years old. "Ah, madam," he replied, "you may add to that six many more naughts, and still it won't be naughty enough!"

Pengelly expressed his amazement that the really religious mind of England had not welcomed Darwin's discovery. "If you tell me of a mechanic who has made a remarkable steam engine I may admire his skill; but if you tell me of a man who has made an engine which can of itself produce another engine, and that another, an engine from which is evolved an endless series of steadily self-improving engines, I might say that inventor was a god."

At Lamorna, the house of the Pengellys, I met an invited company, and learned that Torquay had been schooled in science by Pengelly and his assistants. Assistants? Yes, — some old bones which he brings out, and makes them tell all about Torquay as it was a billion years ago, and the people that lived here, and huge creatures that no longer exist. It had become *de rigueur* in Torquay for gentry to recognize Kent's Cavern as the tomb of their ancestors. One lady told me in confidence that Mr. Pengelly had gone to that cavern every day for years, except one day so frightfully stormy that he staid at home; but on that day his big cavern-boots were distinctly seen tramping through the streets as usual out to the Hole.[1]

Soon after the discovery at Abbeville, Sir Charles Lyell delivered his address as president of the British Association at Bath. I remember well the enthusiasm with which he was received. His long labours for scientific freedom, his establishment of a new Genesis, his brave assertion of truth against sanctified traditions, — all these were now corroborated by a consensus of the competent. With his refined face, his gentle, unpretending look, as he glanced around with childlike surprise at the multitude of elegant ladies and gentlemen whose applause acclaimed him as if a conquering hero, he was in my eyes as fit a figure for the Laureate's verse as ancient Arthur.

---

[1] In a letter from Mr. Pengelly, January 4, 1874, he said : " A lady visitor said to me one day, ' I 've a story to tell you about Kent's Cavern. We overheard the following discussion the other day between our cook (who, you will remember, formerly lived with you), and the nurse. Said the cook, " Mr. Pengelly calls the bones what they brings from Kent's Cavern possel bones; but I don't think he can tell the bones of the possels from the bones of other people ! " " I don't know 'bout that," said the nurse, " I 've 'eerd say he 's oncommon clever that way; and I shudden wonder if 'e cud tell 'em then ! " " But," said the cook, " how cud the possels' bones get over 'ere ? That 's what I want to know. Tell me that if you can ! " " I don't see much in that," said the nurse. " They tell me that nobody knows where Paradise was, and therefore it might as soon 'ave been 'ere as anywhere else; and if 't was 'ere, where else should the possel's bones be ? " Cookie was silent.' "

He began by reminding men of science of the necessity that they should enlarge their ideas of geologic time, in order to realize the operation of the forces of natural selection. He said that a rich man, reproached for the smallness of his donation to a charity, answered that in early life he had been very poor, and could never get the chill of poverty out of his bones. Sir Charles reminded men of science that they had so long been restricted to the pittance of six thousand years as the world's age that even now they were apt to go on adding a mere million years or so where boundless time is needed.

On the Sunday of this meeting of the association at Bath I preached in the Unitarian church a sermon on the text "Nothing but leaves," which had pleased my most thoughtful friends in America and London. The Lyells and many other scientific people were present, and my acquaintance among the members was extended. I attended the annual meetings of the association pretty regularly, and saw the discussion about the antiquity of man steadily fossilized like the Abbeville and Torquay bones. It is digging in an exhausted Kent's Hole of theology to talk of that once burning controversy.

Mention of the Abbeville jaw reminds me of a skull at Halifax, England, which I saw after giving there a lecture before the Philosophical Society. Mr. Layland, an antiquarian, offered to show me through the historical places and institutions of the city. He guided me to the ancient church, and while pointing out the old black canopy over the font said: "It originally had rich colours, but was blackened by the darkness of the Reformation." My scholarly friend thus revealed himself as either a Catholic or a philosopher. He and Professor Tyndall had together served a scientific apprenticeship in the institution at Halifax.

In the museum there is a collection of Egyptian skulls. A manufacturer of Halifax visited Egypt and purchased a large number of mummies, whose heads, each enclosed in a box, were shipped to Hull for Halifax Museum. I remarked the whiteness and shapeliness of one skull, the rest being brown, and Mr. Layland told me an incident about it. It was necessary to boil the mummied heads and scrape them, this task being entrusted to himself and others in the institution. While they were so engaged a strange odour filled the room. It proceeded from an untouched box, which they saw was moist. Hastily opening it they beheld a beautiful female face. The eyes were as if alive, the cheeks plump, the flesh rounded and full. They called to Tyndall and others in another room, but when they arrived the face had collapsed and was oozing away. It was concluded that this lady, probably of high rank, had been mummified with more potent chemicals and unguents than the others, and that these had been relaxed by contact with sea-water while on the ship.

That evening I wrote a Lucianic dialogue between this Egyptian lady and the learned Catholic who saw her, and whose religion had also certain beautiful features in my historic imagination. I was able with all sincerity to sympathize with Mr. Layland's feeling against the art-destroying Puritans, and he on his side loved our much anathematized Professor Tyndall, and had a faith in science not found in orthodox Protestantism at that time.

It has been my privilege to know the leading scientific men in America and England personally, in many instances in their homes, and I can recall none that are not associated in my memory with sweetness as well as light. None of them were orthodox, and what could bigotry say against a tree that bore such fruits? The creeds that academically damned these men, yielded to their characters before adapting themselves to their discoveries. There was not one murmur from any pulpit when Sir Charles Lyell, under whose revelations the Mosaic cosmogony crumbled, was buried in Westminster Abbey.

After the burial of Lyell I walked from the Abbey with Tyndall, and said I was somewhat disturbed by the unreality of some parts of the service. But Tyndall had not listened to the service with a professional ear. It came to him from a remote era when it was genuine. "When I think," he said, "what the old Abbey means, what historic memories and sacred associations have consecrated it, and that now at length it should gather among the great men of the past the great man of the present, without regard to his disbeliefs, why, the whole thing is so grand and so affecting that I did not heed the details." Tears were in his eyes as he spoke, and I took his words to heart.

Sir Charles Lyell remembered well the ordeals through which the discoveries of his time had to pass. "Theologians first cry, it is n't true; next, it is n't new; finally, we discovered it ourselves." Once, when he was talking in this way, Sir William Grove came in and was not so hopeful as Sir Charles and Lady Lyell and myself about the advance of rational ideas. "I have a notion," said Justice Grove, "that it will take about as long for the superstitions to pass away as it took them to grow." I suggested that there are now enlightening agents that did not exist when they grew; and though Sir William was rather incredulous he perhaps became more optimistic when Lyell was buried in the Abbey. That was the first salient proclamation that English Christianity was detached from the Bible so far as science was concerned.

Professor Huxley was a man of conservative temperament and conciliatory disposition, but in defending great scientific generalizations he was drawn into the polemical attitude. There was not a pulpit in England from which issued instructions bearing on religion of such profound importance as those heard from Huxley. I never missed one of his lectures, whether at the Hunterian, Royal, or London institutions, or at workingmen's institutes, and at St. George's Hall. He also lectured at times in my chapel, not on religion, but in Sunday afternoon courses we arranged for the people. Huxley was a perfect lecturer, — as artistic and finished in speaking to workingmen as when addressing a learned audience. Without notes, without a hesitating or a superfluous word, simple, lucid, he carried every mind with him. He did not gesticulate nor emphasize, and without any tone of paradox he swept away fallacies without seeming to know it.

Huxley studied the religions of mankind in their philo-

sophical bearings. In conversation he expressed to me his
belief that the English people were fundamentally simple
deists, as their "pagan" ancestors were. Their deity became
more civilized as they themselves did. In nature he found
both good and revolting things, suggesting, he said, that if there
were any creator he must be deemed a Demiurgos. He said
he had not been bothered in early life about Bible-reading as
a duty, and consequently used to enjoy the Bible stories. This
may account for Huxley's concession that the Bible might
be read in the public schools. His freethinking friends were
distressed by this, but when I spoke of it to Leslie Stephen,
he said, "What made us freethinkers? Why, reading the
Bible!"

Huxley and Tyndall threw themselves with zeal into the
struggle for opening the museums and art galleries on Sunday afternoons. Nearly all of the clergymen of the English
Church in London aided our movement. At a meeting presided over by Dean Stanley, many clergymen being present,
Tyndall in the flow of his argument said, "We only want
half of Sunday for intellectual improvement!" Whereat the
dean began the laugh; the delighted audience caught the
unintentional joke, and would not allow Tyndall to apolo-
gize.

An important side of Huxley was his scientific imagination. Who that listened to his lectures could ever forget how
in his hand the little piece of chalk swelled to a world populous with animal life, or the bit of coal became a diamond
lens through which were seen the trees, ferns, and giant
mosses of the primeval forest? I remember listening to him
on an occasion when he invited us to take our stand with him,
in imagination, on London Bridge; with him we remarked
the current of the Thames, the slope of its banks, their distant
curving; then passed on beyond its boats, barges, and ships,
to its sources and its mouth, varied by glances at primitive
tribes on its shores; till we traced the old river, its tides, its
geologic work, back to a different world and to the confines
of the solar system. All this was the work of imagination

interpreting scientific fact, and a finished literary art jointly working on the material of thorough knowledge.

The most far-reaching hypothesis ever made by any one, since the discovery of evolution, was, in my opinion, one originally made by Huxley concerning the vast chasm, moral and mental, between man and the highest of the lower animals. This was first given in a lecture to workingmen : —

"Well, but," I am told at once, somewhat triumphantly, "you say in the same breath that there is a great moral and intellectual chasm between man and the lower animals. How is this possible when you declare that moral and intellectual characteristics depend on structure, and yet tell us that there is no such gulf between the structure of man and that of the lower animals?"

I think that objection is based upon a misconception of the real relations which exist between structure and function, between mechanism and work. Function is the expression of molecular forces and arrangements no doubt; but does it follow from this that variation in function so depends upon variation in structure that the former is always exactly proportioned to the latter? If there is no such relation, if the variation in function which follows on a variation in structure may be enormously greater than the variation of structure, then you see the objection fall to the ground. Take a couple of watches, — made by the same maker and as completely alike as possible, — set them upon a table, and the function of each — which is its rate of going — will be performed in the same manner, and you shall be able to distinguish no difference between them ; but let me take a pair of pincers, and if my hand is steady enough to do it, let me just lightly crush together the bearings of the balance-wheel or force to a slightly different angle the teeth of the escapement of one of them, and of course you know the immediate result will be that the watch so treated from that moment will cease to go. But what proportion is there between the structural alteration and the functional result? Is it not perfectly obvious that the alteration is of the minutest kind, yet that, slight as it is, it has produced an infinite difference in the performance of the function of these two instruments?

Well, now apply that to the present question. What is it that constitutes and makes man what he is? What is it but his power of language, — that language giving him the means of recording his experience, — making every generation somewhat wiser than its predecessor, — more in accordance with the established order of the universe? What is it but this power of speech, of recording experience, which enables men to be men, — looking before and after, and in some dim sense understanding the working of this wondrous universe, — and which distinguishes man from the whole brute world? I say that this functional difference is vast, unfathomable, and truly infinite in its consequences; and I say at the same time that it may depend upon structural differences which shall be absolutely inappreciable to us with our present means of investigation. What is this very speech that we are talking about? I am speaking to you at this moment; but if you were to alter, in the minutest degree, the proportion of the nervous forces now active in the two nerves which supply the muscles of my glottis, I shall become suddenly dumb. The voice is produced only so long as the vocal chords are parallel, and these are parallel only so long as certain muscles contract with exact equality, and that again depends on the equality of action of those two nerves I spoke of. So that a change of the minutest kind in the structure of one of these nerves, or in the structure of the part in which it originates, or of the supply of blood to that part, or of one of the muscles to which it is distributed, might render all of us dumb. But a race of dumb men deprived of all communication with those who could speak would be little indeed removed from the brutes. And the moral and intellectual difference between them and ourselves would be practically infinite, though the naturalist should not be able to find a single shadow of even specific structural difference.

I remember asking Huxley whether, if the throat of a fine opera-singer like Jenny Lind and the throat of a person of coarse voice were given to an expert scientist to dissect, he could tell by great care which vocal chords belonged to the singer and which to the rude voice. He replied that it would be as difficult as for a musical expert to determine between two violins, outwardly alike in color and shape, which was the Cremona and which an ordinary violin. He must first hear a note sounded.

Among the beautiful things in my memory are the garden

parties of Sir Joseph and Lady Hooker at Kew Gardens. Their house and garden, adjoining the great gardens of which Sir Joseph was the scientific superintendent, were an ideal place for the social gatherings of scientific and literary people. Such from all parts of the world were met there.

Lady Hooker was an attractive and gracious hostess. She was the daughter of the Rev. Mr. Symonds, rector of Malvern. I had the pleasure of passing a few days at the rectory of this clergyman, and could readily comprehend how Lady Hooker came by her scientific tastes and knowledge. Her father was accustomed to form the young ladies of his parish into a class of scientific ramblers. On a certain day of the week they repaired to some locality rich in fossils or in botanical specimens. Under his direction they became experts. On my arrival there the rector was absent, and could not return until dinner, but he had arranged that some of his young ladies should take me on a scientific ramble. They appeared in a handsome wagon, all in pretty gowns, each armed with her little hammer. When we had ascended a height overlooking the valley of the Severn, one of the ladies pointed out to me the hills where the sea had left its record in sea-shells, and, without any allusion to the Deluge, described the river's work in making the valley. At certain stony passes we alighted, and small stones were picked up, in each of which the hammer's tap revealed a crustacean fossil. The young ladies handled delicately these tiny monuments of their ancestors. In the evening Mr. Symonds went over them with us in his charming way.

After I had built my house, Inglewood, at Bedford Park, I planted in my garden two slips of the famous Glastonbury thorn. It had been mentioned in some lecture of mine, reported in a way that appeared to a gentleman in Glastonbury too sceptical. He wrote me that a tree descended from the ancient "Holy Thorn" was in his garden, and that it flowered twice annually, the second time about Christmas. I answered that I did not doubt that there was a biannual thorn, but only meant to study the legend of its miraculous origin at Glastonbury, where it was said to have flowered from the staff of Joseph of Arimathea when he laid down to perish in the snowstorm, protecting him with a canopy of leaves and blossoms, and thereby converting the heathen. He sent me two slips of good size, which I planted. One tree I named St. Patrick, because the same legend is related of him in connection with the " Holy Thorn " at St. Patrice in France ; the other I named St. Christopher, because his legend was that he converted the heathen by sticking his staff in the ground, where it at once flowered. The tree named after St. Patrick withered, but Sir Joseph Hooker used to come over from Kew and advise me about St. Christopher, and the tree is flourishing to this day. But it is not exact in its legendary reverence for Christmas.

A member of my South Place society, Mr. Klaassen, an accomplished geologist, having invited me to ramble with twenty geologists of his club, I gladly accepted. The ramble was through the Weald (Sussex), the time Whitsuntide, when the landscape was in full glory. Arrived at Battle, we began at the extreme surface of the Weald, the Duke of Cleveland's place, where the duchess came out to see us, and offered the courtesies of her mansion and freedom of the antiquities within and around it. For geologists, however, William the Norman and his ferocious fauna are creatures of yesterday. We were also visited on Hastings cliff by the nut-brown nymph of the place. This sun-tanned beauty of seventeen begged us in the usual gypsy tone to buy photographs of Dripping Well, Ecclesbourne Glen, Lover's Seat. " What is Lover's Seat ? " inquired our chorus. " I 'll tell you," she cried, and, sure-footed as a chamois, she leaped upon a rock overhanging the precipice of one hundred and fifty feet, and began her recital in hereditary sing-song. " There were two lovers," also a cruel father, a leap, a rescue, and a " large family 'appy ever hafter."

Descending to the beach, we came to a good point for observation, and all sat down on the shingle. Dr. Busk and his daughters, Professor Tydemann of the Geological Coast

Survey, and others joined us, and we listened to the full story of the Weald. From his rock the clear-headed geologist, William Topley, spoke for nearly an hour. As I lay on the shingle, listening to graphic descriptions of hills no longer existing and rivers no longer flowing, I felt myself in the presence of realities whose vastness and sublimity reduced to fantasies the visions of Dante and Milton. The instructed eye here beholds a mighty ocean, and even while it looks the ocean dries up and disappears, leaving its record in vast deposits hardened into rocks. A continent rises, is covered with plants and animals; and now a great lake forms over it; then the whole of it sinks, and again an ocean flows over all; presently once more the land emerges, to be denuded by the sea, planed by glaciers, and worn by rains. Every page of its history is laid bare.

There is something strangely mystical in the appearance of the great downs spreading inland from the white chalk cliffs which gave its name to Albion. They are like vast billows rising to their crests. They have a long, gradual slope on one (and the same) side, and on the other a precipitous inward curved escarpment. The effect is that of a sea that has been suddenly solidified. And down on the beach the small rocks are found with similar incline on one side and escarpment on the other. The high downs will be laid low some day; but for those who try to think in geologic time, the placard of " Danger," set on the cliff's edge, appeals to generations billions of years ahead.

We lunched at the house of Sir John Peyton, — to the Virginia branch of whose race my great-grandfather, Dr. Valentine Peyton, belonged, — and at the inn where we passed the night our excellent dinner was followed by comic speeches and uproarious fun. It was delightful to see these geologists who had all day been travelling through immemorial ages — seeing dried-up seas in a shell and extinct fauna in a bone — come now to their own time and good-fellowship.

When I returned to my own religious field of study I found it all Weald; elemental floods of Norse and Teutonic delusion, streams of mythology from East and South, stratum of superstition piled on stratum, natural and unnatural selection co-working to produce an average man whose weald-brain is the world of Christendom in miniature.

CHAPTER XXXVIII

MY first article in "Fraser" appeared in August, 1864, and
in the ten years following I worked pretty steadily for that
magazine. My twenty-eight articles in that time were mainly
on American subjects, though there were others, — the most
important of these being two on plant-lore ("Mystic Trees
and Flowers") and articles on "Demonology," made of four
lectures given in the Royal Institution. I wrote also occasional articles for the "Fortnightly Review" and the daily
"Morning Star." Subsequently I was invited by Mr. Walker
of the "Daily News" to join his staff, and also wrote a good
deal for the "Pall Mall Gazette." All this, with my South
Place discourses, my letters to American journals and magazines, and lectures in various halls about London and to philosophical societies in Hull, Newcastle-on-Tyne, Edinburgh
and other Scotch cities, kept me busy. And yet I worked
little in the evenings. We mingled a good deal in society, and
enjoyed the theatres.

The manuscript of my first article in "Fraser" was sent by
me to Carlyle, at his suggestion, and by him to the editor,
James Anthony Froude. Thus began my long intimacy with
Froude. This friendship made much of the charm of my
London life. Nothing appeared lacking in Froude. Noble
in appearance, a perfect gentleman in manners, simple and
unassuming, frank and friendly, sweet and equable in disposition, he and his intellectual wife associated their house in

Onslow Gardens with an elegant hospitality which those who enjoyed it can never forget.

But if there was anything more attractive than an invitation to the Froudes', where we were sure to meet a fine literary circle, it was my afternoon walks with him. In every such confidential talk I was enriched by his knowledge and the suggestiveness of his thought on subjects that most interested me.

My own experiences gave me a sort of key to Froude. Always conscious that my fruits had been stunted by the barren dogmatic field in which they were planted, by the years occupied with clearing away theologic rubbish, by the further years of struggle with slavery, and not yet mature enough to estimate the compensations of such experiences, I was able to recognize in Froude a spirit touched to finer issues than those that first laid their weird upon him. This man had nothing to do with the clerical life, nor with the cinders of tradition in which he delved with Dr. Newman. In " The Spirit's Trials," and " The Lieutenant's Daughter " (1847), and in " The Nemesis of Faith " (1849), was signalled a unique genius. Such a bold and original imagination, had it reached its own fruitage, must have given to the world works incomparable as the novels of Balzac or Goethe. But Froude had his vulnerable point ; he could not resist the bow and spear of a figure that captivated his imagination : as Newman had captured him at Oxford, Carlyle captured him in London. It was Carlyle who persuaded Froude to renounce imaginative work and write history. The surrender might not have been made but for the clamour with which " The Nemesis of Faith " was met by most of Froude's Oxonian friends, who for their unorthodoxy were paying a special tax to conventional morality. The book was burned at the close of a lecture by Professor Sewell in Exeter College, Oxford, of which college Froude was a Fellow ; he resigned immediately, and no voice was heard in his defence. So he left Oxford to return no more until he went there as a professor.

The graphic portraiture in " Nemesis " of Dr. Newman's

preaching at Oxford, and of the man himself, shows how Froude's heart had been almost torn out of him by parting from the great preacher whose beloved collaborator he had been. He was in a spiritual loneliness like that of the scholar in " Nemesis." In that time of isolation, and amid reproaches for his novels, the one man who could be to him in his scepticism what Newman had been in his old faith was Carlyle.

In boyhood Carlyle, because of his father's horror of fiction, read novels surreptitiously; but even rebellion does not free a man from parental fetters. Had it been otherwise, Carlyle would have held Froude to the form of expression which his genius had already selected. But as he discouraged the poetic form, he disliked also the form of fiction. Froude had indeed shown, in the book that enjoyed the distinction of being the last book burned at Oxford, that the truth most needed in English literature could be told only in the form of fiction.

Farewell, then, my genius! Yet a man's genius does n't leave him so easily. Froude's " History of England " is one of the most brilliant works of his century, but even those who have no sympathy with the carping criticisms upon it rarely fail to perceive that picturesque events and striking figures at times overpower the imagination of the author at the cost of historical judgment, although the charm of the work may be heightened. All of his historical works involved original research. He would leave his magazine in Charles Kingsley's hands and run off to Spain or elsewhere at times simply to examine one or two documents ; but when the document appeared, it was sometimes suspiciously alive and entertaining. If one takes account of that, more can be got from Froude than from any other historian of England.

Personally he was enigmatic to those who were best acquainted with him. " Did you ever notice Mr. Froude's eyes ? " said Mrs. Carlyle to me. " Yes," I replied, " I have observed that they are brown and clear." " At times," she said, " his eyes appear to me like those of some wild but gentle animal." Something prevented her at the moment from saying anything further, but she meant, I think, the serenity

of his look, which nothing seemed to disturb. He had humour, and at times smiled with his eyes, but, however stormy
the talk around him, his eyes expressed no emotion. He was
intent, as if observing each one who spoke rather than what
he said. I never knew him to be vehement on any point.
He impressed me as profoundly sceptical on all general subjects, but rather credulous concerning persons. Once, when
we were talking of some recent works directed against Christianity he said, " I should as little think of attacking Christianity as of attacking a horse. It will continue so long as it
is of practical utility to a large number. But there does n't
appear to be a single command ascribed to Christ that can
be really obeyed to-day without qualification." He nevertheless had no belief that Christianity as a system would be
supplanted by anything really better. What is called " Reform " amounts, he said, to one rusty nail driving out another.
Or if the driving nail be not rusty, it soon becomes so. At
the time when the " Liberal " and the " Conservative " parties
were competing as to which should be first to enfranchise
the masses, we were walking in Kew Gardens and talking
about " Progress." We came upon a fine century plant which
had mounted up high from joint to joint, and was near to its
time of flowering. " That plant," said Froude, " thinks it is
making great progress ; it has grown much this spring ; next
week it will blossom, and that will be the end of it. A week
later its flower will be on the ground, and thenceforth no more
growth or blossom. I fear," he added, "that will be the
result of what is now called political progress."

Nevertheless Froude sceptically balanced the good and evil
in every question. In a note to me he casually said : —

Unless I am mistaken, we are observing the death struggle
of the great Anti-Reform party in England. Merchants and
such like have become so rich by such bad means that they
are in terror of the people, — and the conflict which is only
beginning will witness changes of which no one living can
foresee the magnitude.

Froude had a very high esteem and affection for Motley,

and he repeatedly referred to the way in which Motley had changed front on the subject of secession in America. He declared that while the States were seceding, Motley, then in London, welcomed the separation. It would relieve the nation from complicity with the wrong and do away with the perpetual discord of the country and corruption of its politics. " But the next time I had an opportunity to converse with Motley, and alluded to what he had said on the subject, he simply foamed at the mouth. He was all for uncompromising coercion and war. On thinking over the matter, I felt myself more inclined to his original arguments than to the foam."

Froude was generous in permitting me to write with perfect freedom in his magazine on American politics. In a note of December 23, 1864, concerning an article of mine already in the January " Fraser," he says : —

I fear that on the slave question I agree more nearly with Carlyle than with you. At least I look at it, and have all my life looked at it, as a thing to be allowed to wear itself gradually away as civilization advances. You cannot treat an institution as old as mankind as a crime to be put out by force. If you do, you are unjust and the injustice will recoil upon yourselves. You make wrong into right by treating it unfairly. You are playing over again on a new stage the old game of Philip the Second and Alva. You cannot be more persuaded of the wickedness of slavery than they were of the wickedness of heresy. The universe does not allow a section of mankind to inflict its views upon another at the point of the sword, — if the sword is pressed into a service beyond the common service of ordinary average men it will kill the man that uses it.

You won't believe any of this, — but you will find it to be so unless the laws under which we live in this world are suddenly altered.

Froude did not change a word of my article (January, 1865), but merely placed at the top — " By an American Abolitionist." His phrase concerning the sword, " it will kill the man that uses it," soon had a literal and fearful fulfilment. The death of President Lincoln rendered another paper necessary. A note came from Froude (April 28) : —

" Will you dine with me *alone* on Sunday evening, to talk over this terrible business? I shall want you to write something about it in June ' Fraser.' When the Devil is once born there is no foreseeing what will happen. The only safe prophecy is an increase of madness and sorrow.

" I shall dine at 7.45. My house is in confusion, as we are moving, but we can have two quiet rooms, and in the evening, if you like, we will go down to the Cosmopolitan Club."

I had already been engaged to write some personal recollections of Lincoln for the June " Fortnightly," but there remained plenty to say. The article in " Fraser " duly appeared in June, — " By an American Abolitionist," — the task being difficult, on account of my animadversions on the administration in the previous article.

At the Cosmopolitan Club — a Sunday evening association — there was, after Lincoln's assassination, an exceptionally large gathering. The bullet of Wilkes Booth had destroyed the discord between parties. I was besieged with questions concerning President Andrew Johnson, and I shared the general apprehension that the wrath of America would be wasted on individual victims instead of on slavery.

The feeling of England concerning the assassination is historic ; the conversations in private were remarkable. Louis Blanc was astonished at the self-restraint of the American people. He said to me, " If such a thing had happened in France, one half of the people would have tried to get the other half in prison before night." English republicans were somewhat disturbed at discovering the extent of American loyalty to a person, especially as the President had for some time been regarded as reactionary. In one small dinner company, an eminent clergyman and author, whose name I withhold, said that, shocking as the event was, it could hardly be wondered at, as Abraham Lincoln was caught between contending principles and forces with which he was incompetent to deal. " He could not go to the bottom of a thing either in the South or North. In this conflict of great forces involving all humanity, Lincoln was a Polonius behind the arras, and suffered the penalty of being out of his place."

The able gentleman who said this was not aware that among his listeners there was an antislavery American, but the others knew, and either on that account or because the opinion was unwelcome to all, the subject was dropped. But what a despot is Death over the faculties of man! One week before I would have sanctioned that estimate of Lincoln; but the words now sounded like blasphemy.

When the odious epoch of reconstruction arrived, — as Southerners said, "when peace broke out," an irony some antislavery men and many slaves equally appreciated, — Froude and Carlyle urged on me the absurdity of enfranchising the negroes. But, I asked, who else was there in the South to enfranchise? Were the whites to be now given the balance of power in the government they had for four years been trying to murder? Carlyle did not suggest any alternative to negro enfranchisement. But Froude argued that the rebellion was not begun in a spirit of treason to the United States. It was in defence of what certain States believed their constitutional rights. Personally they were honourable people, still convinced that they were right, and the Northerners would find in the end that their Union had a South on its hands like the Ireland that England had. In one of his many notes he says : —

Our Irish experience is that the *people* (the *peasantry*), whose manifest benefit our administration was calculated to produce, who were ground into slaves by the native landowners, yet preferred and still prefer the tyranny of their own people to English patronage. It was so before the church difficulties rose; it is so at this day in matters with which the church is not concerned. On the estates where the agents enforce English methods the land is improved. The rents are thirty per cent. lower, the wages rise, the people are better housed and fed. Yet they shoot the agents and curse the landlord and believe themselves the most oppressed of mankind. The Squireens who will let them go their own dirty way — squat, propagate, subdivide, and multiply, into dens of pauperism — may and do grind death rents out of them, impound their cattle if they don't pay, — even take their hunting-whips and thrash them like dogs, — and they will go through fire and water for them, die for them if necessary, and think themselves honoured in doing it. Our Indian experience is exactly the same.

That you have killed slavery is certain enough. That the negroes will remain devoted to their old masters, and serfs as much as the Irish peasants are serfs, that the poor whites will cast their lot with them to whom they have always looked up, seems to be equally certain. The masters may accept the results of the war and return quietly to the Union under such conditions as they can get, but that they will never forgive New England and will watch for the time to be revenged under the forms of the Constitution flows necessarily from the common laws of humanity. Do what you will, the whole South will be Democrat. The New England Republicans will again be in a minority, and secession next time may come from them.

I thought of writing for " Fraser " an article on the American poetry inspired by the struggle with slavery, and submitted examples. After reading them, Froude wrote : —

The American originality in the author of " Margaret " I can enjoy and admire most heartily, and so I can Lowell, — but these new people fill their sails with the whirlwind of the last six years ; and I am still heretic enough to regard all that not as a perennial trade wind of humanity, but as a lone tornado generated by temporary electricity ; an outburst not of intelligent but of the brutal forces.

Nothing violent is long-lived, and these all-absorbing, all-sweeping passions blaze like prairie grass, sweeting the ground, indeed, for a future crop, — but not things in themselves proper to sympathize with. I do not recognize *poetry* in either of your friends except Howells, — and he is the one of the four who has caught the disease most mildly.

Froude talked freely with me on religious topics. His brother William, the civil engineer, whom I sometimes met, maintained fraternal relations with Anthony, but remained loyal to Cardinal Newman. Carlyle did not like talk about theology, and his contempt for Cardinal Newman and Tractarianism sealed up a third of Froude's experiences. Francis

William Newman's unimaginative way of dealing with Jesus repelled him. " I heard Francis Newman preach this morning at Voysey's service," Froude wrote me. " The sermon will be printed ; the more important parts of it being invectives against the moral character of the unfortunate son of David. It may be absurd to make an idol of a man and worship him. But that is no reason why, when we have left off worshipping, we should kick him out of doors." Mr. Voysey's theism he found " dreary and passionless."

I tried to entice Froude into the committee of a contemplated Liberal Congress. But he was too skittish to be bridled. When the committee met at Huxley's house, Froude was expectedly not there. A note came explaining the cogent reasons for his absence : " Huxley reports that your meeting was a very rational one. I was detained by the *ice*. It was the last good skating day, which I could not abandon."

We used to converse on theological points in a purely historical way. Concerning a theory of mine, that Jesus had been wealthy and was of Hillel's College in Jerusalem, Froude wrote : " I cannot quite reconcile myself to a *rich* Christ. Merivale insisted once to me that the disciples were Jews of good family and position ; and when I said they were fishermen — ' Fishermen,' he said, ' yes, like you and me. They had their villas on the lake, and went out fishing for their amusement." He felt, like you, that they were cultivated and educated men, or they could not have done what they did. You and he may be right, and my hesitation may be only prejudice."

Froude had discovered that he could best express his heresies as it is done in his " Short Studies of Great Subjects." For the ordinary lay reader the essays are instructive and amusing, but for those experienced in sceptical inquiry these volumes abound in historic episodes which are far-reaching parables. His analyses of Lucian were outlined to me before publication, and he drew my attention to the correspondence of Lucian's situation amid old superstitions withering and new ones growing with the situation of scholars in our time.

His "Divus Cæsar" I regarded as one of the most pregnant works ever written. "It has been on my mind since 1850," he wrote me, "and belongs, as you see, to the old cycle of my ideas."

Although Froude was so severe on the Irish in his writing, Ireland had a fascination for him. His fondness for sport and for wild beauty made him happy there. In 1873 he took for the summer the beautiful mansion of Lord Lansdowne at Derreen, and in August I passed a fortnight with him.

I had been going over my old tracks during the Franco-German war, and Froude had engaged me to write an article about it. It appeared in "Fraser," October, 1873, under title of "Gravelotte Revisited." Fortunately it was nearly finished in France, for the yachtings and excursions Froude had arranged in Ireland along with Lord Ducie and others left few hours for work. Meanwhile, some article of Froude's on the Irish question had brought demonstrations of wrath against him, though few in that region had genuine knowledge of the subject. Probably residing in Lansdowne House was Froude's real offence. After the battle of the Boyne the estate was taken from a recluse named McSweeny, and the Lansdownes bought it for a small sum. The family sent McSweeny a present of wine to soften the blow, but he brought all the bottles before the house and smashed them on a rock. So a vendetta existed against the mansion itself.

The country around Derreen is populous with beings that do not exist, — spooks, fallen spirits, imps; the peasantry get little glimpse of actual nature and fact. I could never see any hope for the southern Irish masses but transplantation; yet the Irish gentry are delightful, and their ladies among the fairest and sweetest in the world. Mrs. John Rae (wife of the late Arctic explorer) and her sister, Miss Thompson, a fine writer, I knew for many years. They are gentle and beautiful ladies; but one year they advised their own tenants in Ireland not to pay them any rent in order to make common cause with the movement against English landlords.

I met with a learned and titled Irish physician who was a

materialist. When, however, I began to talk about the " banshee " superstition, I found that old Celtic sentiment, which requires every famous family to have a preternatural servitor in its livery, was too strong for him. He told some banshee anecdotes that he called "strange," but was contemptuous towards religious superstitions.

The last time I met Froude was at the burial of Carlyle at Ecclefechan, Thursday, February 10, 1881. Mr. Arthur Johnstone-Douglas, a connection of the Marquis of Queensberry, had invited me to visit him at Glen Stuart, and I travelled to Scotland on Monday the seventh. The weather was then bright, and we drove about to the places associated with Carlyle, — Craigenputtoch, Dunscore, Annan. Much to my astonishment Mr. Johnstone-Douglas did not know even the day of the funeral, and we had to drive some miles to the residence of Mrs. Austin, Carlyle's sister, to discover it. With this lady I had an interesting conversation. She said that her brother had been in boyhood and youth devoted to his mother, and affectionate towards his sisters. He was continually going with them to carry bundles, and was their always willing messenger. She and the other surviving sister, Mrs. Aitken of Dumfries, had always remembered that even in his later youth, so troubled with doubts about the path on which he should enter, his love for them and their mother was unfailing. He was of very sweet disposition, she declared. Mrs. Austin was a woman of veracity, and was perfectly calm when she told me this, — which indeed, I did not need to be told.

Why secrecy was made about Carlyle's funeral I could only conjecture. It had been announced that the Dean of Westminster's proposal that he should be buried in the Abbey had been declined, because Carlyle had expressed a wish to be buried among his own people ; but it was not certain whether this meant at Ecclefechan or beside his wife at Haddington cathedral. Neither the day nor the place of the funeral reached the public. No religious service, of course, was admissible, but it seemed to be carrying privacy too far that the coffin should be conveyed to the station in London, and from the station in Scotland to the churchyard, without any opportunity for an expression of feeling even by his friends. Johnstone-Douglas said the Scottish gentry were proud of Carlyle, though their tenants were fairly represented by one who had said to him, " What a pity yon man Tom Caerl was an infidel! " He thought that if the day had been known, the fox-hunt would have been suspended, and many gentlemen been present at the funeral. He himself did not feel entitled to enter the churchyard, having had no notification from the family, but remained in his carriage outside the gate. At the hour when Carlyle was buried, many of the villagers were off at the installation of a new minister in a neighbouring church. Only when the bell began tolling did those remaining know the hour.

At noon the hearse drove up, followed by five funeral coaches in which were Carlyle's relatives ; about a hundred other persons straggled up in the snow and mud, apparently peasants ; presently Tyndall arrived, and after him Froude and Lecky, all on foot.

The snow and rain now fell furiously. Several hundred children from the schools were pressing their faces through the railing of the graveyard, while only about a hundred of us surrounded the grave. The flowers on the coffin could not relieve the scene, — desolate even to weirdness. Not one word was uttered. I supposed that Tyndall and Froude or Lecky would speak, — but no! the patriarch of English literature was hurried into the grave in absolute silence. When I thought of the man, of what he had been to England and America, it filled me with pain, and had I not been a heretical minister, I should have uttered a farewell. Arthur Johnstone-Douglas told me that the burial was in accordance with Scottish usage, and perhaps Carlyle had ordered the silence, which might not have been so depressing had the weather been fair and everything less bedraggled.

But alas, what were sleet and snow and mud falling on the great man's grave compared with the blizzard that presently struck Carlyle's fame, and chilled the hearts of multitudes that had looked up to him! There was deep and universal feeling at the death of Carlyle, and the publications that swiftly followed froze the tears as they were falling.

As we started off for the night journey to London — Froude, Tyndall, Lecky, and myself in one compartment — we were all suffering from the dreary funeral of the man two of us certainly loved with personal tenderness. Tyndall began to say something to me, but his voice broke ; my tears also were falling. With Mr. Lecky I had no intimacy, though I sometimes met him. Froude had a sad and weary look. We all sank into silence, but I think got little sleep. For myself I had enough to think of, as on the following Sunday (13th) my chapel was to be the place of a memorial discourse which would be attended by the veterans of Carlyle's times.

The " Nemesis " of Carlyle's quasi-hypnotic influence over Froude fell on the memory of Carlyle himself. After the death of Carlyle the imaginative genius of Froude resumed possession of him, and he wrote a " biography " so marked by dramatic situations, thrilling scenes, and startling effects, that I discover in momentous chapters the hand that wrote " Nemesis of Faith " and " Shadows of the Clouds." The reputation of Carlyle was so unconsciously overthrown that, had I been superstitious, I should have personified Froude's imaginative genius as a *dæmon* which, having been exorcised by Carlyle, returned to wreak posthumous revenge on his memory.

When the excitement about Froude's publications was at its height, I was one day at the London Library, and soon after Lord Tennyson's son entered and told me his father wished to speak to me. He was in his carriage at the door, and said, " I saw you go into the door there, and wished to tell you an incident of some interest. When Carlyle's appointment of his literary executor was announced, I asked him why he had chosen Froude. He answered, ' Because of his reticence ! ' "

I should certainly have equally ascribed that character to Froude, and said so to Tennyson, whose distress at the publications was extreme. But I could not give any theory of the astounding affair. Tennyson's main trouble seemed to be that the bones of Carlyle should be flung about, and one evening he repeated to my wife and myself a quatrain he had composed about the delight of apes in seeing a man dragged down to their own apehood. The lines impressed me as mistaken. The people generally were as much troubled as Tennyson at the lowering of Carlyle. Carlyle had never flattered the people, he had become the great representative of antidemocratic tendencies, and they had paid him homage.

I had been haunted by apprehensions about Froude's fitness for his great task even before Carlyle's death. One day, when he was already at work on the papers, I called. He gave me the letter written me just before her death by Mrs. Carlyle which I had given Carlyle. Froude read me from one of Mrs. Carlyle's letters to her husband a merry anecdote about a titled lady in London, and then said gravely, " I hardly feel that I can print that story." I was amazed that the thought of publishing it could even occur to him. It was a fair enough bit of gossip for a wife to amuse her husband with, and decidedly witty, but quite unprintable. I went off with an uneasy mind. As Froude got deeper in his work his friends saw less of him. I have often mourned that William Allingham and I, who had so long and intimately worked with him on " Fraser," did not together offer our assistance in assorting the enormous mass of letters and papers by which Froude was overwhelmed.

In going over again the miserable events that followed the publication of Carlyle's " Reminiscences " and Froude's biography, I have reached the conclusion that Froude never really knew the man. He appreciated his intellect, but not the by-ways of his genius, nor the depths of his heart. In talking over the matter with Tyndall, we agreed that the Carlyle we knew is not in the biography at all. I always, indeed, had observed Froude's simple awe in the presence of Carlyle ; I never knew an instance in which he uttered any difference of opinion from him.

With a mountain of material to master, and the most complex tangles that ever beset a biographer to be unravelled, — all requiring the utmost calmness of mind, — Froude fell into a panic lest some one might publish a biography of Carlyle before his appeared. He feared two or three writers, among them probably myself. He knew that I had a large collection of Carlyle's letters, and for seventeen years had been making notes of his conversations, and that in Edinburgh he had given me an outline of his life. Alas, Froude did not know how I loved him, and how gladly I would have made over to him every scrap I had, and furthered him in every way. The immensity of his task overwhelmed him; he could not keep a level head under it; he hurried unnecessarily. Carlyle's "Reminiscences" appeared full of *errata* and of things never meant for publication. In the biography, said Tyndall, "Froude damaged Carlyle and damned himself."

The burden of correcting two of the most serious errors in the biography fell on me. It was the most grievous burden of my literary life, but laid on me by every consideration of honour. One of these involved both Carlyle and his wife. Froude and I were once passing an evening with them, when I told Carlyle of a visit I had made at Ostend to George Catlin, the American artist, who had lived among the aborigines in the West and made pictures of them. Carlyle then told us of an early pamphlet by Catlin entitled "Shut your mouth!" In it Catlin related that the Mandan Indians believed that diseases entered by the mouth, and that the squaws took care to close the mouths of their sleeping children, who consequently never had measles, scarlatina, etc. Catlin adopted this theory, and Carlyle said he read his brochure with interest. Then Mrs. Carlyle told us a merry story. Once, when more ill than usual, she hid it from Carlyle, whose work was very hard. One evening just after tea Carlyle began to read and she lay on the sofa gasping, when he turned and said, "Had n't you better shut your mouth?" She said she felt like throwing the teacup at him. It turned out, however, that

Carlyle had perceived the trouble she was trying to conceal, and in his anxiety it had occurred to him that Catlin's
prescription, "Keep your mouth shut!" might help her.
Froude forgot the essential part of the story, said nothing
about Catlin and his book, and, instead of the narrative by
which Mrs. Carlyle told of her husband's anxiety for her,
made it an example of his rudeness in bidding her shut her
mouth. As I was the only witness who could tell the true
incident, I felt bound to do so. Carlyle was never rude to
his wife. Even if she made a provoking remark he took it
meekly. When Carlyle stormed about anything it was about
some large question; he was gentle and submissive in simply
personal matters.

The other case I had to correct was a mistake of far-reaching effect. Froude wrote: "His mother early described him
as 'gay ill to live with.'" This became a sort of proverb in
Froude's mind; in his biography he four times winds up a
statement with the sentence: "Gay ill to live with." The
family were astounded; nothing could be more untrue. As
Mrs. Austin had told me on the day before the funeral, and
Dr. John Carlyle many a time, Carlyle had been in childhood, boyhood, youth, of amiable disposition, and always the
delight of his mother. Mrs. Alexander Carlyle (Mary Aitken)
told me that it was notorious in the family that her uncle
was pleasant to live with. Whence, then, came Froude's four-
times repeated proverb? In one of Mrs. Carlyle's letters to
her husband (afterwards published) she humorously puts
in, "Thou's gay ill to deal wi'." To this Carlyle added the
footnote: "Mother's allocution to me once in an unreason-
able moment of mine." It will thus be seen that a fond mother's momentary expression to a momentarily naughty child,
that he was hard to *deal* with, had been transformed into
her "description" of a son, who was the joy of her life, as
hard to *live* with. "Mother's allocution to me once," not forgotten by the devoted son, is taken from his own pen and
hung up as the maternal portraiture. That it was retouched
by Froude with such intent is not to be thought of. He had

long believed that such a genius, sometimes strong and lucid, must be hard to live with in the domestic circle, and, having projected the man into the child, read the word " live " instead of " deal," — assisted no doubt by Carlyle's penmanship. After my letter in the London " Athenæum " the misquotation was of course altered in the next edition, but alas, the error can never be overtaken. For on that error, that Carlyle was " gay ill to live with," Froude's whole theory was founded ; his work is pervaded by it. Carlyle has passed into history as a bad son. Also as a bad husband, though this is as far from the truth as the other notion.

An old physician related to the Welshes, who knew Mr. and Mrs. Carlyle well, told me that though they might have been less liable to occasional fretfulness if there had been a baby, they were by no means unhappy ; and Mrs. Alexander Carlyle, who often staid with the Carlyles, said to me, " If uncle and aunt lived unhappily I never discovered it, none of their relations knew it, and I am sure they did not know it themselves. Mr. Froude alone knows it."

As to this, I could not doubt that Froude's imagination had been misdirected by the imagination of Mrs. Carlyle, who not only printed a fairy-tale, but wove a little romance around herself which she made the mistake of confiding to Mazzini. The great Italian, also romantic, could readily take her confidence seriously — especially as Carlyle was indifferent to his cause. In all that Ashburton affair Carlyle was, I am sure, intent solely on the exaltation of his wife. He had vowed when he married her against the wishes of her proud relatives that he would place her in society far above them all. When finally the doors of that society were opened to her a meddlesome friend excited her suspicion that she was invited simply by social necessity as Carlyle's wife. It was untrue ; Mrs. Carlyle, though she had not Carlyle's depth of feeling, was attractive and piquant in society. But she refused the position he had achieved solely for her, and compelled him to fulfil certain social obligations alone. Mrs. Carlyle was ill advised, and was morbid under the consequences of her social action, but I feel certain that she never fell into the insanity of suspecting her husband's moral character.

The two instances of inexactitude in the biography in which I felt bound to testify seemed to classify me with all of Froude's censors. Knowing well how the sensitive hearts of Froude and his children were being torn, I grieved deeply during the affair. While deploring his lack of judgment which had thrown us all into such distress, I knew well Froude's veracity, and my love for him remained as unchanged as my love of Carlyle ; the break in our relations gave me abiding pain ; for a long time I met him in my dreams and would awake with tears. It gave me profound satisfaction when he was appointed professor of history in Oxford.

The last time I ever saw this beloved friend was in Westminster Abbey, October 12, 1892, at the funeral of Lord Tennyson. From my seat in the choir I could see the pallbearers some distance away, but so changed was Froude that only when he was a few yards off did I recognize him. Again I went home to have my dream, and in it clasp his hand once more. That was the last.

NOTE. — This chapter, and all relating to Carlyle and his wife, were written before the publication (1903) of *New Letters and Memorials of Jane Welsh Carlyle*, and of Froude's posthumous pamphlet, *My Relations with Carlyle*. I conclude to let my testimonies stand without alteration, and shall not here mingle in the revived discussion further than to express my certainty that if there were ever any " blue marks " on Mrs. Carlyle's arm caused by Carlyle it was not done to inflict injury but to save her from it.

CHAPTER XXXIX

Belgium at the outbreak of the Franco-German war (1870) — Paris and theatrical war — Strasburg camps — Basle — The International League — Freiburg — The female telegraph corps — Rastadt, Carlsruhe, in war-time — The King and Bismarck at St. Avold — Talk with Bismarck — Incidents at Pont-à-Mousson — The battle of Gravelotte — Otto Gunther — A dreadful night — Travelling on the car roof — Wiertz' painting of "Bonaparte in Hell."

In 1870 I was looking forward to a happy vacation, the main pleasure of which was to be the Passion Play at Oberammergau. But the year was to be marked by a great Passion Tragedy. In the middle of July I received by cable a request from Manton Marble of the "New York World" to be his war correspondent on the French side. I consented to act through August. I tried to reach the French army near Metz by way of Belgium. The first note of war had desolated Ostend. In quiet old Bruges and other towns drums were beating and soldiers drilling. On July 24 the London "Times" printed, by Bismarck's authority, a treaty proposed to him by France, involving the absorption of Belgium. The Grand Duke Vladimir of Russia was enjoying King Leopold's hospitality in Brussels, and his serene face was in contrast with that of the King. There was ill feeling toward the King because the stock of a national bank had been removed to Antwerp; also it was rumoured that the King and Queen had sent their jewelry and treasure to London for safety. I saw the tall monarch with his big nose, heavy beard, and swarthy face pass before his troops without exciting enthusiasm; but later his lovely wife with her soft eye and pure complexion received loud plaudits on her drive.

The American minister was then at Spa, and our consul being always out, I sought advice of the French minister. He informed me that France was entirely open as before to travellers, with exception of the immediate circle of military occupation.

The preliminaries of the war repeated those in America. Every hour rumours of fights that proved fictitious; of desertions from this side or that; of the romantic female spy; of immense bribes refused or accepted by statesmen; of secret treaties. For one glad hour cheers rent the air because some mediator had secured peace at the last moment; it shone like a rainbow, like a rainbow vanished.

I made my way to Paris slowly. The city was in a state of enthusiasm. There was a childlike confidence in the chassepot that could " kill at five or six hundred metres farther than the needle-gun ; " and faith in the supernatural mitrailleuse was religious. The theatres were crowded, and in every one appeared some finely draped " La France," bearing the tricolour, always amid the choral " Marseillaise." I went to the Grand Opéra, where " Masaniello " was performed. All the most rebellious lines were cheered wildly. At the end, when the " Marseillaise " was called for, there was tumult because the orchestra did not strike up at once; but the manager had prepared a fine surprise : the stage was presently filled with a genuine troop brought from a neighbouring station. Then all shouted out the revolutionary song. The beautiful " La France " was heroically draped. I went to my hotel remembering a sentence I heard from Emerson : " The French will have things theatrical; God will have things real." I did not feel enthusiastic for this Jehovistic realism. How much pleasanter it would be all round if the conflict could be limited to fine parades of pretty girls and tricolours and red lights and *tableaux vivants*, instead of those horrible *tableaux morts* of the real field !

While getting out my passport and other certificates to go to the front I encountered my old friend Murat Halstead of the " Cincinnati Commercial," and we became comrades.

We started on July 31 for Metz, and for most of the way had a compartment to ourselves; but at length a fine looking gentleman entered. We went on talking about old times without noticing the Frenchman, who, however, opened his coat, revealed his official riband, and asked if we were going to Metz. We explained our purpose and showed our passports; but he warned us of disappointment at Metz: we would be unable to approach the camps or to learn any news, and would be necessarily under surveillance. Despite this discouragement Halstead determined to go on, but I alighted at the next station, where I got a train to Strasburg. There everything was so open that I made up my mind that the military commander there, McMahon, must consider himself on a picnic. Early in the afternoon of the next day appeared Halstead, coming fortunately to my hotel. He had a dismal story to tell of Metz. "It was hard to find a lodging. At last I was conducted to a hotel where, after considerable persuasion, the landlord consented to be answerable for my remaining for one night only. Early next morning officers were at my door, and after careful examination of my papers said I might remain for a time inside the fortification. One step beyond was death. This amounted to being corked up in a bottle. I could not move without being watched; one individual was met at every step. The people there are furiously patriotic and eager to show it. There is anxiety lest an assassin should be lurking about; dread of spies, and special dread of correspondents. I was not satisfied with my bottled condition. I decanted myself."

We were surprised at the freedom with which we moved about Strasburg. We visited the suburban camp (Kehl) of the many-coloured Turcos, most of them, however, walking rather tipsily, *grisettes* on arm and bliss on their shiny faces. There was a sensation one day over the arrest of a woman found on the French shore of the Rhine where she had been set down by a German boat which swiftly glided back. The operation was observed; the officers stationed near the scene found a woman closely veiled; the veil was withdrawn and a heavily bearded face revealed. The spy in woman's clothes was hurried to the guard-house where only men were lodged. But this prisoner's clamorous alarm at being left there all night caused an investigation. She turned out to be a famous " bearded woman " exhibiting at Mayence when the war broke out. As she was a native of France the Germans had carried her out of their lines.

When Halstead left Metz a telegram about him left also, and at dawn (August 2) he was awakened and his papers overhauled. We found during the day that we were suspected of writing for journals; wherein we were sustained by the sweet consciousness of guilt. It was difficult to imagine the function of a French correspondent under the circumstances. Edmond About was there in Strasburg representing the " Figaro," and I have little doubt that one of his charming novels chiefly occupied his time. Not being willing to let my friend Manton Marble be unrepresented altogether, I resolved to go to the Germans. We were astonished at the ease with which we got to Basle. Just before reaching the frontier a family of poor people were set down on the roadside with their bundles, far away from any house. But our passports were not inquired after. I was afterwards assured by a French official that the exact facts concerning every person on the train were known to the authorities before it left Strasburg.

The excitement in Switzerland was intense; and indeed I was often reminded here, as in Belgium, of the divided condition of Maryland and Kentucky in the civil war. After we had passed the frontier a Swiss fellow-traveller said : " You see, sir, we Swiss love freedom. That is our bond with Germany. Then we have German blood in our veins. So you will find that the working people in Switzerland are not fond of the French dynasty. But our rich men — oh, our rich men make all their money out of France! Do you see those magnificent houses ? " — we were now in Basle — " the men in them own millions of money and all in francs and napoleons. They are for France."

There was continual danger that there might be an outbreak. There had just been held in Basle a *congrès extraordinaire* of the International League of " Peace and Liberty."

The chief centre of this league was in Basle; as I took them more seriously than my comrade, I left him to other objects of interest and sought out the peacemakers. I found it difficult to discover the Capitol of the United States of Europe, of which wayfarers had never heard. Nevertheless it was discovered, — being simply the neat little parlor of a Swiss workingman who had begun the work of union by marrying a brilliant Frenchwoman. This lady appeared to me as one who was high-born and had made a marriage similar to those of royal personages, that is, for the sake of the European situation. I soon found, however, that her husband was a man of ability and worth. He hastily summoned for my benefit the leaders of the Basle branch, which bore the name of the "International Association of Workingmen." This was because the general "Ligue Internationale de la Paix et de la Liberté" frightened some of the working class by their extreme radicalism, especially by their disposition to do away with old-fashioned ideas of marriage.

The lady was eloquent even in English, and must have been the chief speaker at their assemblies. I wrote down at my hotel the subjoined notes of her conversation : —

There is not even a grain of truth in the charges made against us, or against our members in London and Paris. We generally hate Napoleon, but assassination is not our plan. We should be glad if every throne in Europe and every aristocracy were overthrown, and we would join in a revolution against them; but to kill this or that man, however odious, would not serve our purpose. Until the people are ripe, the death of Napoleon would but vacate the seat for some other Napoleon, and it would be the same with Bismarck, whom we also hate. Our dependence is on the press; that is, on the education of the people to know their rights and to appreciate their power to secure their rights. Some of us belong to the *bourgeoisie*, but the vast majority of our six or seven thousand members are poor working people — very poor. Yet they put together their little means and give them freely only for two purposes: one, the support of our newspapers; the other, to support the families of labourers on strike in any part of Europe. We are all freethinkers. We have nothing to do with the churches, but have a Sunday gathering, where freethinkers lecture and debate.

The president, J. H. Frey, gave me a good photograph of the five leaders, who were all present: Volckardt, treasurer; Schmidli, standard-bearer; Starki, secretary; Vetterli, vice-president. Behind them in the picture is their banner, the device a triangle with rays; above it written *Keine Pflichten ohne Rechte;* and beneath, *Keine Rechte ohne Pflichten.* I was sorry the handsome lady was not in the picture. They also gave me a copy of the appeal put forth in all European languages by the recent International Congress. Above it is their motto: *Si vis pacem, para libertatem.*

APPEL AUX PEUPLES DE L'EUROPE!

A horrible, a barbarous war has been declared between two great civilized peoples.

We cannot prevent it; it will take its course. Meanwhile, we have regarded it as our most sacred duty to proclaim anew, on the immediate frontiers of the two belligerent nations, that such wars, which have not for their end the liberation of peoples, but the satisfaction of dynastic ambitions, can never be avoided until the peoples shall possess free self-government, and decide their own lot.

In this supreme moment, when, it is said, the only word to be spoken must come from the cannon, we will add one also for right, for reason, and for humanity. We make our appeal to the people: that in the face of burning villages and smoking battlefields, in the face of the frightful butchery made by new engines of destruction, amid the ruins, the miseries, the crimes of all sorts which make up the hideous cortège of war, they shall swear with us to labour to conquer for themselves such forms of government as shall render forever impossible the renewal of these fratricidal strifes, and shall secure, in conformity with the principles of our league, the arrival of the *United States of Europe.*

In the name of the Congress:

> Jules Barni, president; Armand Goegg, vice-president; John Rollanday, secretary general; J. Gerber, president of the Basle Committee; J. J. Bohny, secretary; Mme. Mary Goegg, in the name of the women.

This proclamation was laughed at by those who were leading France into war " with a light heart," but before a year had passed they were appealing to that same international society to try and lower the demands of the German conqueror.

That famous phrase of Olivier about the "light heart" had seemed at Strasburg to pervade all the air. There was universal laughter, universal sipping of absinthe, and the music halls were in their glory. At Freiburg a deathlike silence reigned. Halstead and I were the only guests in a hotel generally filled with summer tourists. The cathedral was silent; its famous organ found no listener; the peasant women in their yellow stove-pipe hats or bow-knot headdresses sat desolate in the market-place beside untouched pyramids of fruit.

Finding that we must wait until after midnight before travelling farther, I went to visit a family connected with a Cincinnati friend (Mr. Garlichs), and passed the evening with them. The head of the family was a distinguished citizen and scholar, and the ladies refined and gracious. But they were in dread of the " ferocious Turcos ! " The accounts were so exaggerated that I made a note of them for my studies in demonology. The demons of the Black Forest may partly have been developed in imaginative terrors of threatening and unknown invaders. As we sat on the veranda in the evening sipping our wine, I gave an account of my visit to the Turcos' camp, and my report of their merry ways and their countenances, indicating less cruelty than those of the whites, somewhat soothed their fears.

The chief monument in Freiburg is that of old Schwartz, discoverer of gunpowder. Its bas-reliefs represent him in his laboratory, and one of them shows him starting back in terror at the explosion of a mixture. But how would the old chemist have started back had he seen all that was to come of his damnable invention ! What would he have said had he seen that cloud of smoke taking shape as the genius of destruction, and known that it would hover over the happy homes of those who honoured him with this monument !

My credentials and the Freiburg gentleman secured for us the confidence of a commander at the station. We had several hours to wait for a train to Carlsruhe, and sent telegrams to our wives and our papers.

All the amusements of Freiburg were closed, but none of them could have been so entertaining as the large military telegraph room on the station platform. Its walls were glass, and we saw inside long past midnight more than a hundred busy operators, — all young women. One or two fine-looking women moved about from point to point for supervision, but no man approached nearer than to convey authorized despatches through the wicket. Gazing in at these damsels working like bees in their hive, I felt as if I were seeing amid the desolation of war one little oasis of civilization. The commander told me that in such service they employed only women. I inferred that it was because the young men were all bearing arms, but he said, " Men cannot be trusted in this kind of work like women. Every fräulein in there feels that on the exactness and promptness of the despatch she is sending the fate of Germany may depend. They are more conscientious than men ; you might watch here a month and never see one of them dozing."

We reached Offenburg by rail ; thence on the top of a poor old stage started across the country by way of Achern and Bühl, seeing in every village crowds of people in their picturesque Sunday costume gathered around old trees on which posters announced " Great Victories " at Wörth and Weissenburg. In the distance we saw the minster of Baden-Baden. Poor Baden ! The little railway that had borne to it so many pleasure-seekers was now cut off. Five hours short of Rastadt our vehicle broke down. We secured a wagon that Halstead found nondescript, but which I recognized as one of the sort that used to carry wheat in old Virginia, — fifteen feet long, five wide, without springs, and with plank seats.

It was about ten at night when we rumbled into Rastadt. It was silent as a tomb. Strasburg, just across the river, was noisy until one o'clock. In all the German towns through which we passed there was this sad silence, and it was reflected in every face. I telegraphed to Manton Marble, New York, that he might prepare for the defeat of France.

The war minister of Baden warned us that the road on which we were about to enter was fearful, — lined with confusion and terror, every village crowded with the dead and wounded. On the way to Homburg we travelled on a long, crawling train of freight wagons, seated on the floor with soldiers whose main talk was of the hoofed and horned Turcos. We entered France in a luxurious first-class car, the only fault of which was that after a good sleep we awoke before daybreak to find our compartment motionless on a side track and solitary. We were in little Faulquemont; and in the still car began writing our narratives. At length our car moved on and overtook the royal headquarters at St. Avold.

The French in evacuating St. Avold had left there no food or drink, nor even a cigar. The curses heaped by the German soldiers on the French for carrying warfare to such an extreme of barbarity as the removal of tobacco may be imagined.

An amusing little difficulty arose in our way. Halstead's first name was Murat, and had been given him in honour of the famous French soldier. His father had not foreseen that his son would one day be dependent on German favours in a war against France. There had been no way of escape from that unfortunate name Murat. Had he used only the initial "M" that must have stood for Monsieur, and indeed the first name had to be in the passport. This difficulty was enhanced by the disposition of the few French people remaining in St. Avold to regard us (being without uniform) as countrymen.

We wandered into the ancient church. In it were three men, fourteen women, and three children (French), while two German soldiers said their prayers near the door. The pale priest went through mass with a scarce audible voice, and the little assembly vanished like a mist.

As we came out we saw the King at his window. While we were looking at the King there passed by us and approached

the royal headquarters a shapely giant in dark blue uniform
faced with gold, swiftly recognized as Bismarck. Before entering the door he scanned the street. Among the uniforms
we were the two black streaks. The chancellor held up his
forefinger to us as we were moving off. We approached him,
and he met us half way. "Where are you from, gentlemen,"
he asked, "and whither bound?" (Woher kommen Sie, meine
Herren, und wohin gehen Sie?) I said, "We are Americans,
and are writing for the press of that country." He then said
in English, "You are welcome. We are very glad to have
American writers among us and with our army. The only
thing that the officers will expect from you will be proper
papers of legitimation. You have these?" We showed them,
and he said, "Very well; the freedom of everything will be
accorded you." Halstead said that the one thing he needed
was a horse, for which he would gladly pay whatever was
demanded. Bismarck said, "I fear that is the one thing we
cannot help you to; we are in France a nation on horseback,
and need every conveyance that can be obtained." "It seems
hard," said Halstead, "that an editor who desires only a horse,
and has money to pay for a horse, cannot get one." Bismarck
responded with a smile, "Have you not found it so in life,
that what one most desires is just that thing he cannot obtain?" He presently added that if we would go to an officer
whom he named, and show him our papers, he would assign
us seats in some conveyance. Bismarck then inquired about
our journey from Paris, and appeared surprised that we had
come so quickly. When we told him that we had had such
remarkable freedom among the forts at Strasburg he smiled,
and we observed that he put no questions to us about them.
He gave us several practical instructions. We would be quartered along with their officers and soldiers, and it might be
in private houses; the German officers always took careful
account of the services received from the French quarters,
and would repay them; but it was important that we should
not pay anything or give any fees, however small, to persons
who waited on us or gave us food; the soldiers were unable

to pay such fees, and if we should do so they might be jealous or suspicious that we were receiving favours. We must be careful not to carry any weapon, — otherwise if taken by the French we might not be treated as correspondents ; at any battle we should stay near the King, which would always be the safest place. We thanked him, bowed to the King, who returned the salute, adding a little gesture with his hand, and started off ; but were presently overtaken by General Kranski of the King's household, who told us that if we should be unable to procure food it would be given us at the King's headquarters.

The night at St. Avold was uncomfortable, the only bed in the hotel to be obtained being the edge of a billiard-table, the better portions of which were occupied by more fortunate sleepers. I was apparently the only one in the crowded room who could not sleep. About two in the night there was a knock at the door opening on the street. It was not answered, and was repeated several times with increasing loudness. At length I went out to the door, and a messenger thrust into my hand a large envelope, said something I did not understand, then disappeared quickly. By the light of a dim lamp in the hall I made out the name of Moltke on it. Going softly upstairs I found a German soldier sitting outside a bedroom door. I inquired for General Moltke's door, and was told it was there. I waited to see the soldier take the envelope into the room and return, then went off to my billiard-table edge. (My reader will, no doubt, ascribe this incredible incident to nightmare.)

In the morning we sought the officer who was to aid us, and found a spectacled young man reading a volume of Shakespeare (English), who took us in charge. He was in command of a telegraph corps, and gave us a seat in his buggy. His function was to keep up a telegraphic connection between the King's headquarters and Germany. Our polite friend was eager to air his English.

We several times found ourselves in an American atmosphere ; we had been drawn the day before successively by two engines, one labelled "America," the other "Philadelphia;" and now, as we started, a troop passed singing in English the John Brown song; they were Germans come from America to fight for the Fatherland.

On our journey through Nomény and Remilly to Pont-à-Mousson we came upon some French tents. The officers there had been captured by the Prussians just as they had sat down to a fine champagne dinner. I got out of the buggy to look at them, and felt pity at their doleful faces, especially that of one handsome young officer. On returning to my seat I missed my fine new overcoat. An order was given for an exchange of these French prisoners, and as they drove off I saw my overcoat on that same handsome French officer who had so moved my compassion! The movements were too quick to make any reclamation, and I had to put up with my loss.

At Remilly our telegraph corps had to part from the main army and go across country. We had a small military escort, for we were in danger. It was beautiful weather, and we passed picturesque villages which on such fair Sundays once knew only gaiety, but were now silent as cemeteries. We had need of information as to the road we should take, but it was difficult to coax any one close enough to give us direction; at one time we started on a road that would have led us upon the batteries of Metz. On one occasion, seeing a pleasant-looking young woman sitting some twenty yards off at a door in a village, our leading officer called out: —

"Come here, my dame!"

The woman was frightened and began to retreat.

"Come, come," said the officer.

The woman began to weep.

"Have no fear, good woman; you shall not be harmed; I only wish to ask you the way."

The officer's voice was so pleasant that the woman became encouraged a little, and having approached very timidly still, gave the best direction she could in her confusion. Having received this, the officer said: "Why did you weep when I spoke to you?"

"Oh, sir, I am in great fear; my poor husband has been taken away from me; I am alone."

The simple pathos with which she said this was what the most accomplished actress could not surpass.

"Your husband taken away?" asked the officer; "and by whom?"

"By the Prussians."

"How taken? For what purpose?"

"To drive a wagon to No-mény."

"Ah," said the officer, relieved; "we have now and then to use the men as well as the resources of the neighbourhood we are going through; but you need have no fear whatever; your husband is much safer than if he were not working for us; he will be paid, and I promise you, my good woman, that he will return to you in a few days at most. You will find that the Prussians are by no means such barbarians as you have heard."

The woman looked up with swimming, but now smiling eyes.

The German troops did not behave well in Pont-à-Mousson. In other towns they had been unable to obtain anything, and on arriving here they rushed to the tobacco shops and helped themselves, in many cases without paying, and in some breaking the glass over the tobacco. They felt that they had a right to do this, tobacco in France being a government monopoly. But very little tobacco had been left, and nothing to eat. In our hotel was a cellar of Moselle wine, but not an atom of food, and as the German sutlers had been held up by a French force, Halstead and I had to pass thirty hours without even a morsel of bread. We breakfasted, dined, supped on wine.

One evening, to our joy, a French beer saloon opened. We hastened to it and took several courses of bock. In payment I handed the proprietor a napoleon. He immediately folded up the gold in a bit of paper and gave it to a woman who disappeared. When at length I asked for my change the saloon-keeper angrily declared I had given him only a franc, and opened his drawer to show that no gold was in it. "Just because I am French and alone, and you surrounded by friends, you wish to impose on me!" I concluded to lose my francs rather than make a fuss, and left. We explored what few shops were open, with the hope of finding sardines or olives; in vain! We had to live on sparkling Moselle. How poor it had become beside beer! Were not four bocks worth a napoleon? So we asked ourselves, in reconsidering a resolution to withhold our patronage from that saloon-keeper. The August sun melted me to forgiveness. As soon as I entered the saloon the old man rushed at me from behind his bar, raised his hands, put them on my shoulders, and said, " I have not slept, because in making up accounts last night I found your louis. Monsieur, it was genteel of you to leave it instead of getting me into trouble with my enemies." The old man as he handed me the napoleon actually shed tears. It was forenoon, and no other person was present. He said, " Do you need anything to eat?" I told him that we were starving. " Then, messieurs, if you cross the bridge at one o'clock this day, turn to your right at the other end, go on till you come to the second gate, enter and walk to the house, you will find something to eat." We remembered the offer of food at the King's headquarters in case of need, but felt shy about it, and though warned against snares we made our way half a mile out of town to the house indicated. He and his wife received us with effusion, and there was set before us a dinner of lamb-chops and vegetables which I always remember as the most delicious meal I ever tasted in my life. Thirty hours of starvation can turn chops to terrapin and onions to canvas-back ducks and claret to nectar. Nor could we induce these two grateful people to receive money for a dinner worth to us at the moment so much more than the restored nineteen francs. In the late afternoon, however, when we took coffee at their saloon in town, I laid down a napoleon and said, " This time, monsieur, I refuse to receive any change." The old man and his wife bowed low, and their smile amid the terrors surrounding them was cheaply purchased.

The King drove rapidly into Pont-à-Mousson in a plain

open French voiture, preceded by an escort bearing drawn swords. The soldiers crowding the streets gave loud cheers, and Moltke saluted. Bismarck had previously entered the town incognito, but now walked on the street. I was in a chocolate shop when in it the word was caught from tongue to tongue — " Bismarck! " All crowded to the door, and sure enough, there was the great tall man, apparently taking notice of nothing.

Although the delay of the sutlers had not prevented the soldiers from having their rations, it had withheld the supply of tobacco. I inquired of an officer at our quarters the reason for the unusual delay in that town ; he replied that it was because no army could be sent into a field of battle without plenty of tobacco. Thus the " Great Plant," which had played so important a part in the political history of America, England, and France was still determining events.[1]

About four miles beyond the bridge there is a superb hill crowned with a picturesque ruin. Halstead and I had gone up there with a number of German officers who were taking a military view of the country. A troop of soldiers were stationed on the height, which commanded a view of the Moselle up and down for a great distance, and an officer near me spoke of that river as " the natural boundary of Germany."

At Pont-à-Mousson I strolled into the old church (St. Martin's). A few women were there, who did not lift their heads from their prayers. I gazed upon a fine old window representing princely St. Martin on his steed, dividing his cloak with his sword to give half to the beggar. The solemn quiet was invaded but faintly by martial sounds, and I sat dreaming of the happy era when swords shall be beaten into scissors and needles to make cloaks for the shivering.

One day when I was in a shop a German soldier entered and managed to indicate that he wanted a pocket-knife. The price was named ; he put down a few groschen, much less than the price, and went off. " This is the way we are

---

[1] See my " Barons of the Potomack and the Rappahanock," *Tobacconalia*. (Grolier Club volume, 1892.)

robbed," said the woman at the counter, bursting into tears. I told her I thought the difficulty had been that she had not been understood and that it would be well to study the German coinage. The husband who had just entered said to me, "You seem to belong to some other country." I explained that I was there as a neutral to write an account of events. "Ah," he replied, "it may be well we should know this. Any little turn of affairs might bring about wild scenes in Pont-à-Mousson, and if any riot should occur you had better come to my house, and my wife and I will see that you are safe."

On the day of the Virgin Mary, August 15, there was the fête as usual, but on the 17th a great number of peasants came into the town, and had the battle of Gravelotte turned out differently the wild scenes might have occurred.

Halstead and I were now supplied with food but suffering from the tobacco famine. While strolling on the bridge we saw the first sutler wagon entering the town, ran to it, and bought each a bundle of a hundred cigars. Hurrying back in triumph to deposit our treasures in our room, we met four soldiers, who incontinently rushed upon us, snatched both bundles of cigars and took to their heels. We had to conclude that the cigars were bad, also a valuable contribution by us to the German cause; but found it more consoling that the tobacco famine was at an end.

We had been assigned a room over a barber's shop, previously occupied by an English correspondent, who had left English papers, the only ones I had seen for a fortnight.

Having time on our hands, we resolved to visit again the Pont-à-Mousson castle on its height. Taking our lunch we walked to the summit, where we were amazed to find absolute solitude. We at once felt it imprudent to venture so far from the protection of the army and turned to go away. Just then from behind the ruin came forth a huge man in labourer's blouse, who had menace in his eye and a sickle in his hand. Presently two other men, one armed in the same way, advanced and stood squarely across our path. One of them spoke German and asked, "Are you Germans?"

"No," I answered in French, "we are Americans."

We now saw a fatal steel-like look in the eyes of these men; their voices trembled.

One of them held a little piece of a German paper in his hand, very dirty, and evidently picked from the ground. He held it in one hand, his other being kept behind his back.

"Will you please," he said to me in French, "read me what is on this paper."

I took the paper and stumbled along with the German text. I fear I hàrdly did the instructions of my old teacher justice in my pronunciations. We showed our passports, but there was no French visé on either and one of them remarked that it was easy to get passports in any land. The man who talked German observed closely the little bundle under my arm; it was our luncheon, which I had wrapped in a copy of the London "Sunday Times" found in our room, and I placed it in his hands. He examined the paper carefully, tried to spell out the words; his countenance lost some of its darkness, and he said to his comrades, "They are not Germans." Thereon they all moved off about forty feet behind a wall of the ruin perhaps for consultation. We needed no consultation for retreat, and when we reached the edge of the hill saw the men emerge with three sickles instead of the previous two. Instead of going along the road we entered into a field thick with tall hop-vines which were friendly enough to two unarmed journalists.

When we reëntered Pont-à-Mousson there were terrible scenes. Wounded men were pouring in from the front, where there had been a sharp engagement. Bismarck had told us that when it was known that a battle was to occur he would notify us, and about one o'clock in the night a messenger knocked at our door and informed us that the army was advancing towards Vionville, where there had been fighting. We at once found our telegraph buggy, but at the tail of the vast great army it moved too slowly and we concluded to walk. After a substantial meal at a peasant's house on the roadside, we travelled on until we came to the foot of a range of low hills covered with thick woods, the Bois des Ognons. It was hardly daybreak, but the thunder of cannon suddenly began, rolling up as if from the interior of the hills. Passing through the village of Gorze, twelve miles from Pont-à-Mousson, to the high plain beyond, we reached fields strewn with bodies, some not yet dead — the battlefield of Vionville. Seeing on a particular hill the King and his Cabinet, we approached them.

Looking thence over the vale, I saw against the horizon a village of bright houses gathered around a pretty steeple and all the bright sky dotted with white fleecy clouds, as if at some fête numberless little balloons were sent up. We could even hear music, and on the meadows beneath the garden terraces of Gravelotte multitudes seemed to be dancing. Ah, the field-glass reveals another picture : the snow-white balloons are bursting shells ; the music is ground out of the revolving mitrailleuse ; and on the meadows beneath is the dance of Death. Forever filing out of the Bois des Ognons is an interminable German line, crawling like some huge black snake towards the high village, but in its farther part are many gaps ; only segments of the serpent are struggling up the terraces. And how slowly !

The chieftains near us sit on their horses, nearly a score ; among them I recognized the King, Von Moltke, Bismarck, Prince Adelbert the King's brother, Adjutant Kranski, and the American General Sheridan. Every now and then a messenger from the front rides up furiously and hands a paper to Von Moltke, — who looks like a fleshless death's-head beside the florid King. Von Moltke passes the new missive unopened to the King, who opens and formally glances at it, then returns it, really unread, to Von Moltke. The great commander reads it and makes a suggestion to the King, who declares that opinion to be his own, and the messenger rides off swiftly with it.

A company of cavalry dashes up from behind, and in passing salutes the King and his Field Cabinet. One of them by a wave of his hand exchanges a special salute with Bismarck : it is his son. Several of the grand personages dismounted, among them Prince Adelbert, who spoke pleasantly to me, and dotted on the back of my passport the positions of the various corps at the front. Bismarck sheltered himself from the burning sun for a time under a picket tent.

Then came from some mysterious region behind us, as if sprung from the earth, an army that marched forward only some thirty yards on our left, all singing the "Watch on the Rhine." Afterwards we saw many of their foremost men in death agonies on the ground, while still behind us were advancing and singing their comrades, who a little farther on must suffer the like fate.

The mounted commanders had sat almost still as statues, but in the late afternoon there was a sensation among them — excitement — rapid words. The French had abandoned Gravelotte for a farther ridge. Not long after, the royal party dashed off towards Rézonville, a village on our left nearer Gravelotte. Halstead and I started to walk that way, but gave it up after a time and moved about the battlefield of the previous day, Mars-la-Tour and Vionville.

The dusk had begun to fall, and it became a serious concern where we could get food, and where lay our weary heads. At that moment I saw a young man without uniform seated on a stone about fifty yards from us. In his grey dress and stillness he was hardly distinguishable from the stone he sat on. On his knees was a portfolio, and guessing that he was a journalist, we approached. It was Otto Gunther, artist for the "Illustrirte Zeitung." He said he was assigned a place at the King's headquarters, and had been making sketches all day. He had noticed us. He spoke but little English, but I knew enough German to perceive that he was an interesting man. He promptly solved our personal problems by saying that in Gorze he had a room with two large beds and would be glad to have us share it. On our way we passed many dead bodies, and on the ground were strewn many knapsacks and weapons, — from which each of us took a French sword (kept, by the commander's consent, as souvenir of that

tragical eighteenth of August, 1870; for Germans will use
no sword that has been raised against their country). The
house to which we were assigned was the largest in Gorze. It
belonged to the leading citizen, an intelligent notary, who,
with his attractive wife, received us amicably, and provided
an excellent supper. They held their house under orders, and
no doubt hoped their burden would be restricted to us three
civilians. Since my arrival in France I had not enjoyed any
conversation so much as that of our attractive hosts, over
cigars and coffee. It was, however, necessary that we should
write our letters, and three tables were provided for us in our
grand room, just above the room opening on the street, which
it overlooked. Here Otto Gunther showed us the picture he
had made that day for his paper. It represented the King
and his entire Field Cabinet on their horses and the entour-
age. It was a fine drawing and I wanted it. He had to send
it off early in the morning and expressed his regret that he
could not gratify me. " But what would remunerate you, Herr
Gunther, for making another copy for the ' Illustrirte Zeitung' and letting me have this?" "Ah, I should have to
charge you fifty thalers." "I will pay it." And that night
till three Otto Gunther sat up copying the picture whose
original is now before me.

But indeed there was little sleep for either of us that night.
Between twelve and one began noises in front of the house,
and leaning out of our window I beheld a ghastly scene. A
bright full moon lit up the blood-stained features of many
wounded men, and had it not been that Gunther in addition
to his special assignment from the King's Cabinet had accommodated us, — authorized correspondents, — his room would
probably have been taken for the wounded. Going down-
stairs to find if I could be of any assistance to our gentle host
and hostess, I was told by the German surgeon that their aid
was ample.

But oh, the pity of it! There were the lovely lady and her
eighteen-year old daughter wiping blood from the wounded
bodies, half of them their countrymen. At dinner the ladies

had been able to smile, but now all smiles were gone out : their ashen faces and starting eyes were as if some engine of torture were sprung on them.

Leaning out of our window I beheld the whole street filled with ambulances, and at every door the horrors borne into homes whose quiet beauty had charmed me in the morning.

After our literally sleepless night the rosy dawn greeted us with a smile that seemed mockery, and in our pretty garden the flowers were blooming and the birds singing.

Even amid the frightful surroundings madame did not fail to give us an excellent breakfast. We decided that for once we must disobey Bismarck's warning not to offer any money for our entertainment ; but our hostess shook her head, and could hardly be persuaded to receive our contribution for the sufferers in the village. Presently, as we were leaving, I heard her say to a German officer, with a flash of her eyes, " we cannot receive money from Prussians." She had recognized my look of sympathy, and in parting expressed the hope that some day I might visit them in peaceful times.

Another thing to be remembered : as we passed through the front room it was crowded with wounded men, several of them conversing with each other, Prussians with Frenchmen, in friendly tones. I thought of the song of Jeannette to her soldier lover : —

> All the world should be at peace;
> And if kings must show their might,
> I 'd have those who make their quarrels
> Be the only ones to fight.

Returning to the field where we had stood the day before, I picked up a large number of letters scattered from torn knapsacks. Near one fine-looking German who lay dead was his diary, in which were verses full of devotion to his Fatherland. There were also some pathetic sentences. " I tremble when in the face of death, for it is hard to become a mere part of the soil of a foreign land." " We are all brothers marching perhaps not to return, but we shall at last be happy together." Most of the letters were from French wives and mothers giving tender details about the little ones, and their messages to papa, and some were from sweethearts. They were all affecting. I afterwards sent them in a package to the French government.

While strolling across the field a bullet sang close to my head, and I perceived that it came from a German who was collecting weapons scattered about the field. He fired off every rifle before pitching it into his wagon, and when I went to suggest that it were well enough to be cautious, he appeared to be surprised at my thinking any one man's life of such importance.

We passed through several of the little villages along the beautiful highroad to Metz, for the possession of which the battles of August 16, 17, and 18 had been fought. Houses were still burning in several of them, and of poor little Flavigny only a few blackened walls remained. It was pitiful to see the villagers there, the aged and demoiselles near their burnt houses. I spoke to two young girls, pretty enough to have been village belles. One of them had in her apron a little rice, scraped from the ground, — all she and her sister now possessed save the clothes (little enough) then on them. "*Ah, mon Dieu ! mon Dieu !*" one of them exclaimed, "what shall we do ? " "Do you live here ? " I asked. "We did live in the house at the corner there," pointing to some blackened walls, the interior of which was just sinking to ashes ; "now all we had is burnt up. Our friends have all run away, and we know not where they have gone. All last night we lay on the ground in the field out there." They then sat down on the side of the street and wept. "Here is some bread," said a rough German soldier, drawing his whole ration from his haversack.

Moving on towards Gravelotte, thirst tempted me to descend a precipitous bank where there was a spring ; but other thirsty souls had preceded me and it was difficult to ascend the slippery path. Just then the handle of a cane was extended to me, and I came up to find the famous correspondent, Archibald Forbes. He had not reached the place in time to witness the battle of Gravelotte, because of the incompetency of the horse he had somewhere bought, and which he was still leading rather than riding. We three walked together to Gravelotte, in our ascent to which we had to pick our way to avoid treading on the dead. The gardens were open sepulchres. We came at times on points where there had been struggles for the possession of some gun, the corpses were massed together. Beyond Gravelotte we came to a deep ravine where there had been a cavalry charge ; for a hundred yards it was a grave of Germans and their horses. The King and his generals were moving about the fields, and we had opportunity to converse with Sheridan, — an old friend of Halstead. He said, " The Prussians are winning, but it costs them dear."

Rézonville, being the centre of the Red Cross organization, suffered less than other villages. There we entered a restaurant to try and get something to eat ; we did not succeed ; but through an open back door I saw three grand officers enjoying a repast of fat bacon, black bread, and claret.

We had learned from Sheridan that headquarters would return that night to Pont-à-Mousson. That was the only route by which I might hope to reach home. Not only had I seen enough of war, but on the first Sunday in September my chapel would open. After a good supper at Gorze we started on foot for Pont-à-Mousson. It was not a pleasant prospect to walk the twelve miles of that road all night. Should we encounter another company of French peasants we might not escape as we did at Pont-à-Mousson Castle. A French peasant with an empty voiture drawn by a fagged-out horse was appealed to, and said he was going only five miles of our way ; but once in, gold did the rest. The weariness of the poor horse, which we relieved at every hill, did not weigh against the safety of being in charge of a French peasant. But the pace was very slow, and as we neared the town we could hardly move because of the enormous number of ambulances. When we entered in the small hours of the morning the scene was frightful. Moaning Germans with fearful wounds swarmed in the streets, entreating to be carried to their homes. The large square was an open-air hospital, where women were nursing the soldiers in their agony.

The excitement of the French in Pont-à-Mousson was tremendous. I saw a crowd of French people — peasants, bourgeois, women of all degrees, bareheaded and in dishabille — following a wagon in which were four grievously wounded French officers. On the front seat sat upright and stately General Latour, on his face an expression of self-respect mastering the agony of his head-wound. When the wagon stopped the street was blocked by the French and many wounded Prussian soldiers. The women rushed out of the houses with wine and other delicacies, hitherto hidden away, and the wounded Prussians began to grow angry. The French kissed the general's hand again and again. At the windows women and children were weeping and calling out with expressions of enthusiastic devotion. No attempt at repressing these demonstrations was made by the Germans, but one thing startled me: when the wagon stopped the French general hastily took from his pocket a large package and handed it to a woman without a word. The woman vanished with it.

Before leaving Pont-à-Mousson I went to take leave of the Frenchman and his wife who had been kind to me. " Ah," said the man with tears, " this has long been the most beautiful town on the Moselle, and the happiest. You see what it is now. For many years it will be a picture of war. But if it be still standing when peace comes, come hither again, and we shall take our coffee and cigars together, and talk of many things. For me, for my wife there, our lips are now sealed; we know not who is friend, who foe ; but we know how to do well by strangers, and shall not forget those who spoke to us in kind tones during this frightful week."

On our homeward journey we found at Remilly ghastly crowds of wounded Germans who had straggled seven or eight miles to this nearest station, hoping for places on the home-bound trains. It was here a contest between the claims of war and the cries of humanity, in which of course war had its way.

Along this road thousands of fresh soldiers were still pouring into France, and provisions for them, and only now and then could a train be got with its groaning freight the other way.

The scenes of agony at the stations on our road to Saarbrücken were heart-breaking, but the ministrations of mercy were heart-restoring. Everywhere were tables covered with the viands, delicacies, cooling drinks, freely given to all sufferers. Physicians — among them several English surgeons — were kneeling with anxious devotion by every couch of straw, and large numbers of refined young women were bathing and bandaging naked bodies and performing repulsive services with the gracious dignity of madonnas.

It was only with great difficulty that we made our way to the German frontier (Saarbrücken). The only train going that day was so crammed with the wounded that we could not ask places on it as travellers, but having provisions and cigars and wine we offered ourselves as nurses, and to give what we had to the wounded. This being found impracticable, we got behind the train as it was starting and climbed to the top of it. " The bridges are low and will knock you off ! " shouted an official who caught sight of us ; but it was too late. The front edge of the car-roof was flattened enough for seats, and there was no difficulty in lying on our backs to escape the bridges, so long as daylight lasted ; but the cars started in the late afternoon, and two thirds of our ten hours were passed in thick darkness and chilling mist. So we had to lie flat and keep awake.

It was after two o'clock in the night when we reached Saarbrücken. Numb with cold and painfully sleepy, we left the station to find a place to sleep, but the town was dark and silent. After much wandering we perceived a glimmer at one window, and though the house was small and repulsive we knocked at the door. It was opened by a surly old man who did not ask what we wanted, but silently pointed to a back door. Just as silently we went to that door and entered a large bare room, whose floor was covered with sleeping men. There were neither pallets nor pillows ; all lay on straw in their clothes, and we were joyful in finding a corner in which we could enjoy this experience in equality and fraternity.

We waked to a beautiful Sunday morning, and started on the great military train for Trèves. But alas, the terrors and pangs of war were not left behind. The train halted long at every station, each crowded with the inhabitants, — chiefly women and children, — pressing to hear tidings from their husbands, sons, brothers, fathers, who were in the war. We were creeping along the road, distributing wounded and dying men to their once happy homes, and dropping heavy tidings, answered with shrieks, till it seemed as if our wheels were crushing human hearts. Before our train could come to a stand in any place, women were clinging to its side, darkening every window with haggard faces, fiercely demanding, " Where is he ? " The fatal tidings might be conveyed by silence, hesitation, tears, but shriek after shriek all along the train told how many hearts were pierced. So far reaches every bullet! At times I was sick and faint. The earth yawned into one vast grave, the blue sky was a pall, the sun had turned to blood.

The railway bridges having been burned, we journeyed by voiture from Trèves to Luxembourg. It seemed shocking to find the people happy and peaceful; sipping their wine, playing écarté or billiards, talking of the war as if it were a big game of chess. On conversing with some at Luxembourg, I perceived that they were on the side that was to win, whichever that should prove.

At Brussels I met a gentleman who had been at Châlons when the Emperor arrived there after his escape from Metz. As he passed along, the soldiers of the Garde Mobile darted from their ranks and cried, "Assassin ! " The Emperor passed, with indescribable misery in his face, grasping the hand of the little Prince Imperial, who was trembling and weeping.

One of the most interesting things in Europe is the Wiertz Museum in Brussels, and the most powerful picture in it is that of " Bonaparte in Hell." On the large canvas the famous Corsican, with darkened countenance and starting eyes, moves through a fiery gulf whose surging waves on each side take the forms of ghastly, fleshless women, with outstretched arms holding out the bones of the husbands and sons slain in his wars. After witnessing the battle of Gravelotte, and the continuous moans and wailings on our homeward journey, this picture engraved itself upon me with the added pigments of my month on battlefields in a way ineffaceable.

Halstead went on to Paris. I reached the night-boat at Ostend, and on Monday morning was in London. No paper contained any news about Gravelotte. Having cabled my letter (the last) to the " New York World," I went to the offices of the " Daily News " and wrote a description of the great battle which was telegraphed throughout Europe and translated into all languages. It occupies ten pages in the first volume of the " War Correspondence of the Daily News, 1870 " (pp. 63–73).

For several weeks after reaching home my dreams were haunted by the dreadful scenes I had witnessed on the battlefields.

CHAPTER XL

In 1871, on the roof of University Library, Berlin, I saw the King review his victorious armies. Here expanded the million-leaved *Victoria regia* whose roots had been fed by that red flood in France. Minister Bancroft, whose hospitality I enjoyed, was full of enthusiasm at the rise of a Teutonic United States, and I was in joy that the Napoleonic nightshade had perished, but I could not enjoy the magnificent festival of the conquerors. From the moment when the bugles sounded the approach of the splended cortège, — those bugles that sounded the call to the slaughter at Gravelotte, — I saw the triumphal march of the King, princes, warriors, and their fine steeds trampling human beings. Just opposite University Library a dingy man had climbed up fifty feet and sat on the head of equestrian Frederick the Great waving his hat to every personage and equipage passing beneath him. I put that aspirant in my note-book ; he suggested to me the necessity of viewing the scene from the historic head of Germany's far past. But I could not rid myself of the thought of Mencius of China : " When a man says I know well how to draw up an army he is a great criminal. To be elated with victory is to rejoice in the destruction of human life. Those who have been victorious in battle are disposed in the order of a funeral."

The Berlin theatres were blazing with patriotic scenes, but at Kroll's there was a strange little play, " Berlin nach Paris."

A German soldier courts a French maiden, who accepts him because she knows "the Germans are always faithful." At that moment a German girl, the cross on her arm, appears and finds her lover in that "faithful" youth. It was well acted, and moved many to tears. Most of the pieces, however, were spectacular. The performances at the opera on Sunday evening were indescribably magnificent. All the royal family, the German princes, the military chiefs, the diplomatic corps (I sat with the Bancrofts), were present; the finest artists and dancers had been searched out for the ballets and tableaux. These represented the legend of Barbarossa, who after his slumber of ages awakens to find a united Germany. The awakened Barbarossa was an admirable make-up of the King, who from his box bowed in response to the plaudits. Beautiful Fräulein Erhart, as Germania, in a Greek war-dress, spoke finely the Prologue, during which she unveiled statues of Frederick the Great and Frederick William III. The final tableau represented the King — proclaimed Emperor — mounted on his horse in Paris; and suddenly unveiled all the States of Germany, — beautiful women, with heroically displayed forms, bearing the various ensigns.

At the desire of my friend, Mathilde Blind, I called on Frau Lewald in Berlin, who in the five years since the suicide of Ferdinand Blind, brother of Mathilde, had laid wreaths on the youth's tomb in the cemetery. Frau Lewald, a beautiful and accomplished lady, did not oppose me when I deplored the young man's attempt on Bismarck, but she regarded the Chancellor as the evil genius of Germany, and felt some satisfaction in his having alluded, in the Reichstag, to the decorating of that tomb by "ladies in high position." She said, "There are sorrows beneath all this joy. There will be no reaction in the movement for freedom in Germany. As for Christianity, no educated people in Berlin have real belief in it. The other day a preacher told the children of a school which my son attends that *belief* — in the New Testament sense of the word — was no longer expected. They must try to be good."

In one respect war had been more discriminate in Germany than in the Union war in America; it did not sweep off the youth of the universities. In America, war appealed to the brilliant and cultured young scholars with a pretext of liberty and humanity, but the Franco-German war was a mere duel between old antagonists on a quarrel about succession to the Spanish throne. It was a pawn game. But how close is hid the future! One sentence I find in my note-book of the royal cortège remarking, because of his youth, "The crown prince's son on a little dark grey horse." That is all. The evil fate of German literature was riding on that little dark horse.

At the house of Lepsius, to whom I brought letters, I met Curtius, the brothers Bunsen (Carl and Heinrich), Professor Alban Vorstadt, and others, — Gelzer of Basle and Blackie of Edinburgh being also there at a special evening company. The German professors were rejoicing that the war was over because of the turmoil, but were less inclined to talk about its results than we foreigners. When I asked Lepsius about the Egyptian devils he was amused, and said, "The living devils seem so numerous just now that one has hardly opportunity to study the dead ones — or anything else." But he gave me useful information for the lectures I was preparing on Demonology.[1] Curtius, too, was evidently tired of war-talk. He spoke excellent English, and had studied all English works on Greece. Grote he thought without taste for Greek art, while Thirlwall was better, but without feeling for Greek religion. Curtius had a fair, beardless, somewhat feminine face, and was an engaging man in conversation. I was rather surprised by those university men being so fine-looking. There in the elegant house of Lepsius — himself handsome, with his silken white hair and face full of sensibility — the German

[1] He said the forty-two judges of hell were the seeds of evil spirits. Every sin has a special spirit in Egypt. The serpent is there generally an agathodemon, but on some papyri seems to be evil. The serpent is called Uro (king), equivalent of basilisk ($\beta a\sigma i\lambda\epsilon\upsilon s$). On German demons I had the advantage of consulting Dr. Dorner, whom Bancroft knew; he gave me a list of useful works on my subject.

guests were all noble in appearance and polished in manners.

I carried on my merry devil hunt in old towns, — especially
in Leipzig and Auerbach's Cellar, — but was now and then
saddened by coming across tracks of the real devil — war. I
travelled with haggard Germans returning to their homes
from French prisons or hospitals, and French invalids trying
to reach home. I arrived in Munich just in time to witness
the first performance of Wagner's " Rienzi." All the people
of rank and fashion in Bavaria were present. My confession,
that after having heard all of Wagner's other operas I prefer
" Rienzi " above them, will excite the laughter of Wagnerians,
and I must conciliate them by acknowledging that the spell was
woven about me by the Messengers of Peace. The nightmare
that followed my journalistic tramp on battlefields had been
revived by the apotheosis of war at Berlin, but they were dis-
pelled by the troop of beautiful olive-bearers and their wondrous fraüenchor. We hear their gentle theme in the distance,
rising as they approach ; clad in pure white, each bearing her
olive branch, they slowly file upon the stage, — and oh, the
tenderness and exaltation of that chorus ! They disappear
slowly while singing, their voices are heard more and more
faintly ; the song ceases. After a little silence the strain is
wafted back again as on a fitful wind. Again silence. Yet
once or twice more the theme reaches us, as if the peaceful
messengers were passing here and there an open space. The
spectators, — the most brilliant assembly I ever saw, all the
ladies in court dress, — sat breathless, too profoundly moved
to applaud. In another scene I recognized in the composer a
Prospero creating a fairer world than that hard and heartless
imperial realm whose barbaric splendours I had seen in Berlin. Amid the appropriate gorgeousness of ancient Rome the
gladiators appear in the Coliseum and perform their combats ;
when lo, the " eternal feminine ! " Gathering by hundreds
from every part of the vast stage the dancers come, — no man
among them, — like lustrous fleecy cloudlets : dance follows
dance ; now they are spirits in hues of heaven, now sea-tinted

nymphs, or again green-girt goddesses of the forest. All nature transfigured in their shining faces and forms, they draw the gladiators after them with ropes of wreathed flowers; the phalanx throw each his shield upon his head, making thus a floor beneath which the gladiators stand as pillars, while upon this shield-floor the hundreds of beauties dance in the art-created era when all chains shall turn to flowers and shields into dancing floors. This resplendent ballet was almost too much for the audience; they stood up, waved handkerchiefs, and shouted with one voice for Wagner.

But the Prospero had hid himself; he had long been working with Conductor Willner on the mighty orchestra, he had personally concerned himself with every detail of scene and costume, he had mounted tableaux unequalled in the history of the German theatre; and neither he nor any of the great artists (Nachbauer, Frl. Leonof, Kendermann, Frl. Stehle) could be induced to thrust their personality upon the stage.

I carried to Munich a letter to Kaulbach, but had found in his decorations of Berlin Museum, his paintings of Goethe's Faust in Auerbach's Cellar at Leipzig, in the splendid curtain (" The Muse ") in the Munich opera-house, and the Christian and Pagan legends with which he had covered the edifices of the " City of the Monk, " a cumulative introduction to him. Kaulbach was, in the largeness of his work and the character of his subjects, a sort of Wagner. And in personal build and immortal youthfulness he was not unlike Wagner, though finer looking; and he had happiness in his face which Wagner had not. Naturally, for in his magnificent house and park were beautiful ladies, — his wife and daughters, — whose intelligence and taste surrounded him with all charms congenial to an artist. I passed a happy evening with them, and was especially interested in the artist's account of the Oberammergau Passion Play to which tourists were crowding, — the war having deferred it to 1871. Kaulbach said that he had long ceased to attend it. Thirty years before it had charmed him. It was a series of pictures that moved the heart, presented with intense feeling, beheld by the peasants with silent fervour. The homeliness of the acting rendered it the more impressive. Around us, said Kaulbach, were the solemn mountains with their snow, the primitive forest, the songs of birds. But it has been adapted to the tourists, it is given over to sophisticated people, and has lost its early charm.

At Munich I met a charming American artist, David Neal. Born poor in some New England village, he made a living by carving little engravings for newspaper advertisements, found his way to San Francisco, and while engraving pictures for books was told by a fellow workman that he ought to aspire to higher work. Neal found his way to Munich, where he found employment under the artist (afterwards count) Ainmüller, who presided over the Glasmalerei. Ainmüller sent him to Piloty, and Neal became a fine colourist. He married Ainmüller's daughter. Neal had among his small pictures one representing Watt as a boy seated in a chimney-corner in a kitchen, studying the phenomena of a kettle. His comely mother opens the door to call him to supper, where the other children are seen. I persuaded Neal to put this on a large canvas, which he did and sent it to London. I offered it to the Royal Academy, where it was hung, and was bought for a substantial sum. The grateful young artist presented my wife with the original small picture.

David Neal took me to the Hofbrauhaus, an official brewery, where eminent personages were drinking bock (from Einbock, Brunswick, where it was first made). Among the charcoal sketches on the walls two were new — Bismarck, with three aggressive hairs upright on his bald head, and Napoleon III swinging from a gallows. Pius IX was caricatured leading a fat pig with the features of the Archbishop of Munich. The Passion Play actors were also caricatured, — each woman very *décolletée*, — some of these being apparently of the previous century. Such was the outcome of a town given over for centuries to the sway of mönchen (monks), whose name it bears. The Old Catholic movement could not be saved from such Mephistophelian antics in the city of its origin. And, by the way, I believe it was the favour shown to the devil in

Munich as a subject of caricatures which led to the withdrawal of Satan from the Passion Play.

Professor Piertz of Munich — brother-in-law of Lady Lyell,
who introduced me to him — informed me that he had found
in the archives indications that the Passion Play had been
preceded at Oberammergau by plays representing the gods
and goddesses of mythology. The plays were, however, originally merely incidental to the main industry of the place —
wood-carvings of holy figures, explained by the venders; under
Christianity the play became the main thing, but the carving
industry continues all the year round. I voyaged up the
Wurmsee (making notes of its dragon legend), and was jolted
in a primitive wagon with primitive folk to Oberammergau.
I found comfortable lodgment in the house of the Langs, —
whose daughter Josepha had the part of "Mary Magdalene."
The art of the librettists in making the wrath against Jesus
and the whole tragedy turn on the assault on the temple merchants was notable though not scriptural. It was comic to see
them picking up their coins. But there are venders of holy
candles in the churches also. The automatic Christ of Joseph
Mayer was meant for automatic worshippers. A few relics of
the former simplicity recalled by Kaulbach were visible, —
e. g. the Greek style of the chorus, the naked legs of Adam
and Eve, the disciples drinking beer at the noon entracte.
Jesus was more finely dressed than the disciples; he was robed
in red and wore silk stockings. John also wore stockings, the
other disciples being barefoot.

An interesting event for me at Munich was an interview
with Dr. Döllinger, on whom the eyes of Europe were fixed
more than on the new incarnation of infallibility at Rome.
He felt that this dogma of 1869 was fatal to his church, but
could see no hope in Protestantism. He spoke of the Protestants as consoling themselves for the disintegration and ineffi-
ciency of their visible churches "with thoughts of the assumed
glory of an invisible church, possessing in fanciful perfection
all that is lacking in the visible." This reminder that a suffering world is not to be comforted or saved by a disembodied

Utopia made me feel that he, too, with his Old Catholic staff, was on his earthward pilgrimage.

There was little about the man or his library to suggest the priest. From between the loaded book-shelves looked down faces of the great of all ages and churches, the chief picture being a Madonna and Child. The doctor was simple in his manner; he was dressed in plain black without any ecclesiastical or other badge; head and face were freighted with force, his voice gentle and winning. His English was excellent. His seventy years were recorded only in such lines as long study furrows; they had hardly touched his dark hair, and only added vivacity to his large eye. I was delighted with his humour. It was excited by a story I had heard of Archbishop Purcell of Cincinnati, said to have gone to Rome as an opponent of infallibility. Introduced into the presence of the Pope, the Archbishop fell on his knees: the Pope bade him rise. He then tried to kiss His Holiness's toe; the Pope took him by the hand and raised him up. He would next kiss the Pope's hand; the Pope opened his arms and clasped him to his breast. Döllinger's laugh at this evidence of infallibility was hearty. "The hardest thing I have had to bear," he said, "was the closing of the room where I have lectured more than forty years. My trouble was increased by messages of kindness and confidence from the students. They wished me to meet them in indirect ways, but this I would not do. This ending of an old man's customary work is hard; but it cannot be helped." I thought again of his sad look when I heard afterwards that the students had unanimously demanded that Döllinger should be president of their university.

His chief disappointment was that the American bishops, once against ultramontanism, had gone over to the new dogma; the adhesion in England he considered the work of Manning. He showed me a Catholic paper just received from New York containing a bitter attack on him. "In this article," he said, "there is just one thing true. It accuses me of having conceived the hope of a union of Christian churches throughout the world. Of that I am guilty. Nothing has interested me more than the letters I have received from Protestants in all parts of the world confessing that their several churches are in an unsatisfactory condition, and hoping that our struggle here may give rise to a larger and more spiritual organization. I am unable to see any basis for such an organization except the Christian idea, and that has been for Europe historically shaped in the Catholic Church. Whatever situation in the evolution of a universal Church shall reveal itself must be dealt with as it arises. At present so far as my horizon extends the struggle against this new dogma is vigorous. But that has already called about it false principles and political designs. Many things must fall with that dogma of infallibility — the whole machinery by which it was imposed, for example. We have enough work cut out for us without looking farther."

On my asking what were the opinions of the lower classes, he smiled at the idea of their having any opinions. " After the priest has spoken, it would never occur to one of them that there could be any other opinion. The chief difficulty we have is not the opposition but the utter apathy of the people. It does not affect them personally, and they find the question uninteresting. Possibly the increasing complication of the issue with politics may give them more serious impressions."

As to the effect of the new dogma on Catholic theology, he said, " The question which has arisen between us and Rome is one of life or death to theology. Should the dogma of infallibility be accepted, there could be no such thing as theology. No man with self-respect would put pen to paper only to bolster predetermined opinions that might not be his own. The rewriting of decrees is not theology."

Tom Hughes and his wife received their friends on Sunday evenings at " high tea," and high matters were discussed. There are still a few grey heads like mine in which are cherished memories of that lovely family. At their table I sometimes met William Evelyn, who dwelt in historic Wotton House, Surrey, and was heir to the virtues and intelligence of his ancestor, the author of "Sylva," who lived there two centuries before him. Among the most beautiful days of my life I count several passed in the grand library left by that scholarly gentleman who passed unstained through the storms of the seventeeth century. William Evelyn drove me about to the homesteads of the Noels and Byrons and other old families, and we even called upon Tupper.

On one of my visits to Wotton, Rev. Thomas Arnold and his wife were also guests there. Their daughter, Mrs. Humphry Ward, as yet unknown, did not inherit her mother's beauty nor her sparkling humour, but I have often reflected that with such parents she could hardly escape a notable career. Thomas Arnold, slender, superfine in countenance and expression, nervous, — his delicate mouth sometimes twitching, — was more striking in appearance than his brother Matthew, and resembled more their sister, Mrs. W. E. Forster. It has always been a matter of regret that I did not then know of the fair dreams of a new society with which in early life he had been inspired by the writings of George Sand, and which had carried him away to New Zealand to found there his Utopia.

In September, 1871, my wife and daughter were invited with me to Wotton harvest home festival. The work people being mostly dissenters, the sermon was given by a Baptist preacher, and was poor enough to excite my regret that the intelligent vicar who was present did not preach. The parable of wheat and tares was turned to the sorry sense of good and bad people dwelling together — under one roof, sometimes husband and wife — till one should burn in hell and the other sing in paradise.

Afterwards there were sports, — cricket, croquet, racing, — then a fine dinner in a grand marquee, young ladies of the neighbourhood waiting on the labourers. After the usual toast to the Queen, the bailiff gave the toast to Evelyn, — "Our Master, — more important to us than the Queen!" After Evelyn had spoken, — with his characteristic modesty and tact, — I was called on, and contrasted the death-harvest I had witnessed at Gravelotte the year before with the happy harvest home in Surrey.

Alas, so closely are the wheat and tares bound together that in these later years the conclusion is forced on me that it is precisely because those toilers in English fields never look on the face of war that England can freely send out armies to mow down men in every other part of the world!

Wotton's nearest town is Dorking, where in a deep and floral glen the " Flint House" hides itself and gives a pretty hermitage to the fine literary artist George Meredith. In the few times that I have met him he was delightful, his imagination putting out his fancy to represent it in sparkling talk that could hardly prepare one for the depth and passion of his poetry. For I always love Meredith's poetry better than his novels, these impressing me as too often containing involved intimations of vital things in order to escape the deletions of Mrs. Grundy, to whom all proof must be submitted.

CHAPTER XLI

EVER since my tractate "Natural History of the Devil" was published (Albany, 1859), I had continued my studies in demonology, and I was pretty well prepared for the four lectures which I was to give at the Royal Institution. In 1866, on Washington's birthday, February 22, I had given in that august place a Friday evening lecture on New England, but a full philosophical and anthropological course was a more serious matter. I had studied the demonology of Russia, Germany, and France fairly well, but learned that I should see some old images in Rome, where I had never been. So in February, 1872, I passed a fortnight in that city.

Robert Browning told me to be sure and see an ancient fresco on the front wall of the church Bocca della Verità. It represented, he said, Ceres amid the corn on one side and Bacchus amid grape-vines on the other; from Ceres was sent down a stream of meal, from Bacchus a stream of wine, which together formed the eucharistic bread and wine on an altar below. On my arrival in Rome I was met by my cousin Frederick Daniel, former secretary of legation, who spoke Italian fluently; he was my companion during my sojourn. But we found no picture on any wall of Bocca della Verità. The façade had been whitewashed, but I detected at one or two edges traces of colour. I mentioned to W. W. Story, the American sculptor, what his friend Browning had told me, and he sent me to Signor Rosa, Minister of Fine Arts. Rosa, — descendant of Salvator Rosa, and an able man, — learning that we had been sharply told by the sacristan and a priest that there had never been any such picture, accompanied us to the place, and was satisfied that the fresco had been covered over. He had hopes that the whitewash (rather old) could be removed, declared the fresco's destruction criminal, and said he would at once make an effort to recover it. But twenty years later the fresco was still hidden.

Bocca della Verità, — " Mouth of Truth," — thus suppressed a truthful pictorial witness to the sanctity of Ceres transmitted to Mary the mother of Jesus. The long devotion of women to Ceres rendered it necessary for the early Christians to exalt some woman in her place, the continuance of the old cult being represented, no doubt, in the word *ceremony*. To Mary Magdalene passed the cult of Venus, preserved probably in the word *venerable*. At Oberammergau I observed on the stage architrave a painting of the Madonna holding the rose of Bertha, the Teutonic Ceres, the crimson flower symbolizing the heart ever watching over the household. Jesus called the Holy Spirit his " Mother." [1]

In Rome I visited a schoolmate of my childhood, a lovely and lovable Virginia lady whose husband was a clergyman preaching to an American congregation in Rome. She told me that some years before, on her arrival in Rome, she made the acquaintance of a sweet neighbour, — a devout Catholic lady, — to whom (for she knew Italian) she became deeply attached. " After a year of warm friendship I was troubled by the reflection that this exquisite lady should be under the delusions of Catholicism, and felt it my duty to converse with her on the subject. What was my surprise to find that she had long felt the same concern about me ! After our long talk

[1] See *Gospel according to the Hebrews*, Nicholson, pp. 74, 79. See my *Solomon and Solomonic Literature*, p. 187.

she said with tears, ' Alas, you do not know the happiness of communion with our blessed Mother!' Then throwing arms around me she cried, ' Promise me, O my dear friend, promise me — if only for my sake — that this night you will offer up one prayer to our blessed Mother! Ah, what happiness and peace will fall on your heart!' Now what could I do?"

I did not venture to ask my friend — the clergyman's wife — whether she promised and offered the prayer, but said, " Did you desire to deprive the Italian lady of her blessed Mother?"

" Oh, no!" was the reply.

General Sherman was in Rome, and Signor Rosa invited me to go out to Ostia with a small party gathered for the American officer. I could not regard Sherman's famous " march " — destroying the homes and fields of poor and undefended families — as heroic, but *inter arma silent corda*. Though not so interesting as his brother the senator, General Sherman was good-natured and sociable. He was a tall, handsome man as Rosa was, and it was interesting to see the military general learning like a child from the art-general meanings of ancient symbols and figures. Here were pre-Christian monuments, — Isis with serpent, Mithras slaying the Bull, Apollo Sauroktonos (lizard-slayer), and other antique forms which may have suggested to Sherman that these heroes were his forerunners crushing ancient Confederate rebellions. But the realm of mythology is harder to conquer than Southern villages.

Heine in his delightful essay, " The Gods in Exile," shows the classic divinities out at elbows, wandering in wood and wilderness ; but had the brilliant genius been in Rome in 1872 he might have discovered that the gods and goddesses had found new and gayer temples and worshippers than any priesthood ever gave them. The Carnival was in full fling. On the site of a temple of Jove the French theatre was displaying all the gods and goddesses in Offenbach's " Orpheus," — the goddesses being costumed seductively enough to attract the wealthy and fashionable while the poor were sparsely kneeling in churches. At two fancy masquerades which I attended,

— one at the Apollo, the other at the Argentina, — superb beauties from all parts of the world were dancing as Bacchanals, Graces, Nymphs, Aphrodites.

One of the handsomest women I saw in Rome was Madame Ratazzi, — of the Baltimore Bonapartes, — whom my cousin John M. Daniel loved, but left for a Confederate grave in Virginia.

One day (my cousin was not with me) I directed my driver to the Lateran Museum, but he took me to the St. John Lateran chapel, where I began lightly walking up the sacred stairway. Finding a woman going up on her knees, it flashed on me that it was the Scala Santa on which no foot must tread because thereon Jesus ascended to the judgment-hall of Pilate. I hurried down, but it was too late; several guardians were screaming at me from below, not daring to come up even to arrest me. I was taken to the bureau, and having found some one who could talk English explained and deplored the accident, offering to obtain a certificate from the American Minister, Marsh, who knew me. My apology was murmuringly received by the keepers of the stairway, who ought to have been on hand when I entered.

My impression was that the excitement was not so much because of the sanctity of the stairway, as on account of the fact that it was while going up on his knees Luther had revolted, descended on his feet, and abandoned Rome forever. I once had the misfortune to go into a mosque without taking off my shoes, but the admonition in that case was gently given, and no vexation caused.

In Rome I was afterwards cautious, but nevertheless irritated the sacristan at S. Georgio. He showed me the relics of St. George, — the spear, vexillum, saddle, wherewith he met the dragon. But so great was my interest in dragon-slayers that I imprudently asked him if there existed any relic of the dragon. Without any reply he swiftly shut the case and hurried away, slamming the door after him.[1]

[1] My inquiry was not so impertinent as it may seem; for in my French guide-book it was stated that at Cimiez, near Nice, the dragon slain by

On my way back to London I stopped a day in Florence to see the venerable sculptor Hiram Powers, with whom I talked about our mutual friends in Cincinnati, and about Hawthorne. The evening was passed at the house of Professor (now Senator) Villari, the most interesting Italian I met, his wife being an accomplished English lady. Villari told a curious anecdote concerning an American poet whom I knew, — Thomas Buchanan Read. He had come to Florence many years before with his attractive young wife and brought him (Villari) a letter of introduction. One night — it was Mardigras — he was called up in the night by Read, who told him his wife was dead. Hurrying to the lodgings, he found there two physicians who declared that she had died of Asiatic cholera. Mrs. Read was the first victim of the last plague in Florence. Villari sat up beside the dead lady all night with Read, who read aloud all of his own poems. " It was a fearful night," said the professor. " There I sat, feeling that the dread plague was in our city. The street was filled with noisy masqueraders, their lights and figures flashing across the walls of the room, their laughter and shouts mingling with Read's voice steadily reading his poems. It was awful, like something from Dante's Inferno."

An exceptional amount of work awaited me in London. Each week in March had to be devoted to the rewriting of the lecture of that week at the Royal Institution, and my

the pious exorcisms of the saint who converted a temple of Diana into the church there, was suspended near the altar. I visited Cimiez, but no dragon was there. The attendant priest said it had never been there, but I discovered above the altar two hooks, showing that something had hung there. An aged man in Cimiez told me that many years before the dragon had been removed to the lycée in Nice. Repairing to that college, I saw its president, who told me that the alleged dragon was simply a crocodile. It was in the museum when he entered on his office, and was valued solely on account of its Cimiez legend, as an example of ancient superstition. But two years before it was found necessary to clean the museum, and as soon as the old crocodile was touched it crumbled literally to dust. Not even an inch of it remained. The college is the Apollo Sauroktonos. The fabulous monster of the altar becomes a lizard in the lycée, and passes to the dust-hole at last.

wife had to attend to our social duties almost alone. Every year the spring brought to our doors friends from America, or persons introduced by them, and every week we gave a dinner that they might meet English people. Meanwhile our three children, the girl aged four, required attention, and we were uncommonly glad when August vacation brought us opportunity to seek the seaside. We had pleasant remembrance of a fortnight at Trouville in 1867. Its Arcadian simplicity inspired an article in " Harper " — " Trouville: a new French Paradise." We had lived in a charming hotel, taking our meals out under the trees, and all at an absurdly low price. But when we arrived in 1872 at the same hotel the cost was nearly doubled. Mine host said he had many applicants from America, and showed me my own article in " Harper " in which I had imprudently mentioned the name of his hotel. When I told him I had written the article, I was not sure that he believed me; it certainly did not affect my bills.

Finding that George Sand was in Trouville I obtained a note of introduction to her from Louis Blanc, and meeting her is among the cherished memories of my life. She had no apartments in which to receive any one, but only two bedrooms, — one for her two grandchildren, who made pleasant acquaintance with my children. Our own situation was similar, so our natural place of meeting was on the sands where she walked daily. She had her grandchildren to look after, — those for whom she wrote " Le géant Yéous " and " Les ailes de Courage," — and we had ours, and our meetings amounted to little more than salutations and appreciations of the scenery and seaside play of life. We conversed a little about our beloved Louis Blanc, with whom she had shared the visions and hopes of 1848; but these had long vanished, — leaving her at sixty-eight the serene happiness of a genius which having created a beautiful world for mankind, who had refused to enter it, found it now returned to her as her own palace, its walls adorned by the faces and forms with which her supreme art had transformed to beauty the stocks and stones of nature.

I did not try to have a philosophical or literary conversation with George Sand. I had no such mastery of her language, nor she of mine, as would have enabled me to give any expression to my homage, which those searching eyes of hers could recognize better without my trying to stammer. But I told her that I had made her acquaintance through " Lélia," which the most intellectual of American women, Margaret Fuller, had given to the greatest of American philosophers, Emerson, who had given it to me.

With her uncanny reputation I had made acquaintance in boyhood, for I remember my mother and some other ladies conversing with bated breath of one Madame Dudevant, of whom an engraving had appeared showing her in man's dress. Why was that shocking? A problem was then (about my fourteenth year) grafted in me. In May, 1853, Emerson gave me " Woman in the Nineteenth Century," in which Margaret Fuller reveals that she is fascinated by George Sand ("noble in nature, but clouded by error, and struggling with circumstances ") and quotes Mrs. Browning's two sonnets to her. Ten years later, when I was leaving Concord for England (1863), Emerson gave me " Lélia" to read on my journey. It is the edition of 1841, with the prefatory apologia; but this I needed not. Margaret Fuller and Mrs. Browning were both in this brain of George Sand; nay, all the aspiring and discontented women known to me in America, — poets, orators, reformers, — were the offspring of George Sand, endeavouring to build in the New World a palace for Woman so perfect that the monastic retreat of Lélia, tossed between faith and atheism, and the pavilion of her courtesan sister, Pulcheria, with her cult of pleasure, should vanish away forever. In the storm and stress of antislavery struggle and grapple with dogma I did not go farther into George Sand's writings at that time. " At a more convenient season I will call for thee." But I knew she was the peer of the greatest of her contemporaries, — Carlyle, Emerson, Dickens, Thackeray, Browning, Tennyson, Hawthorne. And I was conscious of a certain awe when I stood in her presence.

She was not beautiful, but much more than that, — fair, refined, candid, with a countenance of queenly elevation mingled with gracious simplicity and sensibility. " Ne cherchez pas en moi ces profonds mystères," said Lélia to Stenio; " mon âme est sœur de la votre, vous la contristez, vous l'effrayez en la soudant ainsi. Prenez la pour ce qu'elle est, pour une âme qui souffre et qui attend."

It was enough, then, to meet this admirable lady on the sands, to exchange salutations, to see her smiling with my wife as her grandchildren and my children made acquaintance. But I could not help recalling the old gossip about her terrible male attire when we were looking upon the ladies of fashion disporting themselves in the sea, some in diaphanous costumes, or racing along the beach with bare legs.

It was part of my duty as an American correspondent to call on President Thiers in his villa at Trouville. At an appointed hour I was pleasantly received by his four secretaries, of whom neither spoke English, and ushered into the presence of the President, who was conducting momentous negotiations with Germany and England without knowing the language of either country. Thiers' thickset form supported a brachyocephalic head and intellectual face. He was precisely the same cheery old gentleman I had seen five years before at the Emperor's reception, as if the wars with Germany and the Paris Commune were only a passing nightmare.

I could not take the old monarchist seriously as the President of the new Republic. He was a name from the defunct firm commissioned to carry its good-will to the new one. I had desired to talk with Thiers of the evils of the bicameral legislature in America, — as France was about to frame a constitution, — but I could not argue the matter in French.

When the Convention was in prospect I expressed to Louis Blanc my hope that they would not follow that fatal example of the United States in instituting presidency and a bicameral legislature. He had already resolved to oppose those measures, and at his suggestion I wrote my little work entitled " Republican Superstitions." Proof-sheets were sent him, and I received the subjoined letter dated October 7, 1872: —

As early as 1846 I published a paper in which I endeavoured to show that the establishment of a second chamber was fraught with unmitigated evils, and afforded but a sham remedy for the political dangers it was intended to ward off.

By the end of 1848, just at the time when Louis Napoleon Bonaparte was coming forward as a candidate for the presidential office, I thought it my duty to point out the direful consequences likely to flow from the election of a president. The solemn warning I then gave to my countrymen was expressed as follows: " Whenever a man and an Assembly stand face to face, that Assembly brings with it a 10 Août, and that man has behind him an 18 Brumaire."

But, as you have rightly observed, there are political as well as religious superstitions, nor are the former more easily uprooted than the latter. At the time alluded to it seemed next to impossible that there should be a republic without a president. A strange aberration this — more especially on the part of the French, as they had been taught by experience how readily a president or consul is turned into an emperor.

However, the warning was disregarded, and on the 2d of December, 1851, we had to undergo the unspeakable humiliation of another 18 Brumaire. My prediction was thus fulfilled, even sooner than I expected.

Whether we shall know how to turn to account the lesson we have repeatedly received remains to be seen. I hope it will be so. Certain it is that nowadays many are they in the republican party who consider the presidential office as a mere stepping-stone to ascend the throne. If others have some doubt as to the necessity, both of a president and a second chamber, it is because they are under the impression that that system works well in the United States. To correct such an error is to do good service to the cause of republican institutions.

In the autumn (1872), when my " Republican Superstitions " was in press, Charles Sumner passed through London. He had been spending a month in Paris, to regain strength, and was on his way home, feeling better. He said that before leaving Paris he had a conversation with Gambetta. " I said to him that the great trouble of France was that they had no religion." What Gambetta's answer was Sumner did not tell me. I asked what he meant by religion, but he only talked about the pleasure he felt in listening to the Litany. When I knew him in Washington (1854–1863) I never suspected him of being interested in religion, nor of church-going, and now reminded him of the hostility of nearly all American churches to the antislavery movement up to the war. He was thinking, however, of the French leaders like Gambetta, and no doubt felt that their republicanism was too merely political and not religious enough. But I was left a good deal to conjecture, for he seemed hazy on the matter. I then told him of my forthcoming book. With regard to the bicameral legislature, he said that all the American States had the system, which worked fairly well, but I reminded him that our state senates were not, like the federal Senate, the creatures of disproportionate representation. He had never gone into that subject, but with regard to presidency he had much to say, which he was glad to have me make notes of and use as I pleased. For all my former criticisms of one or another action in the past were erased by the stand he had taken against the usurpations of President Grant. The old emotion with which I had sat at his bedside in Washington when he was felled by the bludgeon of slavery had stirred in me again when, fifteen years later, he was struck down officially by a military president whose warlike scheme he had defeated. And not only officially ; the vindictive blow which had degraded him from his committee chairmanship in the Senate, and degraded his friend Motley in London, thereby shattering that historian's health, had brought back the sequel of slavery's blow. He stood there in London, telling me all that story, — with a quivering lip when he mentioned Motley, — and his words were only less eloquent than his white hairs and haggard face at sixty.

Sumner had no need to refute the accusations made by Grant against him and Motley. In "The Golden Hour," 1862, I wrote, "To-day, should the war end, the masses would seize the man whose hand reeked most with human blood and bear him to the White House." It could not surprise me that the warrior's civil administration should be marked by the craft and deceptions that won victories in the field. I omit, therefore, Senator Sumner's narrative of his struggle with President Grant and quote, as written down at the time, his closing words : —

" We have arrived at a period when the personal power of a president is almost irresistible. For many years the powers of checking his will in Congress have been becoming weaker, until a single act of resistance now requires every sinew and nerve which the nation can bring to bear through its representatives. The evil has gone on until the Chief Magistrate has come to regard constitutional opposition to any scheme of his own in the light of a rebellion or a crime which the Executive must punish. We fairly parallel the condition of things in Great Britain nearly a century ago when the House of Commons adopted a resolution declaring ' that the influence of the Crown has increased, is increasing, and ought to be diminished.' The military spirit fostered by the late war, and increased by the election of General Grant, has brought this formidable tendency to a climax. If Grant be reëlected, no one can contend that it is because he is regarded by the American people as the worthiest citizen to be their head. It will be due entirely to the army of office-holders, representing a complete organization of drilled and interested persons who, having forced him on the country as a candidate, are devoting the whole resources of the government, and a power of patronage not possessed by any other monarch in the world, to the one purpose of his reëlection."

" What remedy is there for this ? " I asked.

" It is a long work — longer I fear than our people are aware of. The first step would seem to be the limitation of every president to a single term. This would prevent his using his enormous patronage to prolong his power."

" But," I said, " might not an ambitious or selfish president, if unable to secure reëlection, use it for some other advantage, perhaps pecuniary, or perhaps to elect some favourite to be his successor, — a relative, perhaps his son ! Would not an executive commission be safer ? "

" It is by no means certain," said Sumner, " that the republic may not be eventually compelled to preserve itself by the total destruction of the one-man power."

And so I parted from the brave and true statesman, never to see him again ; but rejoicing that as his first speech in the Senate was against slavery, his last was against the pomp of war. No warrior ever showed more courage than Sumner when, on his return from Europe, he moved in the Senate that the names of the battles won by the Union army should be removed from the army register and from the regimental colours. This was the sage Mencius saying once more, " Let those who have conquered an enemy be not elated, but dispose themselves in the order of a funeral ! "

The array of historic facts in my " Republican Superstitions " was utilized by Louis Blanc, and he had some following. But Gambetta would not lead in the matter. Gambetta's speaking from the tribune was captivating, but in private and in conversation he impressed me as a French Disraeli, — brilliant, subtle, cynical, and without faith in principles.

The engineering of the Constitution was in the hands of M. Dufaure, an insidious man, who did not attempt to answer arguments against presidency and bicameralism, but simply appealed to the example of the United States. Without any criticism at all there was adopted in the new Constitution a principle which would enable a president to make a *coup d'état* like that of Louis Napoleon with perfect security. The Constitution, after providing that any member of the government may be impeached, provides also that the act and articles of impeachment shall be signed by the President. As the President would not of course sign an act for his own impeachment, he is practically unimpeachable. I found even Renan without any knowledge of this clause. At the house of Theodore Stanton, in Paris, I dined with two French senators, old workers of the extreme Left, who had been in the

Convention that framed the Constitution. When I expressed my surprise that the President was secured from impeachment they both exclaimed, "You are quite mistaken, monsieur: every official in the government can be impeached." When Stanton had produced a copy of the Constitution and I had pointed out the clause requiring the President's signature to authorize any impeachment, the two senators were astounded and also humiliated. They confessed that this clause had been embodied in the Constitution without any discussion and without their notice. Landor represents Thomas Paine as saying that the French were more interested in the making of a salad than in the framing of a constitution. Fortunately the presidents are apt to be as little versed in constitutional law as others, and perhaps few of them have been any more aware of their immunity than the two old senators. But I have no doubt that Dufaure and his clique meant to restore a certain absolutism under the title of President, and to do away with *coups d'état* by making them constitutional.

The prophecy of the Parisian I met at Brussels, and cabled to the "New York World," that if Paris fell into the hands of King William it would be amid a carnage unparalleled in history, was fulfilled in the so-called "Communard" reign of terror. The Napoleonic column in Paris had been pulled down, and the monument of both Napoleons had risen in the graves at Gravelotte and Sedan, the blackened walls of the Tuileries, and the loss of Alsace and Lorraine. With such a record Napoleon III came to England, an exile in the land where for twenty years some of the best men of France had found asylum. About the same time that this Emperor was being courted by snobbery, "communards" were finding asylum in that world-metropolis, London, impartial as Nature between good and evil. I had no sympathy whatever with any violence, but some conception of the terrific sufferings of those long-oppressed people. Among the exiles in London was Elié Réclus, a brother of the eminent geographer, and himself an accomplished *savant*. He and his family were charming people, and the narrative he gave us of the tragedies he saw, and from which he narrowly escaped, were thrilling. He declared that he and others who were momentarily expecting to be carried out to execution were in such a state of exaltation that they were almost disappointed when the massacres were stopped. Some of the groups of communards ranged along a wall to be shot to death sang cheery songs and laughed aloud; yet not one of them believed in any future life.

Réclus was a learned anthropologist, and read to our society in London a paper of great value on the rite of circumcision.

Elie Réclus took me one evening to a room in Bloomsbury where the communards who had escaped were wont to gather. A poor place, and they were poor people; but I was impressed by their intelligent and benevolent countenances. Several told me of the means by which they had escaped. One very striking individual had been saved by two women who had no interest whatever in the agitation, but saw him trying to evade pursuit along their small street not far from the Porte St. Denis. They were respectable young women who had closed the windows and doors of their shop below, and were looking out of an upper window. They managed to arrest his attention, and he was admitted at their door just in time, for the pursuing gendarmes had appeared in the street which he had been seen to enter. The women concealed him under their mattress. Soon after there was a knocking at their door, which they opened with a string from their bedroom. There were one or two other families in the building. When the gendarmes came to the door of these maiden sisters, they had undressed, and opening the door just enough to be partly seen, they said, " What is it? you can't come in here, we are half naked." The gendarmes knew that they were respectable people and departed. He stayed until late at night, during which time the sisters had gone off to an address he gave and secured him a passport to England. They made up some disguise and he left at midnight, made his way to the coast, and reached England in safety.

Elie Réclus was interested in my researches on Demonology, and mentioned to me that one of the communard generals, De Cecilia, was a learned scholar in Eastern tongues, and might be of service to me. He was in London, and wanted employment.

De Cecilia was indeed a useful assistant. I have received from his widow, on whom I called in Paris in 1900, an account of his life and his escapes, and hope to publish it some day. But I could never comprehend how that learned man, delicate and refined, feminine as his name, could have been a " general " of any kind, or been mixed up in any violence.

From the time I reached London, after my adventures during the Franco-German war, my burden against war was repeatedly uttered. My narratives and descriptions were listened to by large audiences, reported in the papers, and generally welcomed. But at length one discourse brought some censures upon me. This was on " The dead Emperor."

As a journalist I attended the funeral of Napoleon III at Chiselhurst (January, 1873), but it was with reluctance that I incurred such risk of being mentioned by some reporter as paying homage to Napoleon III. It was a memorable scene. There in an old English mansion lay in state, surrounded by candles, covered with lilies, honoured by the Queen's family, the man whose perjured, blood-stained throne had appeared to me in youth a seat of the real Satan. I had tracked his career of treasons and massacres, and witnessed the slaughter of thousands on the altar of his ambition. As he lay there dead, while the victims of his oppression breathed freer, I could now look upon him with a certain compassion as himself a victim. He was born under a star that was not in the sky but in his own deluded consciousness; his superstition had deprived him of free agency. He was chained to his guilty phantasy, and had to fill the measure of its iniquity. Let it go at that.

Yet it could not be left to go at that. He had bought the favour of England with the hush-money of a commercial treaty, and now the balance was being paid at his grave out of the treasury of English honour. The press was largely filled with effusive eulogies which all had one keynote: " Our customer is the immediate jewel of our soul." The terrible crimes were accorded silent condonation, the desolations of France forgotten, and out of the tomb was raised a soul to march on again amid the enthusiasm of youth, to wield again the sceptre of tyranny. For this was the evident aim. There was no real mourning for the Emperor; the abjectness at Sedan alone must render him an impossible emperor; hardly was he in his tomb before Britannia was putting on all her smiles for his son.

That nothing but good must be said of the dead is an axiom totally inapplicable to those who do not remain dead, but are raised out of their tombs to be exemplars, standards. With such preface I told my congregation (January 11, 1873) the plain history of the dead man. No newspaper resented my statement, but I received angry letters.

In the summer of 1873 I was introduced to Emile de Girardin and to Prince Napoleon, and had some conversation with them. The great editor was very interesting as a genuine organism of past epochs looking forward to their return under new names. To Prince Napoleon I carried a note from Charles Bradlaugh, for whom he expressed friendship and sympathy. The Prince was a fine looking and able man, and spoke good English, but I did not trust his Bradlaughism. I also on this visit met Victor Hugo, of whom something is said on a farther page. From Paris I went to wander over my old tracks as a war correspondent. In Gorze I stopped at a door where I had been kindly received by a French family. The house was then filled with wounded Germans, and madame and her young daughter, refined ladies, were sleeplessly nursing the sufferers. Madame was now an invalid. Her husband took me to her room, where she lay in bed. She told me that of the many wounded men brought to their house, twenty-six had remained for six months. Though up to the battle of Gravelotte she had never known any illness, she had since not known a day of health. This lady, whom I remember as beautiful, was now pale and her hair touched with grey: her kindly eyes filled with tears as she recurred to the tragical events that had desolated her happy life and home. She was a picture of France.

I revisited the fields and groves where I had witnessed the terrible strife. The battlefields were golden with ripe corn, and only peaceful reapers were seen there where the dreadful scythe of death had mowed down men. The fields exhibited no red spots but the poppies, and in the distance even the groups of white crosses were like parterres of flowers. In the foreground were the cheerful gardens with their burning bushes, — roses and fuchsias so large and deep-hued that it may have been such that caused Nizami to say, " Every flower in the garden of the earth is the heart's blood of a man." Nature was hiding her scars with flower and grain, as if to persuade her human children to forget theirs. The only thing missed from the cheerful scene was the songs of the birds. Three years before, even in the intervals of the cannon, the air was filled with their music. In Rozerielles I observed on several houses boughs and bushes, and was told that this village had been famous in times past for its pigeons, constituting its special merchandise. But since the war few of the birds had returned, and the inhabitants had hung out the boughs to lure them back.

But the efflorescence of the war on the French stage and on the walls of the Paris *salon* was very different from that of the flowers on the battlefields, and for some years reminded me of the departed songsters. Pictures of war, bloodshed, cruelty had replaced the scenes of happy peasant life and the dreams of repose. French literature was indeed stimulated, but a tone of despair began to pervade it. The mixture of self-contempt at having been led by intriguers like Napoleon III to slaughter and disgrace, the bitterness of inglorious sacrifices, the irremediable bereavements felt throughout France, were powerfully expressed in a volume of poems by Louise Ackermann. One of her poems impressed me deeply — " Les Malheureux." The last day has come ; the trumpet has sounded. A great angel descends, uncovers all the graves of the dead, and bids them come forth for everlasting life. A few eagerly come forth, but the larger number refuse. To the divine command they answer, that they have had enough of life in his creation ; they have passed through thorns, and over flinty paths — from agony to agony. To such an existence he called them — they suffered it ; and now they will forgive him only if he will let them rest and forget that they have lived.

A pleasanter visit than that to the battlefields was made to another region of France with my dear friend Henry Bacon, — an American whose ancestors fought at Lexington, who had himself fought for the Union, and who was leading the life of a happy artist and littérateur in Paris. Not long after my settlement in London, the chief American artist there, G. H. Boughton R. A., introduced me to Huntington, Paris correspondent to the " Tribune, " and collector of " Frankliniana." He introduced me to Henry Bacon, whom he had inspired enough to paint " Franklin at Home." At that time Bacon was living in the Rue Newton, I think, and had a grand studio. It is, however, chiefly in his apartment in the Faubourg St. Honoré that I saw most of himself and his (first) wife. Bacon was charming company, and in every sense artistic. Full of good sense and tact as well as humour, and very hospitable, he and his first wife — still more his present wife — were my helpful friends during all my life in Europe.[1] He united literary with pictorial art ; he not only was best company, but his dainty imagination was expressed in some sketches he wrote and graciously loaned me which remain graven in my memory. Many years ago I saw in his room a wonderful picture of a young man in evening dress dining alone in his fine room, standing, bending forward and touching his glass against an empty glass across the table. It was a touching and weird picture. Some years later I asked him

---

[1] Mrs. Bacon, under the name of Lee Bacon, has written the best book I know about picturesque Egypt, which is admirably illustrated by her husband. They now reside in London, but for me Paris is hardly Paris without them.

to show me this picture again, but he had sold it. A man had come there — an aeronaut — and given a large price for the picture. This man ascended in a balloon and shot himself. In 1893 the same idea was represented in a powerful cartoon by Gibson which appeared in the Christmas number of " Life," accompanying a story by the accomplished editor, J. A. Mitchell. The story, entitled " A Bachelor's Supper," is extremely poetical, and no doubt Gibson's picture was inspired by it. The bachelor is much older than the man in Bacon's picture, and his fine nature is reflected in the faces of the seven ladies loved and lost who smile upon him.

Boughton had been a pupil of Frère, and had loaned me some of the engravings used in my article in " Harper's Magazine " on " Edouard Frère and Sympathetic Art in France." Some years later I desired to see Frère, and to buy a picture straight from his easel. Henry Bacon, also a pupil of Frère, cheerfully accompanied me to Ecouen. Frère had received my magazine article from Boughton and welcomed me cordially ; he called his wife, who was delighted to see Bacon again, and gave us a repast. Frère was a small man with bright, black, penetrating eyes. He and Bacon talked over the time when the Germans occupied Ecouen. Soldiers were quartered in other large mansions, but the German commander had called on Frère and told him that he should not be disturbed.

Frère had finished a number of pictures, but a contract with Gambart prevented his privately selling one. " But, " he said, " it does not forbid my giving one, and although these new ones are already ordered I have a little sketch here which I pray you to accept as a souvenir." He then brought out a drawing of a " Girl feeding rabbits," also a pen-and-ink sketch of a village school interior, and at the bottom of both wrote his presentation. His friend and pupil Von Becker came in, and we all visited his atelier to see a picture just completed of an humble interior in Finland (Von Becker's country), a child taking her first steps in dancing, — since widely known by engravings. Von Becker was a noble gentleman ; he afterwards held some high office in Finland, and

I believe painted little. When Bacon and I were setting out for Paris a package was handed to me through the car window. It proved to be a gift to me from Von Becker — a life study of the favorite Ecouen model, a beauty of eighteen years. My enrichment was increased in Paris, where Bacon gave me a charming little sketch of a scene in Ecouen, — a German soldier plodding along with hands full of ducks and geese, and two children, — a little boy shrinking behind the skirt of his sister. It is a beautiful picture, and now in my son's house.

The cruelty with which the French government pursued the artist Courbet on the accusation of having led the riotous Commune to pull down the Vendôme column in Paris excited a great deal of sympathy for him. For myself I regarded the intensity of feeling among the new Republican rulers about that column as measuring the depth to which Napoleon-worship was rooted in France. Both of the Emperors bearing that name had by blunders brought their country bleeding and desolate under the feet of conquerors and ended their meteoric careers in miserable exile. If ever there was a pardonable thing for the victims of Napoleonism to do it was to pull down that memorial of their shame and of the baser elements in France. Courbet, chosen Minister of Fine Arts by the Commune, had managed to save the collections of the Luxembourg and of M. Thiers from the mob, but made no effort to save the Vendôme column.

Among those who shared my feelings about Napoleonism was my dear friend Judge Hoadly, afterwards governor of Ohio. Towards the close of 1872 he requested me to order a picture from Courbet. In answer to my letter came the following, in French : —

Ornans, Dp. du Doubs, 11 February, 1873. — My dear Sir, I have received your letter, and the order you have given me in it for your friend in Cincinnati, with the greatest satisfaction ; but, imagine then in what an exceptional situation I find myself. I am ill and have been so all winter. You will understand it easily when you know of the shocks and troubles I have had to undergo.

Beside other unheard of things, here is the French Chamber trying to make me raise again the Vendôme column, else they will seize all my property, my studio, and perhaps my person. How could you, pray, expect me to paint a picture in such a situation?

We must hope that all this will pass. It is an ineffable insanity, all the more that I have once already undergone all the condemnations, which have been carried into effect. After all this ends or when I am free, so soon as I can I will hasten to execute the kind order you have given me for your friend.

Be sure I do not forget you and that I hope to be satisfactory to your friend so kindly intentioned toward me as well as toward yourself who have been so kind in this matter.

Please be patient and take into consideration my present exceptional situation. Accept, I beg of you, the expression of my most distinguished sentiments. With my compliments to yourself and your friend — GUSTAVE COURBET.

When Courbet was in exile at Vevay I travelled from London (midwinter) to select a picture for Judge Hoadly. His atelier was near famous Chillon, and he alluded to the notable prisoner in speaking of his own banishment. This he felt keenly. The few pictures he had completed were neighbouring mountain and lake scenes, powerful but with a sombre tone. No human figure was in any of them, and when I expressed preference for a picture with some figure he said, " I cannot insert a figure in the presence of these grand mountains. It would belittle them. And indeed since I left Ornans I have had no heart to paint human figures." The look of this portly Courbet was that of an overgrown boy, — very blond, quick in movements, full of emotion, too. He was not eager about the price of the picture selected, but Hoadly wished it to be full. He said nothing about the Vendôme column.

Looking back from the opening twentieth century on the past, with the eyes of a disillusioned reformer, it appears to me that the nineteenth century reached its apotheosis in the Centenary of Voltaire at Paris, May 30, 1878. That day the playing fountains, the expanding blossoms, the cloudless sky, combined with festivals of the splendid Exposition to overlay the scars of war, put to shame tinsel of the dead empire, and welcome back the banished brains of France.

The festival opened in the circus at the Château d'Eau. In the vast building six thousand people assembled. In the centre was a flower-wreathed chariot surmounted by symbolical statues of France and Liberty. Winged genii held wreaths above the head of a veiled figure. Music and banners greeted the Municipal Council, bearing aloft the arms of Paris and the motto: "*Fluctuat non mergiter.*" Around the veiled and laurelled figure shone the names of the fathers of printing and of Voltaire's great contemporaries. The eloquent Senator Laurent-Pichat gave his brief oration, the veil vanished, and there was Voltaire holding his pen. The enthusiasm of the six thousand was overwhelming. "*Vive Voltaire! Vive la Republique!*" began the continuous *vivas* for everybody and everything brave, free, human, ended only when Hubans' cantata to words by Paul Avenal broke out from the choir.

Having to leave in order to hear the oration of Victor Hugo, my wife and I could only get out through vaults, led by attendants with candles. She was unequal to another function and I went alone to the Théâtre de la Gaiété. The standing crowd was so great that I could not reach my appointed seat near the front, but my friend Howard Paul the actor saw me, and having to leave managed to get me into his seat.

A more brilliant auditory never gathered. Eloquent as were the orators, more impressive was it to see the statesmen and authors of France assembled in homage around the flower-wreathed bust of Voltaire — the original bust by Houdon.

When Victor Hugo arose, and his head haloed with snowy hair was seen just in front of the bust, a cry of joy broke from every heart. It was not a cheer, not a *bravo*, not a *viva*, — simply a cry of joy. It began with a long-breathed-out satisfaction — Ah–h–h! — easily interpreted as "here is our man!" With what delight the plaudits followed, how eyes glistened and hands waved in the air, cannot be described. The assembly beheld in Victor Hugo the avatar of Voltaire. The poet and the bust were apotheosized together. When he spoke of Voltaire's "smile," which he traced to the very stars, the thin lips of the statue seemed to move, and the penetrating eyes of the stone beam on the assembly. The listeners became as a thousand-stringed harp, which the master swept with æolian accents of a voice pure and flexible, capable of every range. When he spoke of the one weapon which Voltaire wielded, a weapon soft as the zephyr, strong as the storm — a Pen — I could only think of the voice to which we were listening. His gestures were as unique as they were graceful. When he had recited the two terrible examples of priestly tyranny, and said, " Then, O Voltaire, thou didst utter a cry ! " his hand with outstretched finger pointed straight before him, and for the moment one could hardly help turning to see if Voltaire were not in the dress circle. Every movement was realistic ; and yet even his emphatic gestures were surpassed by the wonderful changes of colour that played about the face of this wonderful man. The denunciation of war, the arraignment of it — and it seemed to stand before him personified as some Ghoul preying upon Humanity — was matchless. And when he had spoken those glorious sentences, had pictured all the happy and peaceful toilers and enjoyers of the world compulsorily gathered " to that dread international exposition which is called the battlefield," there was but one thing which would not have been an anticlimax, and that one came — tears. The orator's voice was choked with an emotion which spread through the house, and when he next essayed to speak, and for an instant faltered, the whole assembly, half rising, burst out with acclamations.

The banquet in the evening at the Grand Orient of France was radiant with the prevailing joy, the happiness of the hundreds of radicals at being free to utter their whole mind. They touched glasses, they were filled with laughter, they rose up and sang the " Marseillaise " again and again, repeating the verses as if they could never have enough of it.

Peace was not only the cry of Victor Hugo. On that very stage where he so impressively denounced war there was a grand spectacle of the "Age of Gold, and the Golden City." In it the *première danseuse* came forward waving an olive branch. Then all the flags of the world blossomed out — waved by the *corps de ballet—except that of Germany*. Then the *première danseuse* went back a little, and pirouetted forward waving in front of all the German flag. The reception given it by the spectators was cordial enough to be favourably felt on the Bourse. No more Franco-German war!

At the banquet I was called on for a speech. I could fairly understand a speech in French but not make one, so Dr. Chapman, editor of the "Westminster Review," translated my address. I was introduced and welcomed as an antislavery American and a freethinking lecturer in London; the chairman (whose name I forget) privately explaining to me that he omitted any allusion to my chapel because the word "chapel" had in French minds a theological connotation and would convey a false impression.

On the following day I visited Victor Hugo. When I first came to Europe I had brought him as a gift from George L. Stearns a life-size marble bust of John Brown. We did not converse, however, about John Brown. For he had said in his oration, "Voltaire is the nineteenth century." And Voltaire wielded the pen as his only weapon. John Brown belonged to the century of Joshua and Gideon; or so it appeared then, — for alas! it looks as if his violence may march on in the twentieth century while his love of freedom is left in the nineteenth.

In the above account of Victor Hugo's oration I adhere pretty closely to my notes made at the time under an enthusiasm inspired not only by the orator but by the European situation amid which he spoke. England had been for some months on the verge of a war with Russia, and only five weeks before the Voltaire Centenary Gladstone had been mobbed, and he and his wife dragged from their house into the street, because of opposition. On Sunday, March 31, the danger had appeared so imminent that I laid aside my advertised subject and preached on " The Peril of War." This discourse was widely circulated in pamphlet form, and I received from Mr. Gladstone the following, dated 73 Harley Street, April 13, 1878, a few days before his house was mobbed : —

I thank you for your kindness in sending me your able and outspoken discourse on " The Peril of War." I have read it with great satisfaction.

We are, I fear, widely separated on matters which I regard as of deep moment to the welfare of mankind. I am on this account not the less but the more thankful to find that we also are in accord upon the paramount and essential principles of " justice, mercy, and truth " in their application to the great question of the East. This pleasurable sentiment does not relieve the pain with which I observe that many of those who are good and supergood are entirely at issue with us, and in my view, as also probably in yours, have altogether lost the clue which should have guided them to a right decision. I remain, sir,   Your very faithful servant,

W. E. GLADSTONE.

The war-cloud had not indeed disappeared when Victor Hugo uttered his oration ; the song of the Jingo was still heard in the land ; but the uprising of the moral sentiment was sufficient to check Lord Beaconsfield, — if indeed the whole thing was not a theatrical stroke. It ended with the grand London ballet " Aphrodite," in which Cyprus was the scene, Beaconsfield and the Queen of Cyprus the hero and heroine !

73 Harley St
Apr. 13. 78.

Sir

I thank you for your
kindness in sending me
your able and outspoken discourse on the Peril of War. I
have read it with great satisfaction.
We are, I fear, widely separated
on matters which I regard as
of deep moment to the welfare
of mankind. I am on this ac.
count neither the less but the more

thankful to find those who also
are in accord upon the paramount and essential principles of "justice mercy and
truth" in their application to
the great question of the East.
This pleasurable sentiment does
not relieve the pain with which
I observe that many of those,
who are good and supergood,
are entirely at issue with us,
and in my view, as also probably in yours, have altogether

lost the clew which should have
guided them to a right decision
        I remain Sir
            Yours very faithfully servant,

                Wyld Melton

(I beg you to forgive me if in igno
rance I address you otherwise
than according to custom or
your wish.)

Moncure D. Conway Esq

CHAPTER XLII

George Peabody — Sir Sydney Waterlow — "Fairseat" and "Lauderdale" houses — Julia Ward Howe in London — Professor Seeley — Mrs. Duncan Maclaren — Garrison at a woman suffrage meeting in London — Mrs. Stanton's sermon — Annie Besant — Mrs. Besant pleading for her daughter — Rose Mary Crawshay's gift for a woman's college at Oxford — A conference at Oxford — Emerson at Cyfarthfa Castle, 1872 — Symposium at Rose Cottage, Wales — The poet R. H. Horne.

IN the year of my arrival in London (1863) I met the American banker, George Peabody, — a simple, strong-browed old gentleman, whose large and wise benefactions won him the gratitude of the poor. He seemed to have been less bothered by applications for money from America than by the deluded families who fancied there were accumulated fortunes (e. g. Jenkins) awaiting the discovery of heirs. Professor Marsh of Yale College told me in London that when he called on his uncle Peabody the old gentleman was cordial, but when he (Marsh) hinted that he had a request to make, smilingly said, " For money, I suppose." " No," said Marsh, " not a penny for myself, but I wish you to endow Science at Yale College." That reached George Peabody's heart and his purse.

The Peabody scheme of homes for the poor was taken up by Sydney Waterlow, — afterwards Lord Mayor of London, knight, baronet, and member of Parliament. Sir Sydney, a trustee of South Place chapel, founded the society in Camden Town, where for many years I gave evening discourses. When he first stood for Parliament his connection with South Place chapel came near defeating him (the constituency being in Scotland). Tory journalists came from Scotland on the Sunday before the election to report my sermon, which, however, happened to be without anything that could help them.

Sir Sydney's homestead, "Fairseat," was at Highgate, on the road associated with "Dick Whittington." Whenever I passed the stone marking the traditional spot where Whittington leaving London in his despair heard the Bow bells calling him back to be "Thrice Lord Mayor of London," I recognized in Sir Sydney himself an illustration of the typical London tale. He told me that even when he came of age he was almost without means. On that day he happened to be in Paris with a young friend, his health being drunk with soda-water because wine cost too much.

When Emerson was in London (1872) Sir Sydney requested my intervention to secure a visit from him and his daughter, saying that he ascribed his success in life mainly to the inspiration of Emerson's essay on "Self-Reliance."

I remember a droll circumstance connected with Fairseat. Before the Waterlows' residence there it was a small frame house occupied by an humble widow. She had for many years reverently preserved a room in which she and her husband passed their evenings just as it was when he died. The old lady's sentiment about that sacred room was such that no pecuniary inducement could secure the house until Sir Sydney contracted that whatever alteration was made, that room should remain intact. He built grand rooms, verandas, conservatories, but at the centre remained that memorial of the widow's love and happy life. Whether since the building came into the hands of the London Corporation the contract has been fulfilled I have been afraid to inquire. In this world of disillusion I do not wish to part with even one instance of the power of love to rise above its grave. That widow of Highgate was in her humble way a sister of Mary Magdalene, in whose loving vision, "while it was yet dark," Jesus rose again; and for a light so imperishable that even after philosophers have enlarged their temples, deep in their heart remains a room where sentiment cherishes the beloved man.

Sir Sydney owned also Lauderdale House and grounds, a historic place adjoining Fairseat. In July, 1872, this house was the scene of a function by the Prince and Princess, now

King and Queen, which our intimacy with the Waterlows enabled my wife and myself to witness. Sir Sydney gave to St. Bartholomew's Hospital for seven years Lauderdale House, fully furnished as a convalescents' home. Near by, the Whittington Stone reminded me of the half-legendary lord mayor who gave a grand entertainment to the King who owed him much money spent in his French wars; the Queen having expressed admiration at the fire of cinnamon-wood kindled in her honour, the lord mayor made a costlier fire by throwing into it all certificates of the royal debts. Lauderdale House was the very mansion that Charles II fitted up for Nell Gwynne. In the grounds remained the large marble basin in which the orange girl was said to have disported herself. We saw the traditional window where Nell held out her infant, and cried to the King in the garden, "Unless you do something for him, here he goes!" The King cried, "Save the Earl of Burford!" The Earl of Burford became the Duke of St. Albans, the fortune of whose house found its way to the benevolent hands of Miss Burdett-Coutts, who accompanied the Prince and Princess when Lauderdale House was opened as the Convalescents' Home. Lady Waterlow told me that she had not ventured to invite the Princess, who, however, wrote her a note saying she would like to attend. At this fête we entered under an archway inscribed: "Friend to all Nations," — the allusion to the hospital's hospitality to the world being appropriate also to the cosmopolitan Prince.

In that same month (July, 1872) Elizabeth Chase of Rhode Island and Julia Ward Howe, delegates from America to a prison congress in London, summoned a peace congress. It took place in St. George's Hall just after we had been celebrating that Fourth of July which has done so much to consecrate the sword. About three hundred were present, but every one a source of influence. Only ten years before Mrs. Howe had written her hymn, having around Washington city "seen a fiery gospel writ in burnished rows of steel" (most people find something divine in a war for their side), but her plea for peace was eloquent. She considered that the old

Peace Society had been shown useless by the Franco-German war, and women must now do something. She had come to England to knock at their door and say, " Sisters, arise ! The bridegroom cometh — go forth to meet great Duty on the way ! "

Mrs. Howe, who twenty years before had put forth her poetic " Passion Flowers," showed that the wand in her hand could blossom with passionate love of freedom and justice. While she spoke I cast a glance at my friend Professor Seeley, in whose " Ecce Homo " men of differing creeds found a common watchword — " The Enthusiasm of Humanity " — with a feeling of joy in his being there to witness this manifestation of American moral genius. The almost boyish-looking scholar — smooth-faced, flaxen-haired — was looking on the speaker with an expression of happiness. And very happily he followed her. There were few more charming speakers than this professor, — and I think his marriage with one of the accomplished Phillot sisters may have assisted in the large view he held with regard to " the eternal feminine." He pointed out the many Utopias that had been realized, and declared that all ideals had their chances. He welcomed Mrs. Howe's aim as directed to bringing forward women to aid the cause of peace ; it was appropriate at a time when women were claiming a larger relation to public affairs.

Mrs. Howe on the Sunday following preached eloquently in my chapel to a great audience. Indeed, several American ladies preached for me, — among them Mrs. Livermore and Mrs. Stanton. Ernestine Rose gave us one Sunday her reminiscences of Robert Owen. These American ladies were more eloquent in the popular sense than the English female orators, — and Elizabeth Cady Stanton was not surpassed by any congressman or commoner of her time, — but in what is called " parliamentary " speaking the English ladies excelled. I do not believe that John Bright ever made a finer speech than I heard from his sister, wife of Duncan Maclaren, M. P. It was at a woman suffrage meeting, — her husband in the chair, — and Mrs. Maclaren without betraying emotion moved us all by her gentle accents and her thought, for she had no gestures. Alluding to a recent charge that women were not practical enough to vote, she referred to the message Pilate's wife sent to him as he sat in judgment, " Have thou nothing to do with that righteous man ; for I have suffered many things this day in a dream because of him." For once I felt that I was listening to a lady worthy to be compared for beauty of thought to Lucretia Mott, whom only thirty-seven years before Quaker orthodoxy doomed to sit silent in a gallery at the World's Antislavery Conference in London.

William Lloyd Garrison, who was present at this meeting (1877), had told me he was resolved not to speak ; but he was so inspired by speeches of Mrs. Maclaren, Lady Talbot, Mrs. Fawcett, and others, and by the revelation of the new age that had arrived in London since Lucretia Mott was forbidden to speak there, that he was presently making a brilliant speech. The grey-haired American went a step beyond all the radicalism of England by proposing that there should be established in London a woman's parliament, at whose session every measure of importance brought before the men's parliament should be discussed. This sentiment so delighted the crowd of young ladies present, and their applause was so prolonged, that the venerable member of Parliament who presided was constrained to remark, though he did it smilingly, that a woman's parliament was not yet included in the programme of their movement.

At that time I did not take so much note of Garrison's idea as I did of his felicity in the speech. But in after years I reached the same idea (the woman's parliament) and printed articles about it. Only recently I was reminded by my old notes that the plan had occurred originally to Horace Greeley and later to Garrison ; in each case probably as in mine it was thought out independently.

In November, 1883, while I was in Australia, Elizabeth Cady Stanton gave a discourse in my chapel on the question, " What has Christianity done for Woman ? " It was her first matured declaration of religious independence. She showed by the facts of history, as she says in her autobiography, "that to no form of religion was woman indebted for one impulse of freedom, as all alike have taught her inferiority and subjection. No lofty virtues can emanate from such a condition." I have had talks with her on the subject, also with the equally freethinking Susan B. Anthony, and with the eloquent Rev. Anna Shaw, and distressed these "suffragists" by my belief that the disfranchisement of their sex had made them individual thinkers and orators. As for suffrage, the masses of men are unfit to vote, and womenkind are under coverture of mankind. It is impossible, save in a few cases, to get at the real sentiment and conviction of the woman: her vote would always be that of her parson or of some man. Even the most emancipated ladies in London, demanding suffrage, did not dare to utilize for their cause the most eloquent among them, — Annie Besant, — because, I suspect, of her repudiation of Christianity.

In 1873 my wife and I were much interested on hearing that the Rev. Frank Besant, of the English Church, brother of Sir Walter Besant, had separated from his wife on account of her unorthodox opinions. In their village religious scandal had been caused by the abstention of the vicar's wife from the communion. Soon after a pamphlet by her was printed in the rationalistic series edited by Thomas Scott. Both husband and wife found the situation embarrassing and peacefully separated, a deed being drawn up assigning their little boy to the father except for one month of each year, when he was to be with his mother, while the little girl was to remain with her mother under the same condition.

Mr. Besant had but a small income, and could give his wife nothing. My wife at once invited her to come with her child and stay in our house until she could make satisfactory plans. The invitation was accepted. It filled us with astonishment that a young man should be willing to part from this beautiful and accomplished wife for the sake of any creed. She could not be more than about twenty-seven years of age; her face was beautiful, its delicate oval contours and feminine sensi-

bility were heightened by the simplicity and sincerity which
come of good breeding and culture. Her little girl Mabel
was as lovely a child as I ever beheld; our three children
were in utmost delight at having the little companion with
the mother. After some weeks Mrs. Besant became troubled
about remaining, but I was able to quiet her fears of staying
too long by engaging her to do some work for me. Being
occupied with my " Demonology and Devil-Lore," I had a
number of German books gathered from obscure places in
which there was some mention of local legends. Mrs. Besant
knew German (also French and Italian), and gladly undertook to sift them. I still have the book in which she translated
the desired items.

Meanwhile Bradlaugh discovered that Mrs. Besant's opinions were inclining towards secularism, and she was invited
to write for " The National Reformer." He could not pay her
much, but her assistance improved the paper and enlarged
its circulation. She wrote under the *nom de plume* of
" Ajax." Mrs. Besant gave an excellent discourse at South
Place, and it was evident that she was entering on an important career. There was even greater charm in her speaking
than in her writing.

After her first visit Annie Besant was often with us, and
the affection expressed in her " Autobiography " for my wife
was always returned. In 1877, when Charles Watts was
arrested for publishing " Fruits of Philosophy : An Essay on
the Population Question," by the American Dr. Charles
Knowlton — which had been on sale in the Freethought
Book Establishment for forty years — he (Watts) declined
to defend the pamphlet, which was charged with indecency.
Mr. Bradlaugh regarded it as necessary to defend the honour
of the worthy freethinkers — James Watson and the Holy-
oakes — who had printed the really medical Malthusian
pamphlet, though he admitted that if it had been offered to
him as manuscript he would have refused it for the bad taste
of a few phrases. Mrs. Besant had become a partner in the
Freethought Book Establishment, but we all hoped she would

not associate herself with the case. My wife and I entreated her not to do so, though we regarded the pamphlet as legally defensible, because we foresaw that evil tongues would be busy with her reputation. But she felt it a point of honour to bear her part in the defence. She largely prepared the case; she went through many standard medical works, comparing them with the Knowlton pamphlet, and during the trial acted as a solicitor for Bradlaugh, whose conflicts had made him for such issues one of the ablest lawyers in England.

Although the first condemnations were quashed by a writ of error, the consequences to Annie Besant could not be escaped. Her husband demanded their daughter on the grounds that the mother was an atheist, that Mabel had no religious teaching, and that her mother was not a proper person to bring up a child, because she had published a pamphlet teaching people how to regulate the size of their families, that being an immoral book. On Saturday, May 10, 1878, the Master of the Rolls, Sir George Jessel, devoted four hours of his Jewish Sabbath to this case between an English clergyman and his wife. Mrs. Conway sat beside Annie Besant in the court-room, Wentworth Higginson and myself accompanying them. Annie Besant, simply and elegantly dressed, pleaded her own case alone. She spoke with quietness, point, and moderation, and with such adherence to the points of law, that although the judge had expressed annoyance at her not having counsel, her conduct of her case elicited from him a compliment. She pleaded that so far as her atheism was concerned, the recent Public School Act allowed parents to withdraw their children from all religious education; that it was unprecedented in any court to deprive a parent of a child because of any speculative opinions. She also argued that as her separation from her husband was on account of her heresy, he had parted with the child knowing that it could not be educated in orthodoxy, and consequently could not come into court on that ground.

With regard to the " Fruits of Philosophy," she cited her preface to it, disclaiming agreement with much in the book, which she published to prove the right to discuss the Malthusian question of population ; she contended that as the Lord Chief Justice had already decided that the " Fruits of Philosophy " was no worse than many other medical works, a physician might on such grounds be deprived of his child because he had published such works.

Up to the year 1873 the law did not permit a man to part with the custody of a child by any arrangement such as that made between the Besants ; since then, however, it was left to the discretion of the judge to enforce such agreement or break it, but solely on the ground of what would be for the temporal advantage of the child. Mrs. Besant said she was prepared to give evidence that she was better able than her husband to provide for the physical comfort and the education of her child ; but the judge said that Mrs. Besant had acquired such a reputation by her propaganda of sentiments shocking to the community that he was convinced that the worldly interests of the child would be more secure in the house of an English clergyman. It was not, he said, to be expected that respectable ladies would associate with her.

When the judge said these last words many eyes in the court-room were turned upon Mrs. Conway, who sat beside Mrs. Besant. Mrs. Besant sat with burning face. When the two ladies came out of court, accompanied by Wentworth Higginson and myself, we passed through a crowd of several hundred who broke into applause. Mrs. Besant had entered the court-room young and beautiful ; she came out old and hard. She said to me as she moved out of the courtyard, " It is a pity there is n't a God ; it would do one so much good to hate him."

Here then was a Promethea — the beak of Jehovah's vulture in her side !

The taking away of the little girl, who clung passionately to her mother, was intolerable even to many English Christians. A barrister told me that although the decision was within the scope of the law, its principle would compel the eminent Jew who affirmed it to take away, under similar circumstances, the child of a Jew, which in most cases would enjoy more social advantages in a Christian home.

Mrs. Besant enjoyed the friendship of a larger circle of ladies in high society than before, but when she applied for admission to a science class open to both sexes in University College, London, it was refused. My younger son, Dana, with two others in the college, prepared and circulated a students' petition for the admission of Mrs. Besant and a daughter of Bradlaugh excluded with her, but such was the feeling of the majority of the boys that while my son was going about with the petition he was attacked by a larger fellow who, after a severe fight, managed to tear the petition to pieces.

It being Passion Week when the trial was under discussion, I wrote a note to the " Daily News," satirically unctuous, reminding Christians of the ancient Jewish mother whose heart was pierced by the loss of her child; and suggesting that such sacrifices as that exacted from Mrs. Besant were necessary to supply the place of the bullocks and burnt offerings by which souls of pagans used to be saved, " infidels " being now won to Jesus by the sacrifice of their daughters. To this irony I signed " Cha. D. Band," assuming that everybody would recognize in it " Chadband," the proverbial hypocrite of Dickens. To my surprise, however, the " National Reformer " extolled the letter of " Mr. Band," especially as he had been bold enough to sign his name !

At a debate between Mrs. Besant and Rev. Mr. Grant — a polemical clergyman — held in my chapel, I presided. The issue was Supernaturalism. In contending against the clergyman's doctrine of successive creations Mrs. Besant found, with Tyndall, all life potential in so-called " inorganic " matter. Despite my general concurrence with her, I thought she pressed too far the scientific imagination in finding in the phenomena of crystallization, and in the vegetal forms of transitional organisms, evidences of continuous evolution. On thinking it over, I reached a conclusion that Mrs. Besant's acute mind, more constructive than sceptical, found definiteness on that point necessary. My own imagination was so strongly attracted by the ideal unity of nature that I revised the whole subject with extreme care, reaching the conviction that Organic and Inorganic are essentially separate and co-eternal. My friend Annie Besant followed, no doubt, what appeared the logic of her monistic conviction into theosophy. This, however, is largely conjectural on my part, and if I have in any way misinterpreted her she will, I know, feel sure that it is with loyalty to our long friendship.

Little Mabel suffered grievously by the separation, and on coming of age at once went to live with her mother, with whom she remained until marriage.

Annie Besant never spoke to me with any bitterness concerning her husband. I never met him, but the whole affair remains in my memory as a striking instance of the tyranny on earth of beings that do not exist. If there is anything certain it is that there is no deity who could desire a young man for his sake to dismiss out of his life a lovely wife and burden his children with lifelong sorrow.

Sir Walter Besant, whom I often met, never alluded in my hearing to his brother.

In conversing with Frederic Harrison on the subject of woman suffrage, I referred to the hope that Emerson had of the purification of politics by the " moral genius " of woman. Harrison said that one might see in the political societies then newly formed by ladies of high position what women would do with parliamentary suffrage. The " Primrose League " — so named after Lord Beaconsfield's favourite flower — and its antagonist " Liberal League " (Gladstonian) were blindly partizan. They seemed ready to advocate any policy whatever of their respective chieftains, however unjust or warlike.

On the other hand, that suffrage agitation did not decline without having caused lasting effects. It called attention to the unjust laws relating to women, and these were repealed ; it opened the professions to women, and it built colleges for them at Cambridge and Oxford. Some of us regarded it as a stigma on the sex that these colleges were not in regular relation to the universities, and that women could not have the same degrees as men. But I learned that there is another side to this.

In 1876 Mrs. Robert Crawshay, a lady connected with my South Place society, desired me to go to Oxford with the offer from her of a thousand pounds towards founding there a college for women which should be regularly incorporated with the university. Professor Max Müller had misgivings about the scheme, but desired me to stay in his house, and invited to dinner those likely to be interested in my mission, — among them Mark Pattison and his wife, Mr. Green (author of the "Short History of the English People") and Mrs. Green, Miss Arnold (afterwards Mrs. Humphry Ward), and Rev. Dr. Talbot, Master of Keble College, and his wife. To my surprise the master of Keble and his wife (intellectual as she was beautiful) took my matter up with enthusiasm, and arranged that a conference should be held in his college. He also invited me to lunch with him just before the conference. Thus the first step towards a college at Oxford for women was made in the house of my heretical self in London, and the second in High Church Keble College.

There was no reporter at the conference; the subject was dealt with freely. There was a universal desire to try at Oxford the experiment already proceeding at Cambridge (England), but the difficulty evidently was whether girls should be encouraged to give time and toil to the regular studies of the male students. There were virtual admissions by one or two that for a large proportion of these students the dead languages were nearly useless; that in those, and perhaps other studies needed only by specialists, young men had various ways of getting through examinations without having mastered them; but that young women might take all courses of study to heart so seriously and toil so hard as to injure their health and devote some years of their youth to things that would prove valueless in after life.

The partly optional curriculum has been largely introduced since then, but it became evident to me at the conference, and in private conversations, that ancient Oxford had become an antique and ornamental frame around its contemporary culture. No doubt women were so conscientious that they would be liable to take the frame as seriously as the picture, which would involve in most cases failure to comprehend the picture.[1] The matter was presently settled in the best way; I agreed to try and persuade Mrs. Crawshay to give the money in trust to a good commission with discretion as to conditions, and Oxford now has two admirable colleges for women.

The Crawshays resided in Cyfarthfa Castle, Merthyr Tydvil. The late Mr. Robert Crawshay was an able man, but his hearing having been destroyed, I think by some blast in his iron works, he rarely went away from his immense castle. Mrs. Rose Mary Crawshay, his wife, passed part of the year in London, where her friendships were chiefly among scientific people. We were sometimes guests at the castle, once (1872) in company with Emerson and his daughter Ellen. The most notable people of Merthyr Tydvil were invited to a grand dinner at the castle, and I remember Emerson's amusement at finding in one wealthy gentleman a relic of Welsh antiquity. The conversation fell on Merlin (the mythical theme of a poem by Emerson), and it appeared that a folk-belief lingered that at a certain place the voice of Merlin could still be occasionally heard from the prison of air in which the spell of Vivien had bound him. But the elderly gentleman who sat beside Emerson confided to him in low tones, " I have passed that spot at every hour of the night and day and never heard any voice yet." I saw a twinkle in Emerson's eye as he replied, " You must be a bold man ! "

[1] In a talk with Professor Thorold Rogers he quoted some queer oaths that had been steadily taken at Oxford from about the time of Edward III until about 1830. " You will not wear boots," " You will not lecture at Stamford," " Nec initis in gratia cum Henrico Simeone." Professor Thorold Rogers said it was surmised that there was some secession to Stamford, and that Simeon had got a degree by underhand means. How boots had offended was a mystery. It seems that the absurd oaths were abolished because some consciences were wounded by taking oaths that not even antiquarians could understand ! But that was in 1830.

Some time before, when the woman suffrage question was about to come up in Parliament, being at the Castle I was invited to address a society in Merthyr Tydvil to promote that measure. Mrs. Crawshay presided; and I remember her youngest son Richard (then perhaps fifteen) confiding to me when we returned, "It is a shame that my mother's men-servants should go off to vote while she cannot." That bright boy touched the only point in the subject that for me retained interest after the movement was submerged by the flood of democracy, — the stigma on woman, however intelligent, in the eyes of her own sons and of her inferiors. However, the vulgarization of the political vote rendered it inevitable that many thoughtful and scrupulous men should retreat from the mob-ridden polls and form with ladies a non-voting *élite*.

The women for whom suffrage was demanded by Mill, Fawcett, and other leaders in England were not those under coverture either as wives or domestics, but tax-payers, — widows and spinsters who would have votes if they were men. But when manhood suffrage arrived in England (practically) the correlative would be womanhood suffrage, — the vote of every lady swamped by those of her domestics. The English ladies of intelligence and means, having under the reformed laws all the liberty they need, and all resources for culture, have been steadily turning their attention to things within their reach.

Mrs. Crawshay could not have secured with a hundred votes so much realization of her personal aims as she did in forwarding female culture at Oxford, founding a prize for literary essays, promoting cremation, and surrounding herself in Wales with congenial guests. After her husband's death she resided at Rose Cottage, not very far from Bwlch, Wales, where she used to invite her London friends. My wife and I always remembered a particularly happy week there with the Cliffords and Richard Henry Horne. This poet, so dear to the Brownings, was a charming man. Though considerably over seventy, he swam across the large neighbouring pond and back before breakfast, however chilly the day, delighted us by his literary reminiscences, and sang us Spanish songs (some also of his own) accompanied by his banjo. He was a well-informed freethinker, with racy humour, and it was a rare experience to listen to the wit and wisdom of two men of unique genius — Clifford and Horne. And as Mrs. Clifford was there too, the charm of our symposia at Rose Cottage may be imagined by those who knew the company. Alas, how few are left!

CHAPTER XLIII

IN February, 1874, the Rev. Brooke Herford, minister of the
chief Unitarian church in Manchester, invited me to visit that
city and preach to his people. Brooke Herford's invitation
was not given in spite of but for the sake of my rationalism.
He wished me to give two sermons representing my differences from Unitarian Christians. The invitation was timed
in connection with several Unitarian meetings and events in
that region. A pleasant programme awaited me.

Brooke Herford said: " I hope you are not afraid of busy
family life! We swarm with children at our house — and do
things in very homely and plain ways — but are *very* glad to
see our friends." This did not prepare me for the peculiar
delight I found in the family. My host and hostess welcomed
me as if I were a kinsman, and I made acquaintance with
their children, — bright and vigorous. The household was
conducted on principles of mutual helpfulness; work was
a kind of play; it never surprised me that from that household should come the artistic reciter Beatrice and the witty
writer Oliver now known to the world.

Early Saturday morning Herford and I started for Etyal,
where was to be a ministerial conference. The brother of
a profound author whom I knew, W. R. Greg, had built on
his estate, " Norcliffe," a pretty Unitarian church. There
we were to meet. On our road we stopped at Knutsford, the
village Mrs. Gaskell made famous as " Cranford." Brooke

Herford, who edited " Cranford," knew the ladies identified as characters in that delightful story, and we were told merry anecdotes. There was no suggestion of the resentments once felt at Knutsford against Mrs. Gaskell. It broke the monotony of little Knutsford to have doubles, and I believe there was a merry competition for one or two characters.

We went on to the conference, and to a grand dinner at Norcliffe. The weather was brilliant, the ministers friendly, the conference interesting.

On Sunday I gave my discourses in Manchester to large congregations. In the evening the " Jubilee Singers " came, — a choir of coloured people from Fisk University, Tennessee, who were travelling about England, and singing in chapels. As their hymns were of the old Baptist and Methodist kind, their attendance at the Unitarian church was less embarrassing than might be supposed. They had come probably because the papers had spoken of me as an antislavery Virginian, and the front pews near the pulpit were given to them. For these simple souls I drew several things from my Methodist heirlooms. Their singing came at the close, my anti-theological manifesto ending with hymns I had heard in childhood. I knew them by heart, and joined in some from the pulpit. No oratorio could be half so sweet. The singers shook hands with me, and I hoped that my negations had turned to bread of life in their happy hearts.

Returning to London, curiosity to see the " Tichborne claimant " drew me one morning to the court-house. Already there was a large crowd waiting, and I concluded that my only chance of obtaining any glimpse of the phenomenal trial was to petition Lord Coleridge, whom I knew, to secure me a place on another day. Coleridge was to make his first speech for the Tichborne family that day, and I was turning away with disappointment, but caught sight of the American jurists W. M. Evarts and Chief Justice Waite in the crowd. I forced my way to them, and learned that they had arrived the night before, and had come on the bare chance of hearing Coleridge. They were about abandoning the attempt, but I

wrote on my card a note to Lord Coleridge with the names
of these eminent men on their way to the Arbitration at
Geneva, and gave it to the first man whose wig secured him
entrance. Soon after an usher came to the door and shouted
my name, and made a passage for our advance — all three.
We had excellent seats, and heard from Lord Coleridge that
wonderful invective in which the only mistake was that it
opened instead of closed his argument. I was in such measure identified with England that it was a satisfaction to me
that Evarts and Waite should see and listen to such a noble
specimen of the English barrister as Coleridge. Dr. Kenealy
grew red under Coleridge's speech, but the claimant, a huge
mass of fat, was unmoved, and it occurred to me that he
must have had previous experience of that kind.

The mental confusion of the British populace was such that
a political agitation about the claimant arose among the Nor-
thumberland pitmen (twenty thousand), unconsciously confessing their feeling that the claimant was one of their own
class.

There is no knowing where this case might have ended had
not the claimant made the mistake of bringing forward as his
comrade on the ship Bella a witness proved to have been during all those years a convict in England. Sir Bartle Frere
told me that after this he asked his usual cabman, a warm
believer in the claimant, what he thought now? " It looks as
if he is n't Tichborne," said cabby. " But what ought to be
done with him then ? " " I think, sir, they ought to give him
something for his trouble."

On my return to America (1875) I at once started for Virginia, but staid in Washington over Sunday. I did not let
any one know of my arrival, knowing well that my friend
Shippen, minister of my old society, would insist on my
preaching. Hardly to be recognized was the town of twenty
years before in this huge Washington! I took an early walk
to look at my old church (now a police court), paused before
the frame house where I had lived, and went on to the new
Unitarian church, a solid, handsome edifice, and entered.

My old negro pew-opener, who would have thrown his arms
around me, had long been dead; I was shown by a white
functionary into a pew for strangers; I listened to tunes and
hymns unknown to me; my eyes searched through the congregation in vain to find a face I remembered. Shippen
preached one of his usual solid sermons, after which I lingered about the door without recognizing any one or being
recognized. When I reflected on my ministerial joys and
griefs in old Washington, and how completely all traces of
those events were obliterated, and how unknown I sat there
in the new church and new Washington, I had a lesson in
lowliness. What a tiny ripple can our seeming whirlpool
turn out to be in a few years! Strange to pass even one
Sunday in Washington without exchanging a word with any
one![1]

At length I was at the old Virginia home again! Of the
young men in Falmouth who had compelled me to leave the
place because of my abolitionism in 1854, hardly one was
left; they were in Confederate graves. Conway House, which
had been used as a hospital during the war, was now occupied by some Northern work people, its once beautiful gardens and terraces running to weeds. After ten years the
footprint of war was everywhere traceable in desolations.
They killed the fatted calf for me, so far as any was left,
without hinting that I was a returning prodigal. Indeed, they
opened their churches for my lectures (paid for), drove me
about in their carriages, and Mayor Little (eminent ex-Con-
federate) gave a dinner in my honour. But no honour equalled
the delight of finding my old father, to whom my religious
and political heresies once gave so much trouble, advanced to
a sweet tolerance, and even finding pleasure in reading my
"Sacred Anthology."

My brother Peter and I rode out on a Sunday to old
Aquia church, fifteen miles away, in Stafford, and heard a
sensible sermon from our cousin, Rev. John Moncure, given

[1] After visiting my parents in Virginia I was welcomed in Washington
by old friends, and gave them an ethical sermon.

from a pulpit beside which his great-great-great-grandfather, Rev. John Moncure, and his wife were buried. The inscription on that altar tomb of our two Moncure ancestors says that they founded a numerous race, and on that morning I counted about fifty of my cousins, most of them connected with the first and this last " parson Moncure." The young clergyman was handsome, unpretending, and without cant.

I heard from my father some interesting incidents connected with the war. When Virginia seceded the governor warned all who meant to adhere to the United States to leave the State by a certain date. A surprisingly large number of farmers and their families passed in procession through Fredericksburg to the wharf to take the boat for Baltimore. " They were," said my father, " poor countryfolk, travelling in wagons with wives and children, — some on foot, — all moving on in silence, gloomy and frightened. Everybody crowded to see them, and some near me began to jeer ; but I moved away from these with disgust. I was touched by the sight of these humble people sacrificing their homes and solemnly following their old flag."

Six months after the close of the war an old farmer from a remote region near the mouth of the Rappahannock travelled up to Fredericksburg, which he had not seen for years, and entered a dry goods shop to buy clothes for his negroes. He actually had not heard that the negroes were free. Being quizzed by the salesmen, he came to my father and said, " They tell me down the street that the servants are all free. I suppose they are poking fun at me. My hands are working down there just the same as for the last twenty years." I suspected that his negroes knew all about the situation ; the controversies about them were still raging, and they probably preferred to remain with a kind master rather than rush into the uncertainties of a much complicated " emancipation."

Before the war my father possessed, in addition to Conway House and gardens and his two farms stocked with negroes, about $100,000, — a good fortune then in little Falmouth. The war turned the money to ashes. But before secession was thought of he had reluctantly accepted, for a bad debt, a quantity of cotton stored at Mobile. The cotton having risen to great value after secession, my father ordered it to be shipped to New York, and there stored, and an insurance made at par value. A few days after, the New York storage-house was burned and the cotton with it. When the war was over my father supposed that his connection with the Confederacy would render it useless for him to seek through the New York courts for the insurance money, — which had been refused, — but his brother-in-law, Chief Justice Moncure, urged him to try. The insurance company fought the case in every court, but ultimately had to pay the money with costs. The sum was large enough to repair his fortunes more than he had hoped.

I learned from leading gentlemen that during all the " reconstruction " time, when the negroes were required to have an official representative, those of Fredericksburg unanimously elected my father. Other offices were offered him, but this alone he agreed to accept. Without any salary he served them with justice. " When your father entered the board," said a friend, " his first speech was, ' Gentlemen, henceforth I know neither white men nor blacks.' "

The two races were getting on pleasantly together, in 1875, in northern Virginia. No white man desired a return to slavery, which indeed would have been ruinous to people who had more than they could do to support their families without having to clothe and feed negroes they did not need.

My welcome at Fredericksburg was renewed at Yellow Springs in Ohio, when I went thither to visit our family negroes, colonized there during the war. Their patriarch, Dunmore Gwinn, and his wife Eliza — who had been in our family before I was born — were " shouting Methodists," — or Baptists, when these were meeting in the neighbourhood. Dunmore had a good house, five well-kept acres, poultry, and pigs ; he and his family were the coloured gentry of the region. They gave a banquet in my honour, with old Virginia luxuries on the table, and there were present all the coloured preachers and prominent brethren and sisters of the neighbourhood in addition to our own former servants. The dinner began before one o'clock and continued during the afternoon, with a new set of guests at each successive dinner with exception of myself, who had to be present with each company, — Eliza being near as chamberlain to suggest my rôle and support me in it. How I was to go through the 'grace before meat' required of me was a grapple with the unknowable until I bethought me of the desire each parson present must have to contribute a blessing to the feast, and dexterously passed my privilege to one after another.

But the trial came when the feast was over, and the house prepared for a grand prayer-meeting. Fortunately I was not in 1875 without a sufficient amount of collectivist theism to utter as my prayer one of the " meditations " which had taken the place of prayer at South Place. If my memory serves me, I recited part of an old hymn from a Persian litany to Ormuzd, which was glowing enough to elicit " Amens." When the prayers were over all was plain sailing, for I loved the old Methodist hymns and could join in the singing.

But the awful thing was when old Dunmore Gwinn, a practised speaker, gave an elaborate address to the large company concerning myself and the circumstances of my becoming an opponent of slavery, and having to leave Virginia. I was dumbfounded by the size and completeness of the mythology which had in twenty-one years formed in the minds of these humble friends. I was pictured standing in the centre of Falmouth with the whole village raging around me, and as pointing to a poor negro and crying, " That woolly-head has in him an immortal soul ; he is a child of God ; he has the same right to freedom as any of you have," and so forth ; for the speech was long and admirable. Still more graphic was Dunmore's description of how the mob was cowed by my eloquence, and the blacks encouraged. For there were visions and prophecies and manifestations. As a matter of dry fact the whole thing occurred just as related in chapter xv. No negro was present and no speech made.

But was I to humiliate poor Dunmore and Eliza, their children and grandchildren, and call it all fabulous? I made a rather extended address, saying that Dunmore had praised me higher than I deserved, and telling the more meritorious story of him and the others who had amid all the troubles and dangers of war toiled until they had earned enough to find their way to Washington. I dwelt on what each one had done for our family while in servitude for many years, — services that could never be requited. I did the best I could, but had not the courage to attack the mythology outright; the effort of so doing would have undermined the repute for good faith of our whole colony, and diffused more untruth than it dispersed.

I gave a lecture at Yellow Springs; the students of Antioch College being curious to hear the lecture on Demonology, that was selected, and the wall behind the desk duly covered with illustrative pictures of demons, dragons, and devils. Front seats in the gallery were reserved for our negroes, who all came in finest raiment and occupied the position that in Europe would have been accorded to royalty. It was by no means a lecture suited to them, but I had tried to throw in as many good stories as I could for their sake. However, the scientific study had to be made, and when I got into the depth of my subject an incident occurred. While with my pointer I was describing the evolution of demons, I came at length to a figure drawn for me in London from a gnostic gem.

"This," I said, "is the only known representation of Satan."

"Give it to him, honey!" shouted old Eliza from the gallery. "Give it to the old devil hot and heavy!"

Of course there was prolonged laughter in the assembly, to most of whom the gaunt figure of our prophetess was well known. Eliza had made the hit of the evening so far as the fun was concerned. But alas, I was unable to give it hot and heavy to my gnostic Satan; he was my pet figure, being of severe beauty, — the Satan of Job not yet fallen from a legal prosecutor to a punisher. As I proceeded ejaculations of others came from the gallery, — " Right too! " " Ain't it good! " " True 's gospel! "

On the following day when I was talking to my coloured friends again I was pleased to find that the heresies pervading my lecture had passed entirely over their heads, and that their love and loyalty had discovered an amount of good old Methodism in it which I had not suspected. When they talked about the old serpent and the devil, and his way of going about like a roaring lion seeking whom he may devour, and anon changing himself to an angel of light, I felt a warm sympathy stirring my heart. My optimism had been for some time weakening; the Unitarian doctrine that all evil is good in disguise must have been for some time receding; and I listened with philosophic attentiveness to the experiences of trial and temptation told by these simple friends, in which I heard again the word of Jesus concerning the tares, — " An enemy hath done this."

The most intelligent of our negroes was James Parker, a handsome mulatto, who had been my father's valet. In those days James had held the noisy piety of his race in quiet contempt, but he had been "converted," although he did not lead in prayer, and could not sing. I had learned in Fredericksburg that in 1862, when James was left within the lines of the Union army, he penetrated into the Confederate lines, at risk of reënslavement, to find my father and continue in his service, but was told he must return to freedom. He now told me he had never been happy since parting from my father, and would gladly return to his service. It was touching to me to observe the eagerness of all of the negroes to hear about my parents and their family, of whom they spoke with affection and emotion.[1]

1 When Eliza was dead and Dunmore aged, I gave him a rather larger Christmas gift than usual, and he used it to travel to Fredericksburg, Va., simply to see once more "the old folks at home." His visit was made

In New York I was given a dinner by the Lotus Club, Whitelaw Reid presiding; and a breakfast was given to Lord Houghton and myself in the Century Club, the venerable poet Bryant presiding. At this breakfast Dr. Bellows made a felicitous speech, full of literary anecdotes. He delighted Lord Houghton by relating that when Thackeray was there he whispered to him at breakfast, "You know, Mr. Thackeray, that your Colonel Newcome is borrowed." From whom?" asked Thackeray. "Oh, he is plainly a mixture of Don Quixote and Sir Roger de Coverley." "Good God!" exclaimed Thackeray. "How did you find me out?" At Boston and Cambridge I was welcomed by old friends, and also at Concord; but, alas! aphasia had sadly invaded the brain of Emerson, and he was painfully conscious of it. I felt in all this region that there was some desolation more or less related to that I had seen in Virginia. In conversation with Alexander Little, a brilliant but *intransigeant* editor in Fredericksburg, he said, "This old town was captured, but there is the receipt for it," — pointing to the National Cemetery. But ah, what a price it was! There lay the youths who would have continued the traditions of the literary age of New England.

Among the few of the younger generation who had risen to eminence was Professor John Fiske. I saw a good deal of him. Fiske was trying hard to recover his earlier beliefs in a personal deity and personal immortality, and I was trying to do the same. I told him that my difficulties arose from the evils and agonies of the world, — such as the horrors of the war which had ruined a large part of the South and so afflicted France. Incidentally he told me that he had recently had the most remarkable optical delusion of his life. He had seen in his library the Devil, — the regular mediæval Devil with hoof and horns, hideous face and fiery eyes. I told him that it was surely the coinage of his pure reason: he

happy there, but the journey proved too much for him. He died soon after his return to Ohio; and since then the so-called "Conway Colony" has dispersed.

could never have a benevolent and lovable deity until he had some means of relieving that deity of all responsibility for the evil in nature. Fiske's spectral Devil, identical in form to that at which Luther hurled his inkstand, was utilized by me in a sermon before the Parker Memorial society. I preferred Luther hurling his inkstand at the Devil to the academic optimist using his ink to prove that evil is good. But I did not yet trace the confusion of Good and Evil to its root in Creationism. He who creates a thing out of nothing creates all that comes out of that thing, both the good and evil. Always anxious to "believe" as much as I could, I found refuge for a time in utterly renouncing the possibility of gaining any religious idea from nature, and trusting solely to the ideal in mind and heart.

My lecture on "Demons and Devils" was well received. At Portland, Me., Governor Washburn, my host, suggested to the leading Methodist preacher that he should come and hear what I had to say on the Devil. The old preacher said: "If, as they say, the lecturer left the Methodist ministry, no doubt he is well acquainted with his subject, but I have no desire for any acquaintance in that direction."

A lecturer in the Western States thirty years ago was well paid, — $100 or more. At Columbus I got $300 for a lecture before a society there on "London Men of Science." But the lecturer had to give good measure: on the morning after his lecture he had to go through the big school and address the children in several rooms. At the first town where I lectured in Ohio some scientific gentleman gave me a small rude carving of a woman's head found near the place. In going through the public school next day I showed it to the children, and spoke of the importance of antiquities. It produced such a good effect that I carried the little thing in my pocket. At the next town I spoke to the children of the importance of observation: all through their fields were Indian arrows, and perhaps more interesting relics, — such as this (producing the Indian head). At another time my pocket squaw illustrated the tendency to art implanted in the human bosom.

The image did me good service; I became attached to it; but, alas! lost it, and had to get up a new school-piece.

But ah, what delightful people I met in that western tour! Studious, educated, hospitable, they gave me an impression that a new and nobler America was arising in the West, and I returned to England with a burden of happy prophecies.

CHAPTER XLIV

Max Müller at Oxford — His services to mankind — His tolerance — Max
Müller and the phonograph — Personal traits — Extracts from letters —
His American friends — Professor Whitney — Bayard Taylor meets Max
Müller and Carlyle.

" THE day cannot judge the day," said Goethe, and the remark finds illustration in the history of many a great scholar
and educator. The student reads with a kind of envy old
stories of Alcuin founding seats of learning in France, with
Charlemagne and his noblemen for pupils, of Roger Bacon at
Oxford, or Erasmus at Cambridge, but too often fails to
recognize the same men when they reappear in his own teachers — his Agassiz, Jowett, Max Müller.

Having for more than thirty years known Max Müller personally, I was impressed by certain characteristics of the
memorial meeting after his death held at Columbia University. The assembly was addressed by educators in different
institutions, men occupied with various branches of learning,
and the most striking feature of every tribute was its pervading sentiment of personal debt. He had opened for one his
field of research ; he had stimulated others to their tasks; he
had enriched all. What are incidental *errata* of a pioneer in
unexplored regions compared with this creation of a scholarly
race able to correct the mistakes? The master had sat at his
task, assiduous, unwearied ; now his hands were folded on his
breast ; his case was before the jury of scholars, and their
verdict was that of the professor of philosophy at Columbia :
" In a generation rich in scholars no one could be called
greater than Max Müller."

Especially impressive were the simple words of the Hindu
speaker, the Swami Abhedananda, who spoke always of the
deceased scholar as " our friend." Max Müller was indeed

the greatest friend India ever had. He not only exhumed for the young Hindus whom England was educating the literature of their race, but gave them the means of understanding it. Wherever I went in India I usually met the students and the pundits, and a number of the titled men, and all of these, of whatever caste or sect, regarded Max Müller as the greatest of mankind, and I was charged with messages entreating him to visit India. This enthusiasm of the cultured influenced even the illiterate, insomuch that when his illness was announced in India, special sacrifices were offered in the temples for their " friend." For the many Hindu students in England Max Müller's house was a shrine. His hospitality to them was pathetically noble. Most of them spoke good English, but he could converse with them in their mother-tongue, and it was beautiful to listen — occasionally I enjoyed that happiness — to his sympathetic talk with them on their studies and their ideas. These pilgrims sometimes carried to him even their personal sorrows.

Max Müller had a mission to individual minds. To every thinker his heart and home were open, and intolerance was absolutely unknown to him. " You know I do not mind difference of opinion," he wrote me in relation to criticisms on his Hibbert lectures; and concerning some comments I forwarded he wrote : " I liked Bradlaugh's articles,— they show one of the many possibilities of misunderstanding." He never showed heat when discussing a religious question, however fundamental.

Dean Stanley remarked (I quote from memory) : " In my early life few knew even the name of Buddha ; now he is second to but one other." It was this Oxford scholar who created audiences for such studies, enthusiasts for " The Light of Asia," and devout readers for the Sacred Books of the East which he has placed in our hands — the most important ethical service ever done by any man for mankind.

When the phonograph was invented, one of its first appearances was at the house of J. Fletcher Moulton Q. C. (now M. P.). A fashionable company, among them men eminent in science and letters, gathered around the novelty, and Max Müller was the first called on to utter something in the phonograph. We presently heard issuing from it these sounds: *Agnim ile purohitam yagnasm yadevam ritvigam hotâram ratnadhâtamam.*

There was a burst of merriment at these queer sounds, but a deep silence when Max Müller explained that we had heard words from the oldest hymn in the world — the first in the Vedas: "Agni I worship — the chief priest of the sacrifice — the divine priest — the invoker — conferring the greatest wealth." And then the young people gathered around the smiling scholar, to learn, no doubt, that the hymns had all passed through thousands of years, in a phonographic way, each generation uttering precisely what was poured into its ear by the preceding generation, until their language died, to be recovered in the West, where for the first time the real meaning of Agni, and human significance of the hymns, were studied and known. However, I did not hear exactly what the professor said to the eager inquirers, but stood apart observing the picturesqueness of the scene, and finding in it something symbolical of the whole career of the polite scholar. He had evoked from the oral Sanskrit phonograph the ancient Aryan literature and mythology; the thin, metallic voices became real and cast their poetic spell alike on the learned and on the fashionable in drawing-rooms throughout Europe and America, adding vast estates to their minds, delivering them from the mere pin-hole views of humanity to which their ancestors were limited.

I read in a New York paper that Max Müller was "somewhat vainglorious." This is contrary to my own impressions of the man, whom I have known in his home and in my own, and whose most famous lectures I heard. I can imagine a stranger on first seeing him, especially if in university or court dress, associating some hauteur with his erect mien, his handsome, courtly look, and a certain military air characteristic of most high-born Germans. He was a very peculiar man: his virility was expressed in his ruddy face and sparkling eye, and

some ancestral huntsman survived in him to such an extent
that when on a walk with a friend he would at times unconsciously point his cane as if it were a spear, levelling it to his
eye. The cane was aimed at nothing, unless at some point
emphasized in discussion.

Max Müller was a man even of humility ; he listened to the
humblest person addressing him with strict attentiveness; he
looked up to some who were really his inferiors. For his great
contemporaries his love and reverence were boundless. Here
are a few notes from the many private letters before me : —

I heard to-day that Emerson has sent £10 for the Carlyle
monument in London. Could you not work a little among
your friends and countrymen in London ? I have read your
paper, and I feel certain that no gossip could shake your loyalty to Carlyle's memory.

I cannot tell you what a loss Kingsley is to us. I feel as
if another cable had broken that held me fast to this life.

I have been reading your article on Emerson with great
delight. He is a man I love, and grudge to America.

Emerson's stay here was very delightful. Oxford has been
proud of his visit.

I send you the new edition of my Hibbert Lectures and
of my "Introduction to the Science of Religion" (considerably altered and enlarged). It was dedicated to Emerson,
but he was beginning to fade away when last he was here.

I feel cast down like yourself [at the death of Emerson],
and have many more names to add to the death-roll of this
year [1882] and the last. There seems no one left to work
for and to look up to now. Ruskin is the only star of the first
magnitude left, and he, I hear, is setting.

Emerson and his daughter Ellen were guests of the Max
Müllers at Oxford, and he was there surrounded by the best
men in the place, — Ruskin, Jowett, Dodson (author of " Alice
in Wonderland "), Vice-Chancellor Liddell, and others. Dr.
Holmes and his daughter were also their guests (1886) for
some days, and in " Our Hundred Days in Europe " there is
a true little picture of the home in which so many Americans
have been welcomed. Max Müller and his wife were touched
by the tender allusion to the death of their daughter.

That indeed was a heart-breaking event. "Life to me can never be again what it has been these fifty years of unbroken sunshine — but it may become something better." In January, 1888, he writes: "I became very fond of Wendell Holmes. I liked his books, and now I love the man — only life seems all over, and nothing remains but some duties to fulfil."

The Max Müllers had many American friends, and were kept well posted in transatlantic phenomena and literature.

"I saw," he writes in August, 1883, "that Howells has been staying with you — a great artist, to judge from one or two sketches which I have lately been made to read by some American friends who are staying here at Oxford. I wish you would tell me what you consider his best book. Sacred books, you know, are so long and tedious that they leave me little time for other reading, and I can only afford to read the best. I want description of real American life, not that constant theme of American novels — international episodes — metamorphic confusions produced by American volcanoes breaking through the smooth and hard stratification of European society. Please give me a few titles of such books — not too long, and worth reading."

It appeared to me nothing less than a calamity that there should be any discordant note in the relations between Max Müller and his American confrères. Knowing well how eager he was to give credit to the humblest of us working in fields connected with his own, I felt that the personal attacks directed against him must be some curious survival of the old grammarian's curse, "May God confound thee for thy theory of irregular verbs!" I believe that Max Müller also had a feeling that it was his theory (that language and thought are inseparable) which had elicited the animadversions. But in 1874, when he opened the International Congress of Orientalists in London with an admirable address, he became conscious of the personal ill-will felt by Prof. W. D. Whitney's particular friends in Germany — notably by Weber of Berlin. Max Müller had distributed in the assembly a printed copy of the last hymn of the Vedas, — close of the great work on which he had been engaged for twenty-five years. In his address he had honoured the names of the German scholars present, — Weber, Stenzler, Windisch, Spiegel, Haug, Pertsch, and all looked for some response from the great Sanskritist, Weber, who spoke English. But he remained silent. I believe Max Müller then believed that Professor Whitney was doing him mischief.

In 1875, being for some days the guest of Professor Whitney at New Haven, I listened to his grievances, and took careful notes of them to convey to Max Müller on my return to England. This was done with his approval, and in the following May (1876) by Max Müller's request, I wrote to Professor Whitney urging him to accept the proposal previously made by the Oxford scholar, that all the points in dispute should be submitted to arbitration. Professor Whitney was to select three professors from any country in Europe, and Max Müller pledged himself to abide by their decision. This proposal was urged in such terms as my esteem for Professor Whitney suggested, but he declined to say more than that if Max Müller chose to organize a tribunal he would appear before it with his defence. I never doubted that Professor Whitney had sufficient reasons, in nowise arising from any misgivings as to his own case, for virtually declining the proposed arbitration. The personal question was bound up with scientific questions, as he said, and a scholar might naturally be as unwilling to submit his opinions to arbitration as any thinker to so submit his creed. I have letters from both of these eminent scholars which I do not feel at liberty to print, but must do Max Müller the justice of declaring that it was not his fault, if fault there was, that the miserable misunderstanding was not healed in the only way that appeared open to him.

In all the severe talk of Whitney and Weber (whom I knew) concerning Max Müller, I was impressed by a certainty that they knew not the man they were talking about. He was not that kind of man at all!

In the early spring of 1878 Bayard Taylor landed in England on his way to be United States Minister at Berlin. I

managed to reach him before landing with a telegram inviting him and his wife to dinner the same evening at Hamlet
House, where Max Müller was staying with us a few days.
Max Müller was delivering his Hibbert Lectures at Westminster Abbey, and we had a large company to meet him
that evening. Taylor and Max Müller, sitting on the right
and left of Mrs. Conway, struck up a friendship almost hun-
grily. They talked briskly while others listened, now rolling
out German, now English, and when they parted it was with
a promise exacted by the professor that Bayard should visit
him at Oxford. Bayard said afterwards that after meeting
Max Müller he understood the secret of the value he had
derived from the professor's works in his own poetic studies:
"It is the *humanity* underlying his scholarship." After
dinner Taylor went about charming everybody — scientist,
artist, littérateur. President Hayes seemed to have been acting as still a member of our old Literary Club in Cincinnati
when, entirely to Taylor's surprise, he requested him to be
minister in Germany, assuring him that he should be given
every furtherance in the work he was known to have on hand,
the Life of Goethe. When Bayard told me of this, and of
the festivities that accompanied his appointment, his happiness almost overflowed his eyes.

Many years previously Bayard Taylor had met Carlyle,
and wished to see him again, but was not sure he would be
remembered, and wished me to go with him. On our way he
told me that when he first saw Carlyle the old man set a trap
for him. "I told him that I was gathering materials for a life
of Goethe. Carlyle in a disparaging manner said, 'But are
there not already Lives of Goethe? There is ——'s Life of
Goethe; what fault have you to find with that?' I began
pointing out errors here and there in that biography, when
Carlyle interrupted me with a ringing laugh and said, 'I
could n't read it through.' From that moment he knew that I
was searching my subject seriously and was cordial."

Carlyle was again cordial and more animated than was
usual in those declining years. He discussed minutely pro-

blems in the private life of Goethe, and I recall especially his
warm accord with a solution given by Taylor on a point made
by a German writer, which was simply that the said writer
"lied." Carlyle responded with a hearty laugh, which was
indeed provoked by the dramatically gentle tone in which
Bayard pronounced the judgment.

I never forgot the solemnity with which Carlyle bade Bayard farewell. With an evident feeling that his own life must
soon terminate, he repeated Goethe's ode : —

> The future hides in it gladness and sorrow ;
> We press still thorow,
> Naught that abides in it daunting us,
> Onward !

His voice trembled a little when he came to the lines : —

> Stars silent rest o'er us,
> Graves under us silent.

Then Bayard took up the strain, and in warm, earnest
tones repeated the remaining verses in German. Carlyle
seemed deeply moved. As we left he took Bayard's hand and
said, " I hope you will do your best at Berlin to save us from
further war in Europe."

At that moment the danger of war between England and
Russia seemed imminent, and Carlyle was strenuously opposing it, — as indeed he always opposed war.

Bayard Taylor had many devoted friends in England, and
the mourning for him was profound. It was already arranged
that he should be the chief figure at the Oxford Commemoration in 1879. " How very sad," wrote Max Müller, " the
news of Bayard Taylor's death. He looked so strong in body
and mind when I saw him at your house. He is the second
who is gone before I could send him my [Hibbert] Lectures,
out of those few for whom they were specially written, and
whose approval would have been a real reward. I send you
his last letter to me. I thought you would like to see it, but
please take great care of it and let me have it back soon. I
feel deeply obliged to you for having enabled me to know
your great countryman face to face."

CHAPTER XLV

THE friendly intervention of Thomas Hughes brought me an invitation from Professor Jowett to be his guest in Balliol College at the Oxford Commemoration (June, 1863). The pro-fessor was a great man to us in America; we pictured him as a martyr, starving on forty pounds a year for having written one of the " Essays and Reviews." It was more important to see him than to witness any commemoration.

My welcome began at the foot of the long stairway leading to the professor's apartment in Balliol: the wall beside it was hung with large photographs of the great teachers of the time, among them Darwin, Carlyle, Browning, and Tennyson.

A dignified valet met me with messages from the professor; he must be busy with examinations all day, and could not even be back to dinner. I must make myself at home, and should go to the great garden party, for which he left cards.

The old wainscotted room — that of an absent tutor — set apart for me was not only elegant but had in it a friendly odour of tobacco, — true Virginia hospitality.

After seeing the beautiful garden party and strolling among the colleges, I returned for the half-past seven dinner. I pre-pared for possible eventualities by donning evening dress, and thus all alone I feasted in a grand room on a dinner so excel-lent that I felt nervous. Had Jowett supposed me an ambas-sador?

About an hour after dinner the professor entered with a

quick, light footstep, and said he had come before going to
a committee to ask if I had all I needed, and to say what I
might expect next day — the great day. He was forty-six
and slightly grey, but his blond complexion — somewhat rosy
— and his happy look and voice were not suggestive of ordeals. Only the February before he had been summoned
before the vice-chancellor's court on account of " Essays and
Reviews," but had successfully denied its jurisdiction.

Jowett knew nothing of me except what Tom Hughes told
him, — that I was an antislavery Virginian come over to give
some addresses concerning the struggle in America. My religious heresies were as yet unknown. Jowett was interested in
the American conflict, and at breakfast eager with questions.
When I resolutely changed the subject and began to talk about
Harvard, Emerson, and " Essays and Reviews," he responded
with more personal interest, and the conversation became
what I had hoped for. Or was becoming such — but lo! the
old oaken room was invaded by a bevy of young ladies, fresh
as morning roses, who circled around the scholar, delivered
messages from old friends, talked about brothers and cousins
about to graduate, until the grave professor was transformed
to a flaxen-haired youth. He graciously introduced me, and
the various companies of the day were thereby rendered pleasanter ; also it was some compensation for the interrupted conversation to see the grave professor (the martyr!) entering
easily into all the affairs and pretty gossip of the young
dames and arranging their day for them.

In after years when the persecution had ended, and Jowett
had become master of Balliol and vice-chancellor of the university, I saw him at times and wondered whether he might
not be regarding those burdensome honours as the martyrdom
and looking back to the forty-pound years as the happier.

Jowett appeared to me different from other religious liberals. Those called " advanced " thinkers in both America and
England were moving forward on a kind of track laid down
by the science and scholarship of their time, but Jowett impressed me as a man who belonged to earlier and greater reli-

gious ages. When thorns first sprout the camel may browse on them, but when they are old they tear his lip. So said Sheik Saadi, and it is a fair parable of the church which in the seventeenth century nourished the free minds and hearts of Jeremy Taylor and George Herbert, of Tillotson and Dean Swift. Jowett belonged to their race. I never heard him preach, but I heard him lecture at the Royal Institution on "The Dæmon of Socrates," and I doubt if any other clergyman since Swift was so free from the clerical accent. He was keenly interested in the persons engaged in the religious movements going on around him, but did he take the movements themselves seriously? It is true that of the positivist church he reported that he found there "three persons and no God." I was told another story that I can almost believe. Before the new era of open university doors for unbelievers a young man came to Professor Jowett in distress on the morning of the day for subscribing the articles, and said, "Alas, I have studied and searched and can find in the universe no God!" Jowett pulled out his watch and said quietly, "You must find one by quarter past four."

I have one or two anecdotes about Jowett that may be mentioned. I asked him about Socrates' last words, "We owe a cock to Æsculapius," whether they were genuine, and, if so, whether they should be interpreted as a tribute to health, or to the healing art, or had any philosophical significance. He thought the words genuine, and that Socrates meant only what he said.

During the trial of the Rev. Charles Voysey for heresy, I was present at a dinner given by the Hon. and Rev. Mr. Freemantle. Dean Stanley and Jowett were present, and when the ladies had retired the conversation fell on the exciting case. Jowett said, "Voysey looked too far over the hedge."

Dr. James Martineau told me that when he received his degree of LL. D. at Oxford, he was the guest of Dr. Jowett, master of Balliol. "George Eliot" and G. H. Lewes were also guests at the same time. "One day," said Martineau, "when I was alone with Jowett, he said, ' I don't think much of George Eliot's religious ideas: she merely denies the authority of the Bible, — and there stops.' "

Dr. Martineau mentioned this in a talk on intellectual honesty. That a clergyman, and master of Balliol, should regard denial of the authority of the Bible as but rudimentary filled him with wonder. But I could not look at it in that way. Jowett was not another Martineau, he was himself; and the thing needed is that a man should be his single genuine self.

I had many provincial prejudices to get rid of after settling in England. It appeared at first the plainest duty in the world to unite with the dissenters in their agitation for the separation of Church and State. After a year or so I began to wonder at never seeing at their meetings any of the great liberal thinkers, none of the scientific men. My South Place people even, all trained in reforms, though listening respectfully to my discourse in favour of disestablishment of the church, never joined the society organized for that end. I began to suspect something wrong about the cause, and caught some light from an incident that occurred at Zion College. Dr. Tait, then bishop of London, presiding over a discussion on the national Church, said in his opening address that it was proved in America what sad results came from disestablishment, — "the people went off into Socinianism." The bishop did not know that the greatest of Socinians was present — James Martineau — and could not understand the amusement caused by his remark until, to his embarrassment, Martineau was called for. The Socinian began by saying: "Notwithstanding the temptation offered by his lordship, I am an Englishman before I am a Socinian, and not prepared to advocate disestablishment." He then proceeded to present his idea of a national Church freed from its antiquated creeds and enlarged so as to include all of the serious religious organizations in the country. I did not and do not now hold the views of Dr. Martineau on the subject, but I revised the whole matter carefully and reached the conclusion that I had been cheated by the phrase, "separation of Church and

State." No genuine separation of that kind has ever taken place. In America the separation of Church and State has invariably meant merely the separation of the State from one particular Church, — the English Church, — to the extent only of establishing all sects along with it. By the exemption of Church property from taxation the whole community is taxed in the interest of those churches. Then by the legal establishment of the aggregate Sabbatarianism of the churches, by appointing and paying national chaplains, by supporting in treaties and by military force the propaganda of missionaries in foreign lands, orthodox Christianity is made a national American institution. Sectarian churches are indeed all enjoying established privileges in America unknown to the English Church. For in England the Established Church has only a life interest, and a very limited interest, in its endowments and edifices. The property belongs to the secular State, it is under the control of a parliament containing Jews, Catholics, pagans, freethinkers. The whole country participates in the disposal of every pound sterling. No citizen can be excluded from its vestries. No subscription to creed or article is required of him. But in the United States, while the taxes of a wealthy freethinker, like the late Robert Ingersoll, are larger because church property is exempt, — he being thus taxed for sects and dogmas he repudiates, — he cannot sit in synod or conference and say what shall be done with his money. It is taxation without representation.

Matthew Arnold having written an essay criticising the attitude of the English dissenters, James Martineau answered him with severity in a lecture given at Manchester New College, London. This I heard; it was able, but I did not find it satisfactory. I happened to meet Matthew Arnold the same day and told him something about the lecture. He said, " Oh, Martineau is not one of them; he is one of us." He then went on to explain that Martineau did not wish to set up an antagonistic church to overthrow and supplant the Church of England; he was simply a rationalistic critic of the intellectual errors of the church, aiming to liberalize it. Not long

2, Chester Square. S.W
November 8th 1865.

My dear Sir

I have only just returned
after a seven months absence on
the Continent, visiting schools.
It is very kind of you to
have taken charge of the
Emerson Book for me: pray send
it to me here, I shall be
very glad to have it. Emerson
has always particularly interested
me by retaining his reason
while Carlyle, his fellow-prophet,

lost his; Emerson for some time
suffered in "popularity" from his
sobriety, but as the rôle of
reason in human affairs begins
to get more visibly important,
what he lost is being made
up to him.

What you say about my
being read in America is very
kind. Perhaps your countrymen,
from their greater variety and
curiosity of temperament, are
more likely than the English public

to care for what I have written:
but even with you, I suspect,
if I have my tens the Country
Parson has his myriads, so
one must work mainly for
one's own delectation after all.

I hope we shall some day
meet again, either at Rondles
or elsewhere — and meanwhile
believe me, with renewed thanks,
      Sincerely yours,
         Matthew Arnold. —

M. D. Conway Esq^n

after, travelling in a railway compartment with Martineau, I
told him what Matthew Arnold had said. He admitted that
he did not sympathize with the dissent detached from the
Established Church merely on the grounds of its traditional
institutions, episcopacy, etc., while holding the same creed.
This was an admission that Arnold was substantially right.

When the Voysey case came on, and many theists were
uniting with churchmen in declaring it his duty to resign the
clerical profession, I wrote to him expressing the opinion that
when a clergyman reached views different from those he had
honestly held on receiving orders, he should throw on the
church the burden of dealing with him. It was not his duty
to resign, but the reverse; he should avail himself of the
opportunity honourably come by to compel the church to define the limits of its toleration. The existing articles and
creeds had been for many generations so modified by legal
decisions and interpretations that it was not just to the youth
of the nation, liable to enter on clerical life, for any heretical
clergyman to constitute himself an ecclesiastical court, and
determine that he had no lawful right in the church.

This view was paradoxical to Unitarians. Dr. Martineau,
who had retired from the pulpit, attended the chapel of the
Rev. Stopford Brooke after the latter had left the English
Church. Brooke had been the most brilliant clergyman in
London. I had sometimes heard his afternoon sermons, and
used to meet him and his handsome daughters in society,
chiefly at Mrs. E. Lynn Linton's receptions. His leaving the
church impressed me as a calamity, and I expressed my regret.
He was surprised, and told me he had felt himself in the
wrong place. He said that Dean Stanley had urged him to
remain and preach his whole mind with freedom. "But,"
said Mr. Brooke, "I asked the dean: 'Could James Martineau be made Archbishop of Canterbury?' He answered,
'No.' Then said I, 'The church is no place for me.'" My
reply was that if men like himself were to remain in the
church, preach their convictions boldly, and omit every formula they did not believe, the church must steadily become

such that a Martineau could become archbishop. Even if, after the church authorities had decided either to expel or to tolerate one or another phase of unbelief, the heretic should find that his sphere of influence was elsewhere, he might then leave with a feeling that he had done his whole duty by the national institution. Stopford Brooke then said that each individual must necessarily decide on the duty of his particular case ; with this I agreed, with the reservation that each individual should be careful lest he should lay down a precedent or rule for the consciences of others.

When Cardinal Newman in the latter part of his life visited Oxford, a distinguished company was invited to meet him. A generation had passed since he left Oxford. A friend who sat near him at table told me that Newman inquired of a master, " What changes have come over Oxford since I left ? " The answer was, " Greater than I can enumerate ; chiefly this, the university has been largely secularized."

Such a happy result is inevitable in a State Church. And as the experience of the United States proves that Christianity cannot be really disendowed, it is better that a Church historically evolved along with the secular State, and receiving its living through the State, should be established. A single Church also can be controlled, but not a combination of all Churches.

Voltaire said, " All religions are equally untrue and equally necessary." Substituting " inevitable " for " necessary," and regarding all the denominations with an eye solely to general human benefits, I saw that disestablishment would silence the only independent clergy. Apart from the debatable ground of theology, the English clergyman can say what he thinks. He may have been appointed to his living by some nobleman, yet may rebuke that nobleman to his face. My lord cannot touch him. He may criticise his bishop, or the government which appointed him, or condemn every prejudice of his congregation ; they cannot remove him. If he be accused of immorality or heresy, he can be tried before a court; otherwise his pulpit is his castle.

Through this independence the clergy have developed what dissenters call their worldliness. The Catholic Church in Europe began with asceticism; holy men fled from the world as a city of destruction to cavern or convent, and women shut themselves in nunneries. By that means the species was left to development by the more worldly. Outside convent walls the Catholic Church was thus gradually drawn into sympathy with popular festivities, the May-pole, the dance. Protestantism swept all this away with its Sabbatarianism and Puritanism. Puritanism was a relapse far behind Catholicism. Socially it recovered the ascetic thorns which Catholicism had overlaid with roses of art and mirth. It burnt pictures and built chapels that were models of ugliness. The English Church alone retains some of the artistic beauty and the humanities developed by previous centuries, and it was the " worldly " head of the English Church, even Charles I, who reached his hand across the Atlantic and stopped the pious murder of " witches " and Quakers.

The English clergy do not object to lawn tennis and cricket on Sunday. At Eversley Charles Kingsley formed a Sunday cricket club for his parishioners and played with them. In clubs to which bishops belong the billiards cease not on Sunday. Thus the English Church shields cultured society from Puritanism. If a rationalist preacher takes his family to the theatre, the puritanical might call it the natural result of his heresies; but as some clergyman's family may be in an adjoining box they cannot ascribe that to heresy. This easy relation between the English Church and the world, which protects the young in their gaieties, is felt in many parts of the world.

During the long struggle for the Sunday opening of museums and art galleries the orthodox dissenters were against us, and even Quaker John Bright, though he voted for the opening, did not revive the testimony of George Fox against the Sabbath. I told him once that a speech in public like his talk in private would unlock the galleries. But he said that the matter had been damaged by being involved with Christianity itself, and by Sunday not being a day of rest in France. But at that very moment the clergymen of the English Church were with us. I once was a member of a deputation to the government to plead for the open Sunday, and of the twenty-seven parishes in London all but three were represented. At a meeting held on the subject in the Lord Mayor's mansion, a dean of Rochester, seeing Henry Irving present, said he would be glad to see him performing one of his grand dramas before the people on Sunday.

The most active leader in that movement was the late Septimus Hansard, rector of Bethnal Green. This admirable man I knew well. He was liberal enough to use my "Sacred Anthology" as a prize in his night school for working people. So devoted were his labours among the poor in that lowest quarter of the city that he was stricken down successively with scarlatina, typhus, and small-pox caught during his parish visits. In the last case he sank in his pulpit while preaching, and when a physician pronounced it small-pox he refused to go to the hospital in a cab for fear of infecting the cab, and called for the hearse, and was taken to the small-pox hospital some miles away stretched in the hearse.

Nor are the charities of the clergy restricted to ordinary relief. They minister to the higher sense of the poor, whose only contact with art and beauty was then in the music and ornamentation of the church. In Shoreditch, in the heart of London, the Rev. Mr. Noble, a ritualistic clergyman, every year pressed his independence to the extreme of getting up a miracle play at Christmas time. My wife and I were invited (there were no payments), and I remember the horrible evening in which we first pressed our way through sleet and fog to his church. Beautiful tableaux of the Nativity were presented by members of his congregation, — with a chorus of angels in luminous raiment who sang the ancient hymns and carols to poor people, who beheld through happy tears these visions shining amid their moil and sorrow.

For a good many years I wrote for "Harper's Magazine" articles about various regions of England, personally exploring them, and I also made investigations in all the counties associated with the Washington family,—Northampton, Yorkshire, Durham, Westmoreland, Cumberland, etc. In all of these places my main dependence was on the clergymen. They alone were competent to assist my researches, and interested themselves in them; and although I had become rather notorious as a heretic, and was careful to let them know that I was the minister of a rationalist society, this made no difference in their hospitality. They invited me into their houses, unfolded their church registers, and accompanied me to historic places. At Epworth, town of the Wesleys, the Wesleyan minister knew nothing about them; he sent me to an old man of his flock, who told me that the only man who knew all about the Wesley family was the rector. This gentleman, Canon Overton, and his wife took me away from the inn and devoted two days to my researches. And even when I was investigating the life of Thomas Paine at Thetford, the venerable Rector Fowler did all he could to assist me. In no instance was I ever treated with disrespect by a clergyman. In some places the people were ignorant and rough, the clergyman and his family being the only persons of refinement and education among them. No such family would bury itself far away from centres of culture and pleasure were not the clergyman a functionary of the State. He is there for the culture of the country, for the humanities — a scholar and a gentleman, — and if his Church were disestablished, reduced to a mere sect in competition with vulgar sectarians, the clergyman would not be there. He has no training at his university for such work. Disestablishment would be like a toppling down of lighthouses on rough moral coasts. As for the creeds and formulas, they have no more effect on the masses than if they were in Latin; they offend only the few that can understand them; altogether, with the music and the responses they make a pretty Sunday concert. It is the refinement and the benevolence of the clergyman and his family that practically make his gospel.

I used to submit these views to the most exact thinkers

among my friends, and especially to James Sime, editor of
" Nature " and author of the " Life of Lessing." He was
brought up among the Scotch Calvinists and was a critical
sceptic, but entirely concurred with me. And one evening
when our little Sunday evening club of " Calumets " met at
my house in Bedford Park, I made this the theme of the talk,
— not one of our dozen was a member of any church or
chapel, — we agreed that disestablishment would be the means
of throwing the masses under the influence of illiterate and
superstitious sects. Yet all agreed that our freethinking societies were performing a necessary function in criticising the
creeds, enlightening educated people, and thus surrounding
the Church with restraints on clericalism and assisting its
broad and tolerant wing. Had there been no Martineau there
had been no such Archbishop of Canterbury as Frederick
Temple, and no such Dean as Stanley.

I was once walking through Westminster Abbey with Rev.
Phillips Brooks (not yet bishop) and we came upon a large
placard, hung on a column, on which were printed solely the
eight lines of Emerson beginning, —

> O'er England's abbeys bends the sky,
> As on its own with kindred eye.

The brilliant American's eye sparkled, and when we were
presently joined by Dean Stanley at that spot, and all talked
of Emerson with love (neither being Emersonian save by the
leaven of his spirit), I remembered the power Emerson
ascribed to Thought. It could raise " a whole Popedom of
forms." I listened to the conversation of two men who had
carried their church to a liberal height beyond Unitarianism.
Some friends of mine in Boston left Unitarian King's Chapel
and joined the church of Phillips Brooks with the same progressive feeling and pains of separation I had in leaving
Methodism for Unitarianism.

As we sauntered through the Abbey Dean Stanley explained to us, with his quiet humour, why deans of Westminster have exceptional immunity from episcopal interference.

It is because the first dean of that Abbey was consecrated by St. Peter himself. Late in the night before the consecration by bishops was to take place a boat came up the Thames, and from it there landed a mysterious man, dressed as a prelate, who knocked at the Abbey door, and when admitted sent the keeper to awaken and bring there the priest about to be consecrated. After consecration the new dean said, "But how do I know your authority?" The man from the boat opened a basket he had brought, revealing a large and peculiar fish, and said, "When the archbishop comes to-morrow present him with this fish; he will know who has consecrated you and the ceremony will not be repeated." The dean added that at one time there was a discussion as to whether a dean of Westminster might not claim a seat in the House of Lords. At any rate, none of his predecessors — so I understood him — had ever been interfered with by a bishop.

When Colenso, the heretical Bishop of Natal, visited London, some of the evangelical prelates, whose deprivation of his bishopric had been set aside by the courts, forbade clergymen in their dioceses to open their pulpit to him. But Dean Stanley defied them by inviting Colenso to preach in Westminster Abbey. There were intimations in the press that for once a dean of Westminster was to be grappled with. A short time before the sermon was to be given Lady Augusta Stanley, the dean's wife, was prostrated by the illness that proved mortal, and Bishop Colenso would not risk adding to his friend's anxiety any trouble of the kind threatened. "There had been no prohibition sent to the dean nor to me," Colenso told me, "but there were probabilities of bitter controversy, and Stanley is in such trouble about Lady Augusta that, persistent as he is, I have resolved to leave London sooner than I had intended."

Colenso was a gentle and modest man and disinclined to become the central figure of a conflict. He had come to England simply to secure justice for Langabalele. He gave us a lecture in a small hall, and in beginning said, "I have for so many years been speaking in the language of another race that I do not feel sure of being able to address you rightly in my native tongue." The words were said with simplicity and an entire unconsciousness of their pathos.

Somehow, after knowing Colenso and listening to him, I found a certain felicity in the "nonsense verse" written when his heresies first appeared: —

> There was a My Lord of Natal
> Who had a Zulu for a pal :
> Said the Zulu, " Look here
> Ain't the Pentateuch queer ? "
> Which converted My Lord of Natal.

This learned and eloquent Englishman, with his superb head and figure, giving heed to the awakened doubt of the dark-skinned " heathen " he went out to convert, was a typical figure of the new generation. We were summoned by great scholars — even by some like Professor Legge who had been missionaries — to sit at the feet of those vulgarly called " heathen," — Buddha, Zoroaster, Confucius, — through whom the genius of other races was expressed.

In 1853 at Concord I had begun making extracts from Oriental books in Emerson's library. I continued to add to the collection, and in 1860 printed at Cincinnati in my "Dial" every month selections of the kind under the heading, "The Catholic Chapter." After my settlement at South Place (1864) I began taking my second lesson from some Oriental work, and after a year or so the two lessons were selected without any discrimination in favour of the Bible. The innovation was from the first much commented on, and in a few years my accumulation of extracts was sufficient to enable me to respond to the desire of my people for a volume of them.

Although I put a great deal of labour into my " Sacred Anthology," it was charming work. Sometimes I was reminded of the way in which we used to hunt over the shoals at Narragansett Pier to find one pebble that was precious. The dear old librarian of the India House, not yet housed in its palace at Kensington, sympathized with my purpose. That man, Dr. Rost, remains in my memory as a character that ought to be portrayed by a Nathaniel Hawthorne — were another possible. Unworldly and unselfish, carrying in his head treasures of learning, remote from roaring London, he manifested surprise and pleasure that any one should need exactly that counsel he could bestow. He pointed me to the great masses of unpublished translations, and there I passed many days. The larger portion was useless for my anthology. There were endless details concerning body and mind mingled in the sacred instructions.[1]

I employed several Hindus and Persians to search books not translated. I was encouraged by R. M. Childers, and shall never forget the delight I experienced when he sent me Buddha's "Excellencies." My hunt for Eastern flowerets brought me into further acquaintance with Professor E. H. Palmer of Cambridge University (England). He revised several Persian translations for me, and but for him I might have known nothing of several fine pieces of Nizami. He said that he regarded the Persian ideas as the finest, and had repeatedly told people that when they had thoroughly studied those books they would "begin to know something about religion."

The "Sacred Anthology" was not compiled for Orientalists nor for critical scholars, but to provide thoughtful readers with some idea of the ethical and religious geography, so to say, of the world ; and also to provide myself with a book of ethnical scriptures from which to read lessons from my pulpit. Type-writing was unknown in 1872–1874, and in order to distribute the selections under their various headings my wife and I fairly carpeted the floor with them. Nevertheless, the volume did please the eminent scholars, and brought me

---

[1] When (1903) I heard of the suicide in New York of Ida C. Craddock, to escape going to prison on account of her two pamphlets, *The Wedding Night* and *Right Martial Living*, I managed to get these tiny pamphlets — in the title of which she describes herself as " Pastor of the Church of Yoga." I was amazed to find that this refined and educated lady had written in exactly the same devout way about the bodily functions as those ancient Hindus.

cordial letters from Martineau, Tennyson, Tyndall, Professor
Newman, Miss Cobbe, and many others. But that which was
most gratifying was the immediate use to which it was put in
various regions. Walter Thomson, a member of my society
who had lived in India (where Oriental writings are less accessible than in London), paid for an edition to be distributed
gratis among the Brahmos and scholars there. Dean Stanley
spoke of the work in a .sermon in Westminster Abbey and
quoted from it these Sufi sentences : " If thou art a Mussul-
man, go stay with the Franks ; if a Christian, join the Jews ; if
a Shiah, mix with the Schismatics : whatever thy religion,
associate with men of opposite persuasion. If, in hearing their
discourses, thou art not in the least moved, but canst mix with
them freely, thou hast attained peace and art a master of
creation."

The " Sacred Anthology " was used in several Unitarian
churches in England and Scotland, and in a large number in
America, for pulpit lessons. The press notices were universally favourable. But one, by Professor Weber of Berlin, began with the words, " Vox populi vox dei," so interpreting the
Greek motto in my title. The lines are from Hesiod (" Works
and Days," bk. ii, end), the translation being : " The utterance does not wholly perish which many peoples utter ; nay,
this is the voice of God." I was distressed on finding that
the plural " peoples " — which so widely separates the thought
from the utterance of any populace — was overlooked by
Professor Weber. Thus Hesiod's saying was exhumed (I
never saw it cited) only to travel the road to corruption previously trodden by the phrase of Cicero, " Res publica res
populi " (Cic. Rep. i, 25), which may have suggested the *Vox
populi* invention. For this is a comparatively modern invention, — European democracy putting on a classic mask. The
irony of it is that Hesiod's lines refer to the care of people
in various countries not to pollute with excrement streams
flowing to the sea ! It occurred to me that the trivial superstition might have grown out of a sanitary precaution, and
that Hesiod wrote more wisely than he knew.

In 1873 I did not believe that the voice of any populace was inspired, though I did not then realize that in every nation the majority are always wrong. But I did — and do — believe that when many different peoples (races) unite in a belief of principle, local egotism and provincialism are sufficiently withdrawn for some moral or physical common law to be implied if not expressed. I had long been convinced that the Bible, ignorantly called Hebrew, owes its place in human interest to the fact that it is an anthology of many peoples, though largely altered by the doctors of one race in their attempt to adapt all the contributions to their own dogmas.

The first copy of the "Sacred Anthology" was sent to Max Müller; it happened to be just before the meeting of the international Oriental Congress in London (1873), and the first public mention of the work was made (to my surprise) in the address with which he opened the proceedings. He said : —

A patient study of the Sacred Scriptures of the world is what is wanted at present more than anything else, in order to clear out ideas of the origin, the nature, and the purposes of religion. In the end we shall be able to restore that ancient bond which unites not only the East with the West, but all the members of the human family, and may learn what a Persian poet meant when he wrote many centuries ago, — I quote from Mr. Conway's "Sacred Anthology" — "Diversity of worship has divided the human race into seventy-two nations. From among all their dogmas I have selected one — the love of God."

Professor Max Müller also wrote a signed review of my work in the "Academy" which attracted the attention of scholars everywhere. The popular success of the "Sacred Anthology," and the applause of the journals, led to a much more important kind of success, — of which I may speak freely, as I wrote nothing in my book but its brief preface. Max Müller told me that the interest in Oriental literature stirred up by the anthology inclined him to undertake the publication of the "Sacred Books of the East," and asked me about the financial support likely to be obtained. My anthology was printed and bound at my own expense, Trübner selling it on commission ; my outlay was covered by subscriptions, and my profits were good, though I gave many and contributed my royalties in the edition donated by Walter Thomson to India. I expressed to Max Müller my delight in his enterprise and willingness to help in obtaining subscriptions. I am thus carrying into my closing days the reflection that my " Sacred Anthology " contributed something to the publication of the " Sacred Books of the East," — the chief religious achievement of the nineteenth century.

CHAPTER XLVI

IN my ministry Theology was naturally replaced by Anthropology. This science had not in 1863 been recognized by the British Association; the facts with which it was concerned were brought out in other sections, and the society in London discussing the negro with an eye to America had not yet merited recognition. But my combat about the negro in that society was the means of giving me a place in the Anthropological Institute when it arose. The works of Tylor and Lubbock and the generalizations of Herbert Spencer concerning primitive man breathed on all the dry bones in the museums, and Anthropology presently leaped into the front rank of sciences.

The materials for such investigations were largely supplied by Colonel Lane Fox, an officer who, having won promotion in the Crimean war, found that his genius was for the study and not the destruction of man. He then conquered tribes and races by friendliness ; he had gained their confidence, and returned from his official expeditions with a vast number of guns got not by capturing but captivating the tribes. He had even learned the arts of primitive man : he was probably the only Englishman who could make a primitive flint arrow and throw a boomerang so as to make it return.

Colonel Lane Fox and his wife (a daughter of Lord Stanley of Alderley) were aristocrats without airs. They were free from dogmatic notions and often came to my chapel. We found them delightful neighbours. They were not wealthy, but one day we were startled by the tidings that Colonel Lane Fox was henceforth to be known as General Pitt Rivers, having inherited Rushmore, the magnificent estate of his grand-uncle Lord Rivers in Wiltshire. He told me that nothing could have appeared to him more improbable than this succession, there being two sons of Lord Rivers to inherit the estate before it could pass to the female line represented by himself.

The unexpected death of Lord Rivers's sons as they successively approached majority could not fail to start a local legend : it was said that a noble maiden whom Lord Rivers was expected to wed died of a broken heart on hearing of his marriage, her last words being, " None of their children will inherit Rushmore." If scientific men had not lost the Eastern faith they might have believed that the angel of death had been commissioned to secure for science the inheritance of Rushmore. To science it came. The vast estate was rich in barrows and other relics of primitive man, and all these fell precisely to the man most competent to summon them from their slumber of ages and interpret their story of an extinct human world. The six large illustrated volumes recording his researches, distributed to those who could utilize them for the advancement of knowledge, the museum he built at Farnham, and his great collections given to Oxford, constitute the fit monument of General Pitt Rivers. Had not his modesty been equal to his merit, or had he been capable of partizanship, he would have been made Lord Rivers. But, as Schiller said, " The question is not, art thou in the nobility, but, is there nobility in thee ? "

General Pitt Rivers was conservative in temperament, and my admiration was not due to any special sympathy on his part with my opinions. Even where we generally agreed — that is on religious subjects — he inclined to think that a little admixture of superstition was more useful than I thought, — if the superstition were not cruel, like the biblical ferocities. I was afraid of even the so-called pretty superstitions.

The estates and revenues of Rushmore came into the possession of General Pitt Rivers freed from entail, and it was a droll circumstance that several Church livings came into the absolute ownership of this scientific rationalist. He asked me if I would like to have one of them! He told me that the bishop once came for some official duty and staid at Rushmore. On Sunday they drove to church, where the bishop preached, and one of the lessons for the day happened to be a belligerent psalm. On their way home the general remarked, " That lesson seems rather more related to my profession than to that of your lordship." The bishop smiled but said nothing.

In walking through the Anthropological Museum at Oxford, presented to the university by General Pitt Rivers, in company with my friend E. B. Tylor, we recalled at every step the illumination given to the various objects at the Institute in London when the general was its president. His military knowledge was utilized to show us the " survival " of the cross-bow in the Oriental rifle ; and he had collected a variety of Patagonian paddles painted with queer fragmentary designs, utterly meaningless until by putting them together they were shown to be the gradually distributed parts of a sacred image — a tribal totem. But he did not omit regions nearer home from his researches. He made a collection of the caps of women in Brittany ; and I well remember how the mirth caused by their display to a company of ladies and gentlemen in London changed to grave interest as he revealed to us the significance of these caps. The peasant or villager of one parish must not wear the cap of another parish to which she has casually gone. The parish caps vary, and each has in itself arrangements for variation : some ornamental appendages are let out when the wearer attends a wedding or a fête, and some usual fringes are turned in for a funeral. A nun's headdress was shown, and the general pointed out the indications that all of the French caps were developed from that of the nun. Nothing was too small for his study.

I do not think the general ever printed anything about these caps ; his theory of their origin (the nun's headdress) he regarded as conjectural. It was his way to suggest things in conversation which lasted in the memories of his friends. One day when we were talking of the precipitous way in which the French had hurled themselves against the Germans he remarked that it might be due to the brachyocephalous character of the Gallic cranium. In their heads the blood flies straight up like a fountain. In the long-headed man the blood has to go a roundabout way before it mounts, and gives him time to think twice before he acts. But he liked the French and highly appreciated their anthropologists.

In presiding over any discussion in the Anthropological Institute the general showed as much skill in getting at the ideas of his colleagues as in securing secrets from remote tribes. And they were men whose ideas were worth having. There sat Huxley, Busk, Lubbock, Tylor, Leitner, Francis and Douglas Galton, Palgrave, Sir John Evans, Professor Newton, and generally some eminent man from America or from the continent. Professor Whitney once addressed us, and Eugene Schuyler described curious manners and customs in Turco-Slav regions.

A motion to admit ladies to membership sprung on the Institute a " burning issue," and an evening was devoted to it. There had been receptions of members in private houses, and the intelligence of many of their ladies was well known. The Hon. Mrs. Pitt Rivers, Mrs. Tylor, Mrs. Huxley, and others were felt by best men to be persons of serious interest in our pursuits, and these would have been admitted without controversy. But to admit only a few was hardly possible. Professor Huxley made a vigorous speech in favour of the admission of women ; he spoke with unusual animation, brushing away some of the objections made on the score of feminine delicacy. Several members feared that readers of papers on manners and customs of distant tribes might, were ladies present, suppress pictures or details of importance. Professor Huxley did not believe that any lady interested in science could have mock modesty ; she was as much entitled to know the facts of nature as a man. Tylor, to whom we looked for an appreciative anal-

ysis of the points made in any discussion, made in his graceful
way the summing up, which for a time delighted the group
opposed to the innovation; but he closed by saying, " Should
the society conclude to admit ladies, I beg to propose the
name of Mrs. E. B. Tylor." This of course raised a laugh
and ended the discussion. Ladies thenceforth began to appear
at our meetings, and there was no reason to suppose that any
narratives were modified or pictures suppressed because of their
presence.

One day I accompanied General Pitt Rivers and Sir John
Evans on a day's exploration in the Thames valley, where
some flint implements had been newly discovered. We moved
along the sharp flinty roads, softened only by enthusiasm,
never removing our eyes from the ground, however the larks
might sing or the gorse blossom. I gathered sundry bits of
stone whose smooth sides or points suggested manipulations by
man, and, separately others I thought more doubtful. But
Sir John no sooner put them beneath his spectacles than all
my unquestionable ones were hurled into the air, while of the
doubtful ones two were thought to bear some trace of work-
manship. We entered the house of a gentleman not without
some skill in such things, who had accumulated six hundred
specimens. The stones were laid out on a table; Sir John sat
at the head, Pitt Rivers at the foot, and their eyes sparkled;
but of the six hundred pieces only two or three dozen had
been touched by primitive man.

The numismatic knowledge of Sir John Evans was unsur-
passed; he was a charming speaker, and I never knew an
audience at the Royal Institution more enchained than by a
lecture of his on " Coinage of the Ancient Britons and Natural
Selection." From pictorial representations he read us a connected story of evolution: the forms of ancient coins had
grown, changed, passed into totally new species, occasionally
relapsing into the original type, and generally preserving some
trace of their origin. One series — picked up in odd places
and fitted together — told a very quaint story. The original,
struck under Philip of Macedon, had a laurelled head of Her-

cules on the obverse, and on the reverse a chariot with two horses driven by Victory. This was the most important Macedonian coin commercially, and the engraving fine. As trading communities sprang up in the western regions whither the race was migrating, it was necessary to have a coin interchangeable with that of Macedon, but impossible in new centres to engrave the figure so perfectly. The result was mere indications of the devices on the coin sufficient to identify its value, and these gradually reduced. A stage was reached when the chariot was represented by one wheel; another when of the two horses remained eight amputated legs. In time the original meaning of these signs was lost. But skilful engravers had appeared in the West, one of whom made a guess at the meaning of the horse-legs and produced from them a head of Medusa. On the reverse, from the laurelled head of Hercules the face gradually disappeared, leaving only the headdress and fillet. The western engravers supposed this headdress and fillet to be an early attempt to represent the cross, which duly supplanted the last trace of Hercules.

My wife and I enjoyed the hospitalities of Rushmore, and Mrs. Pitt Rivers took us on delightful drives, — among them to visit descendants of the old Lord Baltimore who in 1648 appointed my ancestor William Stone governor of Maryland. But my anthropological interest brought me nearer to the chiefs buried in the Cranborne Chase barrows than to any ancestor, and I enjoyed most my morning walks or drives with the general to the points where his workmen with their picks were digging with tender caution.

I had the happiness of being among those invited to Rushmore soon after the family moved there, to pass some days in witnessing the opening of a number of tumuli which the general believed likely to yield interesting results. The other guests were Herbert Spencer, Norman Lockyer, Sir John Evans, Sir Francis Galton, and Sir John Lubbock (now Lord Avebury, whose wife is a daughter of General Pitt Rivers).

Some of the barrows being far, luncheon was sometimes taken with us, and the visit made a kind of picnic. Near each dead chieftain were little piles of cinders left from sacrifices offered in his honour or for his repose. The cinders, the shape of the mound, the weapons and implements found, were discussed while we partook of the animals sacrificed for our own comfort, — as possibly those represented by the barrow-cinders were for the funeral guests.

In returning from immemorial antiquity our minds were accommodated to the present by watching the ladies at tennis or other sports on the Rushmore lawns, or dispersing ourselves to read or write, and to dress for dinner. For the dinner at Rushmore was a brilliant event. The family was large — six sons and three daughters. The ladies in their artistic dresses, and the men of science (who generally appreciate the time for relaxation better than business men or theologians) made the most of these occasions. Mrs. Pitt Rivers with her culture and entertaining conversation was the fit hostess for such assemblies. In the latter part of the evening we filed into the billiard room, where I observed with pleasure the skill of Herbert Spencer. All have heard that he did not like defeat, and once said to an opponent who easily vanquished him that his unusual skill " argued a wasted life." The legend was probably based on the gravity with which Herbert Spencer made every stroke. Some of my friends were surprised too at my own eagerness if not proficiency in the game. My friend Fletcher Moulton Q. C. suggested for me as a coat of arms a pulpit impaled by a billiard cue. But I never touched a cue before going to England, and at Aubrey House learned to play from grave men like John Bright and Peter Taylor M. P.

The modern man calls himself civilized because of his improved machinery, but Solomon and Confucius and Buddha and Jesus were considerable men without any telegraphs or electric lights. When the archæologists used to speak of stone age or bronze age, meaning thereby ignorant and morally savage people, I knew perfectly well that those several types were living side by side in our great cities. In 1881 London was able to witness the flagellation of Judas in the docks ; a clergyman of the English Church leading a devout procession along the streets in celebration of the " Stations of the Cross ; " a clerical manifesto against the " pagan blasphemy " of eating cross-buns on Good Friday; the opening of a grand Natural History Museum on Easter Day while the cathedrals were celebrating the resurrection of a prophet from his tumulus ; and lectures in the Royal Institution by Helmholtz, Tyndall, and Maine. Stone age, bronze age, age of gold, age of reason, all elbowing each other in that sum total of all epochs called London.[1]

I remember the last appearance of Faraday at the Royal Institution ; he came to hear Dean Stanley lecture on Westminster Abbey, and entered the theatre supported by two friends. The Prince of Wales (now king) presided and gave in his delicate way a gesture of deference to the venerable man. In 1881 Helmholtz came to deliver the annual Faraday lecture before the Chemical Society. This was a grand event. I thought Tyndall particularly happy in his speech, after Roscoe had presented the German with the Faraday medal. Helmholtz, a grand Bismarck-like man, delivered in good English his lecture on Faraday's experiments in electricity, and charmed his learned audience.

[1] Morally and intellectually considered, the " ages " are not chronological, but are mixed up in most brains — even the best. In a note of November 8, 1865, Matthew Arnold said : " Emerson has always particularly interested me by retaining his reason, while Carlyle, his fellow prophet, lost his : Emerson for some time suffered in popularity from his sobriety, but as the rôle of reason in human affairs begins to get more visibly important, what he lost is made up to him." Emerson since his death is the greatest name in American literature, but he leavens the mind of his country less than he is leavened by it. At the celebration of the Emerson Centenary, May 25, 1903, by the Society of American Authors, in New York, the fine dinner was preceded by a " grace " extended into a long thanksgiving to the Lord for Emerson. Although I sat beside the chairman I could not rise with the rest, but sat remembering the line in Emerson's " Threnody " about the " blasphemy of prayer." There were celebrations in various cities, and they proved that the great men can still rise from their graves only at the cost of their special genius. We say they are gods, but they fall like mere princes.

But Helmholtz was not to return to Germany with the impression that Albion is the happy isle of pure science. The Psychical Society sought to interest him in their wonders. The case which then particularly interested them was that of two little daughters of a country clergyman, one of whom held up behind a closed door any playing-card, and her sister on the other side described it. When this was told Helmholtz by a college professor who had experimented with the children the German could hardly take him seriously. The professor named some of his eminent colleagues in the investigation and said they should be credited with common-sense enough to test such things with care. Finding Helmholtz still incredulous he asked, " Would you believe it if you saw it yourself ? " " Certainly not," answered Helmholtz ; " in my investigations if anything peculiar appears I do not accept it on the evidence of my eyes. Before any new thing can be even provisionally accepted I must bring it to the test of many instruments, and if it survives all my tests then I send it over here to Tyndall, and to investigators in other countries. No, I would not believe any abnormal phenomenon on the mere testimony of my eyes."

The scepticism of Helmholtz was justified in the case of the clergyman's daughters, who were detected in their clever trick.

A. J. Ellis, philologist and editor of Chaucer, a friend of Helmholtz, told me that he (Helmholtz) once said, " If an optician were to send me a lens as faulty as the best human eye I would return it to him as slovenly work." [1]

[1] Ellis himself — whose researches on vibration and sound were much valued by Helmholtz — added to what his friend said about the eye a like criticism on the ear and the organ of speech. In a conversation I alluded to the general use by preachers of an old currency of words and phrases which it required special learning to understand, — Atonement, Grace, Faith, Deeds of the Law, etc. Ellis believed that no two minds had ever attached the same sense to such words. " In fact," he added, " I doubt if any noun or adjective conveys precisely the same meaning to any two individuals."

Mr. Ellis was during all my time in London until his death an active member of South Place chapel. He gave us at times Sunday morning

In my discourses at South Place it was not always easy to preserve the calm philosophical spirit necessary for anthropological study. The men of the theological barrows are alive and pugnacious, and a freethinking chapel has to be defended. But there were in London tribes of believers so far away from our theological arenas that I could study among them contemporary folk-lore.

One Sunday I found at my chapel door an old devotee of his visions whom I knew in America, — John Murray Spear, long known in Boston as the " prisoner's friend." He occasionally sojourned in Cincinnati with his little company of disciples. They were interesting people, but I could never discover just what land of promise they were seeking. Mr. Spear was a figure that any old Italian master would have rejoiced in to represent the noblest of his saints. Six feet and several inches in height, slender but shapely, his hair and beard snow-white, his face ruddy or even rosy, his eye exceedingly brilliant, his aquiline nose and other features clearcut, his head rising to a dome, he was a wonderful apparition. He felt himself guided by some familiar spirit. While lecturing in Cleveland, Ohio, he descended unconsciously into the audience, and after moving about paused before a lady and pronounced her the " Leaderess." He had never seen her, and did not know her name She at once left all and followed him. She was present when he told me this. The story was not absolutely incredible to me then, when constantly witnessing phenomenal effects of the elements and

discourses, always printed by the society. For a long time after I settled with the chapel he noted down all the pronunciations and accents in my discourses which had for his critical ear any peculiarity. When these, through my gradual absorption of English peculiarities, had ceased, my dear old friend confessed what he had been doing and went over the list with me. He was astonishingly familiar with American dialects, and made it clear to me that though I had been far from Virginia since my twentieth year my variations were mostly Virginian. Ellis was a theoretical advocate of the spelling reform, and much admired my brother-in-law, Professor March of Lafayette College, but did not always carry his theory into practice.

forces set free by the crumbling of creeds in the West in those years. John Murray Spear was perhaps a hypnotist, and if so, certainly a benevolent one.

In 1882 Mr. Spear and several of his followers appeared in London. He was distressed to find that I was still without the spiritualistic faith, and invited me to attend one evening a séance with a small society for the training of mediums. Curiosity led me to accept, and we travelled to some house far away in Whitechapel. In a large dingy room about twenty men and women sat at an uncovered table fifteen feet long. All except myself were "mediums," and the object of their meeting was that the spirits might develop their powers farther, — each in his or her specialty. There were writing, rapping, pantomimic, and musical mediums. Several had heard me in my chapel and I was graciously received. One of the ladies gently reproached me for my unbelief in spiritualism, and I confessed myself a Thomas constitutionally unable to believe without verifying the actuality of some risen spirit.

" What evidence would you have ? " asked several.

" Oh, any little thing will do. Let any one here tell me how much money I have in my purse " (throwing it on the table).

" I am surprised," said a lady, " that your faith should rest on a thing like that."

" Well," said I, " it happens to occur to me. I do not know how much there is in it."

There was a sudden hush, then murmurs and whispers ; presently one of the seers, confessing that her power was not perfectly developed, said that it passed before her faintly that there were eighteen pieces in the portmonnaie. It was opened by a medium near me and her answer found incorrect. As their gatherings were not for tests, no sceptic having previously attended, I offered some apology for the failure, thus preventing any embarrassment, and the proceedings went on. They became excited. One of the pantomimic mediums (who described one's deceased friend by imitating his manner) began gesticulating before me, clearing his throat, and turning his head on one side. I could not recall any who did that, but said I would think it over.

Presently they became noisy; there were loud raps around the table ; some talked to the spirits that rapped, some uttered their inspirations; they all talked at once. The word " bedlam " arose in my mind, but swiftly resolved itself into its original " Bethlehem," for it was in that eastern region I had read of things like the wild scene before me. I did not need any Peter to tell me these people under their Whitechapel Pentecost were not " drunken," but realized the kind of frenzy that took possession of those early disciples who believed that a dead human being had returned to life. The scene was not ridiculous but pathetic ; its grotesque features vanished under the thought that if I should believe — really, and without any trace of doubt — that a deceased person had spoken to me, I also would be frantic, and my life revolutionized.

Under the silent stars I went homeward seated on an omnibus. From the region of East End poverty and misery, amid which hopes of future bliss supplement the alcoholic anæsthetic, I travelled on past the edifices of Art and Science.

How often in that Royal Society building had I seen the great men of science displaying by their lenses and experiments the miracles of nature ! But how petty would all their wonders appear if one of those frantic mediums could utter a single word proved to have come from another world !

I had another experience in London which suggested to me what variants there may be in spiritistic movements, and the forms they evolve holding the secret of corresponding forms in ancient times and regions.

In quiet Gordon Square there is a remarkable church. Architecturally suggestive of the improved taste of the dissenters, this " Church of the Disciples " is, with its interior complexities, ritual and material, a veritable monument of Edward Irving. Once, after listening to the talk of Carlyle about Irving without getting any clear comprehension of a man so wild yet so loved, I attended a service in the church. I found it incoherent as its founder.

Subsequently I was brought into some contact with it. Rev. H. M. Prior, a young pastor I had never met, entered my vestry one Sunday and requested my assistance. After some years' ministry in the Catholic Apostolic Church he had lost his faith. So far as the peculiarities of his church were concerned he believed it nearer to primitive Christianity than other churches; but his changed belief — simple theism — was regarded by his ministerial brethren as infidelity. The formal notice served on him had raised the question whether he should resign or undergo an ecclesiastical trial. He had decided on the latter, because it would give him an opportunity of giving his former colleagues the arguments which had convinced him, and that appeared to him a duty. Having the legal right to choose a counsellor he requested me to act in that position. Finding that he was to conduct his own pleading, and that I was to give an opinion only in case any question as to fairness should arise, I consented.

The trial took place in a large room under the church in Gordon Square, and occupied an afternoon. My principal and I were punctual, but found no one on the premises. Fortunately Mr. Prior knew the place, for we had to go through complex corridors to the subterranean room, — to which as heretics we might not have proceeded as cheerfully in earlier times. It was I believe the first trial for heresy in the Catholic Apostolic Church. Soon after us the ministers began to arrive; each came separately, to the number of more than twenty. All were in solemn black, with white cravats, and every one bore a black leather valise of precisely the same dimensions. I have a vague remembrance of some slight recognition of the presence of Mr. Prior and myself, but not a word was spoken. As they were dressed alike I was unable to distinguish one species of minister from another, — their ministry being fourfold, — but most of them I think were " Angels." All were middle-aged except the young heretic on trial. I was placed on one side of Mr. Prior and on the other sat the prosecutor, who read out the charge in a perfunctory way. The indictment was disappointingly commonplace; the doctrines mentioned as repudiated by Mr. Prior were exclusively the ordinary dogmas of orthodoxy. I was invited to make any preliminary statement I might desire, but made none. Mr. Prior then entered on his defence, which was carefully written. It was a simple statement of his reasons for disbelieving the dogmas of Scripture infallibility, incarnation, and other things deemed fundamental, but without any repudiation of Christianity. There was nothing acrimonious or irreverent in the manifesto, but it soon raised a storm. An "Angel" interrupted Mr. Prior, saying that the question was whether the pastor was disqualified by the rejection of the doctrines he was ordained to preach. He did not think they were under any obligation to listen to his "blasphemous" paper. Several others made a similar declaration, and it then became necessary for me to act. I requested the representative of the council seated beside Mr. Prior to converse with me privately for a few moments, and found him disposed to peace. I then made a brief address to the assembly reminding them that it was a very serious sacrifice for a pastor to separate from his church and his brethren ; that it indicated convictions really religious on his part, and that before they could decide whether he was irrecoverably parted from them it seemed just that they should listen to his entire statement ; especially as presumably he could not affect the faith of learned ministers who must be familiar with all varieties of theology. After some discussion it was decided that Mr. Prior should proceed. The tribunal then easily reached its foregone conclusion : Mr. Prior was pronounced no longer a pastor of the Catholic Apostolic Church. Naturally he showed no emotion, and did not appear to feel any embarrassment. I had some hope that he would write an important work on the church he had left, but he soon after disappeared from my horizon and I know not what became of him.

The people who can think, investigate, and fearlessly reason on the phenomena of nature, or on the contents of their own consciousness, are always few, and it is as difficult to analyze the causes of change in mental and spiritual fashions as of other fashions. How had the fashion of my own mind changed since I used to follow Bunyan's Pilgrim with heart palpitant with enthusiasm? Seeing it on the stage in London, I realized that in thirty years the change in me was as complete as if I had been born into another race.

Among the many curious products of the transitional condition of religion George Macdonald was one of the most interesting. Liberal at heart, he had not fibre enough to break his old cords. He was not orthodox enough to satisfy the orthodox, nor free enough to satisfy the thinkers. He had a clever wife and a large family of handsome sons and daughters, but they were poor, and contrived to make " The Pilgrim's Progress " into a play, in which they all acted. Just as it was promising well the authorities said they must get a license. That involved paying money. It seemed rather droll that such a diffusion of the plan of salvation should be taxed, but it could not be helped, and so we all began to sell tickets to enable them to give their performance in halls. Here again was the drollery of freethinkers like my wife and myself actively engaged in furthering the gospel according to Bunyan. We got up a good company for them at Notting Hill, consisting chiefly of fashionable church people and sceptics.

The play was well worth seeing. The scenery was painted in Preraphaelist style, and there was a finely embroidered hanging representing the land of Beulah. George Macdonald made as splendid a Christian as if he had been evolved for the part. In his shining panoply he encountered an ingeniously wicked Apollyon represented by his son, and won great applause. But I remarked the worldliness of the younger churchfolk, who were sadly deficient in Bunyanesque ideas. They were liable to titter at points where they ought to have wept. When Christian fled from the City of Destruction and his wife bewailed that she had not heeded his warnings, a devout Church lady, to whom we had sold tickets, whispered, " Are we expected to admire him for running away and leaving his family in the City of Destruction ? "

CHAPTER XLVII

In 1867 I gave two lectures in Sheffield. The invitation was conveyed to me by a distinguished resident of that place, H. C. Sorby. I had heard Ruskin speak of this gentleman as a friend who had shown him " the rainbow of the rose, the rainbow of the violet," etc., and had learned that he was the very genius of the spectrum. He was an attractive gentleman, and in his house, Broomfield, showed me what Ruskin had described as rainbows. From each flower, from every variety of leaf and grass, he squeezed a drop of its color, and threw its spectrum on a screen. The important thing was that each had its own spectroscopic lines, its individual signature, just as the planets have. He showed me the spectrum of a drop of human blood, its dark lines differing from those of all red dyes.[1]

More than seventeen years had passed since in our Virginia town I gave my first public lecture, as related in the seventh chapter : at eighteen I was aspiring to the universe, my theme was " Pantheism," I dealt with the celestial rainbow, and in the three primary colours contained in light I saw a symbol

[1] I have heard that in a trial at Sheffield, when a murderer declared the red stains on his clothing to be from the logwood used in his work, Sorby was summoned as an expert. He soaked out the stains in the court and showed their spectrum beside that of logwood and that of blood. The stains were blood, this being the only corroborative evidence needed for conviction. The story may be true, but has some appearance of a myth grown out of the wonders associated with Broomfield.

of the Trinity. Now at thirty-five, looking not through any Athanasian lens but through that of science, I beheld the rainbows around me on earth, at my feet, with their real revelations. In our Virginia garden where I meditated on the Cosmos and spectral Trinity every flower and grass-blade held a revelation that might have awakened me from the dream in which I was moving.

The morning star of another revelation shone on me, namely, that in my pilgrimage from dreams of the universe to religious interest in things near me on earth I was following the path of the human race. Like the ancient Aryan singing his Vedic prayer to sun and sky, I was such stuff as dreams are made of, and Bunyan surrounded my little life in Virginia with a sleep, — a dreamland. I sang as loudly as the slaves around me their favourite hymn : —

> When I can read my title clear
> To mansions in the skies,
> I 'll bid farewell to every fear
> And wipe my weeping eyes :
>
> Should earth against my soul engage
> And fiery darts be hurled,
> Then I can smile at Satan's rage
> And face a frowning world

Not a dart, not a frown, was suffered by any Christian in our region, but Bunyan had made them all visible on that mystical Milky Way to the Celestial City, beset by Apollyon, which I was preparing to travel.

At sixteen I met with the little travesty by Nathaniel Hawthorne, " The Celestial Railroad," which charmed by its exquisite style, and I believe still more by the freedom with which it dealt with solemn matters in a humorous vein. A year or two later I could smile at finding myself on the side of those Hawthorne made fun of — Giant Trancendentalism, and Mr. Smoothe-it-away filling up the Slough of Despond with volumes of French and German philosophy. Gradually my Celestial City came down to earth, — a world free from Slavery, War, Superstition, Ignorance, — but still it shone far away as the Delectable Mountains and the Land of Beulah. Nevertheless for these ideals I left my comfortable " City of Destruction," — that fair garden in Maryland already described

But alas, youth is awakened from one dream only by another. My ideal world was still quasi-millennial, to be realized by revolutions, and that the world around me was abloom with ideals for eyes withdrawn from the future began to appear (as yet mistily) when Darwin came to enshrine Emerson's ideal evolution in science.

Darwin's discovery made a new departure in my pilgrimage necessary. Emerson had already canopied Evolution with rainbows, but they were optimistic. Optimism and Pessimism are equally growths out of Fatalism. If nature and time are working together for the best, if evil is good in the making, we may fold our hands. But Darwin showed that the principle of selection in nature was impartial between good and evil ; the corollary was that the force he revealed must be controlled by human (i. e. purposed) selection.

I was still a theist, in the attenuated sense of Matthew Arnold's faith, that there is in nature " a stream of tendency, not ourselves, that makes for righteousness." This was an Emersonian " rainbow " cast around " Natural Selection." In my exaltation I everywhere found symbols and parables of this mind in Nature (spelt with a capital " N "). At Christmas time Tyndall performed at the Royal Institution pretty experiments for children, and I took my little boy to them : among the experiments some were on the spectrum; he showed that in the dark space around the colours there was more heat than in the colours themselves. A piece of paper passed safely through the seven colours burst into flame in the dark space adjacent. Behold a parable of the invisible power surrounding visible force and action ! I remembered the rainbow I used to watch bent over the fury of Niagara, and wrote an essay entitled " The Cataract and the Rainbow " which troubled my friend Professor Newman by its Necessitarianism, although it was optimistic.

My eyes once reverently turned earthward, parable on parable !

On a summer excursion I travelled from Glasgow to Oban with Herbert Spencer, one of my earliest friends in England. There were many English tourists on the barge, and barefoot children trotted beside it with the hope of having pennies thrown to them. A good many were thrown, as the scrambles were amusing. The little Scots long continued their pursuit, but presently the smaller ones weakened, especially the girls. " There," I said to Spencer, " is an example of the survival of the fittest or ' fleetest ; ' the weaker fall behind and are getting no pennies." " Yes, for the moment," he said, " but soon the force of compassion will work for their benefit." And so it was ; pennies were showered on the tired toddlers, and equality was established between the weak and the strong. Also Herbert Spencer's phrase, " survival of the fittest," received a connotation of " fitness " congenial with the ethical side of the Religion of Evolution.

Thus even in my summer excursions I must still be a pilgrim. In Glasgow also I found the House of an Interpreter. My friend Professor Nichols took me to see Sir William Thomson (now Lord Kelvin), whom I had heard at the Royal Institution in London. He showed us in his laboratory a box containing a number of metallic cylinders received from Paris. They were small as cans of fruit, but each was a canned thunderstorm. Sir William told us that soon after their arrival a friend mentioned to him the case of a baby on whose tongue was a threatening tumour which he was afraid to cut away, lest there should be too much loss of blood. Sir William was just then experimenting on the various degrees of heat derived from his stored lightning, and it occurred to him that the merest touch of one of his wires at white heat could clear away the tumour. The operation was perfectly successful.

I went off with a good theme for my congregation. It was picturesque for Franklin to draw lightning from a cloud into a bottle, but it charmed me more to think of a thunderbolt so humanized as to remove a baby's tumour by one gentle and painless touch.

Another visit I made was to a lady in the neighbourhood of Edinburgh whose method of controlling the wild forces differed from that of Sir William. This was Mrs. Clement, who belonged to a prominent family in London, — South Place rationalists, — Peter Alfred Taylor M. P. being her nephew. She was educated among Unitarians but in early life came under the influence of Edward Irving, and subsequently founded a religion of her own, to which she made a few converts. She was a wealthy widow without children, and lived in a pleasant homestead a few miles out of Edinburgh. I should hardly have gone so far but for a hope of obtaining some new light on demonology. Every now and then, I was told, an advertisement appeared in an Edinburgh paper announcing to the " Circle of Prayer" that a vacancy had to be filled at a certain hour of a certain night. It was the Clementian belief that wrecks were caused by the imps of Satan, and that the reason why such disasters usually occurred at night was that then all prayer ceased, Christians being asleep. So it was arranged that there should be formed a circle of prayer, each one taking an hour or half-hour of the twenty-four, to the end of circumventing the storm-devils by an unbroken defence of prayer. I was not altogether without sympathy with the ascription of some Scotch winds to the devil, and this with my professional curiosity led me to drive out to Mrs. Clement's house. I was kindly received by the amiable lady but presently felt rather guilty ; for Peter Taylor M. P. her nephew had apparently given her no hint of my being the minister of heretical South Place ; and when I told her I wished to learn something about her religious views she spoke so freely as to excite a fear that she supposed me a possible convert. She told me the points on which she had parted from Edward Irving's views — I think it was mainly on account of her belief that the reciprocal washing of feet was essential to salvation. When I inquired whether she ever saw her London relatives, she answered that although she had kind feelings towards them she had not for some years invited them.

They were all Unitarians, and the last time some of them had staid in her house she had a warning. I at once got ready to leave, but inquired something of the nature of the " warning." She answered with perfect simplicity that the first time she entered the room where her Unitarian relatives had slept some invisible power seized her by the back and hurled her to the wall, and she felt the pain for several days.

Wonderful that one small province could produce at the same time Sir William Thomson with his regenerate lightnings and Mrs. Clement with her assaulting devils !

In 1870 was published in London and New York my volume entitled " The Earthward Pilgrimage : or how I left the World to Come for that which Is."

The response to my book was surprising. " Father Ignatius," an Anglican priest masquerading in monkish dress, perverted a phrase about " the worship of a dead Jew " and made the country ring with it. Beresford Hope M. P. read in Parliament an extract from my advocacy of freedom of divorce to illustrate alarming tendencies of the times. These attacks helped the book in England, and no doubt it would have had equal success in America had my friend and publisher Henry Holt been a man of manœuvres : a fire occurred in his establishment which confined itself strictly to consuming a whole forthcoming edition of " The Earthward Pilgrimage ! " Had that fact been got into the pious papers there is no knowing what demand there might have been for a book selected for so obvious a judgment.

The work was taken seriously and well reviewed ; it brought me many sympathetic letters and new friends. Professor Henry Sidgwick of Cambridge wrote in " Nature " a review that especially encouraged me, and with him a number of eminent Fellows invited me to visit that university as their guest. Among these were Fletcher Moulton (afterwards Q. C. and M. P.), W. K. Clifford (afterwards professor in University College, London), and E. H. Palmer (professor of Arabic and Persian).[1]

[1] I thoroughly enjoyed this Cambridge visit. There was nothing for-

"The Earthward Pilgrimage" represented another stage in a veritable and conscious spiritual pilgrimage. From month to month I still found my mental attitude changing, and always in the direction of a decreasing interest in the universe and an increasing interest in things small and near. The study of folk-lore became the most important part of mythology. In December, 1870, was printed in "Fraser" an article on "Mystic Trees and Flowers," in which after showing that the healing or sacred flora were popularly associated with sun, moon, planets, and celestial potencies, I made a generalization regarded by the editor (Froude) as new and true : —

It is generally supposed that man's earliest worship is represented by superstitions concerning plants and animals ; that it was from these lower objects that his reverence gradually ascended to the adoration of the sun and stars. But a careful examination of the superstitions which I have recorded will furnish many evidences that the case was really the reverse. It is probable that the awe which was the beginning of worship was first excited in the human mind when it gazed upon the mysterious, silent heavens, by the conflicts of night and day, and the wild power of the elements. At a later period, and after man had given greater attention to the cultivation of his own world, the scene of his interest would be gradually shifted from the distant heavens to the near earth, from the cold star to the flower unfolding beneath it. Progress of thought would then, as now, be from minding high things toward condescending to things of low estate — from the unattainable to the attainable.

In my travesty of the "Pilgrim's Progress" most of the incidents occur in "Bothworldsburg." There was irony in the name, but I often had to take it to myself. My feet were well

mal, no speeches, but only good dinners and cigars and conversation. Now and then a humorous song was called for, and I was especially delighted by the "Poor Blind Worm," unctuously crooned by Clifford. One verse could not be forgotten : —

> If you and God should disagree
> On questions of theologee,
> You 're damned to all eternitee,
> Poor blind worm !

planted on the earth academically, but I had not reached the secret of George Fox the Quaker, who said, " It was revealed to me that what other men trample on shall be thy meat." My sentiments, nerves, mental habitudes, did not leave " Both-worldsburg " so readily as my logic, but I had got far enough to take to heart the lessons taught by little things. To this day, when I am grey, I remember the impression made on me by the following incident.

On a visit to Stratford-on-Avon I met at the house of Edgar Flower an attractive lady from Germany. She was acquainted with the best literature of her own country, spoke English, and was an enthusiastic Shakespearian. The bright and pretty little daughters of the family regarded the Fräulein as some wondrous being from fairyland. One fine morning the Fräulein and I went for a walk with the children over to Ann Hathaway's cottage. Our way led over fields decked with " daisies pied and violets blue," along budding hedgerows, and the larks were singing blithely. The Fräulein told me pretty things about Goethe and his circle, and repeated fine bits of poetry and legend. We saw Ann Hathaway's cottage at its best, and altogether had a charming saunter.

A year or so later, while revisiting Stratford-on-Avon, I asked the eldest of the girls, Rosalie Flower, about the Fräulein and whether she remembered the charming walk we had with that lady through the fields. Yes, she remembered it well, but also a disappointment of herself and her sisters. While the Fräulein and I were conversing the children had gathered daisies and violets and wild roses and strewn them on the path before us, and neither of us had taken the least notice of their homage! I took the lesson to heart, and went another stage in my earthward pilgrimage. What after all had Shakespeare and Goethe really been to me if they had not given me eyes to read a poem acted under my very nose as sweet as any they ever wrote? Of what use to stand on their great shoulders if my eyes were so riveted on the shoulders that I could not heed the flowers of living hearts strewn on my pathway? Around each strewn flower was a prettier rainbow than Sorby

had shown me in the spectrum of rose or violet. They had
shone in vain, and the dear little hearts had been humiliated.
The beautiful hour in the fields could not be recalled. Its chief
beauty had bloomed beside me, and withered, and I never
saw it. Had I seen it at the time it would never have withered.

"Let no flower of the spring pass by thee!" Ah, wisest
of men!

The subjects of my discourse were advertised, and one on
"The Pre-Darwinite and the Post-Darwinite World" attracted Darwin. I was told that he listened to it; but he
rarely came to London, and probably the discourse was
reported to him. I soon after received an invitation to visit
him at "Down," his house near Bromley.

I went to Bromley with the Wedgwoods. Hensleigh Wedgwood was a very interesting gentleman, but inclined to put
some faith in "occultism." Mrs. Wedgwood told me anecdotes about her brother (Darwin), one of which is quaint.
Darwin could never realize the world-wide impression made
by his discovery, nor his own fame. Gladstone, then Prime
Minister, being in the neighbourhood of Down, had called.
When he had gone Darwin said, "To think of such a great
man coming to see me!"

The other guests at Down, besides the Wedgwoods and myself, were my friends Charles Norton and his sister of Cambridge, Massachusetts. A sister of Mrs. Charles Norton
married a son of Darwin.

Darwin was not in perfect health, and his wife and daughters took care that he should retire early. My opportunity for
conversing with him came next day. In the soft spring morning before sunrise I looked out of my bedroom window and
saw Darwin in his garden, inspecting his flowers. His grey
head was bent to each bush as if bidding it good-morning.
And what a head! All that the phrenologists had written was
feeble compared with a look at that big head with its wonderful dome, and the lobes above each luminous eye. All the
forms of organic nature had contributed something to repre-

sent them visibly in the constitution of the head able to interpret them.

I was soon with Darwin in the garden, which was in floral
glory. He expressed satisfaction that I had been able to
derive from evolution the hopeful religion set forth in my
discourse, but I remember that he did not express agreement
with it. He spoke pleasantly of W. J. Fox M. P., my predecessor at South Place (whom he well knew), and asked me
about Emerson, whose writings interested him. But he had
not been aware of the extent of Emerson's poetic anticipations of his discovery many years before it was published.
While we were talking of these things the birds began to
insist on his attention. One in particular — a hermit thrush
— perched on the topmost point of a tree, continued long his
marvellous song. From my point of view he was justifying
his " hermit " profession by a Vedic hymn to the rising sun,
but Darwin considered that he was no real hermit or yogi at
all, but had a love affair on hand and was singing a canticle
to his beloved.

When we were presently at breakfast the post came, — a
pile of letters which the daughters began to open, separating
from those of friends the large number from strangers in all
parts of the world. A few of these were read aloud for our
amusement, letters from crude people reporting to Darwin
observations which they believed important. One American
farmer wrote about the marvellous intelligence of his dog, who
always knew when he was about to take a walk, dancing
about so soon as he touched his cane. One had some commonplaces to tell about his new variety of beans, another something about his pigeons. The rest of us laughed, but Darwin
said, " Let them all be pleasantly answered. It is something
to have people observing the things in their gardens and
barnyards."

Adjoining the house was the conservatory in which Darwin
carried on his experiments. Into this he invited me, over-
coming my hesitation by saying that he particularly desired
it. I felt indeed that it was right, because I was minister of

the chief rationalistic congregation and was endeavouring to transfer the religious sentiment from a supernatural to a scientific basis. He took pains to show me everything. There was the enclosure in which he and Sir John Lubbock, who resided near him, conducted their experiments with ants. But Darwin was at that time chiefly occupied with the earthworm, his volume on which impresses me as next to his "Origin of Species" in value.

Darwin's unbelief in all varieties of religious theory was not at that time known to me. Although a letter of his, afterwards printed, shows that he must have thought my vision of "Post-Darwinite" religion an illusion, no word of that kind fell from him. His kindly spirit, his interest in the ideas animating liberal ministers, indicated his desire that we should all work out his discovery in its moral applications in our own several ways. It was not exactly his realm, and he knew its importance too well to venture much even theoretically upon it. In the afternoon we had some drives in the neighbourhood, and no doubt passed by without notice the famous "Tom Paine Tree," which I visited with interest many years later.[1]

The visit to "Down" was charming. It stands in my loving remembrance as an era related to that in which I first met Emerson in his home at Concord. But it involved a new departure in my earthward pilgrimage.

When Dr. Holmes said to me, "You and I have had to spend many of our best years simply clearing away theological rubbish out of our paths," the tone was as of a thing achieved. I so received it with a feeling of being right at last. But alas, how much had yet to be cleared away! Terrible discov-

[1] "There is also a local tradition that Paine used to write on the same work (*Age of Reason*) while seated under the 'Tom Paine Tree,' which is on the (Bromley) palace estate. . . . The 'Tom Paine Tree' is a very ancient oak, solitary in its field, and very noble. . . . Not a limb is dead : from the hollow and charred trunk a superb mass of foliage arises. . . . From this high and clear spot one may almost see the homestead of Darwin, who, more heretical than Paine, has Westminster Abbey for his monument." — *Writings of Thomas Paine*, vol. iv. Introduction.

Naushon
Wood's Hole, Mass Oct 1, '72

My dear Sir,

I am the
slowest of correspondents, ever
deeply in debt. To you more
at this time for your beneficent interest in me &
mine. Yet in my very
broken days & hours in
these weeks, I have waited
long to acknowledge
your letter of September
7 to which I ought instantly
to have replied. And now
I have a new letter from
Edward E. reciting his
happy visit & abode at,

your house, as well
as the recollections
I hear daily in William
Forbes's house, Edith's of your
kind cares for them
in their visit to London.

You found me now
an intimation that
I have friends in London
who would wish to make
me some gift in consideration of my losses by the
burning of my house. Will
you please to say to any
such benevolent friend
that whilst I am surprised
& gratified at such a good
will, I will have no such
thing done, as my friends

at home have already taken care to more than indemnify me for my material losses by the fire. Not the less hearty thanks to these English friends.

I have suffered in health lately & have not therefore prospered with my book. I have yet begun to print,— some fifty pages of proof have come back. But it must be slowlier done than I or the printers will wish My daughter Ellen & I talk of a little travel-ing & perhaps shall make a little visit to England to look after Edward & consult with him & his physician & very possibly go somewhat farther. But our plans are not yet settled nay are often changed.

With very kind regards & thanks to Mrs Conway & yourself for your steadfast good will & good work in our behalf,

Yours,

R. W. Emerson

Rev. Moncure D. Conway

eries awaited me. My devotion to science, and my knowledge
of the veracity of scientific men, had been unconsciously projected into the Cosmos. Nature surely was true ; the laws and
forces of the universe were true, evolution was carrying out
sleeplessly the truth of things. In Natural Selection I seemed
to find a gospel of reality. I had supposed that I had got to
the heart of Darwin's works, but somehow the simple grandeur
of that man beside those little creatures he was studying began to obtrude the shady side of nature in a disturbing way.

Was that nature's truth? What were Venus' flytraps but
deceitful vampires? What were those little insects I used to
watch so curiously in the Virginia woods, which pretended
to be sticks or leaves? Their mimicry was a justifiable strat-
agem to escape their enemies, but why should there be this
predatory character extending to all the byways of nature?
Did every tint on the butterfly disguise an agony? The blos-
som-like flies or the leaf and twig insects may be disguised to
escape an enemy or to lurk for tiny victims of their own: in
either case they represented a predatory universe. Renan took
the generous view — as Darwin did when listening to the
hermit thrush — of the amorous heart of nature: "Nature
decorates herself with a flower to find a husband." But even
in sexual selection there is a suggestion of resort to contriv-
ances and subterfuges, pointing to love's weakness, not to its
omnipotence.

Was my old Methodist hymn not so wrong after all? —

> This world is all a fleeting show
> For man's delusion given.

"Given!" We have imported the all-enclosing delusion into
the world by the phantasy that all is from an omnipotent
Giver. My pilgrimage from Darwin's door steadily carried
me past the last Giant Despair, — a dynamic deity and creator
responsible for the wrongs and agonies of nature.

1882. Darwin and Emerson died at nearly the same time
(April 20 and April 27, 1882). The relation of these two

minds to each other and to their time is striking. In the year (1836) when Darwin abandoned theology to study nature, Emerson, having also abandoned theology, published his first book, " Nature," whose theme is Evolution.

It was a notable circumstance that on the death of these two men who have done away with supernaturalism, no voice of *odium theologicum* broke the homage of England and America.

The scene in Westminster Abbey at the burial of Darwin was impressive. From the chapel of St. Faith the body of the great man was borne by the procession along the remote cloisters. We who had long been in our appointed seats in the Abbey presently heard a faint melodious strain ; nearer the dirge of the invisible choir approached ; and when at length the great door of the Abbey opened, and the choristers appeared, and the coffin laden with wreaths from all parts of Europe, a stir of emotion passed through the waiting company. There were following that coffin more than a hundred of the first men in England and some from other countries. On many faces the grief was visible. Huxley, Tyndall, Francis Galton, Sir John Lubbock, Sir Joseph Hooker, could with difficulty control their grief. It was dark in the Abbey and the lights but feebly struggled with the gloom. There was something almost spectral in the slow moving of the procession with noiseless tread. Around in every direction the throng of marble statues were discernible, as if a cloud of witnesses gathered to receive the new-comer in their Valhalla. But it was an earthly Valhalla. The darkness of the Abbey, only made visible by occasional lamps, might have been regarded by saints of the still radiant windows as emblematic of the curtain drawn by knowledge beyond the grave. To me the gloom deepened when the service thanked God for removing such a man out of this wicked world, but lifted a little when the white-robed choristers gathered around the three graves — those of Newton, Herschel, and Darwin — and sang a new anthem, " Happy is the man that findeth wisdom ! "

Amid the universal homage to Darwin one adverse senti-

ment is widely noted and rebuked. " L'Univers," the Roman
Catholic organ in Paris, said, " When hypothesis tends to
nothing less than the destruction of faith, the shutting out of
God from the heart of man, and the diffusion of the filthy
leprosy of Materialism, the *savant* who invents and propa-
gates them is either a criminal or a fool. *Voilà ce que nous
avons à dire du Darwin des singes.*"

Paris, 1900. How far away appears the year when I
wrote down my impressions of the funeral of Darwin! I cannot discover in history any eighteen years so marked by changes
in the moral condition of the world as those that have followed
that time. It now looks to me like the closing of an epoch,
ominously marked by graves of the great whose ideals are in-
terred with them.

The Roman Catholic organ in Paris, which in 1882 was
denounced for its brutal words on Darwin, has its *revanche* in
1900. On the eve of the International Peace Congress, about
to be held in Paris, " L'Univers " publishes an article that falls
on our midsummer like Arctic cold. The spirit of peace it declares has fled the earth because Darwinism has taken possession of it. The pleas for peace have been inspired by a faith
in the divine nature and origin of men ; they were all seen as
children of one Father, and war was fratricide. But now that
men are seen as the children of apes, what matters it whether
they are slaughtered or not !

So runs through its column the terrible article, — terrible
by reason of the passionate earnestness with which it represents its day of judgment. It is small consolation to defend
moral corollaries of science by saying that where the bee sucks
honey the spider sucks poison. For to those filled with horror
by the murderous aggressions of strong nations on the weak
the proverb can only suggest that the spider is taking possession of the world. Seated here in Paris, while the Exposition is presenting at the close of the century a picture of the
harmonious industrial nation distributed through all nations,
" L'Univers " opens before me a dreary prospect of deciviliza-

tion and decadence. The humanitarian spirit that breathed through the literature and art of England and America for fifty years (1832–1882) is entombed in a sepulchre which few even garnish, while the mourners grown grey, who shared its spirit, are helpless as the women who heard the cry of their dying leader, " My power, my power, why hast thou forsaken me ! "

1903. It has become necessary entirely to revise the bearings of science on ethics. My friend Goldwin Smith, whose eighty years have only matured his wisdom, foresees fatal results to the next generation unless science can construct something to take the place of the failing religious conscience, and Herbert Spencer sees that the fatality has already come. I quote their letters elsewhere. Apprehensions of this kind have long beset rationalistic preachers and publicists, of whom some have been swept away by the floods of Jingoism and Militantism.

Had the Roman Catholic writer in Paris, who said Darwin had slain Peace, followed his own doctrines to their logical result, he would have seen that they include belief in the providential character of all the evils and agonies of the world; also that Darwin and the apes are equally a part of the eternal order with the Pope and his crusaders. Yet I cannot help recognizing the terrible fact under that anathema on science. The basis of democracy is the much misquoted affirmation of the Declaration of Independence — " all men are created equal." Its strictly religious essence has been lost by the substitution of " born " for " created." Republicanism, democracy, negro-emancipation, were all based on belief in the fatherhood of God and brotherhood of man. The religious sanction having broken down its place cannot be taken by science until all human beings are scientific.

No class of men in the modern world are of higher character in all the relations of life, private and public, than the men of science. The man of science lives in the presence of tremendous forces; he is trained in the knowledge of cause and effect; his hourly instruction is in laws that fail not and which no prayer nor penitence can escape; he knows that his every action to man or woman or child is taken up by forces impartial between good and evil, pain and pleasure, and carried on to unending results. Science alone understands the reality in this world of that hell and heaven which superstition has located in a future world where they have lost actuality in the minds they once controlled. The men of science may not believe in the continuance of individual consciousness after death, because, as Darwin said, they are exacting in the matter of evidence; but a very long existence is given by the scientific imagination which travels from the dawn of life on our planet to the reign of man, and anticipates the remotest future of nature which present forces are determining.

Were it possible that the masses of mankind could be developed out of the mass and become individual thinkers, science would surely reach them with its " saving grace " of self-restraint, while delivering them from the ethical fictions which obstruct the moral freedom essential to happiness.

But is this possible?

The masses of mankind have a reverence for science because they live and move and have their being amid its practical results and witness its miracles. They are steadily withdrawn from the ancient miracles wrought by gods and saints for remote lands in other ages, not by criticism or rationalism, but by the miracles of science benefiting the people of to-day.

In May, 1874, the scientific men predicted several weeks before it occurred that the tide would rise to a great height in the Thames on a certain day in June. It happened to be the day of the burial of Dr. Livingstone. Barriers and breaks were built by the river's side; and on the day named the vast crowd which had gathered at Westminster Abbey at the funeral of Livingstone repaired to the bridge embankment to see what would happen. There was a halcyon superstition that the high tide of the Thames could not rise while the swans were nesting. They were just then nesting, and so it was that there was a sort of contest between superstition and science. When the waiting thousands saw that day the great tide steadily rising and beating against the high barriers which protected their homes, I could see in many faces the rising tide of reverence for science. By innumerable experiences of this kind the newer science has supplanted the old, and the institutions founded on antiquated science, the churches and temples, can only maintain themselves by their importance to the practical interests of mankind. How many millions would be impoverished were all temples closed?

But the high personal character of scientific men generally is not due to the results or to the discoveries of science, which is as impartial as nature between good and evil, and as progressive in the instruments of destruction as in those of welfare. Their superiority is derived from the scientific training, the habit of thinking, of reflection, — the philosophic mind engendered.

Even men of science do not always attain the scientific habit of mind. Mr. Crookes adopted spiritism after " experiments " with two women, — one afterwards confessed the other an exposed impostor, — whom he was probably too polite to deal with as searchingly as with his chemicals, or as he would have dealt with male " mediums." One of these " mediums " gave semi-public séances near the British Museum every week, and two scientific assistants of this institution went on one occasion provided with a pocket apparatus for illuminating the room. After the " medium " had been tied in the cabinet the lights were lowered, and the " spirit " moved about in the room. One of the two from the museum clasped the apparition while his colleague illuminated the room, despite the blows of a manager rained on them. The " spirit " proved to be the " medium " herself professedly bound in the cabinet. The facts being undeniable, Alfred Wallace wrote to the " Times " explaining that the " spirits " might conceivably in some cases utilize the body of the " medium ! " That the " spirits " should select for this unusual course an evening when scientific men had come with an apparatus to expose their (the spirits') chief " medium " was an absurdity that occurred to everybody except Wallace. The brain of Wallace is a fair loom, but one could not look to it for any judgment on the soundness or unsoundness of the threads it weaves. As for Mr. Crookes, he remains inexplicable. I last met this agreeable gentleman in a company at the Royal Institution, and Tyndall told me that when in conversation he had alluded to spiritism Mr. Crookes was silent, and it seemed to give him so much pain that he concluded never to mention the subject to him again.

CHAPTER XLVIII

IN October, 1876, we went to reside in Hamlet House, Hammersmith. It was an old but not ancient mansion, built about a hundred years before. It was surrounded by nearly three acres of ground with stately trees, classic statues amid them — large lawn in front, rose-garden at the back, and behind that fruit-trees, of which some were of rare excellence.

The lease made out for this old homestead interested me a good deal, not only because I had to pay for it (twenty guineas, I think), but because of the number of engagements I had to make, such as taking care of bridges and water-courses. As these serious looking contracts referred to things that had been detached from the estate for a century, I had no fear of signing them; but when the lawyer read out that I was to take care of the deadlocks I demanded, What is a deadlock? Neither he nor my landlord could answer, and there being no dictionary in the room one had to be sent for. There had not been a deadlock in Hamlet House since, about sixty years before, it was used as a school for young ladies, who, after their retirement at night, were secured by those external bolts. Although the doors had many times been re-painted, I could see near the top a faint indication of where the deadlock had been. Had everything that had disappeared from Hamlet House and grounds disappeared also from the lease this could have required only two or three pages. But how then could the lawyer get his guineas? My lease rested on a great conservative principle.

Although church-rates had been abolished by Parliament, the collector for Kensington parish called with a bill of seven-and-sixpence for the church. When I expressed my astonishment and said I could not pay such a tax, he told me that I could not be compelled, but that the agreement to pay it had always continued in the lease of Hamlet House. The lease being brought out I found that I had signed an agreement to pay the usual charges and taxes. Perhaps I should have refused to pay an implicit tax of this kind, but during my three years at Hamlet House I paid this annual seven-and-sixpence. I believe the tenant of Hamlet House had some privilege in the selection of a pew in Kensington church, which, however, I never entered except once for a wedding.

In 1878 Sir Charles Dilke requested me to act as one of his committee in Hammersmith, and although I never voted in England, and always retained my American citizenship, I complied with the request. We had long been in friendly relations with Sir Charles and Lady Dilke. This first Lady Dilke was spirituelle and charming; she was appreciative of all public questions without giving herself up to any " Cause." Sir Charles appeared to be the coming statesman. He had in 1878 especially pleased me by a two hours' speech in Hammersmith in which he alluded to recent encroachments by " royal prerogative." It was Gladstone who revived " royal prerogative " to abolish " army purchase," — a very small evil compared with the precedent set by that revival. My only function as a committeeman was to dine occasionally with Sir Charles and listen to the talk of my colleagues.

Our chairman was Mr. Beal, our excellent neighbour, whose two pretty daughters used to assist in our tableaux and theatricals at South Place chapel. For we had such amusements there, and actor Mansfield in his youth managed many a pretty performance at South Place.

When Beal heard that I had taken Hamlet House he said humorously, " You are a bold man." To my delight I heard that there had been a suspicion of its being haunted; but I could find no such story about the house, and concluded that the name " Hamlet " on the porter's lodge had suggested the ghost. The name was that of the famous old jeweller who built the house.

But Hamlet House had its legend. The old jeweller had been rich but was ruined by building the Adelphi Theatre. His family consisted of one daughter, a beauty for whom Hamlet had made the finest necklace in England. She was betrothed to a lord. While the bankruptcy of Hamlet was known to but few, and unknown to his daughter, he returned from the city one afternoon with two gentlemen and strolled with them in the garden. Then he entered the house and told his daughter he wished to show some gentlemen her necklace. She brought it, and never saw it again. Her noble fiancé having withdrawn from the engagement, Miss Hamlet made her living by school-teaching.

Among the happy memories connected with Hamlet House is the coming on a sweet June day in 1877 of the venerable William Lloyd Garrison and his son Francis. It was his last day in England, and we invited to luncheon some of the younger generation to whom it would be a cherished memory to have known the great liberator. He was most gracious and gave us anecdote after anecdote concerning his early struggles and his comrades. He charmed us all, and inspired us with hopefulness for the future of the Southern States and the negroes. He spoke with delight of the meetings he had attended in London and of the eloquent women who spoke at them, and smiled at the early days in which he had been a " Pharisee of the Pharisees " with regard to the participation of women in public meetings. Garrison was a beautiful figure walking through the old garden with the young people clustering around him. There was a radiance about his almost snow-white head like a halo. At the very time that Garrison was drawing around him his circle of admirers, General Grant was being lionized in a very deliberate way. I attended assemblies now for one and next for the other. The man who sowed the seed of emancipation and the man who, having grown grey without ever feeling a throb of sympathy for the slave, yet reaped the official and pecuniary harvest, had no apparent relation to each other.

I first met ex-President Grant at a grand dinner at the Grosvenor Hotel given him by John Russell Young, then representing the "New York Herald" in London. I had some conversation with the ex-President, and he talked mostly of his reception by the Queen the day before. While he was at Windsor Castle a cablegram arrived from Pennsylvania (he did not say by whom sent) addressed to the Queen, thanking her for her reception of him, — the news of which must have travelled very swiftly for the response to be returned before the reception was over. He also spoke of the agreeable dinner given him at Marlborough House by the Prince of Wales.

It was easy to perceive that the reception given Grant in London had no heart in it. The official people wished to please the Americans, and all was properly done. But Grant's administrations were believed to have been marked by corruption, and the removal of Motley, known to have hastened his death, was ascribed to petty vengeance against Sumner.

The general committed a sad mistake at the formal reception given him by the Duke of Devonshire. On this occasion the nobility wore their orders. The ex-President appeared decorated in just the same way, — that is, with a flaming red riband across his breast from shoulder to waist, and a large gold badge. General Badeau wore something smaller of the same kind. There were few Americans present, but we were shocked. I was embarrassed by the inquiries made to me by Englishmen present, whether there were orders and decorations of that kind in America. Of course I could give no explanation. My friend G. W. Smalley, if I remember rightly, told me that the gold medal was engraved with a list of Grant's victories. The incident excited ridicule, and some Americans managed to let the general understand that this bit of imitation had changed the homage of the nobility to an ex-President into an ex-President's genuflexion before them.

At any rate, the riband was laid aside later in the evening, and not worn again in London.

It was a great delight to find ourselves neighbours of the composer Edward Dannreuther. We remembered him as a boy in Cincinnati playing the organ in our Unitarian church with wonderful skill. Many a time I had watched from the pulpit his little head beyond the screen at the other end of the room, admiring his voluntaries. After leaving Cincinnati (1862) we never heard of him until we found him in London in the circle of artistic poets whom we well knew. He had married a Greek lady and fixed his abode at Bayswater, in the house where the poet John Sterling lived. Not far from it lived the poet's son, Edward, an artist, and his two sisters, both of stately beauty. The Dannreuther house was old and full of quaint rooms and halls, and the composer had added a concert-room. The walls were covered with Morris papers — the design lemons and pomegranates — and hung with pictures by Burne-Jones and his school. The furniture was antique, a fine feature being an architectural stove towering to the ceiling. Amid this environment we used to listen to the compositions in which Dannreuther had interpreted poems of his friends William Morris and Dante Rossetti before they were published. There were among his friends ladies and gentlemen enough able to sing these ballads with sympathetic skill.

There was in all this poetry and in the music a certain melancholy. Those present were persons in good circumstances, the ladies refined and fair, most of the gentlemen distinguished in art or in letters. In these charming societies — for there were similar circles in several other houses — I was reminded always of the garden pictured by incomparable Boccaccio outside Florence, where ladies and gentlemen found refuge from the plague in Florence. Their refuge was in the realm of the imagination, and the refuge of these from the coarseness and hardness and despair of London was also in that realm, but they could not attain the joyous freedom of the Italian genius.

When superstitions have vanished, Hell become a vulgar notion, and the god of wrath forgotten, the " Earthly Paradise " begins to arise, but with painful revelations of actual thorns wounding the poor and suffering. Again and again have I stood in Hyde Park with the humble crowd listening to William Morris, while carriages of the wealthy rolled past. He too might have enjoyed his carriage instead of trying to engrave on those hearts his transcendent sociology and to animate them with visions of reform beautiful as the windows he stained for churches. Out there on the grass, a rude bench for his pulpit, rough people for his audience, William Morris raged against himself as one of the class of their non-producing oppressors. " If I were in the situation of most of you I should take to hard drinking." I was a listener solely from interest in the man, having no faith in any socialism except that poor people should unite in communal means for physical comfort, in order that mental individuality may increase.

William Morris impressed me then as a noble but still more a pathetic figure ; as I look back on the scene it appears to me tragical. For I believe his premature death was in part due to disillusion. I think of him now as one who spoke to the multitudes in an unknown tongue, as if Prospero had called up his exquisite masque for a company of comparative Calibans. Meanwhile, those who really understood as well as loved him were forming their oases to make life beautiful in the brief interval of existence. The Prometheus that brought their fire had consumed faith in the future life, and grim, remorseless London forbade any faith in a coming heaven on earth. So they gathered together in their affectionate circles. Among these the assemblies at the Dannreuthers are associated in my memory with the tender melancholy of Morris's ballads, as Dannreuther translated his thoughts into sound. Across the graves of some who were guests in that circle I still hear the voices gone silent of two who sang a duet from " The Earthly Paradise."

> In the white-flowered hawthorn brake,
> Love, be merry for my sake;

Twine the blossoms in my hair,
Kiss me where I am most fair:
Kiss me, love! for who knoweth
What thing cometh after death ?

There were gala evenings at the Dannreuthers' when Wagner visited London (1877). Ferdinand Praeger, Wagner's earliest friend, persuaded him to conduct concerts of his operatic music in Albert Hall, despite his protests that it was against his principles to detach his music from dramatic action and scenery. Wagner brought Frau Materna with him, — the wonderful voice which determined various *tours de force* in his operas. Before the concerts began, Wagner was entertained by the Dannreuthers, the guests being not only musical artists but painters and writers. G. H. Lewes and his wife were present, and I remember. a display of enthusiasm by George Eliot. Wagner performed on the piano a piece just composed, unknown I believe to his nearest friends. It was a song, and in it were one or two passages that one might suppose beyond the compass of any voice ; but Materna mastered them one after the other, the composer's face reddening with excitement until the last note sounded, when he leaped up and seized the hands of the singer. Then George Eliot moved quickly forward to shake hands with her, though whether Materna was aware of the distinction of the woman who congratulated her was doubtful. For George Eliot, who could probably not have been drawn into so large a company by any less attraction than Wagner, had sat in her usual reserve until this brilliant performance by Materna. This German lady was handsome, gracious, and entirely free from vanity or any airs.

By taking Hamlet House we were enabled to supply the South Place congregation with what it had never enjoyed in its long history, a social centre, and to entertain our many friends coming from America. For London was the great place to see Americans, — and we welcomed in those years Higginson, John Fiske, Frothingham, Robert Collyer, Bayard Taylor and his wife, Eugene Schuyler, Hon. Alphonzo

Taft and his family, John Jay, Cyrus Field, and many another. In 1879 Bedford Park with its artistic homes and its circle of literary men and artists charmed us away even from beautiful Hamlet House. We built there a pretty " Queen Anne " house, despite my friend Herbert Spencer's wonder that a " progressive " should go far back in the matter of architecture. Our " Inglewood " — for I had gone back to my earliest remembered home in Virginia for a name — had a pretty garden ; and although it was not large enough for the lawn gaieties of Hamlet House, our Inglewood " Mondays " had the attraction of being attended by the artists and literary people whose residence made Bedford Park a village such as Rabelais dreamed of in " Theleme."

Ah, the happiness of those years at Bedford Park ! The walks and talks with James Sime and John Todhunter ; our choice circle of " Calumets " passing Sunday evenings in such genuine conversation as the presence of Sime and Todhunter, Dr. Gordon Hogg, G. H. Orpen, York Powell, Fox Bourne, and Jonathan Carr assured ; the exhibitions at our art school, the University Extension lectures from Sir Martin Conway, the discussions at the village club (for both ladies and gentlemen) ; the theatricals, tableaux-vivants, masquerades, — these charms for the evenings of days passed in toil made Bedford Park for my wife and myself the ideal place to which we always looked back with a wonder that any ties could ever have drawn us away from it.

Sir Martin Conway I had met at times in Cambridge, as a youth distinguished for his knowledge of the history of art, and the curator of prints, not yet dreaming of the Himalayan heights on which he wrote his grand books and climbed to his title. He was lovable and brilliant, and I was sorry I could not make out some kinship. I would have liked to meet one of the English branch of our Virginia race, and heard with interest that a Captain Conway had come with his family to reside near us. But during my absence from home, my wife returning from a walk found the cook at the door in violent altercation with two officers, and holding on with her hands to some valuables they were trying to seize. She heard the cook cry, "My mistress always pays her debts as she goes; she don't owe anything to anybody." The officers said to my wife, "Isn't this the house of Captain Conway?" On being told where the house was the officers apologized, and told my wife that the so-called captain was a fugitive from accumulated debts, and a warrant was issued to seize the furniture. We afterwards learned that his name was not Conway at all, but that he was a Scotchman with high connections. This was the only disagreeable incident in our residence at Bedford Park.[1]

A famous "Ballad of Bedford Park" appeared in the "St. James's Gazette" (December 17, 1881), in which Jonathan T. Carr, founder of the village, and Norman Shaw, the architect, consult about building "stores" and a church, and in this connection the unknown minstrel made free with my name.

"A church likewise," J. T. replies.
 Says Shaw, " I 'll build a church;
Yet sore I fear the æsthetes here
 Will leave it in the lurch."

"Religion," pious Carr rejoined,
 " In Moncure Conway's view
Is not devoid of interest,
 Although it be not true."

[1] Another experience my Conway name brought me was pleasanter. On my way to Berlin a young German, who spoke English, chatted pleasantly with me, and on arrival was active in getting me a cab and seeing after my baggage. When I warmly thanked him, he said, with a bow, "It is nothing compared with the pleasure I have got from your great novel." He left me to my amazement, as I had written no novel, but on my trunk was my name in large letters; and no doubt he had seen it and concluded that I was the author of *Called Back*, then making some noise. Although I once or twice saw Mr. Fargus, I never had the opportunity to ask him why he selected the name of Hugh Conway as a pseudonym, but some sentiment about Conway Castle may have led him to consult Burke's "Landed Gentry," where he would find the Welsh branch springing from Sir Hugh Conway, transplanted from Yorkshire. The heroine of *Called Back* is "Mrs. March," that being now the name of my only sister.

> " Then let us build a house for her,
>   Wherein she may abide;
> And those who choose may visit her —
>   The rest may stay outside.
>
> " But lest the latter should repine,
>   A tennis ground we 'll make,
> Where they on Sunday afternoons
>   May recreation take."

As a matter of fact the tennis play went on through the Sunday forenoon as well as the afternoon. The clergyman of the church did not disapprove of Sunday tennis, but it thinned his congregation, and he prepared a proposal that it should be discontinued between 10 and 1 o'clock. To this he wished to get signatures, and first of all brought it to me and my wife. From fear that religious discord might arise in the harmonious village, and Sunday recreations be stopped altogether, my wife and I signed the proposal. But no other signature could the clergyman get. The young people, even some that supported the church, protested that Sunday was the only day when husbands and brothers were not at business, and there were not enough afternoon hours to accommodate them all. So we two, the most notorious heretics in Bedford Park, alone signed the clergyman's Sunday petition!

Soon after our settlement at Bedford Park came Edwin Abbey, who took great interest in our village of antique houses, all newly built, in going about which he said pleasantly that he " felt as though he were walking through a water-colour." Abbey charmed everybody there by his wit and engaging personality. We were both working for " Harper's Magazine," and among the pleasantest of my expeditions was our visit together to the English lakes (1879), which resulted in the article entitled " The English Lakes and their Genii." Every illustration in those articles represents to me some delightful adventure. We staid in quaint old hotels in all that region, and Abbey's anecdotes were so full of drollery that I did not feel quite sure that he had not mistaken his vocation, and should not have been either a literary or stage comedian.

In May, 1881, I gave an address before a "Society for Promoting Religious Equality," newly formed by students of Cambridge University. Its object was to maintain the principles of the University Tests Abolition Act. This act of Parliament, opening the universities to persons of any creed or no creed, was not made prospective. Consequently Keble College, to which only members of the English Church are admitted, was built at Oxford, and the organization of a similar one (Selwyn) at Cambridge was announced for June 1. Its promoters meant to demand incorporation with the university, but Fawcett had framed a measure prohibiting religious tests in the universities forever, and it was in concert with him and other leaders in Parliament that the Cambridge society was acting. My paper, therefore, was read in Clare College eight days before the inauguration of Selwyn, as yet unbuilt, by the Earl of Powys, Lord High Steward of the University. About two hundred young men were present. Under title of "The Unbinding of Prometheus," I presented my idea of the cords by which Thought was still bound and preyed upon for serving mankind in ways not authorized by the Christian Zeus. I had naturally alluded to the disfranchisement at that moment of a constituency because of its representative's atheism, and although few present shared Bradlaugh's opinions, the anger against his persecutors was manifest. My enumeration of the burdens on religious liberty which tended to make English thinkers defiant like Prometheus was made on careful data, and in the discussions that followed my paper there was a consensus on the principles of liberty.

During this visit I was a guest of Sydney Hickson, a brilliant student of science, soon afterwards appointed professor of zoölogy in Owens College, Manchester. His rooms were in Downing College, adjacent to the large grounds called the "Wilderness." This Wilderness, carpeted with long grass, fringed with flowering shrubs, and shaded by blossoming trees, was vocal not only at night but during the day with songs of the nightingales. It was all sweet and beautiful, this Wilderness beside the Greek walls and columns of the college.

I was admitted on the floor to hear a debate in the Cambridge Union, whose discussions are conducted as in the House of Commons. About four hundred students were present, the galleries being crowded with ladies and gentlemen. The subject related to the Bradlaugh issue, and was opened with a motion that the parliamentary oath should be abolished. The youth who led in favour of the motion was, I was told, a particularly religious churchman; yet in a speech which would have done honour to any legislature he affirmed that the oath should be abolished as a restriction on honest thought, an encouragement to hypocrisy, and an impediment to progress. He not only objected to the religious formula, but also to the pledge of support to the monarchy which it sanctioned. He preferred the English Constitution to any other, but if the country saw fit to frame a republic it should be free to do so. It was maintained, however, by another speaker, that an oath to support " Queen Victoria, her heirs and successors, according to law " would admit of a legal effort to make a president her " successor." There was a good deal of republicanism manifested, one speaker declaring that the advance of democracy was not to be repressed " by the flickering shadow of a dying monarchy." There was also abundant heresy. One speaker having spoken of atheists as " disgusting, despicable," was called to order on the ground " that no person could be permitted to use such language concerning the opinions of members of the house." The chairman called upon the speaker to withdraw his words, which he did. It was remarkable to observe what an instinct for parliamentary procedure this body of youths had acquired. There was at all times *esprit de corps*, loyalty to the chair, and speeches quiet and simple in language, and to the point.

A few days after my return to London I received a long telegram from the leaders of the Cambridge Religious Equality Society, saying that general consternation had been caused

by the announcement that the new American Minister, James
Russell Lowell, was to assist in the founding of Selwyn College, the object of which was to restore creed tests in the
university. They did not believe that Mr. Lowell understood the situation, and begged me to explain it to him. I
had hardly read the despatch when Lowell called, and I
handed it to him. He had gone too far to recede, and merely
said he did not consider the affair as likely to mix him up
with either party. However, he began his speech at Cambridge with an allusion to the incident. He said that when
he was asked whether he knew what he was about, and if he
was coming down there to join a conspiracy, he felt like the
honest citizen of the sixteenth century who innocently contracted to supply Bonner with faggots. He assured them
that his being there had no political or dogmatical significance. He was drawn there as a native of Cambridge in New
England, with filial respect for Cambridge in Old England.
This was not a felicitous remark for either party, for Selwyn College was not a part of the university for which he
felt "filial respect," but a fortress raised and armed against
it because it was now like Harvard University without any
creed test. His High Church hosts must have winced when
they read next day in the Cambridge paper the following
paragraph : —

The presence of the United States Minister on Wednesday
among the bishops and other church dignitaries at Selwyn
College was unusually suggestive. Mr. James Russell Lowell
is the descendant of an old English Worcestershire family,
who were led to leave England many generations ago through
the persecutions of the church dignitaries of those days ; men
who held (according to Mr. Lowell's own humorous words)
that —

    The right
Of privately judging means simply that light
Has been granted to *me*, for deciding on *you*.

To-day we see the eminent scholar and poet, the descendant of the Puritans and the son of a Unitarian minister of
the younger Cambridge, in Massachusetts, associated with

English ecclesiastics in furthering the claims of an English High Church college. The juxtaposition of Bishop Words- worth and Mr. Lowell, and their concerted action in further- ing the same cause, is just one of those things which no one would have ventured to predict, and which must be seen in order to be appreciated.

Lowell may have supposed that I had some hand in this paragraph; if so, he was mistaken. I had nothing whatever to do with it.

I lectured several times at Cambridge and made interest- ing acquaintances, among these being Karl Pearson, now a professor in University College, London. In 1882 he placed in my hand a poem he had written (anonymously), entitled "The Trinity: A Nineteenth Century Passion Play. The Son; or, Victory of Love. 'God when He makes the prophet does not unmake the man.' — *Locke*." It came about the time when, after having printed a discourse on Mary Magda- lene, I waked up to the perception that in regarding her as an immoral woman I had followed a baseless church tradi- tion; and the fact that the writer of this passion play had taken the same uncritical point of view prevented my return- ing to it at once. But I have since read it repeatedly and find it a powerful poem. Wagner planned a passion play of this kind and wrote the libretto, of which I possess a copy. But he discovered, no doubt, that the Christian world would not tolerate the idea of Jesus touched by human love, and substituted "Parsifal" for it.

On New Year's eve, in a wintry fog, I made my way through the plebeian portions of Bloomsbury, coming at last to a sign inscribed, "The Church of Humanity." Entering by a nar- row hall I found myself in a room that touched my sentiment of reverence. This was the first room in the world religiously dedicated to the worship of Humanity. One might feel here that he was beside the manger from which a great influence might come. It was nearly three centuries after the birth of Jesus before Christianity possessed a temple of its own. Au- guste Comte died in 1857, and within twenty-five years thereafter his philosophy had received in great, hospitable London the vestments of a religion. I had met the positivist priest, Dr. Congreve, at " The Priory," the residence of G. H. Lewes, and had remarked the especial esteem for him manifested by George Eliot. Subsequently I had several interviews with him, and discovered in him a phenomenal man, a refined scholar, with that elegance of look and presence which marks the real nobleman; but his statements impressed me as curiously academic. He had such unquestioning faith in his creed and church that he might have grown on the left side of the stem that bore Cardinal Newman. He showed no disposition to qualify or to interpret in a strained sense any formula. When I urged that humanity as a whole could hardly be worshipped, so many were its crimes and cruelties, Dr. Congreve simply answered that one loves his mother whatever her faults. But a deity must have no faults. He desired to win to his church the common people, and thought it could be done by cult and ritual. " Women especially need symbolical forms and expressions," he said.

At the " Festival of Holy Women," on the morning of December 31, 1880, I counted forty-eight persons, two thirds being ladies of social distinction and wealth. The small room half wainscotted, half blue up to the low ceiling; the walls ennobled by sculptured heads of great men; the small pulpit barely raised above the floor and surrounded with lofty flowers, — above it a very large engraving of the Dresden Madonna: these combined to make a mystically beautiful frame for some great symbol of all that is supreme in nature. The Madonna and her babe floating in the air were too exotic; the portrait of Comte's much idealized Clothilde de Vaux — neither spiritual nor beautiful — was out of place among the persons exalted on the walls. Were all those saints of the positivist calendar detached from their faults, and their virtues combined in one being, would even that miraculous being captivate these forty-eight hearts, or satisfy all of those deep inexpressible longings that stir within us with energies transmitted from myriad forms through immemorial ages?

Dr. Congreve's discourse was about St. Monica, Beatrice, Heloise, Joan of Arc, others being briefly alluded to; and at the close he read the fine lines from George Eliot's "Jubal," —"O may I join the choir invisible!" In the reading he was animated and impressive.

Next day—New Year's day—was the "Festival of Humanity," and that too I attended. The church had only been opened in the previous September, and its little organ for the first time uttered its voice that New Year's day. About sixty were present, among them some fine-looking young men. After the voluntary—there was no singing—Dr. Congreve said that they would be able to translate into their own meaning the words of Isaiah, and proceeded to read the sixtieth chapter, "Arise, shine," etc. Then the company arose and stood with open eyes and without bowed heads while Dr. Congreve uttered an ascription to the "Great Power whom we here acknowledge as the Highest, Humanity," in which the petitional "may we" occurred twice, the audience responding "Amen."

The sermon was an expansion of the benediction:—

> The Faith of Humanity,
> The Hope of Humanity,
> The Love of Humanity,

Bring you comfort, and teach you sympathy, give you peace in yourselves and peace with others, now and forever. Amen.

During all this I was not conscious of other emotion than wondering respect for this small company of cultured people whose religion had entirely turned away from the heavens, and had enshrined humanity. It was all pathetically picturesque; but no more, because this positivist deity was to me another "Incomprehensible" like the triune. No such entity as Humanity do I find conceivable. In the effort my imagination is lost in a vast cloud with many nuclei,—here, of man-faced bipeds devouring or slaying each other, there, of men helping each other,—but can one define humanity without distinguishing those great ones whose busts looked down upon us from the wall, and those who look up to them with reverence, from the vast swarm of irrational man-shaped beings who act as inorganically as the destructive elements ?

At times I had my desk at South Place occupied by one or another of the positivists. Henry Crompton, Dr. Congreve's leading assistant, gave us a memorable discourse, and Frederic Harrison several. But in none of their discourses could I find any clear definition of divine Humanity. I gradually reached a belief that positivist religion is a refined variety of the general democratization of Christianity. Mankind, in worshipping one or another terrestrial being assumed to be of their kind, are really worshipping qualities and powers that could not possibly exist in any actual being. The very names — Zoroaster, Buddha, Christ, Mohammed — are not personal names, but labels for the stored-up ideals of races in immemorial time. While these systems represent a worship by each race of its own humanity, the positivist — such was my theory — has fused those diverse humanities into one ; but in detaching a " religion of Humanity " from its traditional sovereigns it has not relapsed into anarchy but established a ministerial cabinet in its calendar of saints.

Although the positivists are thus not really worshipping an actual but an idealized humanity, this word is ambiguous. Could their system be popularized the collectivist sense of " humanity " must predominate, and above all the great historic men and women of their calendar be raised the unreason, superstitions, and passions of the masses.

But how precious were, and are, these high-principled men and women, with their unique philosophic faith, amid the sea of doubts and polemics mostly aimless ! How beautiful in my remembrance are the homes and the lives of those whom we knew personally, and how enviable at times their faith appeared ! In 1884, when Mrs. Frederic Harrison fell ill, the probability that this lovely and devoted positivist might die filled all liberal circles with alarm, and also the many homes of the poor in which her charities were known. When this danger was suspended over Frederic Harrison he steadily fulfilled his duties as well as hers towards those who depended on them. At this time I received from him a private letter which I afterwards told him I might some day print, and it is here subjoined: it is dated 23 Gutemberg 97 (3 Sept. 1884) : —

I thank you heartily for your friendly letter of sympathy and inquiry. It is quite true that my reply to (Herbert) Spencer was written (or rather printed) under the presence of great anxiety. . . .

It is in a season like this, for this illness has had every element of alarm and distress, that the strength of what is called religion is brought to the test of personal experience. To her and to myself I will say that our belief has been one of unspeakable comfort. At no instant and in no form has it failed either of us. One smiles to think how trumpery and how incongruous at such a season are the vulgar resources of theological convention. I have never before so clearly realized all that a *human religion* means — how completely one's deepest beliefs and hopes coincide with (instead of having mere complicity with) the medical cares and provisions — how one feels to rest on the coöperation of one's fellow beings, consciously and unconsciously, some of them in sympathy, some in the saving and the recovery of health — how the very instruments of science, the morphia needle, and the like, seem revelations, and doctors, relations, friends, and nurses seem transfigured ministers of humanity.

I will tell our secretary to send you the printed programmes. You will see ("Times" and "Pall Mall") advertisements of our doings on the 5th, Friday next. At 5 P. M. I give an address on Comte — very much in the spirit which you indicate and which I largely share. At 6.30 we dine in the Strand, and at 8.30 there will be a social meeting and music at Newton Hall. All are open and we shall be glad to see you and yours at any of these.

I hope to meet you before your return to America, which in common with all your friends I so much regret.

I remember across twenty years the brilliancy of that discourse on Comte, and others by Frederic Harrison. It was one of the great experiences of life to pick one's way along the narrow and dingy purlieus leading out of the Strand and pass by an alley into the little hall with the grand name where Frederic Harrison, without any trick of gesture or rhetoric, made every mind and heart one with his own in sympathy, and for the happy hour one in thought.

CHAPTER XLIX

THE Right Hon. W. E. Forster was the most fair-minded, liberal, and charitable statesman who ever opened a Pandora box. To him, as cabinet minister, was confided the framing of the new public school system. In presenting it in Parliament he said that the government, in trying to deal with the proverbial " religious difficulty," had found itself confronted with the " irreligious difficulty." From that epigrammatic phrase flew out all manner of angry conflicts. The clergy and the dissenting ministers had for generations alike been imbreeding the belief that morality depended entirely on religion and religion on the Bible, and this imported much heat into the controversies. The atmosphere became charged with polemics.

In 1870 an accomplished casuist, Dr. Liddon, preached the Lenten sermons at St. James's, and arraigned the famous Unitarians, quoting their tributes to Christ, then claimed that they could not logically go so far unless they went farther : unless Christ was divine, supernaturally born, and wrought miracles, they must regard him as self-seeking and egotistical, his influence in history a successful imposture. Liddon was made Canon of St. Paul's, whose guns he turned on Westminster Abbey, where Canon Farrar — scholarly and vigorous but rather rhetorical — was repudiating hell and eternal punishment. Professor Huxley as candidate for the school board was assailed by the orthodox, and protoplasm, evolution, agnosticism were discussed at the hustings. In fact, London in the seventies had become a Mars Hill. Then came a scientific apostle.

This was William Kingdon Clifford, appointed professor of applied mathematics at University College, London, in 1871. His coming to London was a great event. At twenty-seven he was regarded by the leading scientific men as their peer, and he had gone through all the phases of religious faith into well-informed freedom. He had a winning personality, irresistible indeed, and in public speaking could charm alike the Royal Society or a popular audience. Our acquaintance made at Cambridge became friendship in London, and my wife and I used to attend the weekly evenings in his rooms when his friends — among them always Lady Pollock and her sons — gathered around him.

With Professor Clifford I had some droll adventures with " mediums." The chief thaumaturgist was Mrs. Guppy, who had séances at her house in Hampstead. At a discussion in South Place chapel I was challenged to test this " medium," and took Clifford along. A dozen sat around the table, but we two were the only unbelievers. Handsome Mrs. Guppy appeared in fine décolletage ; I was placed on one side of her, Clifford on the other ; and we both knew that it was not she who was to do the tricks. There were raps ordering the gaslights to be put out, and each one of the company to choose something to be thrown on the table — " something likely to be near by." The door was locked, the key given me to hold, and before the lights were turned off I examined the room — which was nearly without furniture. Various things were called for : a rose, a slipper, an onion, violets, a sausage, etc. Clifford demanded a small plate of artificial teeth, which were in the pocket of his overcoat in the hall. I said it was necessary to call for something not easily concealed under a dress, and demanded a large bandbox.

When the lights were turned on everything called for was on the table except what Clifford and I had demanded. Mrs.

Guppy admitted the séance to be a failure, and did not venture on any further experiment.

Another experiment was with the famous Williams. The séance was in my house. The method of Williams was that we should surround the table, finger hooked in finger ; then in the dark he would make some excuse for changing the finger, and contrive to get those on each side of him to hook the forefinger and little finger of the same hand, leaving one of his hands free to do the tricks. Clifford had heard of that device and warned me. When we had been seated for some time Williams said his finger held by Clifford was weary, and proposed to change it, but Clifford in a low voice declined on his side, as I did on mine. Whereupon Williams raised the light and rushed out of the house, leaving his accordeon and banjo, which I sent to him next day. Several credulous ladies who had been victimized by Williams were present, and had the detection explained to them. Williams was broken up in London by this exposure, and the last I heard of him was at Rotterdam where the customs officers seized his paraphernalia of wigs, masks, rag hands, and phosphorus.

After the marriage of Clifford in April, 1875, to Miss Lucy Lane, — now distinguished in the world of letters, — we often met them. He was the idol of children as well as of parents. His resources in getting up home entertainments were as inexhaustible as his resources for charming all varieties of minds by his lectures. Scientific men consulted him about their theories, artists about their pictures, sceptical theologians about their speculations.

Clifford had a strong feeling that scientific men were not in sufficient relation with the general intelligence of the country, and not doing enough to liberate the people of all classes from degrading dogmas. In one of our talks it was arranged that there should be summoned a Congress of Liberal Thinkers.

This congress was held on June 13 and 14, 1878, in my South Place chapel. It was the centenary year of Voltaire, and I came to it fresh from the great festival in Paris (May

30). Our congress brought together leading men from all
parts of the United Kingdom, and some from other European
countries, from India, and from America. Nearly all of these
400 congressmen (including several congresswomen) represented some congregation or society. We had Broadchurch-
men, Unitarians, Secularists, Theists; and we had a tower of
strength in my American friend, Wentworth Higginson. At
the end of the two days' discussion an association was formed,
its aim being defined as : —

1. The scientific study of religious phenomena. 2. The collection and diffusion of information concerning religious
movements throughout the world. 3. The emancipation of
mankind from the spirit of superstition. 4. Fellowship among
liberal thinkers of all races. 5. The promotion of the culture,
progress, and moral welfare of mankind, and of whatever in
any form of religion may tend towards that end. 6. Membership in this Association shall leave each individual responsible
for his own opinion alone, and in no degree affect his relations
with other associations.

The presidency of the association was conferred on Professor Huxley, and by him accepted. I remember well the
satisfaction with which, referring to the eminent names in the
membership, Huxley said, " Freethinkers are no longer to be
simply bullied."

Several important men had discouraged our effort. Dr.
James Martineau, who regretted that he could not attend,
being at his summer home in Scotland, expressed his belief
that " Negation supplies no bond. It has its work to do — a
legitimate work, which I am far from depreciating — but, in
my opinion, this work must be individually done ; and, beyond it, a good deal must happen before religious combination becomes possible." Matthew Arnold wrote, " I am
strongly of opinion that the errors of popular religion in this
country are to be dispersed by the spread of a better and
wider culture, far more than by direct antagonism and religious counter-movements." On the other hand, the encourage-
ments were much more numerous. Max Muller, Picton, Karl

Blind, Dr. M. Kalisch, Leslie Stephen, A. J. Ellis F. R. S.,
Professor Estlin Carpenter, and indeed most of the younger
generation of Unitarians and of the Secularists responded
eagerly. Letters full of sympathy came to us from the Continent — from Littré, Professor Hugenholtz (of Holland),
Professor Th. Bost (of Verviers), M. Emile de Harven (of
Antwerp); and M. Fix, editor of " La Religion Laique,"
came from Belgium, and gave an address to the Congress.

But alas, Clifford was not there. His health had broken
down in April, and under peremptory warning he had gone
with his wife to the Mediterranean. While the congress was
in session I received a letter from him, written May 23 on
the Morocco, *en route* from Fiume to Malta, saying how
hard he had tried to write a paper for the occasion. A relapse
at Venice had rendered it impossible, and he could only send
me some notes he had made of the points he meant to enlarge
on. The notes are these : —

Catholics are fond of saying that an age of atheism is approaching, in which we shall throw over all moral obligations,
and society will go to ruin. Then we shall see what is the true
effect of all our liberal and scientific teaching. As a matter
of fact, however, even themselves admit that the public conscience is growing in strength and straightness, while the
catholic dogmas and organism are more and more repudiated.
We may see reason to believe that the former of those facts is
the cause of the latter. Part of modern unbelief is no doubt
due to the wider knowledge of criticism of the so-called " evidence of Christianity," but in all ages sensible men have seen
through that flimsy structure. Intellectual scepticism is not
really more rife than it has been in many past periods. The
main ground of hope for the masses is the moral basis of scepticism, — 1, its revolt against mythology ; 2, its revolt against
the priestly organization of churches.

As to the mythology, the dogma of eternal damnation is
being quietly dropped, as not in the Jewish part of the New
Testament ; but it has been practically taught by the Christian organization for sixteen centuries. Therefore the Christian organization ought to be thrown away with it, for it is

not " an opinion like another," but a wicked thing to believe.

As to the priestly organization, the practical effect of the Christian organization, " the Church," has always been adverse to morality and is now. The clergy is everywhere making more pronounced its revolt from the great principles which underlie the modern social structure. There is a strong antagonism between the Christian organization and the Jewish ethical literature, which our moral sense approves. And I believe that, so far as the Christian organization is concerned, the time has come for heeding again the ancient warning — " Come out of her, my people, that ye be not partaker of her sins, and that ye receive not of her plagues."

The association elected a committee of twenty-four — in which were two Hindus (Dhairyaban of Bombay and Mitra of Calcutta), and also four ladies, with plenary powers. We had several interesting meetings at Huxley's house, but it was found impossible to organize members scattered about the world in any central or definite movement.

In fact the association, so far as any active work had been contemplated, received a mortal stroke within the year of its birth. The life of it as an organization depended on the life of Clifford, which ended March 3, 1879. The scientific and philosophical thinkers — Huxley, Sir Frederick Pollock, Tyndall, Leslie Stephen, and others — had felt that this congress was to open a great field for the admirable young orator, so perfectly equipped as an apostle of scientific thought in its relation to religion and ethics.

The association was never formally dissolved, and Huxley remained its president to the end. The committee met at his house and reached the conclusion that the two days' congress had done what was needed at the time ; also that no further organization was needed or possible in England. Every serious thinker had the means of reaching the public ; magazines and journals were hospitable to all varieties of opinion; and, as Professor Tyndall said, it was always possible to summon another congress when occasion called for it.

I discovered by that congress that despite Martineau's assertion that " Negation supplies no bond," it is the only real bond between the individual leaders of a people in their exodus from intellectual bondage. There were in that congress at least seventy men prominent in their communities either as preachers or writers, several of them clergymen of the English Church ; there were several titled persons, also Hindus, and a learned African, — E. W. Blyden, Liberian ambassador. These persons had here a chance to witness the enthusiasm which atheism could kindle, not only in scholarly men but in cultured ladies, such as Mrs. Ernestine Rose and Mrs. Harriet Law. The venerable George Jacob Holyoake, who in early life had been imprisoned for atheism, spoke amid the children of a tolerant era. There were old friends of Emerson, among them Goodwyn Barmby, who used to listen to his lectures thirty years before. Solitary thinkers who had long sat eating their hearts, feeling themselves in a world to which they had no relation, came from their retreat and made acquaintance with their kindred. To some extent this was even personal; for we gave at the end of the congress a garden party at Hamlet House where we then resided. Wentworth Higginson was our guest at the time, and even his old friends of Worcester and Boston might have been surprised could they have witnessed the combination in him of the radical preacher, the militant humanitarian organizer, the man of letters, and the " society man." Higginson, while sympathetic with every sincere negation, held to his belief in immortality and his theism; he was thus with his extemporaneous eloquence precisely the man who could make the congress a happy and cheerful one.

In a sense the association ended. But as Goethe said, " a beautiful thing never ends." During the remainder of my life in London I continually received evidences of the happy effects of that congress.

Wonderful London ! At the very moment when our assembly was probing the foundations of religion and theoretically abolishing superstition, around us was a recrudescence of wildest fanaticism. Lord Beaconsfield's occupation of Cyprus, the raising of Cleopatra's Needle beside the Thames, and several other things, set off a swarm of apocalyptic apostles shrieking about the gathering of Jews to Palestine and the Second Coming of Christ. There was also a recrudescence of legal persecution. One of our South Place ladies, Mrs. Flora Carnegie, the beautiful wife of a gentleman of high social position, on appearing as a witness in some small case before Magistrate Newton, was bullied by him because she refused to swear on the Bible ; and Edward Truelove, a veteran bookseller, was imprisoned for selling the Malthusian " Fruits of Philosophy."

My " Sacred Anthology " and the Liberal Congress in my chapel brought me the friendship of an increasing number of able men from India, Persia, and Japan. They, too, were pilgrims who had found no shrine. Contact with European thought had destroyed their old faith but offered them only dogmas more repulsive. Tatui Baba, a learned ex-priest and statesman, and his Japanese friends in London, begged me to go and preach in Tokio, and let the people know that cultured people in England and America did not believe the gospel of the missionaries.

I heard rumours of a Moslem scholar wandering about London, and in want, and after a long search found him. His name was Mohammed Bakher, and he told me his story, — which I afterwards verified. He knew Hebrew, and study of the Old Testament converted him temporarily to the Jewish faith. But although he became eminent among the Rabbins of Syria and Armenia for his learning, his convictions were still unsettled; and at last he took up Christianity. The British missionaries at Bagdad sent him to England for clerical orders, to aid his work among Moslems in Persia; the clergy in England received him with delight at his eloquence and scholarship; but they dropped him as soon as they discovered that he simply regarded Jesus as an inspired teacher, and did not accept the Trinity. On Christmas day I found him in a garret without food or fire, shivering over his

Bible and his Koran. His situation was relieved, but he soon died. He was a man of genius, but what of that? It was still a fearful thing for a Moslem to fall into the hands of the living Trinity.

If London in the early seventies was a Mars Hill, towards the close of that decade a Babel in fragments appeared on the top of it. The situation was fairly represented by a large coloured cartoon of "Our National Church" issued by an artistic cynic calling himself "Ion," containing good portrait-caricatures of the principal preachers and lay agitators in Church and State politics. In the centre the dome of St. Paul's was pictured as a sort of huge parachute crowned with a bell, the handle on top being a cross : a gust tries to carry away the dome, and on each side of a split episcopal throne the bishops and canons hold it down by ropes. Some of the clergy are marching toward a tiara sign-post marked "To Rome," Father Ignatius ("Ignatius Fatuus") looking on in monk's garb with clasped hands. In a cave Moody and Sankey are grinding a hand organ, while Salvationist General Booth with drum and trumpet shouts to them, "Why don't yer stick to yer own country?" Beneath is Bradlaugh, liberty cap in one hand and torch in the other. Spurgeon and Miall are trying to drag down the episcopal throne ; Haweis is playing on his violin ; Dr. Parker is trying to drag people to his booth (City Temple) with a drum ; Stopford Brooke, Voysey, Colenso, Herbert Spencer, Frederic Harrison, are all portrayed. By the Church Association a donkey says "Let us bray!" I am in a little tent marked "Conway's Free and Airy Tabernacle," having a white flag inscribed "We move on." Above all is a bust of Darwin, beneath being a stairway of geologic strata on which a gorilla is climbing, and drawing by his tail Huxley and Tyndall. The text connected with Darwin was Gen. xxvii, 11. "Behold my brother is an hairy man, and I am a smooth man." Darwin, the topmost figure in the picture (on a level with St. Paul's dome) is noble, but the artist remembers the face in that of a gorilla ascending to a rising sun clothed in a cloud marked "Protoplasm." To each figure a scripture text is applied, and beneath the whole are the words: " A house divided against itself . . .? "

I was rightly placed in my picket tent on the extreme left, almost beyond it, and associated with the texts: " We have no continuing city; let us go forth without the camp," and " He dwells at large." My isolated position as a minister, despite asperities of a few Unitarians, was no martyrdom personally, and as a public teacher it gave me advantages. I looked on all of the camps as equally struggling for error, and could weigh without bias the value of each for human happiness. For as the vision of heaven faded the importance of happiness in this world became paramount. I could idealize any idol not worshipped by human sacrifices. My " Sacred Anthology " closes with the words of Omar Khayyám: " O my heart! thou wilt never penetrate the mysteries of the heavens; thou wilt never reach that culminating point of wisdom which the intrepid omniscients have attained. Resign thyself then to make what little paradise thou canst here below; for, as for that beyond, thou shalt arrive there, — or thou shalt not."

Some of my experiences as a confidant of troubled souls were such as make most religious novels commonplace. Several " Robert Elsmeres " poured out their hearts in my study long before Mrs. Humphry Ward's romance was heard of; one or two Catholic priests came to relate how their Madonna had " materialized " in a human sweetheart; still more were the young ladies of genius longing for some congenial task for their powers. I once by a timely visit saved a peer from suicide; the pistol was in his hand. Sometimes I received letters from evangelical preachers rebuking me for destroying faith, and read them along with letters from mothers thanking me for having interested in some kind of spiritual ideal sons who had been mere scoffers. Few indeed joined South Place chapel except those whose theological faith had been utterly lost. My reputation for pulling down was due to the travellers through London, chiefly American.

The venerable Goodwyn Barmby, who came to our congress of 1878, was a man of whom the old friends of Emerson will be glad to know something more, and I make room in this chapter for a parenthesis concerning him.

In 1870 John Camden Hotten engaged me to write a biographical and critical introduction to a collection of Emerson's papers. As the collection was to include early papers from the " Dial," I thought it important to communicate with Emerson, who objected to the publication. The old papers were not protected, and Hotten had gone to considerable expense; nevertheless, the thing was dropped, Hotten being rewarded by being the publisher of Emerson's " Society and Solitude." My introduction was extended, and though not published was printed, and proofs were sent to the surviving friends of Emerson in England; they were used by Alexander Ireland in his book on Emerson. Not unfairly used, for I had got from him many facts relating to Emerson in England as he had got from me many relating to Emerson in America. In 1870 I gathered up the experiences of men and women who had known Emerson, among these being Goodwyn Barmby, an unclassed Unitarian minister in Suffolk. From his house, Vines Villa, Yoxford, June 17, 1870, there came a letter which presents a glimpse of that period too entertaining to sink into my oubliette : —

When Emerson came to tea with me at Bayswater he was quite enchanted with the trees in Kensington Gardens. I remember well his frequent question, " Can you show me any men and women ? What life have you got here in England ? " I knew well that he was aiming at the " Being before Doing and Knowing " of James Pierpont Graves. He was after biography — I was for history. I had just returned from the French Revolution of 1848, and had witnessed the inspiration of a nation, and my harmony was jarred by his not appearing to sympathize with the social movement. He afterwards went to Paris, and took up his abode in the lovely little apartment which I had occupied not long before in a hotel in the Rue des Beaux-Arts, and which I think I recommended to him. There he would have seen something of Hugh Doherty.[1]

---

[1] Translator of Fourier's *Passions of the Human Soul.*

My impression of Emerson was that he was the most beauti-
fully simple and clearest-minded man I had ever met with, —
but I then thought that he was too much immersed in biographical ideas, which were after all a certain reflex of egotism,
and that he wanted social sympathy and its gospel of self-
sacrifice to make him a whole man. I have no doubt now but
that your great war has made him greater.

Alcott I personally liked, but he bothered me with his pa-
ganism, as it seemed pedantic, and as I knew it was not
original, although his expression of it was well welded, all his
own, and applicable to modern ideas. We fair-headed ones
were the children of Apollo — the non-multitudinous. What
then were the dark race of men? Alcott was an unconscious
flatterer. He would not be personally unpleasant, but the
moment a pleasant analogy occurred he put it into poetic
words.

Marcus Spring found me out on the strength of my verses
" The Hand of Friendship." He and his wife were in London
with Margaret Fuller. Mrs. Spring was one of the most winning women I ever met, and I was in rapture with her. Several
times I saw Miss Fuller in their company, and she appeared
very plain indeed. On one occasion I was invited for the
evening to a large party (with a magnificent feast of flowers
and fruits and sherbet in true orthodox fashion), but of those
there I remember only two, the eldest son of Thom, the Inver-
ary poet, a fine, handsome boy, and W. J. Fox. Miss Fuller
confined her talk to Fox. I had Mrs. Spring, and was I not
content? Fox would have liked a quiet hand at whist better.
He was fairly badgered, driven up a corner, talked to death.
Miss Fuller had travelled far farther than he had from the
common ruts of learning and literature. I seem to remember
now that it was more Proclus and Plotinus than Plato, but it
came in a shining flow of words, and he appeared to be always
retreating out of it in vain, for as step by step he went back,
on came the bright waters after him. I can understand how
motherhood brought the beauty of Margaret Fuller's soul into
her face. The Springs invited me to spend a couple of years
with them at Rhode Island (?) but I never dared to go.

There in Goodwyn Barmby's memory were the sowers that
went forth to sow in the previous generation, and whose seeds

we seemed to be harvesting at the Liberal Congress some thirty years later. But alas, the seeds had not enough depth of earth; they blossomed brilliantly, but found no fruitage in the field of the world, and in the garish day they wither into illusions.

Professor Clifford at times impressed me as a reappearance of Voltaire; and, as in Voltaire, an after-glimmer of the old faith was visible in his empirical speculations about deity, so in Clifford's conception of "Cosmic Emotion" the religious sentiment survived. When I heard that lecture I was deep in my "Demonology and Devil-Lore," and enough Methodism survived in me to have no "cosmic emotion" but one of abhorrence for half of the cosmos.

Especially when the cosmos was killing that splendid man. What were constellations compared to the genius of Clifford?

Professor Clifford's ailment was consumption; during its rapid progress we were all under illusive hopes excited by his inexhaustible spirits. In September, 1878, it became certain that he could not recover. One day when my wife and I were on our way to visit the Cliffords, we met Huxley just from the house. His face was clouded with despair, and he exclaimed, "The finest scientific mind born in England for fifty years is dying in that house." On entering we found Clifford in his armchair, serene and full of his habitual humour, his wife trying to smile. He had just been writing and showing her a skit after the style of Lucian which he repeated to us. It represented Christ and his disciples strolling through Hyde Park and subjected to questions by suspicious policemen. The talk between St. Peter and a policeman was exquisitely comical. Clifford spoke of St. George Mivart's claiming the favour of scientific men for his Catholic Church on the ground of its evolution from the moral and spiritual forces of the whole world; and also something he had read concerning the superiority of that church in bringing the humble people in contact with pictures and images. "This," he said, "is all ingenious and plausible: families all want some church or other to go to on Sundays; but the man is in doubt between competing sects : the Catholic Church steps forward and says, ' I 'm a pretty woman, — choose me ! ' ' "

Clifford's bequest to the world was in a sense condensed in the epitaph he wrote for his grave, where it is engraved : " I was not, and was conceived : I loved, and did a little work : I am not, and am content."

There was some excitement about the admission into Highgate Cemetery of this epitaph, but such was the love for Clifford that the objectors could not venture to encounter it.

In 1875, on arriving in New York, I learned that Charles Bradlaugh was ill, and his recovery doubtful, in St. Luke's Hospital, New York. I at once visited him. Owing to the skill of Drs. Leaming and Abbey his condition had slightly improved, but he was still weak when I reached his bedside. He had been compelled to cancel many lecture engagements and was eager to sail for England. He felt, however, that his recovery was not quite certain. He had not the slightest fear of death, but remembering the legends about " infidel deathbeds," was anxious lest his memory should suffer in that way. He begged me to make inquiries of nurses and doctors whether he had said or done anything during his illness which could be construed into an alteration of his opinions, and desired me, in the event of his death, to bear testimony to the facts. My own methods differed from those of Bradlaugh, but I needed no assurance about his courage. Nevertheless, I conversed with the physicians and nurses, and learned that Bradlaugh had not uttered a word suggesting regret for his unbelief or his career, and for the rest had been an uncomplaining and grateful patient. Yet Mrs. Bradlaugh Bonner in her excellent life of her father had to record that " although he recovered from his illness in New York, and was alive to contradict such fables, it was actually said that he had sent for a minister to pray with him, and one clergyman was even reported to have specified the ' minister ' as a Baptist ! " As I was certainly the only " minister " who visited Bradlaugh during his illness, it is some relief to have the legend of a prayer with Bradlaugh fixed upon that my-

thical "Baptist." Nobody will ever suspect me of having ever
been a Baptist.[1]

Some one — so I was told — asked Frederic Harrison
whether Matthew Arnold believed in a God, and was answered :
" No, but he keeps one in his back-yard to fly at people he
does n't like." I remember Matthew Arnold speaking slight-
ingly of Theodore Parker's theology, alleging that his deity
was "dynamic." But his own famous definition of deity as "a
stream of tendency not ourselves that makes for righteousness "
is liable to the same criticism. That which "makes" is dynamic.
In our invitations to the Liberal Congress in London the
word "religion" was used. Bradlaugh said "religion" had
no meaning for him except as the label of certain systems and
dogmas. I maintained in our talks that the word "religion,"
though etymologically objectionable, could alone represent the
sentiment all of us including himself had for the cause nearest
our hearts. The freethinkers also had their altar. When they
gave of their substance to build their hall and support lectures,
none of them would propose to devote the money to relieve
the physical sufferings around them. They believed no doubt
that secularism if generally adopted would relieve such distress, but the orthodox also included that kind of happiness
in their millennial dream. So long as we were devoting our
supreme energies to a cause as yet theoretical we had a religion.
Bradlaugh agreed with the substance of my statement, but
dreaded the connotations of the word "religion." It had been
so long and universally associated with gods, ceremonies, superstitions that its use by a freethinker would be misleading
unless accompanied each time by elaborate explanations. Because of this word "religion" in our circular Bradlaugh and
Mrs. Besant did not accept our invitation to the Congress of

---

[1] Bradlaugh was in need of money which I gladly supplied, and which
was promptly repaid on his return to England. I mention this because in
his grateful public allusion to my assistance he omits the fact that he
sent the money to my wife before my return to England and without its
being demanded. He was a man of nice ideas of honour, and exceedingly
appreciative of kindness.

1878. I respected Bradlaugh's ability and character, but still believe that he was, as was said of the Athenians at Mars Hill, " too religious." Hence his thunder and lightning. And some clergymen recognized this when the International Free-thought Congress of 1881 was held.

The metropolitan character of London was shown in its many congresses, and I generally attended them. Large sectarian averages were audible through their delegates as if these were phonographs. The mass acted quasi-inorganically, and its evolution upward or downward could be studied in a congress. In 1881 the Ecumenical Methodist Conference gave a single hour of its twelve days to the great problems of thought in our time, and even that only to consideration of how they might affect Methodism. The English Church Congress, which followed it, gave nearly one of its four days to the discussion of those problems, considered as to their truth and their bearing on mankind. Such was the contrast between the English State Church and a (popularly established) American Church.

Simultaneously with the Church Congress (1881) was held in London the great International Freethought Congress. It was presided over by Dr. Ludwig Büchner. The striking thing was that the Church Congress recognized in the Freethought Congress not an enemy but another Church. In the Church Congress were such clergymen as Sarson, who had resigned his office in a reformatory because of a slight put on Annie Besant; Stewart Headlam, a gallant defender of the rights of " infidels ; " Anderson, fraternal with all men who had ideas ; and Harry Jones, the eloquent spokesman of the Church contingent which carried its left wing into practical alliance with the secularists. The Rev. Harry Jones declared that secularism was growing by reason of its devotion to human welfare, and that if the Church is to prevail over it, it must be by doing more for human welfare than the secularists did. It was revealed in the discussion that some of the bishops sympathized with the spirit which desired to establish friendly relations between the Church and every

ANNIE BESANT

English school of thought. The Bishop of Durham remarked that many past heresies had become present orthodoxies. The sentiment would have been applauded in the Freethought Congress.

Dr. Ludwig Büchner was a man of grand presence. Beneath his crown of silken white hair was a face of the intellectual German type, with eyes clear and large, and mouth of feminine delicacy. His voice was soft and flexible enough to surprise one who looked at his strong brow. At the close of an eloquent speech he said, "Our work is small now, but all things have small beginnings. I trust in the future!"

Why? Why may not the future destroy freethought as Athenian civilization was destroyed? Because it is a religion, and men like Büchner, Haeckel, Bradlaugh its prophets. The millennial illusion survived in us all. The Parliament of religious Man was going on; it seemed a chaos of antagonistic minds, but it was only the distribution in various halls of souls whose fundamental unity worked in the watchword of them all, "I trust in the future!" When we have lived long enough to see what the future brings we are *hors de combat*, and our similarly cheated successors think us reactionary.

Professor Max Müller, in inaugurating the Hibbert Lectures, — for which, though Hibbert the founder was a rationalistic Unitarian, Dean Stanley opened Jerusalem Chamber in the Abbey, — affirmed the honourable functions of atheism in the evolution of religion. I had long before taken this ground, and printed a sermon entitled "Atheism: a Spectre." But Max Müller recognized religious atheism as distinguished from "vulgar atheism." I think he must have had in mind some continental type of atheism consisting in political antagonism to priests and churches, but I doubt if there had been any such type since Heine said that he had been converted from atheism by attending in Paris a meeting of atheists. Such was the pervading odour of brandy, said Heine, that what reason had not achieved was done by the sense of smell. At any rate, there was no such type in England, where the humblest atheists were thinking and reading men and women and bore bravely a heavier cross than any of their accusers.

While Max Müller was delivering that passage in the Abbey I cast a glance at the face of Martineau, who appeared troubled, then at Dean Stanley, who was beaming.

In 1880 (April) Renan delivered the Hibbert Lectures, and on his arrival in London was entertained at dinner by Dean Stanley in his residence at Westminster Abbey. The Centenary of Channing occurred on April 7, and though a function in Guernsey prevented the dean's presence, he wrote two letters which were publicly read, expressing highest homage to Channing, and begging that his absence might not be misunderstood.

These letters constituted the dean's final benediction on Liberalism: on July 25, 1881, he was buried in the Abbey. Dean Bradley was his successor in spirit. One day in conversing with him I inadvertently spoke of " the dean " (referring to Stanley) and apologized to Dean Bradley ; but he said, " You spoke correctly ; he was *the* dean."

Renan was introduced by his friend Lord Houghton to the grand audience in St. George's Hall which listened to his Hibbert Lectures. Through Houghton — as he could not speak English — he apologized for not giving his lecture standing, the English climate having brought on rheumatism. Renan stood, however, while giving his exordium, in this ten minutes showing himself a graceful speaker. His clear, fine voice and perfect French made him easy to follow by his educated audience. The Hibbert trustees advertised as the title of his course: " The Influence of the Institutions, Thought, and Culture of Rome on Christianity, and the Development of the Catholic Church." Renan told me that the title he had sent was: " In what Sense is Christianity the Creation of Rome ? " I remarked that the British Channel rolled between the two titles.

It was an unintentional coincidence that brought the centenary of Channing and the opening lecture of Renan together. In the morning (April 7) Martineau sat by the side of Renan and heard him describe the ascending social development of Rome before Christianity got power over it: the sentiment of humanity was springing up, Stoics were preaching the rights of man, thought was free, woman enjoyed a large degree of liberty and equality, — all this sacrificed to the ascetic spirit of Christianity. In the evening Martineau presided at the centenary of the great American who had endeavoured under the name of Christianity to recover what was lost by its long arrest of civilization.

At the close of his last lecture Renan said that mankind would "always behold in the universe the smile of a father, and that smile would be a reflection of their own." A shadow must have clouded Martineau's heart at that thought so sweetly uttered, and I could not but admire the artistic elegance with which he fulfilled his function of addressing Renan on the eve of his departure. He was seventy-five, but never more sparkling and charming. After so many generations since the scientific founder of the Martineau race in England had emigrated from France, here was his most eminent descendant matching the finest of French writers with that felicity of manner and expression which no unmitigated English man of his time attained.

Renan (whom I had long known) met a number of literary men at my house in Bedford Park, but Madame Renan who was with him had to nurse him through all the lionizing process; her fine English being his means of communication, she had endless talking to do. Madame was alarmed lest this novel experience of receiving universal admiration should break down Renan's constitution, which had thriven on censure.

The Hibbert Lectures of 1882 were given by Professor Kuenen D. D. of Leyden University. Dr. Kuenen, then about fifty-four, was a tall, handsome man with a grand forehead, and with his broad, ruddy face might be mistaken for a solid member of Parliament. He gave his lectures in English, and although one had to listen carefully there was no fault in his choice of words. His lectures were given without gesticulation or mannerism ; every sentence was freighted. He was acquainted with the condition of religious philosophy in every part of Europe. His general subject was the National and the Universal Religions. He began with a pregnant prologue on "the Age of Darwin." This, uttered at a moment when the burial of Darwin in Westminster Abbey had set all Europe to estimating his discovery, was regarded as a judicial summing up of the modifications of religious inquiry by the Darwinian generalization.

I met Kuenen in private and regarded him as a true intellectual brother of Renan in Biblical and Eastern knowledge. He had not the poetic vein of Renan, but was without that desire to conciliate traditional sentiment so transparent in the " Vie de Jésus."

April 21, 1895. To-day, the ninetieth birthday of Dr. James Martineau, I visited him and found him wonderfully vigorous. I was accompanied by Virchand Gandhi, the Jain scholar from Bombay, who was much impressed by Dr. Martineau's conversation on Oriental subjects. Not long before, Martineau had to address a number of nonconformist ministers, many of them orthodox, and his tact was as unfailing as ever, carrying with him the full sympathies of his audience. His latest volume, " The Seat of Authority in Religion," is his ablest work, and the one most advanced in rationalism : many supposed it impossible that an octogenarian could have written any part of such a book, and labelled the whole of it with his prefatory remark, that some of it was early work. But there appeared in the " Nineteenth Century " magazine for this same month his review of Mr. Balfour's ingenious plea for creeds, and Martineau's genius and learning have rarely been happier.[1]

[1] What is there in intellectual freedom which thus embalms so many of its children ? On April 20, Dr. W. H. Furness reached his ninety-third year. On February 2 he journeyed from Philadelphia to New York, on the 3d he preached a deeply interesting sermon in All Souls' church (which I heard), reading his lessons without glasses ; on the 4th he made a happy speech at the Unitarian Club banquet ; on the 5th united my daughter and Philip Sawyer in wedlock (he had married her parents in

To-day Unitarians throughout the country presented Martineau with an address engrossed in an album on whose cover is a silver plate engraved with the Martineau crest, — a Martin; with the motto, " *Marte nobilior Pallas* " (Wisdom nobler than War).

My South Place society requested me to convey to Dr. Martineau " their grateful remembrance of his long and faithful services to truth and knowledge. They recognize the honour of a career which has carried the best traditions of English scholarship to the maintenance of a higher standard of intellectual honesty; and they rejoice that Dr. Martineau has lived to see, did his characteristic humility permit, noble harvests garnered, or still ripening, from seeds sown by him in fields his youth found overgrown with superstition and intolerance."

To this came the following reply : —

35 GORDON SQUARE,
LONDON, W. C., May 5, 1895.

To the South Place, Finsbury, Congregation and Minister :
DEAR MR. CONWAY, — You will not interpret, I am sure, the late date of this letter as any sign of tardy gratitude to your congregation for their truly generous greeting on the completion of my ninetieth year. So profuse has been the shower of birthday addresses from the many public bodies with which a long life has connected me, that, with my utmost diligence, I have been unable to prevent their overflow into outlying reaches of time.

So cordial a recognition of my life-work as you have been commissioned to send me is the more valued for being based, as I am well aware, not on any party sympathy with the cast of my opinions, but on a common moral approval of careful research and unreserved speech on all subjects affecting either theoretic or historical religion. The attempt to find infallible records in canonical books, and permanent standards of truth in ecclesiastical votes, has so hopelessly failed, that honest persistence in it has become impossible to instructed persons :

1858) ; and, after chatting pleasantly with the guests for an hour, went off to Philadelphia. Though it was during the coldest spell of the winter, he was none the worse for that visit.

and therefore in all competent guides and teachers of men a continued sanction and profession of it is not simply an intellectual error, but a breach of veracity. And this tampering with sincerity on the part of instructors who know better than they choose to say, not only arrests the advance to higher truth, but eats like a canker into the morals of our time. The sophistries of unfaithful minds are as strange as they are deplorable. Whoever smothers an "honest doubt" creates the sin, while missing the preluding good, of unbelief. And the conventional outcry against "destructive criticism" intercepts the reconstructive thought and faith which can alone endure.

I can never cease to be grateful to fellow-seekers after God, whose heart is set on following the lead of his realities, and not the bent of their own wishes and prepossessions. And far above all doctrinal sympathies, orthodox or freethinking, do I prize the encouragement which your message presses home upon our common conscience, to "hold fast our integrity," and trust *the true and the good* as alone *divine.*

Believe me, always, yours very sincerely,
JAMES MARTINEAU.

When Professor F. W. Newman reached his ninetieth birthday (June 27, 1895), the South Place society, which he had several times addressed, passed a resolution which gave him pleasure, and soon after I travelled to Weston-super-Mare to pass an appointed day with him. He was vigorous enough to take a good walk with me before luncheon, and although he used a magnifying glass in reading me something, I could not perceive any failure of mind or memory. He was serene in spirit; and he was even elated by the honorary degree conferred by Oxford on Dr. Martineau. He took up Martineau's latest book — the "Source of Authority in Religion" — and read an extremely rationalistic passage. "And now," he said, " I have lived to see the man who wrote that given a degree at Oxford!" There was a tone of *Nunc dimittis* in his voice.

Beautiful he stands in my memory, with his happy eyes, the white halo of his hair, — his look that of one who had already on earth enjoyed his immortality.

CHAPTER L

NOT long after the death of Carlyle I received from Emerson's daughter, Mrs. Forbes, the amazing information that the greater number of her father's letters to Carlyle could not be found. She had long before received a letter from Carlyle, of which she sent me a copy, declaring that he had never to his knowledge destroyed a scrap of paper on which her father's hand had rested, and all would be sent to her. There was also a memorandum to this effect connected with Carlyle's will. But when the package reached Mrs. Forbes but few of Emerson's letters were in it. I also received from my friend Professor Charles E. Norton of Cambridge a cry of distress, he having been long chosen by all concerned to edit the correspondence. We found from Carlyle's letters, carefully preserved by Emerson, that there were more than thirty letters of Emerson missing. I consulted Mrs. Alexander Carlyle, who had lived with her uncle at the close of his life, and she informed me that she had received the package from Mr. Froude and forwarded it unopened to Mrs. Forbes. Renewed searches were made, but in vain.

I was at that time a literary adviser for Harper & Brothers, and one day when I was in the office of Trübner, he introduced to me a small middle-aged man who was trying to sell an important manuscript of Carlyle. The result was that on the following Sunday evening I went to the address he gave me in Kentish Town, — a miserable house, — where I was met at the door by the same man, apparently the only occupant. He began saying he admired and loved me, thereby placing me on my guard. He then brought out the manuscript he wished to sell to the Harpers, — Carlyle's autograph journal of his tour in Ireland. The man was unwilling to part with the manuscript even for the night, or to wait till I could consult the Harpers. The sum demanded was exorbitant, and such as, even had I authority, I could not have agreed to on a few minutes' examination. The man pretended to be acting in the interest of another to whom Carlyle had given the manuscript; and this story was repeated by Mr. Froude in his Introduction to the work printed soon after. I felt certain that the manuscript had been stolen. By inquiry of Trübner I discovered that the man who offered me the manuscript had been for a time an amanuensis for Carlyle. (I suppress the name because I believe he has children.) About that time the London "Athenæum" published four of the missing letters of Emerson. The editor, Mr. McColl, told me that the letters printed were selected by him from a large number, the same history being given of them as of the Irish manuscript, — they had been given to his German secretary. Knowing well that Carlyle had never willingly parted with a letter of Emerson, and that the thief was the one who offered me that journal, I still did not confide my suspicions to any one. I believe it was on a simple conjecture that they would be offered to the American Minister (Lowell) that I consulted him. He had indeed been offered the letters, but declined to buy them. If he had given notice of the offer to Carlyle's executors a good deal of trouble might have been prevented. Unfortunately, Lowell could not give me the address of those who had the letters, so for some weeks I turned myself into a detective. I discovered that the rogue had been negotiating under the *alias* of "Beckerwaise," and that he was one of a ring. Finally I discovered that the letters had passed to the address of " William Anderson, dealer in Autographs and Manuscripts, Toronto Villa, Torriano Avenue, London, N. W."

My friend Mr. Wolcott of Concord was passing through London at the time, and he volunteered to accompany me to the Anderson place. We concluded, however, that the dealers might be timid if we both appeared, so one of us remained near by. The people at this address said they knew the "lady" who had the letters to sell, and she would call on me. My address in Bedford Park was given, and it was promised that she would call next day (Monday).

The woman duly came. My wife and I, fearing that any effort to put the law in motion might cause the destruction of the letters, resolved on strategy. The woman was middle-aged, crafty, and very timorous. Her story that Carlyle had given the letters to a friend, etc., I accepted without hesitation. As she had come all the way from Kentish Town to Bedford Park, my wife hastened to refresh her with tea, and treated her like a lady. Finding that she had brought only four of the letters, I agreed to her price, ten pounds for the four, on condition that next day I might bring them to her and examine others, until I could select the four preferred. She chose, however, to bring the rest herself, and did so, fortunately on a day when we had guests and when it was necessary for her to leave them for examination during the evening. The four first left had of course been copied, and those she took back. My wife and I sat during the entire night copying the rest. The address left by the woman was the same as that where I had been offered the Carlyle manuscript.

Having lost her timidity, the woman seemed to enjoy the negotiation. My wife gave her cake and sherry. I agreed to take an additional letter, and possibly others, if she would bring all she had and let me keep them over night, and in that way we discovered she had twenty-seven. Having closely verified our copies and posted them, registered, to Professor Norton, I at once unfolded the whole matter to Sir James Stephen, — coexecutor with Froude of Carlyle's papers. It was talked over (November 20, 1882) in a long walk, and I received from Sir James the next morning the following letter : —

I always like to put in writing the substance of anything of importance which I may have said, as it saves mistakes and misunderstandings. I write accordingly to remind you of what passed between us this afternoon.

You told me that there had been a correspondence between
Mr. Carlyle and Mr. Emerson for many years, that Mr. Carlyle in 1875 wrote a letter to Mr. Emerson's daughter (of
which you showed me a copy), saying amongst other things
that he wished Mr. Emerson's letters to be given to Mr. Emerson's family after his (Mr. Carlyle's) death. You added
that Mr. Froude had accordingly asked Mrs. Mary Carlyle to
return Mr. Emerson's letters to his family, and that she, and
I think you said Mr. Froude, had accordingly returned all
they had, being only three or four. You further told me that
the rest of Mr. Emerson's letters, twenty-six in number, had
been ascertained by you to be in the hands of certain persons
in London who are dealers in autographs, and who professed
to have received them from Mr. Ballantyne, a publisher, who
they said had got them from Mr. Neuberg, who had at one time
acted as a secretary to Mr. Carlyle. This account was inconsistent with Mr. Carlyle's letter, which implied that he either
had or believed himself to have possession of the letters in
1875, some years after Mr. Neuberg's death. Lastly, you told
me that you had found means to procure copies of these letters, which you had forwarded to Mr. Charles Norton, who
you said is about to publish them, together with Mr. Carlyle's
letters, which had been carefully preserved by Mr. Emerson.
Having thought [over] these matters you asked me both as
one of Mr. Carlyle's executors and as a lawyer, what I thought
of the matter. I replied that in my opinion Mr. Emerson's
letters to Mr. Carlyle were the property of Mr. Carlyle's personal representatives, but subject to the right of Mr. Emerson's personal representatives to prevent their publication,
and that if you were right in supposing that the letters had
got into the hands of the present possessors by fraudulent
means that property still subsisted.

I further said, however, that in the circumstances you
stated it would in my opinion be difficult for Mr. Carlyle's
executors to establish their legal right to the letters and to
gain possession of them by summary means, though I considered it not improbable that something might be done
towards inducing them to give the letters up. I further said
that in my character as one of Mr. Carlyle's executors I had
no sort of objection to the publication of the letters by Mr.
Norton, and that as far as I was concerned as executor I had
only to thank you for what you had done in the matter. I
said finally that if the Emerson family wished to recover the

letters from their present possessors I should be glad to serve
them. I think I went so far as to say I should have no objection to allow them to sue in my name, but if I did I ought not
to have said so ; I do not think I ought to say any more than
that if they show a strong wish upon the subject to recover
the originals I should be disposed to help them, but I should
not be disposed to allow my name to be used, or to advise Mr.
Froude to allow his name to be used, unless evidence of our
title to the letters fully satisfactory to me in a legal point of
view were forthcoming, and of course upon the usual terms
as to indemnity against all costs.

I have written this in order to prevent all possible mistakes, and to serve as a memorandum.

In answer I wrote to Sir James (November 22) : —

I have received yours of the 20th, and shall forward a
copy of it to Mrs. Forbes by to-morrow's mail.

Neuberg died in 1867. Mrs. (Mary) Carlyle wrote me
(August 12) concerning the letters forwarded last year, " I
received this packet from Mr. Froude for the purpose. I did
not examine it, but dispatched it as I received it."

I did not mean to convey the impression you have received
that there were only " three or four " letters so forwarded.
There must have been many more. But there were thirty-four
letters and one document missing. These were offered for
sale at five places known to me.

Among these letters are, or were when I saw them, two
from " Jane Welsh " to Thomas Carlyle.

Mrs. Forbes writes me that these letters from her father
are mentioned in Carlyle's will.

The woman with whom I dealt for the letters did not to
me name Mr. Neuberg first. She said the letters had been
given by Carlyle to his secretary who helped him on his
books. I suggested Neuberg, and she said she thought that
was the name.

The editor of the " Athenæum " told me that when the
letters were offered to him the same history was given of
them as that Mr. Froude has given of the " Irish Diary " in
his preface. This is the Neuberg-Ballantyne story.

When I parted with Sir James Stephen on the 20th he
said he was going to Froude's house, and I was not surprised

by his letter. Poor Froude was in a sad tangle already about
the Carlyle business. My own relations with him, which for
eighteen years had been intimate, had become strained, and
it was on that account that I had resorted to Sir James. I
felt sure that Froude would not touch any new complication.
He may, however, have called to account the fraudulent
amanuensis who deceived him in the matter of the "Irish
Diary," for I think the "ring" became suspicious of me.
When I presently made an effort to negotiate for the remaining originals of the letters, it was replied that they were all
sold. Perhaps, however, it was true. A few months later a
young Emersonian at Cambridge (England) wrote to me of
his joy in having obtained a letter of Emerson to Carlyle. At
my request he sent me its date, and I had to tell him it was
one of the stolen letters and should be sent to Mrs. Forbes.
He wrote back with much agitation, but the letter was never
forwarded. Alexander Ireland printed one of the letters in
his book on Emerson, but it was one I had been able to
supply to Norton from a copy Carlyle allowed me to make,
and Mrs. Forbes concluded not to disturb her father's old
friend by asking for it. On April 11, 1893, four letters of
Emerson to Carlyle were sold at auction (Sotheby's) for
twelve pounds fifteen shillings, of which three were among
those I had copied for Norton.[1]

---

[1] The unpublished letter enclosed a statement by Phillips, Sampson
& Co. concerning Carlyle's proposal for a complete edition of his works,
Emerson's letter being as follows : —

"Concord, 22 Aug. 1856. — Dear Carlyle : Here is the proposal in full
of Phillips, Sampson & Co., in reply to my explanation of your design. It
looks fair and fruitful to me, though I am a bad judge. The men Phillips and Sampson are well esteemed here, have great confidence in themselves (which always goes far with me), and I believe will keep their
word as well as any of their kind, though in all my experience of mortal
booksellers there are some unlooked-for deductions in the last result. I
have neither a right nor a wish to throw any doubt on these particular
booksellers, who mean the best. I hasten to send the letter, before any
steamer from Liverpool can bring me any growl of wrath from my dear
old lion. Stifle the roar, and let me do penance by appointing me to

These letters were from the collection of Mr. T. G. Arthur of Glasgow. The "ring" had also transferred its operations to New York, where the "Tribune" published four of the letters. Little by little Mrs. W. H. Forbes obtained a large number of her father's letters.

My friend Charles Norton wished to dwell largely on this story in the introduction to his volume, but I advised him not to do so lest it should excite the suspicions of the "ring," and prevent me from procuring originals for Mrs. Forbes. So he contented himself with expressing in the preface his gratitude for my having obtained the letters which "had fallen into strange hands."

negotiations and mediations with P., S. & Co. and the printers, which I will gladly and faithfully execute.

"Success to the history of Frederic! I read a slight recent life of Voltaire by Eugène Noël, which touched Frederic; a far better book, *L'Eglise et les Philosophes*, by Lanfrey; but wait for you. Ellery Channing, a dear gossip of mine, told me that he had read your *French Revolution* 'five times'! Send the new edition with more speed.

Ever yours,   R. W. EMERSON."

CHAPTER LI

WEARY reader of a wayworn autobiographer, clasp my hand! We draw near to our place of parting; not because my story is all told, but because it can be told no farther than in the detached memoranda of this final chapter. For it must be a sort of omnibus chapter, in which are to be crowded as many as its limited capacity can carry of memory's latest passengers. They must find places as they can. And alas, how many are left behind altogether!

In the autumn of 1882, while on a visit to Rose Hill, Coventry, I had some conversation with Miss Sara Hennell, author of "Thoughts in Aid of Faith," concerning her lifelong friend George Eliot. We went over to Birdgrove, where George Eliot's girlhood and youth were passed, and in the unoccupied house I submitted to her my theory: George Eliot had grown up mentally at a time when marriage was clerical and connected with the subjection of women to an extent that lost it the reverence of progressive thinkers; but after her irregular union with Lewes the laws were reformed and her position was unhappy; young ladies were, however, able to quote her example; under these circumstances, after Lewes's death she married Mr. Cross in a fashionable church with almost osten-

tatious clerical solemnities, for the express purpose of avow-
ing her mistake in the Lewes union and reversing her example.
Sara Hennell said, in substance (I wrote my notes next day),
" Marian Evans was in youth morbidly pious ; she was melancholy by temperament and often in tears; she suffered from
loneliness. The first thing she wrote was a review of Froude's
' Nemesis of Faith,' in a Coventry paper. It fell into Froude's
hands and he came from London to see her. My sister and
Mr. Bray and I were arranging a tour in Switzerland, Marian
Evans with us, and Froude intended to go with us; but at
the railway station a note came saying he was on the point of
being married and could not come."

I probably spoke to Sara Hennell of the possible bearing
of the " Nemesis of Faith " — wherein a wife meeting one she
loves regards her legitimate marriage as a sort of adultery —
on George Eliot's union with Lewes. " We all regarded this
union as a calamity," said Sara Hennell. " Mr. Bray regarded
it as due to her defective self-esteem and self-reliance, and
her sufferings from loneliness. She continued to suffer from
loneliness, but came to love the characters in her books as if
they were her children. She loved them even when they were
wicked. Once when I was at her house in London, looking at
some sketches from ' Romola,' we paused before ' Tito.' After
a moment's silence George Eliot said softly, as if to herself :
' The dear fellow.' I exclaimed ' He 's not a dear fellow at
all, but a very bad fellow!' ' Ah,' she said, ' I was seeing
him with the eyes of Romola.' "

After the theological and ecclesiastical anarchy that set in
after the Tractarian movement at Oxford there were many
indications of a moral revolt, — for the most part theoretical,
— resembling that which followed the fall of Roman Catholicism at Geneva, which Calvin crushed by beheading brilliant
Jacques Gruet. The " Nemesis of Faith " was one sign of it,
and Hawthorne's " Scarlet Letter " was a reflection of it. The
effort of Swinburne to revive it in England by his audacious
poems was suppressed somewhat in Calvin's way; his head
was metaphorically cut off. He did, indeed, write some bril-

liant poems after that, — notably in his " Songs before Sunrise," — but for his wonderful genius they were songs of
an afterglow. I used to see a good deal of Swinburne in the
time of his controversy with Philistines, and, being a born
lover of liberty, held in horror the conspiracy of critics to re-
press his genius. His poem addressed " to Walt Whitman in
America " affected me as a plaintive swan-song. Walt Whitman took it rather too much as a laudation of himself. Swinburne was really attracted mainly by his audacity ; he wrote
me a long letter about Whitman, but has requested me not to
print it, and I agree with him that it would misrepresent his
maturer thought.

In 1883–4 I made a voyage around the world, studying especially the various religions of mankind, — Buddhism, Brah-
manism, Parsaism, Jainism, Islam, Brahmoïsm, Theosophy,
Mormonism, and other movements. My observations and adventures during this journey, when fully written, proved to
be a record too extensive for inclusion in the present work ;
it amounts indeed to a volume, and must await its time to see
the light.

Now, at the age of fifty-two, I desired to leave the pulpit.
I had been in that kind of work since I was nineteen, my
twenty-one years at South Place chapel had enabled me to
deliver my religious and ethical convictions with a certain
completeness, and I had several works in view that demanded
literary leisure. So we sold our house in Bedford Park, and
on July 27 the last of my seven " Farewell Discourses " (published 1884) was given.

The last months of 1884 we gave to Berlin, where we saw
something of the Webers and Bunsens, and other learned
men, and joined in the homage to the historian Von Ranke on
his ninetieth birthday. His English daughter-in-law enabled
us to converse pleasantly with the charming old man, whose
mind was clear. A herald announced the approach of the
young princes, and the company ranged themselves close to

the walls, while the royal youths handed large white bouquets
to the author.

Our particular friends in Berlin were Herman Grimm
and his wife (daughter of Goethe's " Bettine "). Herman
Grimm, endeared to all lovers of Emerson by his exquisite
essay on his works, was the most attractive gentleman we
knew in Berlin ; we were invited every Sunday evening to
his house ; but I lost this friend by a single sentence in " The
Wandering Jew" which I presented to him. Writing in
1880, during an outbreak of Judenhetze in Germany, I said:
" The retention of the Rev. Mr. Stocker as court chaplain,
while he is leading this agitation so unscrupulously, is a confession that the anti-Semitic movement has the encouragement
of the Emperor and his Chancellor." So we saw the Grimms
no more. A mutual friend told me that Herman Grimm had
no sympathy with Judenhetze nor with Stocker, but that he
could not tolerate a word that might reflect on the Emperor.

Bismarck in the Reichstag impressed me as a finer parliamentary leader than either Gladstone or Beaconsfield. There
was a simplicity in his art, an air of deference in his force,
and a repose in his manner which added moral dignity to his
fine physical presence. One day a radical member made a
fierce and at times insulting attack on the government. Bismarck in his reply made only a brief passing allusion to the
personalities, saying, " We also are capable of such feelings,
and if we do not express them it is for the sake of good manners." What could be more neat ?

The Hon. Alphonzo Taft and his family had been members of my church in Cincinnati, and our friendship with them
had continued for twenty-seven years. Judge Taft having become minister to Russia, we were invited to visit them in St.
Petersburg. The weeks we passed there were always memorable to us ; we were entertained by the Czar and Czarina,
who spoke English (she fluently), and met the diplomatic
people. It was especially useful to me to converse confiden-
tially about Russia with so exact and thoroughly informed a

lawyer as Judge Taft. When we worked together in our church in Cincinnati the Jews were friendly to our society, the Rabbis Wise and Lilienthal paying me much attention, and the reputation of Russia for hostility to that race troubled me. It so happened that Minister Taft was just concluding his interviews with the government on two cases of Russian Jews naturalized in the United States who were desirous of securing " permits of residence " which would enable them to enter Russia. By Russian law no native could leave the country without official permission, and those who had gone without such permission were liable to arrest on their return. This law was applicable to all races, but the discrimination concerning the Jews was that the law prohibited their coming in any case to Odessa and a few other localities. The right of Russia to pass such laws could not be questioned, the minister said, there being nothing inconsistent with them in any treaty. And as for the apparent animus against Jews, he said that after many conversations with the Czar and his ministers he was satisfied that no one in the government had the least ill-feeling toward that people. There was no discrimination against Jews in St. Petersburg or in Moscow (Russia has built many colleges for them in various cities), but in certain remote places it had been found that a fanatical prejudice and hatred lingered which the coming of a new Jew might fan into an unmanageable flame, dangerous not to one but to all Jews. The restrictions are therefore for the security of Jews. The government cannot distribute military companies in all these distant regions to manage mobs.

Observing the adoration of the holy Bambino in the Ara Cœli church, Rome, — the infant Jesus carved from a tree on the Mount of Olives, painted by St. Luke, and decorated by popes and princes, — the doll with its staring eyes faced me with a *Tu quoque*. I, too, had all my life been decorating one Bambino after another, — the Messiah, the Redeemer, the prophet, the martyr, the typical man, the reformer, the altruist, the freethinking teacher. Strauss's declaration that the man once merged in a god is irrecoverably lost seemed to me justified by all the modern " Lives " of Jesus, including that of Renan. It was surprising to find Renan accepting so many incidents related of Jesus in versions that make them inconsistent with his own portraiture, — such as the attack on the money-changers. " Un jour même, dit-on, la colère l'emporta ; il frappa à coups de fouet ces ignobles vendeurs et renversa leurs tables. En général, il aimait peu le temple." If he cared little for the temple, why be so violent with the " sacristans " " fulfilling their functions," as Renan says ? Professor Noyes was careful to point out to us at Cambridge that a right interpretation of the story in John showed that the whip was used solely to drive out " the sheep and the oxen." Unfortunately Dr. Noyes did not recognize that the violence to the money-changers was imported clumsily from the synoptics into the text of the Fourth Gospel, where it was really written : " He made a whip of small cords and drove out of the temple (court) the sheep and oxen, and to those that sold doves said, remove them."

In all my pleadings against war, since my nineteenth year, I have found its chief entrenchment among Christians to be that scourge of Jesus in the temple. The Prince of Peace was always accommodated to that assault, and I have no doubt that the supposed incident has been the chief consecration of bloodshed. Being myself long convinced that the thing was incredible, it appeared to me comic at the Oberammergau Passion Play (1871) that the money-changers should receive their blows submissively from a man they could easily have arrested. But in 1879 Dr. Nicholson (afterwards Bodleian Librarian at Oxford) sent me sheets of his " Gospel according to the Hebrews," and in it I noticed a saying of Jesus preserved from that lost gospel by Epiphanius : " And they [Ebionites] say that he [Jesus] both came and — as their so-called gospel has it — instructed them that he had come to destroy the sacrifices, and (said), ' Unless ye cease from sacrificing, the Wrath will not cease from you.' " The Wrath ($\dot{\eta}$ 'Op$\gamma\dot{\eta}$) is a personification. All sacrifice is devil-worship. But to end sacrifices altogether was to destroy the last remnant of priestly support and authority. Here, then, for the first time I discovered a sufficient cause for the execution of Jesus. He might have repeated the disparagements of sacrifice contained in several psalms and prophetic books; but the very efforts of the early Christians, themselves adhering to the principle of sacrifice, to turn this temple incident into an attack on merchants and zeal for the temple, proved to me that they would not have entirely invented it. The young genius had gathered around him a large crowd of anti-sacrifice reformers, — too numerous for the temple-police to resist, — and driven the sacrificial animals out of the temple courtyard bazaar.

Such is the outcome of reforming zeal! Zoroaster declares an eternal war between the Good Mind and the Evil Mind, and Parsî theology comes to derive both as twins from one mind anterior to both; Buddha says there are no gods, and is himself made a god; Jesus denounces sacrifice, and is himself made the supreme sacrifice!

When I made this discovery my ministry had closed. What a source of light it would have been to me had I been taught that at Harvard Divinity School! I have tried to impress it on liberal teachers, but they generally cling to their *bambino*, — the humanitarian Teacher, — and the freethinkers who do not believe any human Jesus existed have a *bambino* of their own, — some Krishna Christos or solar form. No doubt they will mostly consider my anti-sacrifice enthusiast merely my ninth *bambino*. And practically that is of little importance, but it is of serious importance that the Christian clergy should sacrifice to the letter of scripture the character of Jesus. A violent attack on men engaged in selling sacrificial animals at a temple door would be as immoral, intolerant, and brutal as a similar attack to-day on those who sell tracts in a church vestibule, or the venders of candles to burn before holy pictures. To scatter their money would be robbery. To drive cattle out of the temple precincts may have been lawful, and at any rate it is not inconsistent with generous sentiments.

In witnessing the Passion Play again I remarked more

than on the former occasion the absence from the drama of
any real motive for putting Jesus to death. Humanly speaking it laid upon the Jews the crime of killing an innocent
man through diabolical hatred of his excellence and wisdom,
and at the same time showed that they could not help themselves, the whole thing being divinely ordained for the salvation of mankind.

On our return to America (1885) I went with my entire
family to visit my parents in Fredericksburg, Virginia, who
resided with their youngest son, Peter, and his family. My
other brother, Richard, came from his farm in Orange County,
and our sister, Mrs. F. A. March, from Easton, and for the
first time we had a family reunion. For the first time too I
had opportunity to make some careful investigations into the
history of our region, where the Washingtons lived. But my
most entertaining search was one described in "Harper's Magazine," January, 1886, under the title, "Hunting a Mythical
Pall-bearer." For twenty years following the war there had
appeared in the American and European press an alleged
epitaph in Fredericksburg of one Edmond Helder, in which
it was said that he had been a pall-bearer of William Shakespeare. I had credited the story in 1865 when in England,
had discovered that it was a myth in 1875, when visiting
Fredericksburg, but now in 1885 determined to find out the
origin of the myth. My aged mother remembered that in her
girlhood when driving with her father near Potomac church,
over five miles away, her father stopped and wrote down the
inscription on a lonely tombstone; her half-brother, Dr. J.
H. Daniel, remembered the stone and that it bore the name
of an English "chirurgeon." This word was in the mythical
Shakespeare epitaph. In company with a lawyer, St. George
Fitzhugh, I started out for that region and discovered a
sunken grave, very old, from which a stone might have been
removed. About two hundred yards away we saw a cabin
and found there a poor widow, Mrs. Alexander, a name once
grand in Virginia. She needed a large stone for the back of

her fireplace, and a neighbour brought her this gravestone. She did not use it because a tombstone was sacred, and it was set out of doors against the chimney. A few weeks before our visit her chimney had fallen and covered the old stone with débris. She remembered that the name on it was " Helder," and 16 was in the year of his death. St. George Fitzhugh and myself cleared away the débris and found the stone blackened and broken, with the letters H E, and part of the R in the opening HERE. A week later I learned that the original inscription had been copied for its curious lettering by a New Hampshire soldier, C. J. Brown, during the war, who sent me his copy.

HERE'LIEJIИTE RED
THEBODOOF EDMOИD
HELDERAR\EƏIOИERIИ
PHYJIᏩK·AИDCHYRURᏩE
ІУ BORИIИBEDFORDE
ЈHIREOBIITMARᏩH·II
1618ЈATATIЈЈ·ЦАᏒl

There was no white settlement in northern Virginia in 1618, and no doubt Dr. Helder died while on some exploring expedition. The foot-square stone with two letters on it, now in my brother's house in Fredericksburg, is a fragment of the oldest tombstone of an Englishman in America.

There was a family of Elders in that region, one of whom was a fine portrait-painter in Fredericksburg. It occurred to me that a tale might be written on the subject, and the result was my little novel " Prisons of Air." But a droll fate befell it. After making a first draft of it I concluded to submit that to a publisher, and if he liked the plot to write it in a full and finished way. Being much occupied with centennial work I almost forgot the novel, until one day I received a letter from a Moncure relative in Paris (Mme. Du Bellet) thanking me for the pleasure she had received from my " Prisons of Air ! " Much shocked at this, I wrote to the John W. Lovell Company, — to whom for some reason I had submitted it, — and discovered that the book had been published several months. They supposed it complete, and believing I was in

Europe, did not know where to send the proof, and thus my tale, of which I could have made something, was thrust in mere blocked-out condition on the public.

A beautiful welcome awaited us on our return to dwell in our native land. I was invited by eminent citizens of New York to give a course of lectures in the University Club, and was fairly fêted by old friends. In order that our two sons, already in New York, might be with us, we desired a large house, and found one in Clark Street, Brooklyn, No. 62, not far from my old friends Gordon L. Ford and his family on one side, and Henry Ward Beecher on the other. In the early summer we went to the new seaside village of Wianno, where many of our friends had cottages, and where all the fairies were dancing, and the naiads swimming. My wife fell in love with Wianno, and I presented her with a cottage there, which she named " Pine and Palm,"—the title of my first novel, which Henry Holt & Co. published in New York.

Just as my story of Southern life was published, appeared a romance by another Virginian, "The Story of Don Miff," by Virginius Dabney. On inquiry I learned that he was residing in New York. The book filled me with delight, and I hastened to make his acquaintance. He was a very brilliant man, and I feel certain that he would have had a notable literary career but for his premature death.

My "Pine and Palm" had a fine success in England, but Virginius Dabney and myself both found that the American people could see no picturesqueness in the old South, and were rather irritated by attempts to revive the subject. My Virginia cousin, Lucy (Daniel) Cautley, wrote a tale which I thought powerful when I read it in manuscript; but it has never been published, and I suppose she also found publishers not attracted by pictures of ante-bellum Southern life.

Mr. Kingdon Cautley, an English gentleman, and husband of cousin Lucy, called on me in Brooklyn, and left with me a parcel of documents relating to his wife's great grandfather, Gov. Edmund Randolph, first Attorney-General, and second Secretary of State. I never before realized that dear aunt

Lucy, wife of Justice Daniel, was a daughter of Edmund Randolph. I then made the discovery that Edmund Randolph had suffered the most shocking injustice. I set about writing an article on the subject, but on finding that my friends, the McGuires in Washington, possessed a large number of unpublished letters of Randolph I undertook the larger work, " Omitted Chapters of History, disclosed in the Life and Papers of Edmund Randolph."

At the Harvard Commencement in 1886 I gave the annual address to the graduates of the Divinity School, my theme being the new incarnation of religion which I recognized in the humanitarian tendencies of all churches.

In November of that year we were overwhelmed by the death of our younger son, Dana, who was just completing his scientific studies in Columbia University. He was the darling of his brother and sister, as well as of his parents, and the bereavement was terrible. We could not bear to live in the Brooklyn house, and I purchased an apartment in New York. Before entering it my wife and I made a short visit to Boston, where Dr. O. W. Holmes called on us. He had shortly before lost a son by the same disease (typhoid), and in trying to console us broke down and mingled his sobs with ours.

It was fortunate for me that I had on hand the work on Edmund Randolph. To this I gave much time and toil, visiting Washington, Richmond, Charlottesville, and the chief historical societies of the country. The work elicited fine reviews and articles and brought me many grateful letters from publicists, yet it never paid the publishers' expenses, and of course not one penny did it bring me.

I have often had reason to recall a remark I once heard from Mr. Lecky, — that mankind are largely swayed by "historical" personages who never existed.

If any man wishes to preserve his faith in our political gods, let him not search into the truth of American history. Very few of them — a braver man might say none — can bear the microscope found in his own correspondence without some

smokiness in his halo. And the diabolical horns of the de-
famed — such as Tom Paine, General Gates, Aaron Burr —
are transmuted by unbiased investigation into halos quite as
pure as those of the political gods.

When I was writing the Life of Edmund Randolph, I
talked over with George Bancroft the charges secretly made
by Timothy Pickering against Randolph, then Secretary of
State, on the basis of an intercepted letter written by the
French envoy, Fauchet, obtained from the British Minister,
Hammond. Pickering showed Washington a translation made
by himself containing a mistranslation damaging to Randolph.
Bancroft said, " It is certain that the charges made against
Randolph were untrue, and it would no doubt be made clear
if all of the intercepted letters of Fauchet could be found.
Hammond selected only one from the package to be shown
Washington." My dear friend Samuel Fenton in London
explored the British Foreign Office archives for those intercepted dispatches, but they were not there. I found three of
them in the Pickering papers in the Massachusetts Historical
Society, and my friend John Durand in Paris discovered there
an unintercepted dispatch showing the charges groundless.
But it was not until after my Randolph book was published
that in examining the Pickering MSS. for another purpose I
came upon one of the intercepted Fauchet dispatches, which
had it been revealed at the time to Washington would have
overwhelmed the intrigue against Randolph. This despatch
was bound far away from all other papers and despatches relating to the Randolph-Fauchet case. It had thus escaped my
attention, and no doubt that of the Hon. Robert C. Winthrop.
Mr. Winthrop, in an oration on Washington many years before, had spoken disparagingly of Randolph, but interested
himself to secure for me freedom to use the Pickering MSS.
There is no reason to doubt the statement attached to this
Fauchet dispatch, that it was loaned him (Pickering) by Minister Liston, successor of Hammond, and as this was some
years after the Randolph affair, the document might easily
get among the papers of another year, and so bound up by

the Historical Society. It remained true, however, that Pickering, after supplanting Randolph as Secretary of State, had in his hands a document which would have entirely relieved his predecessor while alive from disgrace. So is history made!

In a list of debtors to the United States laid before Congress in 1887, a balance of $61,355.07 stands against Randolph. In talking of this with Randolph's grandson, the late P. V. Daniel Jr. of Richmond, he assured me that Peter Washington, while in the Treasury, had shown him all the accounts with Randolph, proving that he owed nothing. After being twice told at the Treasury that no such accounts existed, an accountant there, Mr. Garrison of Virginia, hearing what P. V. Daniel Jr. had said, searched them out. They proved that instead of Randolph's owing the United States anything, the government owes his heirs $7,716.61. Before my book appeared I printed the facts in the " New York Evening Post." On this my relative, Senator Daniel of Virginia, induced the Senate to order a report on the Randolph accounts. The report was made. Some years ago it occurred to me to inquire of the Comptroller of the Treasury if the old entry of the Randolph debt had been cancelled. Nothing of the kind! It was contrary to Treasury usage to correct anything transmitted from the past. The utmost that I could secure was a promise that beside the fictitious debt entry should be written a reference to the report of January, 1889. There is no other intimation of the erroneous character of the entry.

It was I think in 1888 that Sir Edwin Arnold visited New York. He fell ill in his hotel, and Mr. and Mrs. Andrew Carnegie took him to their house. After his recovery they invited a number of literary people to dine with him. After the ladies had withdrawn the conversation fell on the question of retaining Latin and Greek in the normal college course. Sir Edwin argued warmly that the retention was essential to the preservation of the elegant and beautiful style acquired by English writers at Oxford and Cambridge. Andrew Carnegie thereon broke out with a vehement protest against the absurdity of occupying the best years of youth with dead tongues. Shakespeare knew small Latin and less Greek ; he and Burns wrote well enough without it ; and Carnegie prophetically declared that the great world growing around these cultivators of classicism was steadily ignoring their existence. The writers listened to were dealing more and more with things, with realities, not with neat phrases and words. I knew but little of Andrew Carnegie, but being substantially on his side was impressed by his vigour, — even eloquence at times, — and thought to myself that had Carlyle been present he would have taken his hand. Arnold, however, was not happy during the rest of the evening

I do not believe that any very rich man ever lived before him with so much and such genuine enthusiasm for literature as Andrew Carnegie.

In returning to America it was among my hopes to renew some intimate friendships of my youth. Helen Jackson, among the earliest of these, — whom publishers had persuaded against her will to adhere to her literary signature, " H. H.," adopted while she was still Mrs. Hunt, — wrote me (1879) a discouraging account of the conditions of literature in America.

There is nothing in America to give you an equivalent for what you would give up in London. There is no such thing here, it seems to me, as a literary class : I doubt if there ever will be. It is because our literary men are not great enough nor numerous enough to create a class, but still more because money is the national gauge of power. I believe if you got at the truth of the inmost feeling of ninety-nine men out of a hundred in what are called the " financial circles " of America it would be found to be eight tenths contempt (for literary people), one tenth pity, and one tenth respect. They think it is well to have a Longfellow and a Whittier, and a few more like them, because other countries have authors, — " a thing no country should be without," — but for anything beyond that? no! Their only feeling about literature is that it is an uncommonly poor way of making a living. If they had to take their choice between being Mrs Southworth and Hawthorne they would be Mrs. S., — unhesitatingly ; she has written fifty-nine novels and made a fortune, — *that* is worth while.

When Helen came through London in 1869 my wife and I called on her in her lodgings, and soon after she wrote to Mrs. Conway, " Will you not come and see me some day without Monk? I want to know you, if you will let me." Wife, who had never seen Helen in America, was of course captivated by her, and so were our literary friends whom we invited to meet her at dinner. In 1880 we had her in our house at Bedford Park for nearly a week, and in 1884 should probably have accepted the invitation of Mr. Jackson and herself to visit their unique home at Colorado Springs but for the accident that befell her (June 28). She wrote to me merrily about her shortened leg and crutches in October, but in the summer following we could only send messages of love and grief to be read as her eyes were closing in death, — August 11, 1885.

I was astonished in reading obituary notices of Helen Jackson to observe that none ascribed to her the famous Saxe Holm stories in any decisive way. Soon after they began to appear she told me that she wrote them, but begged me not to betray her secret during her life. I regarded the secrecy as a caprice, but told her I would keep it, though I would not positively deny her authorship. This was in the summer of 1875, when I met Helen in New York. In November, when I was lecturing in Chicago, I was entertained in the house of Mr. and Mrs. Lewis, who assured me that the Saxe Holm stories were written by a friend of theirs in that city, who was the friend also of Mrs. Celia Burleigh, — whom I knew. It occurred to me that Helen, in order to give her denial of the authorship technical veracity, had persuaded some friend to write some pages of the work, and wrote to her what Mrs. Lewis had said. In reply she wrote me the subjoined letter, dated at Colorado Springs, November 16, 1875 : —

DEAR MONK, — I am glad of even a lie which made you write to me. The history of the false claimants to the S. H.

stories is long and amusing. When you are in New York go and talk with Gilder about it. There is another young woman (in New York) who swears she wrote them, — and her patron and friend, a worthy jeweller in the Bowery, has been to Scribners and pressed her claim; and actually carried them another story to prove her to be the author. Of course the story was trash, — even worse, for it was full of mispelling and bad grammar: but her friend still believes her. "Why," he says, " I 've known her for years and years; she 's the next best woman to my wife."

This woman whom you have just run against in Chicago must be an audacious creature; for a long time ago — two years or thereabouts — Celia Burleigh published a letter in the " Woman's Journal" setting forth her claim; and I wrote to Celia Burleigh (signing myself S. H. and sending the letter through the Scribners accompanied by a note from Mr. Seymour guaranteeing the genuineness of the S. H. signature). I begged Mrs. Burleigh not to allow her friend to persist any longer in a deception which must sooner or later cover her with disgrace, etc. The letter, accompanied as it was by a note from the Saxe Holm publishers, could not have failed to convince Mrs. Burleigh. Whether she had the moral courage to let her friend know of it I cannot be sure, but I think she would. I asked her to acknowledge the receipt of the letter, writing to S. H., care of Scribners, but she never did. Possibly she never received it.

Last autumn a Mrs. Katharine Gray, of Pennsylvania, wrote a letter to the " Commonwealth," making the same claim for a friend of hers. I wrote as before, but had no answer.

Colonel Higginson says I shall get into trouble some day, as I have so positively denied the authorship; but I think not, because I intend to deny it till I die. *Then* I wish it to be known. He is really the only man who can *swear* I wrote them. He read the first three or four, page by page, as I wrote them. Mr. Jackson can swear to " Four-leaved Clover " and " Tourmaline," for I read those to him page by page as I wrote them out here. And I am going to get to work on another as soon as we are established in our home. It will be either " The Lady of Ensworth County " or " Mercy Philbrick's Choice."

Now you can say to the Lewises every word of this except my name. That you must withhold.

All goes well and three times well. I am profoundly glad. I believe the best part of my life lies before me, even now, if only I can be well and strong. I have only one regret; that is, that I did not see two years ago that this thing was best and right. I wish from the bottom of my heart you could see Mr. Jackson; I believe you would recognize him, and be glad for me. Think what it would be now — to come and stay once more under my roof, and drive with me through the Garden of the Gods! I don't believe there is anything in Egypt so solemn or so grand as these red sandstone towers here. I have a paper in the next " Atlantic " you must read, — " A Symphony in Yellow and Red." It is a feeble word for the Colorado colony.

Now write again and say that you do not believe I am S. H. at all!

I wrote to the Chicago family, but cannot remember any reply. And indeed it was absurd to expect people to denounce an acquaintance as an impostor for claiming the authorship of a work on the accusation of an anonymous person supported only by a conceivably interested publisher. On December 15 Helen wrote again urging me to give my lectures at Denver and visit them, and incidentally asked if I had received her " long letter setting forth how I really did write every word of the Saxe Holm stories, and interesting facts relative to the ' claimants ' ? "

In a letter of January 14, 1877, Helen wrote me about her novel, " Mercy Philbrick's Choice," in a way that revealed such sensitiveness to criticism that I better understood her anxiety to conceal her authorship.

I am quite at sea about the book ; and feel, I must say, less heart to write another than I wish I did. I honestly tried my best to write a good story — I honestly thought it was a fairly good work ; but the " Saturday Review," the " Nation," the " Literary World," all abuse it. Of course there has been a great wave of adulation, but from inferior sources. Warner and Curtis are the only men of standing who have praised it, and I have an unfortunate but unconquerable tendency always to doubt the praise and believe the blame. I saw it quoted from a letter of yours somewhere that it was " the cleverest book recently printed in America," and that gave me pleasure. And Hatty Preston wrote a positive panegyric on the book's style and quality for the " Atlantic," and Howells accepted it, — but it does not appear, and I think will not. Meantime the story sells steadily — is now in its eighth thousand. I have had great fun in discussing it, — having intimate friends say, " What utter trash ! Don't you think so ? " I think it is not all universal — the notion that I wrote it. — The new Saxe Holm (a short one) which begins the next Scribner will probably give rise to more interesting discussions and wise sayings. You will see that plenty of the critics will say : " Now it is made plain that Saxe Holm was not the author of ' Mercy Philbrick's Choice.' Nothing could be more unlike than this story and that," etc. Nothing could, that is sure, and the short story is the best. Perhaps I can't write a long story, but I mean to try once more. Colonel Higginson said of " Mercy " " It is much stronger than any of the Saxe Holms, and far better written."

Helen in these tales and in her poems could not get her intimate friends out of her mind : she wrote for them and received their praise. She wished to find out how they would impress persons who had no personal knowledge of her, or even whether the author was man or woman. Hence the secrecy, to be removed after her death. " Then I wish it to be known."

Soon after undertaking the " Life of Thomas Paine " I found that it was a large and arduous task. The anathema on him had been the means of burying masses of important facts. He was the most competent and veracious witness to the events of the revolutionary epoch of the eighteenth century, — in America, England, and France, — and his testimony had been suppressed or ignored by historians because he wrote " The Age of Reason." It was necessary to revise the history of the three nations between 1774 and 1800 in the light of Paine's letters and writings, published and unpublished. Having explored the American archives, I resolved to follow the tracks of Paine in Europe.

This purpose was delayed by a demand from Professor Eric Robertson to write the life of Hawthorne for the " Great Writers " series he was editing for Walter Scott. The writing of this work was a delight from first to last. In the great centennial year 1889, when I acted on the committee for Washington family portraits in New York, and wrote historical articles, I was conscious the while that no president that ever lived interested me so much as Nathaniel Hawthorne. I discovered a Hawthorne enthusiast in Mr. G. M. Williamson, then of Brooklyn, who took me out to his house, where he and his gracious wife entertained me two days while I explored the MSS. referred to in my volume. In the spring I went with my wife and daughter on a sort of Hawthorne pilgrimage, — to Salem, Brook Farm, Concord, talking with all who remained of Hawthorne's friends, especially with his wife's sister, Elizabeth Peabody, and with Dr. Holmes and Wentworth Higginson. Then I began the work at our " Pine and Palm Cottage," Wianno, Cape Cod ! [1]

In October, 1889, we sailed for France, and after seeing the Exposition went on to Rome. In the Continental Hotel, where I had a good room for writing, I had the fortune to find the

[1] Ah, that last beautiful summer at Wianno ! What tableaux and theatricals at the amusement hall, and what memorable Sunday evening conversations at the house of the venerable Elizabeth Chace ! Especially memorable was the visit of Thomas Davidson, biographer and interpreter of Rosmini. Mr. William R. Warren of New York, the most intimate friend of Davidson, tells me (1904) that Professor Knight is writing a life of that marvellous man. I hear it with pleasure, but even the art of my old friend at St. Andrews can hardly convey to those who did not know Thomas Davidson, the charm of the man, his disinterested devotion to high philosophic thought, the happy way in which he went about distributing the riches of his mind among us, every gift suggestive of his abode in some invisible pearl-island in communion with all spirits finely touched to issues too fine for appreciation by a world consecrating its energies to stupendous trifles. Yet no man of the world had finer and friendlier manners, or a more engaging personality.

particular old friend who could be most helpful to me, — Dr.
George B. Loring of Salem, then U. S. Minister to Portugal.
He had known Hawthorne all his life, had thoroughly studied
him, and was glad to give me his recollections. In the same
hotel Dr. George Bird of London was passing the winter; he
was a near friend of Dante Rossetti and an expert art critic.
He entered with eagerness into my plan of visiting every
work of art in Rome mentioned by Hawthorne in " The Marble
Faun " and in his Note-Books. So with Mr. and Mrs. W. W.
Story at hand, and the Stillmans, and the Dufferins (at the
British Embassy) I could hardly have been better situated for
writing about Hawthorne.

When I was called on to give a public lecture on " Hawthorne in Rome," most of the large audience must have felt
that they had helped me to prepare the piece, — especially
the Countess Marone, owner of Hilda's Tower, and Lady Victoria, youngest daughter of Lord Dufferin and Ava, who
guided me about and was the sweetest of interpreters. It was
she who went with me to see the Tarpeian Rock, and asked
the custodian to show us the exact spot where the Capuchin
fell and was killed. " There 's the place," answered the Italian woman ; " but he was not killed at all. The papers said
so, but he was taken to the hospital and is now quite well ! "

While in Rome I was called on to give another public address ; it was on Robert Browning, tidings of whose death
reached us. W. W. Story and his wife were as deeply moved
as myself by this event. Story said to me, " The last time I
saw him was here in Rome ; he was just driving off to the
station but stopped his voiture and looked out ; I went to him
and he placed his hands on my shoulders and said, ' Forty
years of unbroken friendship ! ' That was all. I could not
speak, and he drove on."

While writing the " Life of Hawthorne," published in
1890, I had friends and agents in both America and England
ferreting out for me every letter and relic and old edition of

Thomas Paine.[1] On arriving in England the same year I visited every spot in the country associated with Paine, — as indeed I had done in America and Paris. The two volumes of Paine's life and four volumes of his writings occupied the greater part of five years. In 1892 my old congregation urged such reasons for my resuming my ministry there that I had to consent to give them discourses for a time, and in 1893 wrote the " Centenary History of South Place Chapel," — which in 1793 was founded by Elhanan Winchester of Roxbury, Massachusetts. Originally a stern Calvinist preacher, he had been converted to Universalism by the gentle protest of an American schoolgirl, casually met in a stage-coach, against the dogmas with which he was trying to alarm her. Elhanan published a vigorous reply to Paine's " Age of Reason." The centenary of his chapel was celebrated by a Paine Exhibition there, and now an oil portrait of Paine by Charles Wesley Jarvis, presented by myself, hangs on its wall.

In 1892 my " Life of Thomas Paine " appeared, and to my surprise the alumni of my old college (Dickinson, Carlisle, Pa.) invited me to give their annual address, and on that occasion the college conferred on me the degree of L. H. D.

In an appendix to my centenary history of my chapel I printed an essay on " Liberty," composed of three discourses which had appeared in " The Open Court," Chicago. The Unitarian " Christian Life " attacked me for opposing all laws enacted in the interest of private morality, but I was consoled by letters of approval from Herbert Spencer, who had long passed out of our London circles by removing to St. Leonards-on-Sea. On December 12, 1893, he wrote: —

I am glad to see you still busy with your pen, and it

---

[1] My large collection of Paine editions was some years ago purchased by the National Library at Washington. I possess still an oil portrait of Paine painted during his life (artist unknown), but my most curious relic is a bit of Paine's brain, removed and preserved by Benjamin Tilly, the English agent of Cobbett who carried the body from New Rochelle to England in 1819. I paid £5 for this in London to stop its being hawked about.

seems to me with unflagging vigour. Judging from what I
have seen in the notices (for I have not seen the book itself,
which indeed I should not be able to read), you have done an
important service by your Life of Paine alike in clearing his
reputation and showing his merits, as also by reëmphasizing
some of his views.

I have just been reading in " The Open Court " your first
article on " Liberty," and have read it with great satisfaction.
Napoleon's dictum was perfectly just, and I am startled to
find that he had long ago enunciated a view which I have
often expressed with respect to the French — caring for equality, but not for liberty. Though the same characteristic does
not hold so completely of the English and the Americans as
it does of the French, still it holds in large measure. As you
rightly point out, people do not at all understand the principles of liberty.

But here I think there is a shortcoming in your conception. They have no true *idea* of liberty because they have
no true *sentiment* of liberty. No theory is of much service
in the matter without a character responding to the theory —
without a feeling which prompts the assertion of individual
freedom, and is indignant against aggressions upon that
freedom, whether against self or others. Men care nothing
about a principle, even if they understood it, unless they have
emotions responding to it. When adequately strong, the appropriate emotion prompts resistance to interference with
individual action, whether by an individual tyrant or by a
tyrant majority ; but at present, in the absence of the appropriate emotion, there exists almost everywhere the miserable
superstition that the majority has a right to dictate to the
individual about everything whatever.

I think you could not do a better thing than devote your
energies to enlightening people upon this matter. It is the one
thing about which politicians and people at large are utterly
in the dark ; and to dissipate the superstition that the majority
has unlimited powers is of more importance than anything
else in the field of politics.

The dictum of Napoleon I Spencer referred to I found in
Taine : " The people do not care about Liberty ; what they
want is Equality. Those who care for Liberty are a few

peculiar persons." In a postscript Spencer says, "What a
far-seeing man Turgot was!" This was suggested by my quotation from a letter of Turgot to his friend Rev. Dr. Price of
London, who had written him triumphantly about the revolution in America. "I write you no more about the Americans,"
says Turgot; "for whatever be the issue of this war, I have
somewhat lost the hope of seeing on the earth a nation
really free, and living without war. This spectacle is reserved
for very remote ages."

On January 10, 1894, Herbert Spencer wrote to me —
again spontaneously : —

I have just been reading your third essay in "The Open
Court," and entirely agree with it.

How entirely I agree with its essential principle as set
forth in the paragraph I enclose, you may judge if you will
turn to my first book, "Social Statics." You will find there a
statement of that same position which you set forth, namely,
that no restriction save that imposed by the law of equal
freedom is to be tolerated, since any other restriction is liable
to prevent man's nature from growing into its most desirable
form.

I should be very glad to see your essays in some developed
shape put before the English public. . . . You might take
for your title "Liberty *versus* Equality," and for motto the
sentence you quote from Napoleon. . . .

I agree with you that little is to be done. The wave of
opinion carrying us toward Socialism is becoming irresistible;
but still we ought severally to do our little, if not with a view
to immediate effect, yet with a view to effect in time to come.

The paragraph of my article inclosed by Herbert Spencer
is subjoined : —

Among our faculties the moral sense now alone claims
absoluteness, and in these days, when the moral sentiment is
borrowing the enthusiasm of religion, it is important to consider whether this reinforced power is using scientific methods,
or merely giving new lease to notions related to discredited
systems. The increasing tendency to invoke legal authority
for the regulation of private conduct has succeeded to the

declining authority which regulated religious belief and worship. As it is now certain that the enforcement of creeds retarded religious progress for many ages, it may be fairly suspected that moral legislation will retard ethical, consequently social, progress, unless the enforced morality be perfect and infallible. But it would require human omniscience to determine such perfection ; and by consensus of ethical philosophers our moral systems are defective, their social results unsatisfactory : legal repression of moral differentiation is therefore, so far as effectual, practically prohibitive of improvement, from the danger of the general principle involved in such laws. Of course, the reference here is to strictly private conduct ; that is, to conduct which directly concerns the individual agent alone. Human laws exist only to prevent one from injuring another, or others ; that is, from violating individual rights or public order. The law has no right to enslave a man ; and it does make a slave of that man whose free will is coerced in matters directly concerning himself alone. That amounts to a majority of numbers suppressing, by brute force, a variation which, however popularly abhorred, may be as useful and productive as the variation of a crucified Jesus or a poisoned Socrates. It is truly claimed by moral coercionists that a man's private conduct necessarily involves others ; but the laws cannot justly deal with indirect injuries which cannot be defined. A person may injure his or her relatives by becoming a monk or a nun, or marrying out of their station, or emigrating. Men's virtues even sometimes turn out to others' harm, and their vices incidentally cause some benefit. The virtuous Roman emperors, Marcus Aurelius for instance, were moved by their sincerity to persecute Christians, who were tolerated by the hypocritical, who inwardly despised the gods they outwardly worshipped. The just law cannot deal with inferential and uncalculable, but only with actual, injuries. The greatest legal crimes of history have been done in the name of morality, as in the execution of Jesus for his ' immorality ' in violating the Sabbath laws and blasphemy laws of his country. Many a man has similarly suffered, whose immorality is now morality.

As to Herbert Spencer's idea that Napoleon's dictum was more applicable to the French than to the English and American peoples, I could only regard it as a sort of academic superstition. Even Emerson had his superstition about France, — as shown in his quatrain, " Natura in minimis," first printed in my Cincinnati " Dial," March, 1860 : —

> As sings the pine-tree in the wind,
>   So sings in the wind a sprig of the pine;
> Her strength and soul has laughing France
> Shed in each drop of wine.

Had it not been for France, and especially for George Sand, the pleas of Herbert Spencer and J. S. Mill for personal liberty would probably never have been written. In the very year in which the above letter was written the art students of Paris were engaged in defending their liberty against Berenger, who was trying to import from England its oppressions of all freedom not puritanical.

In May, 1896, my wife was obliged to undergo an operation. During her long illness I wrote my " Solomon and Solomonic Literature," published by the Open Court Company, Chicago.

My wife appeared to be steadily recovering, but in May, 1897, complications supervened, and a consultation of physicians decided that she could not recover. My connection with South Place chapel at once ended, and I brought her to New York, where she died in the house of our daughter, Mrs. Sawyer, on Christmas Day, 1897. She was cremated with the exhumed body of our son Dana. Their ashes are in Kensico Cemetery. I issued a leaflet for the perusal of our friends concerning her life and death. Here I say no more. " That way madness lies."

Broken by personal bereavement, filled with horror by the reign of terror suffered by negroes in the South, alienated from my countrymen by what seemed to me a mere lynching of Spain, — my youthful visions turned to illusions, — I left for Europe. In June, 1898, I gave several discourses to my old congregation in London, but there also the sky was overcast. England too was preparing to enter on a murderous career of aggression, and some of the most distinguished liberal thinkers were following Chamberlain in that direction. He had given to Birmingham the reputation of being the ideal Unitarian city, but was now proving that the orthodox Nonconformists were more humane than the Unitarians. Thomas Paine used to say that the world would never have peace until the English people saw war at their own doors, and it looks as if he were right. Lord Salisbury, under whom the British lion became a mouse when bullied by the President of eighty millions (Cleveland), but became doubly ferocious when it was the President of a handful of Dutch farmers who entreated arbitration, seems to have known this, and orders were sent out to South Africa that no wounded men were to be brought home.

When I arrived in Paris I learned from Professor A. Aulard of the Sorbonne, editor of " La Révolution Française," journal of a society for the study of the French Revolution, that six articles had appeared in that periodical on my " Life and Writings of Thomas Paine," and that there was a desire for the French translation of the biography. The writer of the reviews, M. Felix Rabbe, called on me, and an arrangement was at once made for our working together on Paine. The delightful old gentleman had once been a priest, but had left the church and married. In my Hôtel de Strasbourg we used to sit pleasantly in collaboration, and we were both surprised to find as we proceeded how many coincidences with events of the French Revolution were occurring in the Dreyfus struggle raging around us. Similar principles were involved; Marat, Robespierre, Barère, were easily recognized; daily I read articles worthy of Junius, Condorcet, Cobbett, — nay, even Paine was at times recalled by George Clemenceau's leaders in " l'Aurore."

Of especial value to me in Paris was the friendship of John G. Alger, an Englishman on the London " Times " staff in Paris, author of " Glimpses of the French Revolution," " Englishmen in the French Revolution," and other works of original investigation. A little controversy we had in the London

" Athenæum " brought us together. As others go fox-hunting, Alger and I hunted up the localities connected with revolulutionary characters in Paris. I discovered that the Hôtel de Strasbourg, 50 Rue de Richelieu, in which I was writing about Paine, was but a little way from the Hôtel Philadelphia, where Paine staid when he arrived in Paris, and where he was arrested; and in the same street was the hotel of the Monroes, where they nursed Paine back to life after his release. My hotel was also but five doors from the house (now Hôtel Colbert) where Part II of the " Age of Reason " was printed. I knew nothing of these proximities when I fixed myself in the Hôtel de Strasbourg, nor that it was the house where Madame de Pompadour, as some one said, committed the only fault of her life — that of being born.

My French work appeared (Maison Plon) at the beginning of 1900, under the title : " Thomas Paine (1737–1809) et la Révolution dans les Deux Mondes." It contains much that is not in my English work, and is the only book in which the relations between France and America throughout the revolutions in both countries are given with detail and authentication. One document in it, of extreme historic importance, came into my hands from the late George Clinton Genet of New York. This lawyer was a son of the famous Genet, the ambassador sent to the United States early in 1793. The desire of the revolutionary republic in France to transfer to itself the alliance formed with the decapitated Louis XVI led it to entrust to ambassador Genet two long letters of Beaumarchais, of which one reveals the intrigues of a ministerial ring with Beaumarchais to extort money fraudulently from the Americans. The writings about the French subsidies by French and American historians are proved erroneous by this " Mémoire Secret " sent by Beaumarchais to De Vergennes. The " Mémoire Secret " shows that the king was without knowledge of the intrigue, and believed that his subsidy was going genuinely and gratuitously to the Americans.

In May, 1900, in Paris, I read in an English magazine a touching tribute by Miss Frances Power Cobbe to Dr. Mar-

tineau and sent her a paper of my own, with a letter saying
that I did so in loyalty to our old friendship though I did not
suppose she could agree with some of my criticisms. I received
from her a letter dated at Hengwrt, Dolgelley, N. Wales,
May 19, in which she said : —

That we should renew in our old age the acquaintance-
ship of long past years, and tell each other a little of where
Life's long voyage over the seas of thought has landed us,
seems to me rather affecting, and I can but respond to your
friendly letter heartily in the same spirit. Thank you for writing and also for sending me your article in " The Open Court,"
which I have read with much interest and a good deal of
agreement. Martineau's optimism never commended itself to
me, because he obviously never really *felt* the agony of " the
riddle of the painful earth," and only approached it from the
intellectual side. In particular it would seem as if the wide
and terrible subject of the suffering of animals (to which no
theories of the beneficent purposes of human pain can possibly
apply) had never come home to him, — since he can be satisfied with the explanation that good comes to the species
though the individual creature perishes most miserably. Tennyson went much deeper when his " dream " claimed justice
for each individual sentient creature, however humble : —

> That not a moth with vain desire
> Shall perish in a fruitless fire,
> Or but subserve another's gain.

It is on this side, — and I think only on this side, — that I
have felt Martineau insufficient. But where are we to find the
teacher who will lead us out of this wilderness ? You cut the
knot by abandoning the idea of a moral agent at the helm of
the Universe; and I can quite see how much is to be said for
the view (which was poor Mivart's last expression of doubt or
faith), that the great inscrutable Energy behind Nature is something very different from the God worshipped by Christians
— or theists. But to me, after beating my feeble wings
against the bars for sixty years, I remain a believer in a Father
of Spirits who must be just, else where did we gain this supreme sublime craving for justice ? Certainly not from any
" set of the brain " acquired at any epoch by any generation of
mankind from experience !

But I did not mean to touch on the controversies which have occupied so much of both your life and mine, — only to express my feelings respecting the points on which you criticise Martineau. . . .

I am very old and growing feebler, and losing sight and activity ; and (which is far more sad) I am *alone*, for my beloved friend Mary Lloyd died in my arms three years ago. I am living still — quite alone — in what was her house, which quite unlooked-for riches have enabled me to take on lease for my life. It is a beautiful old place, and I am lucky in possessing excellent and affectionate servants ; and dear beasts in plenty, dogs and horses, cows and herds, — a rookery and heronry in the woods. But old age in solitude, facing forever nearer and nearer the great Dark Door, is a solemn thing indeed.

I rejoice heartily to hear that you have happy and affectionate children, and a little grandchild to cherish and keep your heart young. May you have yet many peaceful and happy years !

Mrs. Daniel Lothrop, present owner of " The Wayside," the pretty home of Nathaniel Hawthorne in Concord, Mass., had the happy enterprise to make the centennial birthday of the unique author, July 4, 1904, the occasion of a literary fête. With beautiful hospitality she entertained in her house Julia Ward Howe, Thomas Wentworth Higginson, and myself, of Hawthorne's acquaintance, and with some of the younger generation, — among these Beatrix Hawthorne, granddaughter of the great man, — we the survivors held memorable symposia. As I had some work to do our hostess placed me in Hawhorne's tower, where I pencilled some thoughts which have connected themselves with a droll incident.

On the first day of the fête Wentworth Higginson spoke out in the grove in his characteristic vein of subtle wit and wisdom, and Beatrix — a lovely maid of twenty, a mystical apparition of her grandfather — drew aside the American flag which veiled a tablet of the author who walked there.

On the second day of the fête, in the hall of the School of Philosophy, I presided ; and while the Hon. Charles Francis

Adams was speaking there was suddenly a flutter of excitement along the front row of seats, all occupied by ladies. A snake, about one foot long, had crept through a hole near the low platform's base, raised its head from the floor, and remained motionless. A gentleman near the side door moved quickly down in front of the ladies, picked up the snake in his hand, and carried it to the door, where he gently threw it out. The speaker had stopped, and when the snake was seen perfectly still in the gentleman's hand there was laughter. F. B. Sanborn increased the laughter by calling out the title of Hawthorne's tale, " The Man with a Snake in his Bosom."

In that School of Philosophy famous teachers have been heard, — Emerson, Alcott, Dr. Harris, and others. No doubt each of them might have found the visit of the snake suggestive. Emerson might have described it as the line of grace, and its harmless beauty an illustration of optimism, — nothing really evil. Alcott might have seen in it a symbol of Hawthorne's demonic genius. Any pious listener might have seen in it a sign of the old serpent still offering man the forbidden fruit of philosophy. To my eyes the snake, and the flustered ladies, and the fine-looking gentleman who took it in his hand and restored it to the forest, made a pretty fable of the author we were talking about. The little garden snake was really as harmless as a riband, but there was just enough shrinking as it passed, and anxiety until the hole in the plank was stopped, to remind us that even in that cultured audience the prettiest and most innocent little snake could not be detached from the bad reputation of its race. It is in our nerves. The little snake made me laugh in the chapel, but that night I dreamed of seeing a big Virginian black snake. In fact, the snake is the consecrated symbol of all purposeless and crafty evil in nature, — that is, of diabolism. And that which has got into our nerves is not so much dread of the serpent's venom, as a subconscious dread of the dark and potentially evil forces within us related to those around us. Now, it was in this dread realm that the genius of Hawthorne moved, with the vision of Dante, but without the superstition of Dante.

The schools of philosophy have eliminated Satan, and optimism even declares there is no real evil; but human consciousness knows that the dissolution of Satan only brings man the more immediately face to face with the perils and passions in his own breast. All the optimism in the world does not prevent us from contending with the tares, — the diseases and agonies and desolating passions, — just the same as if those tares were sown amid the wheat by an enemy of man.

That same day — July 5 — was the centennial of the one story-teller of the nineteenth century who can rank Hawthorne, — George Sand. As I grow older I more and more recognize that the genius of the nineteenth century is stored in the hundred volumes of that miraculous woman. When a man's supernatural faith has departed, and his early dreams of a fair and peaceful world turned to illusions, his haven is Paris. There at least the work of creation continues. Sitting in the atelier of fine sculptors, like Rodin and Spicer-Simson, and seeing clay spiritualized in noblest forms, or among the painters who transfigure humble models into saints and goddesses, I have felt that with these chiefly the wayworn, weatherbeaten pilgrims who have sought shrines only to find them tinsel, and entered temples that crumbled around them, find some blue sky still bending over the world. Here at least is no dogmatizing, no throat-cutting, but master-builders surrounding the human spirit with the truth and beauty of life.

Truth? It was said that Rufus Choate described Truth as "a form of Art." It was quoted with a smile, as if an apology for falsehood. But the great lawyer had probably discovered how much art it requires to convey the truth about any occurrence, and how misleading may be a merely literal veracity. Would any unbiased student of history, theology, and ethics say that the library of such works contains as much truth as the library of so-called fiction?

In Paris I read in "La Douceur de croire," by Jacques Normand, this quatrain: —

Le bonheur humain est fait de mensonges
Qui rendent à tous les chagrins moins lourds :
Que sombre serait la trame des jours
Si Dieu n'y mêlait les fils d'or des songes !

It seemed a pity that the poet could not find to rhyme with
" songes " a more felicitous word than " mensonges," but his
deity mingling in the weft of days the golden threads of illusion appears more attractive than a deity menacing with hell
every mind that cannot take the illusions seriously.

In Italy Nathaniel Hawthorne, moved by sacred pictures,
lamented that Protestantism had never by such means minis-
tered to his religious sentiment. O. B. Frothingham, after
labouring in the field of free thought for a quarter of a century, found that it made no headway, led to nothing, but in
Italy found among the humble parish priests — " ignorant,
unambitious, and superstitious " — a " power which must mys-
tify philosophers." Frothingham asked, " What is this power?
I cannot undertake to say."

But standing on the shoulder of those great forerunners, —
mingling with the humble priests and moved by the sacred
pictures, — I venture to say what I see. The old painters
were potent because they believed seriously the tales of ancient
Hawthornes, who wrote of Mary Magdalene as our great
author wrote of Hester Prynne, and of Judas as he wrote of
" the man with a snake in his bosom." The modern parish
priest has power because he is " superstitious," and still more
because he is " unambitious ; " he neither aims nor hopes to
make any " headway." The humble priest aims not at " headway " for dogmas, but, so to say, at heartway for visions and
dreams that touch the heart, and whose reality he is not learned
enough to question.

Those who think at all think freely. They cannot take seriously the ancient illusions, but believe as genuinely in the heart
of their own illusions. In Boccaccio, Rabelais, Shakespeare,
Balzac, George Sand, Hawthorne, the fiction is the embroidered
vesture of truth in the heart and in the nature of things. We
lose the truth when we seek in it the revelations of other ages,

as we would lose the rainbow in searching for the fabled treasure at its end.

The superstition of to-day is our inveterate belief that the world exists for some other coming world, — in heaven or on the earth. Woman is missing the grand benefits of her disfranchisement in the rage for a franchise that would be found dross if attained.

Men go to war and rejoice in victory. I have witnessed enough wars to cry in my heart *Væ victoribus!* and seeing the intellectual and artistic supremacy of France these thirty years cry *Lætitia victis!* During the conflict about Dreyfus in France, which I witnessed, the admirable author Paul Sabatier said to me, " Avait-on jamais vu dans l'histoire ou dans la légende pareille coalition de toutes les puissances ténébreuses?" Certainly not, I answered, nor in history has there ever been seen a coalition of the powers of darkness confronted by such a coalition of the forces of light. In a single protest against the wrong to an obscure Jew I counted nearly four hundred names of the men highest in French science, literature, and art. That was the victory of France.

The cause of justice in that case was begun and carried on for four years by unofficial citizens; they were resisted and punished by goverment after government; and happily Militarism never yielded its prey. It preferred to degrade itself by perjuries and brutalities which revealed to the world its interior blackness, as well as its brainlessness in not recognizing its last chance of rehabilitation offered at Rennes. That was the only victory worth anything. The restoration of Dreyfus to the army would have been defeat.

Instead of being rescued to be a commonplace man in livery under the orders of base generals, Dreyfus is now one of the most enviable men in Europe. It is a hundredfold compensation for all his sufferings that he has been the means of instructing the French people in the principles of law and human rights more in two years than they had learned in any two centuries, and in administering to Militarism the heaviest blow it ever received.

My dear friend, M. Paul Guieyesse, deputy and ex-minister, wrote me that his son, a rising young officer, was so appalled by the revelations made of the honour rooted in dishonour prevailing among the military chieftains that he resigned his place in the army and abandoned his profession. I was assured that there were other cases of the kind. The military officers, who under the republic had come to wear the mantle of aristocracy fallen from the titled *noblesse*, retain their prestige only among the young vulgarians.

At the Paris Exposition (1900) America had three unique exhibits. Exhibit 1. The American Sabbath. Our pavilion and all our exhibits were closed on the weekly fête of the Exposition, this being equivalent for the masses to closing them altogether. Exhibit 2. Equestrian statue of George Washington, bareheaded, sword pointing skyward, — interpretable as the general deifying his sword or defying heaven. Exhibit 3. One or two thousand angry Americans surrounding a big bandbox-like structure inside which a statue of Lafayette was being unveiled by Lafayette's descendants, and presented to France by the American ambassador in the name of the Dames of the Revolution.

This exhibit 3 calls for a note. These excluded Americans had obtained tickets which they supposed would admit them to the function, but they were only admitted to the impenetrable outside wall where they could see and hear nothing. But we who had seats within could hear them, for their uproar was loud enough to make a discordant chorus to the eloquent French of Ambassador Porter and Archbishop Ireland, and to drown at times the voices of President Loubet and other French speakers. Finally the noises took a harmonious turn ; the disappointed Americans joined in singing — almost shouting — the patriotic hymn " America."

Alas, nothing could have been more inappropriate. The verses being inaudible, there floated up to this company, consisting mainly of the chief personages of France, a strain known to them as " God save the King ! " The previous uproar was musical compared to this discordant tune which proved it an English mob gathered to insult the memory of Lafayette, and heap contempt on the Franco-American *rapport*. There were flashing eyes, and whispers from one to another of " Les Anglais ! les Anglais ! " And although we Americans tried to explain to Frenchmen near us that it was an American hymn, the majority of them went off with the belief that England, which had shown marked coolness to the Exposition, had sent a contingent sufficient for a manifestation of jealousy and spite.

Stupid ? Nay, complimentary. These French gentlemen and ladies could not imagine such a lack of originality in Americans that after all the generations elapsed since their independence they had no national anthem except that sung when they were subjects of the British crown.

In 1900, being in Paris, I was visited by Hodgson Pratt, the venerable leader of the Peace Society in London, where I had long coöperated with him, and president of the International League of Peace and Arbitration in Europe. In view of the approaching Peace Congress in Paris he came to inquire about a proposal of mine mentioned by Herbert Spencer in a letter to Grant Allen quoted in Clodd's biography of Allen. The plan was to secure an unofficial arbitration by the most eminent jurists and publicists of all nations on every dispute that threatened peace, — a court formed of unofficial men like Mommsen, Virchow, Zola, Spencer, President Eliot, — whose judgment, though it could not be enforced, would strengthen the party of peace in each country menacing another. My scheme was stated in an address before the Free Religious Association, Boston, in May 1898, and I wrote about it to Herbert Spencer. In his reply, — from Maidstone, July 17, 1898, — Spencer said : —

I sympathize in your feelings and your aims but not in your hopes. In 1882, though in consequence of my nervous disorder I had deliberately kept out of all public action, my interest in the matter prompted me to join with some others in trying to establish an anti-agression league (and permanently wrecked my health in consequence) which should check our filibustering policy and tend towards peace. The movement failed utterly ; and ever since I have seen that in people's present mood nothing can be done in that direction.

Now that the white savages of Europe are overrunning the dark savages everywhere ; now that the European nations are vying with one another in political burglaries ; now that we have entered upon an era of social cannibalism, in which the strong nations are devouring the weaker ; now that national interests, national prestige, pluck, and so forth, are alone thought of, and equity has utterly dropped out of thought, while rectitude is scorned as "unctuous ;" it is useless to resist the wave of barbarism. There is a bad time coming, and civilized mankind will (morally) be uncivilized before civilization can again advance.

Such a body as that which you propose, even could its members agree, would be pooh-poohed as sentimental and visionary. The universal aggressiveness and universal culture of blood-thirst will bring back military despotism, out of which, after many generations, partial freedom may again emerge.

I remarked in this fatalism of Herbert Spencer some unconscious "survival" of that ancient faith which developed the Devil into a being at once the enemy and the ally of God. Why should partial freedom emerge again from military despotism "after many generations," or ever ?

Although aggressiveness and blood-thirst seemed "universal" in several nations, there is distributed through these and all nations a moral and peaceful nation, and my aim was to organize this moral nation sufficiently to reinforce the peace party in each country threatening war, by bringing to its aid the judgment of the best representatives of civilization as to the path of justice. They need agree in but one thing — that war can settle nothing except which country is the strongest.

The fact that Herbert Spencer had written to Grant Allen something which I had not seen, and that Hodgson Pratt had adopted my idea, gave me a ground for writing again to

Herbert Spencer. He replied (writing from Bepton Rectory, Sussex, August 15, 1900), that he had not seen the reference in Clodd's biography of Grant Allen, and in conclusion said: —

If I was not encouraged to hope for any benefit from your plan at the time I wrote (in 1898) I am still less encouraged now. The process of rebarbarization which has long been going on is now going on at an increasing rate, and will continue to go on. Waves of human opinion and passion are not to be arrested until they have spent themselves. You appear to think, as I used to think in earlier days, that mankind are rational beings, and that when a thing has been demonstrated they will be convinced. Everything proves the contrary. A man is a bundle of passions which severally use his reason to get gratification, and the result in all times and places depends on what passions are dominant. At present there is an unusual resurgence of the passions of the brute. Still more now than a generation ago, men pride themselves not in those faculties and feelings which distinguish them as human beings, but in those which they have in common with inferior beings — pride themselves in approaching as nearly as they can to the character of the bulldog.

Hodgson Pratt recognized that my aim was to control the bulldog in a nation by exciting its pride to stand well in the eyes of the most eminent thinkers and jurists of the world. He agreed with me that the friends of peace must make some "new departure." The old peace societies had been pleading for generations; everybody professed love of peace, but war went on all the same. A company was invited to listen to my statement, in the Republican Club, and they all agreed with it, though one or two French gentlemen could not quite appreciate my insistence on the principle that the arbiters must in no case be officially connected with their own or any government. This principle was essential, and in the pamphlet I was requested to write it was pointed out that it was impossible to secure an unbiased opinion — or one not liable to suspicion — from an official.

My pamphlet was translated into French and German, and

distributed to all in the Peace Congress at Paris (1900). It was vaguely approved in an incidental resolution, but the Congress had gathered mainly to utter triumphal shouts over the Hague conventions.

It was only in the theatrical *révues* that the "tragical comedy" of the Hague conventions was truly recognized. In one a member of the Hague Congress informs the compère, — "Henceforth we are to fight all the same, but fight pacifically." The old peace men were so anxious to believe that their cause had at length triumphed that it was vain to point out to them that the Hague Congress had at best only left nations where they had always been — free to arbitrate or free to fight as their interests or passions might dictate. But for myself I then declared that the Hague Congress had given a new lease to war by including it among civilized methods. It was, I said, fundamental in our issue to affirm that there is no such thing as "civilized warfare." I might have expected some sympathizers after the Hague Court, in the Venezuela case, put a premium on war by deciding that a creditor who approaches his debtor with a gun shall have precedence in payment over the creditor who makes his request like a gentleman. But no! The first National Peace Congress of Great Britain, which met in June, 1904, at Manchester, justified the decision, albeit "with regrets" at the encouragement given to murder as a means of collecting debts.

The venerable apostle of Peace, Hodgson Pratt, wrote to the Congress, "At last I must fall out of the ranks, because old age has overtaken me." His words express the condition of all the old peace societies. They have fallen out of the ranks through the senility indicated in their acceptance of the Hague Court with its "civilized warfare," and debt-collecting by bloodshed as a principle of international law.

In a Gnostic legend Solomon was summoned from his tomb and asked, "Who first named the name of God?" "The Devil," was his answer.

Did reason permit belief in a personal devil, one might

recognize the supreme diabolical artifice in this sheltering under a holy name of all the desolating cruelties of men, all the wars that have degraded mankind into egoistic aggregates, or nations, glorying in their ensigns of inhumanity.

The popular belief in "progress," as something going on in the world under a divine order, sanctions all scourges as the scourges of God, and insures social deterioration. When an evil is pointed out the answer is, "Yes, but things will improve." It is like saying of a habitual debauchee that the longer his bad habits continue the more likely he is to break them. But in big things like nations Deity is supposed to be concerned, and rules of individual experience set aside. "Providence in its own good time" will do thus and so. We shall have a new race of great statesmen, orators, authors, artists! Enough deterioration lurks in that infatuation to interpret the Gnostic legend of a devil-invented deity.

When I visited J. G. Whittier at his pretty home near Amesbury towards the close of his life, I found the beautiful old gentleman, who had faced mobs and undergone ordeals, playing croquet against himself out among the many-coloured autumn leaves. We had a long talk about old antislavery days, and his poetic fire rekindled. The great moral cause had been his inspiration; it made him a poet; from his solitude he beheld in vision the travail of his soul and was satisfied. He remains in my memory as a fruit of the moral spirit that breathed over the nation like tropical air and brought forth every seed of talent to its fulness.

It would be only a source of personal sorrow to those who moved amid the stately growths of literature and art in England, Germany, and America in the last century that they can meet such no more, were their place filled with happy and peaceful populations. But under the air now breathing abroad spring up armed men, eager to strew the earth with dead bodies. The great prizes of the foremost Saxon nations are bestowed for successful manslaughter. There can arise no important literature, nor art, nor real freedom and happiness, among any people until they feel their uniform a livery, and see in every battlefield an inglorious arena of human degradation.

The only cause that can uplift the genius of a people as the antislavery cause did in America is the war against War.

It appears but too probable that my old eyes must close upon a world given over to the murderous exploitation of the weak nations by the strong, — even the new peace treaties between the latter being apparently alliances for mutual support in devouring helpless tribes and their lands. There are indeed a few hopeful signs. The grand victory of the unofficial pen over the sword in the Dreyfus case, in France, and the burgeoning of Spanish genius since the two ulcers — Cuba and Manila — that wasted Spain were removed, inspire my hope that what Lord Salisbury called the decadence of those nations will prove their ascent. My last essays, translated into French by M. Henri Monod, have been well received by the Paris press. One of these was an address, delivered before the Graduates' Club in Columbia University, which aimed to dissipate the delusions about American history which have consecrated the sword.

And now, at the end of my work, I offer yet a new plan for ending war, — namely, that the friends of peace and justice shall insist on a demand that every declaration of war shall be regarded as a sentence of death by one people on another, and shall be made only after a full and formal judicial inquiry and trial, at which the accused people shall be fairly represented. This was suggested to me by my old friend Professor Newman, who remarked that no war in history had been preceded by a judicial trial of the issue. The meanest prisoner cannot be executed without a trial. A declaration of war is the most terrible of sentences: it sentences a people to be slain and mutilated, their women to be widowed, their children orphaned, their cities burned, their commerce destroyed. The real motives of every declaration of war are unavowed and unavowable: let them be dragged into the light! No war would ever occur after a fair judicial trial by a tribunal in any country open to its citizens.

Implora pace, O my reader, from whom I now part. Implore peace not of deified thunderclouds but of every man, woman, child thou shalt meet. Do not merely offer the prayer, "Give peace in our time," but do thy part to answer it! Then, at least, though the world be at strife, there shall be peace in thee.

Farewell!

INDEX

INDEX

Throughout the index C. stands for Moncure Daniel Conway. For correspondence see Letters.

ers, 106; an abolitionist, 106; advises against joining the Quakers, 108; and C.'s Unitarianism, 123; on Paine's "Age of Reason," 123.
Brooke, Stopford, separation from English church, ii. 321.
Brooks, C. T., Unitarian minister, i. 169, 331.
Brooks, Phillips, liberalism, ii. 326.
Brooks, Preston, assault on Sumner, i. 237, 238.
Brookville, Md., culture, i. 103.
Brown, C. J., ii. 422.
Brown, F. M., paintings, i. 439, ii. 135; religion, 134; salon, 134; and his son's death, 135.
Brown, Frances. See Moncure, Frances (1).
Brown, Gustavus (1), C.'s ancestor, settles in Maryland, children, i. 1.
Brown, Gustavus (2), medical school, i. 5; and Washington, 5.
Brown, John, raid produces reactionism in Virginia, i. 71; C. on, 299, 302, 303, 310, 311, ii. 4; antislavery opinions of raid, i. 300; effect of raid, 301; wrought evil, 302, 303; character in "Palm and Pine," 303; and Washington's sword, 311; bust, 389; London commemoration, ii. 4.
Brown, Dr. John, ii. 97.
Brown, Margaret. See Stone, Margaret.
Brown, O. M., death, ii. 130, 134.
Brown, Simon, i. 243.
Browne, A. G., i. 376.
Browne, C. F., in London, ii. 136; funeral, 137.
Browne, J. H., in Cincinnati, i. 293.
Browning, Elizabeth B., poetry, i. 278; marriage, ii. 22, 23; learning, 24.
Browning, Robert, on Longfellow, i. 158; Lowell on, 159; early cult in Boston, 177; C.'s appreciation, 177, 178, 278; on Civil War, 412; and Dickens, ii. 7; on immortality, 13, 30; and C., 18, 21; interest in America, 18; sentences on wrapper of poems, 18-21; and Carlyle, 21, 22, 25; obscurity, 21; marriage, 22, 23; home and family, 23, 24; and clairvoyance and spiritualism, 24; and his wife, 24; and the Queen, 25; courted, 25; American friendships, 25; and the sisters Flower, 26, 28, 29; rationalistic influence, 26, 29; and Fox, 30; religious views, 30; in society, 31; cosmopolitan, 31; sculptor, 31; literary friendships, 32; political interests, 32; and Italian liberty, 64; and Joseph Jefferson, 149; and Story, 433.
Buchanan, James, election, i. 250.
Büchner, Ludwig, at Freethought Congress, ii. 400, 401.
Buckingham, J. T., i. 159.
Buckstone, J. B., as an actor, ii. 8, 146.
Bull Run, battle, cause of rout, i. 329; effect, 334, 335; cause, 335.
Buller, Charles, and Carlyle, ii. 101.
Bulwer-Lytton, E. G. E., appearance, ii. 80, 141; at dinner to Dickens, 141.
Bunsen, Carl, ii. 247.
Bunsen, Heinrich, ii. 247.

Bunyan, John, "Pilgrim's Progress," as a play, ii. 347; travesty, 354.
Burnap, G. W., address at Dickinson, i. 117; discussion, with Durbin, 117; home life, 121; conservative, 195.
Burne-Jones, Sir Edward, Ruskin on, ii. 119; religion and art, 132, 134; piano decoration, 132.
Burns, Anthony, rendition, i. 175, 176, 188, 190.
Burroughs, John, and Carlyle, i. 399.
Bushnell, J. C. A., i. 247 n.
Busk, George, ii. 197; anthropologist, 336.
Buslaef, Theodor, ii. 181.
Butler, B. F., in Boston, i. 375.
Byron, Lord, does not interest C., i. 67.

Cabanel, Alexandre, at Paris Exposition, ii. 174.
Cairnes, J. E., Union sympathizer, i. 406; knowledge of America, ii. 15; personality, 15.
Calamese, Nancy, the witch of Falmouth, i. 23; suicide, 24.
Caldwell, Merritt, as a professor, i. 48; death, 48.
Calhoun, J. C., character and constitutional principles antagonistic, i. 71; last journey, 82; Unitarian, 199.
Call, W. M. W., religious experiences, ii. 154; marriage, 155.
Call, Mrs. W. M. W. (Brabant), translates Strauss's "Jesus," ii. 155; first husband, 155.
"Calumets," ii. 373.
Calvin, John, Carlyle on, ii. 111.
Cambridge University, C.'s visit, ii. 353; question of religious tests, 376-379; union debate, 377.
Cambridge, Mass., Town of Beautiful Homes, i. 156.
Cameron, Julia M., photographs, ii. 33; romance of adopted daughter, 33, 34.
Campbell, Lady Anna, ii. 106.
Campbell, Lord Archibald, ii. 107.
Campmeeting, Methodist, i. 26; secular aspects, 27.
Card-playing, i. 290.
Cary, Thomas, and Agassiz's views on evolution, i. 153.
Carlisle, Pa., fugitive slave riot, i. 50-53.
Carlyle, Jane W., appearance, i. 394; on "Life of Frederick," 394; on "Sordello," ii. 23; marriage, 101, 108; death, 107, 108; note to C., 107.
Carlyle, John, ii. 103.
Carlyle, Thomas, "Nigger Question," i. 61, 409; on Whitman, 219; Holmes on, 384; home life, 394, ii. 214-217; "Life of Frederick the Great," i. 394-396; appearance, 395; and Emerson, 395, 398, ii. 112-115; on Swift, i. 396; humility, 396; on America, 396, 400; on emancipation, 396, 400, 401, 407, 409; profanity, 396; pessimism, 397.399; on suffrage, 397-400, ii. 108; conversation, i. 398-400; and Sterling, 398, 440; on mastery of circumstance, 401; on phrase-mongers, 401; opposed to war, 401, ii. 315; progressiveness, i. 402; and evolution, 402; on re-